DEBATING THE DEMOCRATIC LEGITIMACY OF THE EUROPEAN UNION

Governance in Europe
SERIES EDITOR: GARY MARKS

DEBATING THE DEMOCRATIC LEGITIMACY OF THE EUROPEAN UNION

Edited by Beate Kohler-Koch and Berthold Rittberger

ROWMAN & LITTLEFIELD PUBLISHERS, INC.
Lanham • Boulder • New York • Toronto • Plymouth, UK

ROWMAN & LITTLEFIELD PUBLISHERS, INC.

Published in the United States of America
by Rowman & Littlefield Publishers, Inc.
A wholly owned subsidary of The Rowman & Littlefield Publishing Group, Inc.
4501 Forbes Boulevard, Suite 200, Lanham, Maryland 20706
www.rowmanlittlefield.com

Estover Road, Plymouth PL6 7PY, United Kingdom

British Library Cataloguing in Publication Information Available

Library of Congress Cataloging-in-Publication Data
Debating the democratic legitimacy of the European Union / edited by Beate Kohler-
Koch and Berthold Rittberger.
    p. cm.
  Includes bibliographical references and index.
  ISBN-13: 978-0-7425-5491-7 (cloth : alk. paper)
  ISBN-10: 0-7425-5491-0 (cloth : alk. paper)
  ISBN-13: 978-0-7425-5492-4 (pbk. : alk. paper)
  ISBN-10: 0-7425-5492-9 (pbk. : alk. paper)
  1. European Union. 2. Democracy—European Union countries. 3. Constitutional his-
tory—European Union countries. 4. Law—European Union countries. 5. European
Union countries—Politics and government. I. Kohler-Koch, Beate, 1941- II. Rittberger,
Berthold, 1975-
  JN30.D415 2007
  341.242'2—dc22

                                2006101850

Printed in the United States of America

♾™ The paper used in this publication meets the minimum requirements of American
National Standard for Information Sciences—Permanence of Paper for Printed Library
Materials, ANSI/NISO Z39.48-1992.

Contents

**Part III: The Public Sphere and Civil Society:
Prerequisites for Democratically Legitimate Rule Making**

Part IV: Democracy and Political Participation

Part V: Deliberative Democracy

Figures and Tables

Figures

Tables

1

Charting Crowded Territory: Debating the Democratic Legitimacy of the European Union

Beate Kohler-Koch and Berthold Rittberger

The Aim of This Volume

THERE IS HARDLY A SHORTAGE of contributions to the debate about the European Union's (EU) democratic legitimacy. In the wake of the adoption of the Single European Act which heralded a new era of European integration, a new body of literature emerged which addressed the democratic challenges stemming from henceforth frequent episodes of treaty reform and concomitant transfers of sovereignty to the EU level. The acceleration of the process of European integration—the pooling and delegation of substantial portions of national sovereignty in the late 1980s and throughout the 1990s—have thus prompted a vibrant scholarly debate on the EU's democratic credentials: The notion of the "democratic deficit" has swiftly become the most prominent label attributed to the EU polity; treatises on how to improve the democratic legitimacy of the EU have filled scores of books, academic journals, and newspapers. In the wake of the treaty-amending bargains struck at Maastricht, Amsterdam, Nice, and the drafting of the Constitutional Treaty, the number of academic journal articles addressing the question of the Community's democratic credentials has soared while prior to 1990, the question of the quality of democratic governance in the EU had not (yet) entered the academic debate.

Characterizing the literature on the EU's democratic credentials, Giandomenico Majone argues that "we are still groping for normative criteria appropriate to the *sui generis* character of the European Community . . . Since the legitimacy debate is still in the standard-setting state, current evaluations start from different normative premises to reach different, even contradictory, conclusions."[1] The debate about the EU's democratic deficit and assessments of its democratic quality are thus fuelled by different conceptions of the reality of the EU as a polity on the one hand, and, on the other hand, the application of different standards.

First, there is little agreement in the literature on the basic question concerning context conditions: Do we have to reinvent democracy because we live in a new, postnational era characterized by the decline of the nation-state whereby our traditional conception of democracy within the confines of the nation-state is challenged? Or do we simply have to adapt familiar institutions which have been successful in our domestic democratic systems to the *sui generis* character of the EU? Arguments in this debate are difficult to reconcile and there is little communication between these strands of arguments. Those who claim that governing beyond borders is not unique to the EU either draw from the discussion about "post parliamentary democracy"[2] or the more general debate among those authors who strive to "liberate the democracy principle from the (potentially distorting) confines of the nation state."[3] Their main intention is to pave the ground for concepts such as "deliberative democracy," which marks an ontological shift away from the exclusive focus on the state and its institutions.[4] In contrast, authors who see a future in constitutional design turn their interest to the institutional adaptation of traditional democratic mechanisms and employ benchmarks for their functioning which they derive from current domestic democratic institutions and practices.[5]

The second reason for the lack of consensus regarding possible remedies for the EU's democratic deficit lies in the observation that research on the EU's democratic credentials is inspired by different notions about the essence of democracy: Is it an all-embracing concept concerning all fields of human organization or should it be restricted to the realm of the political? How should we judge whether it is appropriate to give priority to some democratic norm over the other? For instance, can we compromise on input legitimacy as long as output legitimacy is secured? Does a democratic system require a strong sense of collective identity and identification for political decisions to command a high degree of legitimacy? Does government, to be democratically legitimate, have to fulfill the conditions stipulated by Abraham Lincoln's trilogy (1863) on "government of the people, by the people, for the people"?

Furthermore, disagreement about how to respond to the deficiencies of the state of democracy in the EU originates from the different assumptions underlying different theories of democracy. For instance, those who take deliberation to be the essence of democracy rather than the representation and aggregation of given preferences tend to place a high value on political communication within civil society and the emergence of autonomous public spheres, whereas proponents of liberal democracy will place a higher value on participation through voting.

It is therefore hardly surprising that contributions to the debate about how to tackle the EU's democratic deficit do not add up to a coherent picture. When looking for a cure, we are offered very different remedies. Some offer and debate competing models,[6] yet mostly authors are absorbed by their own conceptual system of reference. There is not only the (usual) lack of interdisciplinary discourse and modest exchange across language barriers, distinct communities have emerged even within the Anglo-American political science community and, as a consequence, an intellectual transboundary discourse does not come about easily. The aim of this volume is hence twofold: We intend to offer the reader a wide-ranging panorama of different theoretical approaches to EU democracy, and by doing so we wish to stimulate a broader discourse that cuts across different strands of scholarship on democracy and the EU.

In this introduction we proceed as follows. Even though we are not able to offer a comprehensive state-of-the-art discussion, the ensuing section will chart two key strands in the literature on the EU's democratic credentials. First, we will sketch the conceptual battleground on which the debate about appropriate standards and benchmarks to assess the EU's democratic quality is fought. Second, we demonstrate that the debate about the EU's democratic quality mirrors a broader debate in comparative politics about the challenges the institutions of representative government face in a globalized and ever more interdependent world.

Against this background we argue in the ensuing section that irrespective of rapidly changing socioeconomic and political contexts captured by the processes of modernization, globalization, and European integration, and the concomitant discussions about the challenges these processes pose to the fate of the modern state, there is no compelling reason to challenge the validity of the basic normative standard that any system of democratic rules ought to meet: political equality understood as equal respect for and equal worth of all individuals (which we will elaborate upon below). Thus, the contributions to this volume differ not in terms of their basic normative assumption about democracy's essence but in their emphasis on different *dimensions* of democracy which reflect the pluralism in democratic theory. We then present a three-dimensional typology—a political institutions versus civil society–centered dimension, a voting versus deliberation dimension, and an instrumental versus intrinsic conception of participation—as a heuristic tool to distinguish between the different basic assumptions that enlighten the individual perspectives of this book. Furthermore, we will relate the different perspectives presented in this volume to the dominant social-theoretical approaches in the study of politics, rational choice, and constructivism. Finally, we will introduce the contributions to this volume and highlight what they have to offer to the ongoing debate on the EU's democratic credentials.

Conceptualizing Democracy in a New Environment

Bringing Democracy to the EU: A Conceptual Battleground

The question about which standards should be employed to assess the democratic credentials of the EU crucially hinges on how the EU is conceptualized: Since conceptualizations abound, this equally means that there is no lack of different views regarding the degree to which the EU is suffering from a democratic deficit. We will first briefly elaborate on the claim of those who argue that the EU does not have a democratic deficit before we turn to the counterclaim which views the EU's democratic credentials rather skeptically.

There Is No Democratic Deficit

Two positions have gained prominence in the recent past. According to the first position, democratic legitimacy is not an appropriate concept to assess the EU from a normative perspective. The EU is, first and foremost, an economic and a regulatory community which produces Pareto-improving policies for its citizens. To avoid jeopardizing the output produced by these policies, decision making must be vested in the hands of independent regulatory agents, not of parliaments and politicians: This position has been most prominently defended by Giandomenico Majone who conceptualizes the EU as a "regulatory state."[7] Regulatory policies, such as competition policy, the removal of trade barriers, or monetary policy, are destined to address and redress market failures. For those policies to be effective, they have to be taken in an undemocratic fashion in the sense that they are excluded from the adversarial power play of parliamentary, majoritarian politics. Otherwise, decisions would be unduly politicized whereby their credibility and Pareto-efficient effects would be undermined and the EU's (output) legitimacy would suffer.[8] German legal scholars have made claims that can be squared with Majone's regulatory state–thesis as early as the 1970s. For Hans-Peter Ipsen the then EC constitutes a *Zweckverband*, a regulatory agency or fourth branch of government which fulfils clearly specified functional goals and hence offers no room for political discretion.[9] According to Ernst-Joachim Mestmäcker the community is based on an economic constitution which derives its legitimation from the creation of a free market and the notion of free movement which empowers individuals as it extends their individual rights and free-doms.[10] In both cases, there is no democratic legitimacy deficit: In the first case, the community only executes closely circumscribed functional decisions, which correspond to what Majone considers to be Pareto-improving decisions, which member states have agreed to by democratic means, and in the second case, individuals are better off from a rights perspective (rather than from the perspective of efficient regulation).

Others argue that it is because of the use of overly idealistic standards that the EU falls short in relation to democratic benchmarks, yet these standards are not even met by any modern government.[11] By sticking to these standards, analysts overlook "the social context of contemporary European policy-making—the real-world practices of existing governments and multi-level political systems in which they act."[12] Andrew Moravcsik argues that the constraints inherent in the EU's constitutional settlement prevent the EU from becoming an unaccountable superstate. In his assessment, they "exceed the most extreme constraints imposed in national systems."[13] The treaties impose strict limits on EU activities since the EU's core activity remains regulatory in nature: trade in goods and services, movement of the factors of production, trade-related environmental and consumer policy, monetary policy, and so on. Policies such as taxation, social welfare provision, defense, education policy—despite the modest inroads made by the EU—are still firmly in the hands of the nation-state. But even in the policy areas where the EU has a mandate to act, it is constrained by decision-making procedures which impose high thresholds and require either supermajorities or even unanimity as well as concurrent majorities in and agreement among the three EU organs, the Commission, the European Parliament and the Council. Moravcsik also defends the EU against the allegation that it is an unaccountable technocracy by pointing to the existence of multiple channels of political accountability, both directly via the European Parliament and indirectly via elected national officials. Furthermore, he points out that "there is little distinctively European about the pattern of delegation we observe in the EU."[14] EU officials such as central bankers, judges in the European Court of Justice, and Commissioners enjoy the highest degree of decision-making autonomy precisely in those areas in which policy-makers in modern democracies have also insulated themselves from majoritarian decision making and party political contestation. His point here is that critics should not employ double standards: One may well quibble over the question whether insulation from majoritarian contestation is normatively desirable or justifiable by the standards of democratic theory, yet it cannot be ignored that insulation is an empirical fact both in the EU and in advanced democracies all over the world. Moravcsik concludes that "[a]s long as political procedures are consistent with existing national democratic practice and have a *prima facie* normative justification . . . we cannot draw negative conclusions about the legitimacy of the EU from casual observation of the non-participatory nature of its institutions."[15]

There Is a Democratic Deficit: But Can the EU Be More Democratic?

Most scholars share the assessment that even though democratic structures are in place at the EU level, such as a directly elected parliament, the EU has a democratic deficit. Robert Dahl, one of the most celebrated democratic theorists, even calls it "gigantic."[16] The democratic deficit camp, is, however, divided between scholars who see the democratic deficit virtually insurmountable given the inherent limitations in the EU's democratic capacity and those who claim that it can be resolved or at least attenuated through constitutional engineering in the short to medium term. In order to establish a level of democratic accountability and control that would match those in modern democracies "[p]olitical leaders would have to create political institutions that would provide citizens with opportunities for political participation, influence and control."[17] To use those means effectively, citizens not only have to be informed about policy alternatives, these alternatives also have to be the object of public debate and discussion which, in turn, implies that political competition by parties and individuals seeking electoral office would have to be in place.[18] Scholars, however, disagree starkly about when and under what conditions these objectives are realizable. Kielmansegg argues, for instance, that effective public debate about European policy alternatives can only ensue once a set of very demanding preconditions are met. The "non-demos" camp, as Joseph Weiler and collaborators have called it,[19] claims that the EU lacks the structural preconditions to become a truly democratic polity. For Kielmansegg, the proof of the question as to whether or not a political system fulfils the preconditions for democratically legitimate government lies in the capacity of citizens of any given political system to view majority decisions as legitimate: "Only when all those who are affected by a decision perceive themselves to be part of a common, all-encompassing political identity is it possible to differentiate between majority rule which can be consented to and the rule of strangers which will then be considered illegitimate."[20] Yet, such a "viable"[21] identity which would render majority rule acceptable (or, at least, less threatening), especially when authoritative decisions impose duties and create "winners and losers," does not exist in the EU and will not come into being for a long time to come. Why, asks Kielmansegg, is there not collective political identity shared by the peoples in Europe? Historically, collective identities have formed in the contexts of communities of memory, experience, and communication. The EU is obviously not a community of communication-with multilingualism hampering the emergence of common structures of communication and understanding; the EU is hardly a community of memory even though attempts to construct a common European heritage have been mushrooming in the recent past with the constitution or the question of Turkey's EU membership as focal points. Yet, European states have distinct national histories each with its own interpretations of the past. Last, the EU is only a rudimentary community of experience. Kielmansegg argues that it is this community which has the largest identity-forming potential: The commonly shared threat in the years of block confrontation has been a common experience for (Western) European states. All in all, Europe has been very poor in identifying and defining common experiences which could carry the potential to generate a "We-feeling" among EU citizens.[22]

Kielmansegg's assessment about the democratic capacity (*Demokratie-fähigkeit*) of the EU is much more skeptical than that of those who see a potential to be realized via institutional reforms and societal practice. Follesdal and Hix accept that opinion formation and public debate are crucial ingredients for a political system to command democratic legitimacy. Yet, compared to Kielmansegg's demanding trilogy of preconditions, Follesdal and Hix lower the bar for social underpinning of democratic rule: "[R]ather than assuming that a European 'demos' is a prerequisite for genuine EU democracy, a European democratic identity might well form through the practice of democratic competition."[23] Follesdal and Hix thus suggest that "constitutional engineering" can offer a positive short-term impetus for political debate based on adversarial politics. They claim that the most obvious way of enabling political contestation and triggering public discussions is to allow for competition for the most powerful executive position in the EU, the presidency of the Commission. Simon Hix, for example, suggests a direct election of the Commission President by EU citizens or national parliaments.[24]

The Democratic Challenge and Multilevel Governance

Multilevel governance, by now a well-established label to grasp the diffusion of authority within the EU system, is somewhat ambivalent concerning its potential to enhance the democratic quality of the EU. [25] First, the scope of executive and parliamentary jurisdiction—while improving problem-solving efficiency—varies substantially and hence impinges on democratic accountability. Second, the shift from hierarchy and formal procedures to networking and informality—while allowing for extensive input—undermines political equality and control. In the European multilevel system authority is shared vertically between supranational, national, and subnational institutions which Liesbet Hooghe and Gary Marks label "type I governance" embracing "general-purpose, nonintersecting, and durable jurisdictions."[26] A character-istic feature of this type of governance is that the executive is crossing levels of jurisdiction easily whereas the territorial reach of parliaments is limited. In a "penetrated system of governance,"[27] democratic representation and political accountability become deficient when they are organized through territorial-bound parliaments. In recent years, national and even regional parliaments have made every effort to exert more influence. National parliaments are, however, caught up in a "negotiation-accountability dilemma"[28] since stricter control over governments reduces flexibility and success in Council negotia-tions. Therefore, parliaments, or rather majority factions in national parlia-ments, refrain from exerting formal veto powers and choose informal ways to hold their government accountable. According to Arthur Benz, this strategy sets in motion a "de-institutionalization" of EU decision making which "re-sults in opaque processes with the public being hardly able to control them. It makes accountability of representatives difficult and, hence, deteriorates the democratic quality of representative structures. Thus, despite (or because of) the important role of parliaments in EU policy making, the system fails to conform to the standard of democratic accountability."[29]

Most scholars see the distinctiveness of multilevel governance not just in the vertical diffusion of authority across levels of government but even more so in the horizontal dispersion of authority which comes along with "type II governance" in which jurisdictions are task specific, intersecting, and flexible[30] and in which public and private actors have a "shared responsibility for re-source allocation and conflict resolution."[31] The inclusiveness of EU gover-nance, the omnipresence of negotiations and networks, are well founded both theoretically[32] and empirically. Empirical evidence is best established in re-search on regional/structural policy and, albeit to a lesser extent, on EU envi-ronmental policy.[33]

Dense, though differentiated, patterns of communication and interaction have emerged that channel diverse interests into the political process. Empir-ical evidence supports the supposition that the inclusive nature of network governance has the positive effect of being more open to new interests and innovative ideas[34] but provides a mixed account on the more ambitious ex-pectations concerning participatory governance and democratic upgrading. Where the EU has pushed for more involvement of private actors either in territorially overarching networks or in local networks, it has contributed to the empowerment of weaker actors and a greater awareness of the issue among stake-holders. The implementation of the treaty-based partnership principle in EU policies often, however, ends up in "new configurations of partial participation"[35] which run counter to the stipulated inclusiveness, openness, and transparency of the governance process. Therefore, participa-

tory governance becomes a myth and since the rules and practice of participation do not guarantee equality among actors, the involvement of a multitude of private actors is far from promoting EU democracy. The selectivity of
representation and the deficits of democratic accountability so typical for
network governance are aggravated by the multilevel character of governance
in the EU: "The relations between actors . . . are weakly exposed to public
scrutiny, and to the scrutiny of the legitimate, democratic, and representative
bodies."[36]

Peters and Pierre even call multilevel governance a "Faustian Bargain" in
which core democratic values are traded for the accommodation of a broad
range of interests and purported increases in policy-making effectiveness
and efficiency.[37] They argue that formal rules are crucial safeguards for ensuring a distribution of power and authority which, even they do not guarantee equality among actors, at least they ensure transparency, political accountability, and stability of expectations. Informality, on the other hand,
implies that it is incumbent upon the actors themselves to allow different actors to partake and to define their relative authority. Comparative government research supports the view that informal governance structures, such
as networks, bear the risk of substituting private government for public accountability.[38] The lack of clarity where responsibility ends and effectively
rests has the potential to produce a major accountability deficit.[39] Furthermore, scholars claim that the celebrated informality of multilevel governance structures entails a potential for inequality. Peters and Pierre argue
that in the EU, "multi-level governance may in practice favor the interests of
the nation-states as the dominant players, even though it is conceptualized
as providing greater power to the structurally less powerful subnational actors."[40] Inclusiveness thus need not automatically translate into equal opportunities as far as decision making is concerned.

While scholars who study the EU as a system of multilevel governance see
the participatory and problem-solving potential of the new forms of governance, there is disagreement about the implications for the EU's democratic
quality. While some herald the inclusiveness and informality of multilevel
governance as an impetus for democratization that results from enhanced
participation and higher problem-solving capacity, others—as we have seen—
are more critical of these prospects.

Challenges to the Institutions of Representative Government

The democratic legitimacy of the EU is not only contested because scholars
apply different concepts and relate them to *sui generis* features of the EU; in
this section, we argue that the debate of the EU's democratic legitimacy and

potential cures also reflects a broader discussion about democratic challenges faced by advanced industrial democracies. There is a rapidly growing body of literature addressing the fate of the institutions of representative government which constitute the dominant blueprint for democratic government in advanced industrial democracies.[41] The dominant principle of representative democracy sees itself increasingly supplemented by alternative modes of democracy such as direct democracy and advocacy democracy which imply that citizens participate directly and not via electoral channels in the formulation and administration of public policy.[42] Mark Warren has argued that "[w]hile the traditional concerns of democratic theory with state-centered institutions remain importantly crucial and ethically central, they are increasingly subject to the limitations we should expect when nineteenth-century concepts meet twenty-first century realities."[43] Playing the same tune, the report on "The Future of Parliamentary Democracy: Transition and Challenge in European Governance" stipulates that these twenty-first-century realities are not unique to the EU but reflect broader societal and politico-economic trends in all advanced industrial societies.[44] These trends, it is argued, affect the parameters which have traditionally guaranteed the democratic legitimacy of domestic polities. Among these trends, the increasing scientification of politics (expertocracy), the proliferation of transnational citizen groups and public interest organizations which constitute new governance sites bypassing traditional channels of interest representation and accountability, and the pressures exercised by increasing economic interdependence which reduce the policy options available to domestic politicians have a profound bearing on the democratic legitimacy of contemporary political systems: "Globalization calls in question a number of concepts, perceptions and interests shaped by the historical merger between the Nation-State and democracy . . . The coherence laboriously established between economic space, political space and social space is increasingly threatened. How can the political frontiers inherited from history remain the same when major human, commercial and financial flows no longer take account of them?"[45]

Numerous developments in Europe offer an indication that the transformations which continue to leave their marks on the democratic life and institutions in modern industrialized democracies do not appear to halt before the EU level. The following two initiatives shall serve as illustrations. The Commission White Paper on European Governance contains elements which strongly mirror the tenets of the model of advocacy democracy by emphasizing the prominence of nonelectoral channels for citizen participation.[46] The message is "to connect Europe with its citizens"[47] and to "renew the Community method by following a less top-down approach and complementing its policy tools more effectively with non-legislative instruments."[48] Better information and transparency of EU policy-making shall be supplemented by improving consultation and dialogue not just with territorial and functional interests but also with civil society groups and individual citizens. A range of instruments is suggested and has been put into practice in the last few years: the opening up of advisory committees to civil society, business test panels, and venues for ad hoc and on-line consultation and the like.[49]

The Treaty establishing a Constitution for Europe (TCE), which was prepared by the European Convention and signed by the Member-State governments in October 2004, carries explicit marks of the new concepts of democratic governance mirroring the increasing prominence of upgrading civil society and unmediated channels for citizen participation. Though it is laid down that "[t]he functioning of the Union shall be founded on representative democracy" (Article I-46), the "principle of participatory democracy" now finds explicit mention (Article I-47). The principle extends to an open, transparent, and regular dialogue between EU institutions and representative associations and civil society. In particular, the Commission is called on to carry out broad consultations with parties concerned and be responsive to citizens' initiatives. The element of direct democracy is new but very weak since the initiative can only invite the Commission and is restricted to issues that are required for the purpose of implementing the constitution. The provisions for giving citizens voice and to open a civil dialogue reflect the core ideas of the White Paper on Governance and the follow-up initiatives by the Commission. Just like the White Paper, the incorporation of participatory democracy in the TCE has met a mixed response in the academic EU community.[50] The critical arguments echo the debate on multilevel network governance: An open and transparent dialogue is no guarantee for equal access and no cure for a lack in democratic accountability.

The political discourse supporting institutional reforms in the EU is quite evidently inspired by the mainstream debate in academia that the present institutions of liberal democracy are not operating satisfactorily, that a key problem is the lack of civic engagement and, therefore, a main concern is how to promote effective citizenship.[51] Proponents of the transition thesis discard the idea of the *sui generis* character of the EU but arrive at similar conclusions, namely that hierarchical and majoritarian decisions produce sub-optimal results. They differ from the multilevel analysts by their unfaltering faith in the new modes of governance and the advancement of civic engagement.

In the preceding sections we have presented a panorama of arguments about the democratic quality of the EU which support Majone's contention that the question about the EU's democratic legitimacy is still being fought on the conceptual battleground.[52] Societal and political context conditions are interpreted differently by different scholars. However, we posit that the assessments of the EU's democratic legitimacy and the remedies suggested do not just mirror different perceptions of reality. They are rather grounded in different fundamental beliefs about the essence of democracy and democratically legitimate governance: We argue that the differences in views on EU's democratic quality reflect long-standing differences in democratic theory about what constitute the central characteristics of and preconditions for democratically legitimate governance. Before we turn to shedding light on this point, we introduce a minimal set of normative standards of democratic legitimacy which all proposals for democratizing the EU polity have to stand up to.

The Normative Distinctiveness of Democratic Legitimacy

Research on the democratic deficit of the EU explicitly or implicitly focuses on different aspects of democratic legitimacy from which benchmarks are derived to assess the EU's democratic quality or its democratic potential. The bulk of research focuses predominantly on the input side whereby procedural criteria or requirements for determining the popular will (government by the people) are defined. Another strand of the democratic deficit literature defines criteria to tap output-oriented legitimacy—legitimacy that flows from effectively achieving citizens' welfare and goals—to assess the EU's democratic capacity (government for the people). Those with a focus on social legitimacy point to the role played by the boundaries of a political community and hence emphasize issues of collective identity or social homogeneity (government of the people).[53]

While in the literature on the EU's democratic deficit, these aspects are—jointly or separately—employed as the starting points of analyses and assessments of democratically legitimate rule in the EU, we intend to take one step back and emphasize that the distinctiveness of democratic legitimacy lies not (merely) in realizing a certain kind of combination of input, output, and social legitimacy, but in realizing the fundamental values of democracy. It is the principle of autonomy that stands at the center stage of the democratic project.[54] All modern traditions of democratic thought—from Liberalism to Republicanism to Social Democracy—share the underlying notion that for people to develop as free and equal they have to be autonomous.[55] Autonomy is intimately linked to self-determination: Autonomy implies that people are free and equal in the determination of their own lives. Autonomy qua self-determination is thus set against any notions of paternalistic authority or domination which deny that people are the best judges of their own individual good or interest.[56] Democracy requires more than merely a commitment to popular sovereignty, majority rule, or effective problem solving: All these practices may well be related to the practice of democracy, but "they themselves do not define democracy."[57] A political system is not democratic because particular decision-making procedures are in place which we commonly associate with democratic rule. What democracy requires is a commitment towards realizing a condition in which—negatively defined—people are not alienated from political decisions, and in which—positively defined—people are convinced that they are truly governing themselves. Autonomy and democratic self-determination are hence, as Post aptly argues, "about the authorship of decisions, not about the making of decisions."[58] This condition can only be realized, as stated above, when people are autonomous, that is, when they can reason self-consciously, be self-reflective, be self-determining and thus debate and deliberate different views and courses of action in private and in public life.[59] It is only when people are granted autonomy and the forms of participation that enable citizens to act autonomously that they will identify with the state, that is to say, regard the state as legitimate. Democracy thus requires that people not just enjoy the right to vote, but it also implies that citizens enjoy equal entitlements and rights to participate in communicative processes of debate and deliberation which "empower citizens to participate in public opinion in ways that will permit them to believe that public opinion will become potentially responsive to their views."[60]

How does this perspective on the underlying principle of democratic rule now relate to the institutionalization of democracy? The starting point is that the different aspects of democratic legitimacy—input, output, and social—have to sustain the principle of autonomy. However, this does not predefine how autonomy links up with these different aspects of legitimacy. With regard to social legitimacy, the straightforward answer is that the principle of autonomy does not carry any implications concerning the question of who the people is, that is, how a particular group which must be granted the entitlements to lead autonomous lives shall be defined. Does the principle of autonomy help us specify the meaning of government by the people (input legitimacy)? We have argued that the principle of autonomy does not define democracy in terms of specific decision-making procedures but rather in terms of whether or not the realization of core democratic values and principles—autonomy and its derivates (self-determination and political equality)—can be associated with the application of different procedures. With regard to output legitimacy, the principle of autonomy does not prejudice a particular conception of distributive equality.[61] Some conceptions of distributive equality might actually be at odds with democratic principles. Such inconsistency occurs "whenever the demands of distributive justice compromise the autonomous participation of persons within democratic self-government."[62] Any attempt to dwell on the connection between democracy and different notions of distributive justice inevitably opens a Pandora's box.[63] At the bare minimum, democracy means that the distributive consequences of political decisions as well as the procedures by which these decisions are made must not violate the principle of autonomy. Because of this ambiguity, even agreement on the basic standard of democracy does not produce uniform solutions. In the ensuing section we turn to the different theories which implement the principle of autonomy in multifaceted ways.

Democracy: A Three-Fold Distinction

We have argued in the previous section that the principle of autonomy is the unalterable essence of the notion of democracy. But even authors who accept this as a non-negotiable baseline adhere to different schools of thought and, therefore, put different emphasis on what they consider to be the necessary prerequisites of democracy and the best ways and means to bring it to life. In the ensuing paragraphs we present three different dimensions along which different theoretic approaches can be distinguished and which will make us understand why it is so difficult to arrive at a common discourse.

Dimension I: Political Institutions Versus Civil Society

It is a popularly held view by many democratic theorists that democracy is above all a matter of framing the political institutions of the political system. Democratic theorists, however, differ starkly in the way they put emphasis on the institutions of the political system relative to society. Liberals, for instance, by giving priority to fundamental rights and liberties, attribute central importance to constitutionalism—judicial review, checks and balances, separation of powers—as a means to temper the popular will.[64] Government is central in that its key role is to protect the equal rights and liberties of citizens. Participatory democracy, in contrast, places stronger emphasis on political participation compared to the liberals' emphasis on the protection of individual freedom. Proponents of participatory democracy strive for a polity in which citizens actively participate in the making of political decisions that affect their lives.[65] Deliberative democracy offers a perspective that ascribes both government and society key roles in sustaining deliberative processes. The public sphere, a concept developed by Jürgen Habermas, is an arena where private actors can exchange their views and opinions absent external constraints and pressures. It is the arena in which the civil society deliberates, that is, formulates views and opinions, and expresses its desires vis-à-vis the government. Civil society, in Habermas's words, is the "social foundation of autonomous publics"[66] who engage in a process of informal opinion formation. Informally generated public opinion is—among others—transformed into communicative power via formal channels of political participation (elections) into administrative power through institutions of the state (for example, parliaments who legislate).[67]

Liberals and deliberative democrats both put emphasis on political institutions, yet they differ with respect to the core functions of these institutions: the protection of rights (liberalism) and the foundation (and protection) of a public sphere (deliberative democracy). Furthermore, civil society–centered approaches such as participatory democracy and social democracy attack the focus on political institutions prevalent in much of democratic theory claiming that democracy is (or, at least, should be) a more encompassing concept. Social democrats call for a more widespread application of the democratic principle to include all functional systems of public life. Some scholars have called for universal democratization[68] which ranges from universities, schools, mass media, and churches to the workplace democracy. Furthermore, civil society–centered approaches have a different conception of democratic participation and the role of citizens than perspectives emphasizing the role of political institutions.[69] In their view, the interests and preferences of citizens are not prepolitical—formed prior to political interaction, say, through processes of socialization—but can be transformed in the political process. The picture of the citizen is that of an active citizen who is not only qualified to evaluate alternatives and make informed decisions, but also as one who is capable of learning and thus of enlightened self-understanding.[70]

Dimension II: Voting Versus Deliberation

Democratic theorists also differ starkly with respect to the transmission mechanisms which translate public opinion or public interests into collective decisions. This difference has its roots in the fundamental assumptions democratic theorists make about whether or not citizens' preferences are given exogenously, determined—as we have seen above—in the realm of the prepolitical, or whether they are endogenous to the political process. For liberalism, democracy is about devising mechanisms, such as voting systems, for aggregating the exogenously given preferences of individuals into collective decisions. The key for democratic theorists working in this tradition is to devise voting systems which are considered desirable and normatively acceptable from a set of context-dependent criteria.[71] While voting systems based on majority rule may be appropriate for societies where political attitudes are relatively homogenous, supermajority rules or consensual systems may be considered more desirable and legitimate for highly fractionalized societies.[72] For republicanism and deliberative democracy in contrast, the starting point is different. The preferences of social actors are not fixed but endogenous to the political process. Political views and opinions are formulated and re-formulated in a deliberative style, both in the public sphere and in parliament: "Deliberation . . . refers to a certain attitude towards social cooperation, namely that of openness to persuasion by reasons referring to the claims of others as well as one's own."[73] Though voting is acknowledged as a transmission mechanism in mass society, it does not attract prime attention in this school of thought.

Dimension III: Instrumental Versus Intrinsic Conception of Participation

Political participation is a central theme to most theories of democracy, for participation is considered indispensable to meet a core criterion of democratically legitimate rule: government by the people. Nevertheless, participation is valued in different ways. Differences can be traced back to the differential assessment of participation as an instrument to achieve particular ends or as a concept that is valued intrinsically. The instrumental perspective emphasizes that participation fulfils important functions for endowing a political system with stability and legitimacy: In the liberal tradition participation is meant to restrain tyranny or oppressive rule by subjecting officials to the popular judgment.[74] For those in the "populist" tradition, political participation is central to discover the authentic will of the people which, as a corollary, implies that there is a discernible common good that can be deduced from the expression of the will of the people.[75] Those who emphasize the intrinsic qualities of participation do not dispute its instrumental value(s). The right to self-government is so fundamental to democratic rule that the authors of the Declaration of Independence referred to it as an inalienable moral right. This right to self-government translates into a set of primary political rights which are ontologically separate from and thus superior to the democratic process.[76] These rights—the right to voting equality and equal opportunity for participation, the right to exercise final control over authoritative decisions—shall enable citizens to develop their human capacities to act as self-determining and morally responsible social beings. From this perspective it is not the right to participate but real participation which enables individuals to rise above their private existence and become emancipated citizens, hopefully "more knowledgeable, more attentive to the interests of others, and more probing of their own interests."[77]

In the preceding paragraphs we have distinguished democratic theories across three different dimensions; in the following section we argue that democratic theories broadly fall within two camps that mirror the main fault line

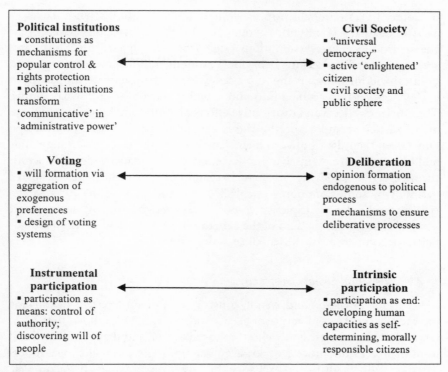

FIGURE 1.1
The Three Dimensions of Democracy

in social and political science more generally: an idealist, social constructivist camp and a realist, rational choice camp.

Realism and Rational Choice

Even though not all realists have fallen victim to some form of anthropological pessimism, they nevertheless share the rational choice notion that the egoistic interests and preferences of social actors which they pursue instrumentally and strategically are the basis of all social action: "Whenever we speak of rational behavior, we always mean rational behavior directed primarily towards selfish ends."[78] According to March and Olsen social action in this tradition follows a "logic of consequentialism": Social actors make rational choices among alternative sets of action options by evaluating their likely consequences (knowing that all other actors do likewise); in interdependent social situations, actors behave strategically in order to obtain their most preferred outcome.[79] This rationalism-inspired literature in political science makes an array of auxiliary assumptions about what it is that social actors actually pursue egoistically. These assumptions range from security-seeking[80] to power-seeking,[81] to welfare-seeking behavior.[82] From the rational choice perspective, political will formation is thus a process whereby citizens' exogenously given preferences get transformed into public policy via voting and/or bargaining. The efficiency effects and distributive effects of voting and bargaining systems are of particular importance for the quality and legitimacy of a political system: Given their distributive and efficiency effects, the rules governing voting and bargaining are themselves hotly contested. The challenge for democratic theorists is thus to devise voting and bargaining systems which are considered desirable by some commonly established criterion, such as the Pareto-criterion or the Kaldor principle which postulates that government decisions are acceptable as long as the sum of the benefits of a government decision are sufficient to compensate the losers of such decision.[83]

Idealism and Social Constructivism

According to Fearon and Wendt, constructivists are interested "in showing the socially constructed nature of agents and subjects."[84] It follows that interests and preferences are endogenous to social action, and they are formed and transformed in the process of social interaction. The rational choice model based on individualism and exchange theories is discarded as an "incomplete bas[i]s for thinking about governance" that does not capture the formative role of institutions.[85] As a consequence it assumes "an interweaving of the two standard logics of human action—a logic of consequence and a logic of appropriateness."[86] This implies that actors may transform their preferences as a response to a perceived lack of resonance between internalized norms and ideas and a social situation which upsets the match (or resonance) between that particular situation and the demands of a position.[87] Social action is thus always a function of the perception or framing of a particular social situation as well as the capacity of social actors to learn, that is, to adapt to new social situations. Deliberative and discursive democrats broadly share this ontological position for they view will formation as a process whereby citizens engage in communicative action (Habermas). This implies that behavior is oriented towards realizing common understanding and not, as claimed by rationalists, towards the realization of success as measured by a set of exogenously given preferences. From the purview of the theory of communicative action, citizens are not oriented primarily towards realizing their own success; they seek to coordinate their individual goals on the basis of a shared definition of a situation.[88] Since in the communicative mode of action, actors' interests and identities are no longer fixed "but subject to interrogation and challenges and, thus, to change" this also implies that "the validity claims of identities and interests are at stake" which, in turn, implies that "an argumentative consensus has constitutive effects on actors."[89] Deliberative democrats' proximity to the postulate of communicative action is evident as they support the assumption that it "induces individuals to reflect on the interests of themselves and others, and also upon the *common interest*."[90]

What Lies Ahead

The present volume offers a panorama of scholarship on the EU and the question of its democratic legitimacy; in this section we will introduce the individual contributions and show how they are positioned on the three different dimensions of democracy—political institutions versus civil society, voting versus deliberation, instrumental versus value-driven conception of participation. It is a special feature of this volume that each of the contributions will be complemented by a commentary—written by first-rate scholars in the field—which critically evaluates the claims and arguments of the individual contributions and relates them to the broader debate.

Democracy: The Constitutional Principle of the EU

The book sets out with a contribution by Armin von Bogdandy in which he charts the development of how the notion of democracy turned from its status as a political demand to endow the EU with an independent form of legitimacy—which was pursued ever more emphatically from the 1990s onwards—to the status of a constitutional principle of the EU. Von Bogdandy approaches the issue from the perspective of a legal scholar, asking how the principle of democracy is defined in the Union's primary law. He shows that the idea of democracy has become firmly entrenched in the EU's primary law within the past decade. Yet, it still finds its most prominent expression in the role of elections which provide two lines of democratic legitimacy (one direct via the European Parliament, the other indirect via the Council and national parliaments). Participatory mechanisms beyond elections have hitherto not found expression in the EU's primary law. Even though the Constitutional Treaty envisages the possibility of citizen initiatives, there is no principle in EU primary law which offers affected parties a right to participate in EU decision making. With a view to our three-dimensional conceptualization of democracy, von Bogdandy's take on EU democracy is characterized by an emphasis on the political institutions of the state which assumes that the realization of the democratic principle is assured by means of reforming the EU's institutional structures. In this context, elections are the most prominent mechanism of popular participation in the political process; consequently, the notion of voting—the aggregation of fixed preferences—also takes priority over the deliberative principle.

What Future for Parliamentary Democracy in the EU?

Despite their often alleged decline, representative parliamentary institutions continue to be bedrock for the democratic legitimacy of democratic polities: Representative democracy as an organizational principle continues to be uncontested, even though direct democratic and participatory elements increasingly come to complement the representative element.[91] The second section of this volume is thus devoted to the question of whether and how precisely the European Parliament and/or national parliaments contribute to the democratic legitimacy of the EU polity.

Katrin Auel and Arthur Benz take issue with the proposition that national parliaments have—as a result of the ongoing process of integration—been weakened vis-à-vis their national executives. Auel and Benz thus seek to answer the question whether (and how) national parliaments can play an effective role in shaping their national government's EU policy or whether they are reduced to symbolic institutions. They show that the two central problems faced by domestic legislatures with regard to their involvement in EU affairs are information asymmetries and the imbalance of power between governments and parliaments. Auel and Benz provide an empirical analysis of the three different systems of executive-legislative relationships (UK, Denmark, Germany) and the concomitant strategies adopted by national parliaments to obtain information and exercise impact upon European policy-making to alleviate the power imbalance.

Andreas Maurer's chapter shifts the focus from national parliaments to the European Parliament and asks how the performance of the European Parliament with regard to its key functions—policy-making, control, investiture of the Commission—affects the popular legitimacy of the European Parliament itself. While the European Parliament has made significant advances with a view to the impact it exercises in its policy-making function in particular, this increase may carry negative repercussions on the institution's popular legitimacy as long as the European Parliament continues to be perceived as a unitary actor whose internal politicization remains obscure to the citizenry.

The two contributions are firmly located at the political institutions-end of our first dimension. Both national parliaments and the European Parliament are considered essential "ingredients" to meet the dual legitimacy requirement which posits that the democratic legitimacy of the EU requires, first, the accountability of Council members to their national parliaments (and through them to their citizens) and, second, a direct form of accountability and citizen involvement via elections to the European Parliament. Both contributions not only emphasize the instrumental character of the contribution of legislatures to contribute to the democratic legitimacy of the EU polity, but also stress the importance of the electoral channel and of bargaining: National parliaments and the European Parliament confront their national executives and the Council respectively to wrest power and influence from them to alter the distribution of information and power.

While Berthold Rittberger's chapter shares with the previous contributions their emphasis on political institutions, voting, and instrumentalism, he moves from analyzing the contribution of European Parliament and national parliaments to the democratic legitimacy equation by means of exogenously given, abstract categories to an endogenous explanation of those very categories: Why have the member states of the EU taken (and continue to take) recourse to the model of parliamentary democracy as a guiding principle for institutional design and reform, as a result of which the member states have successively endowed the European Parliament with control and budgetary and legislative powers? He argues that the lamented democratic deficit is not only an analytical construct which besets academics, political commentary, and to which politicians pay verbal tribute. Once decisions to transfer sovereignty to the EU level loom, normative pressure is generated to counter the threat which policy-makers associate with integration and the concomitant transfer of sovereignty, namely that further integration undermines domestic democratic processes and institutions. As a result, politicians have come to consider both the European Parliament, and—as of more recently—national parliaments, as appropriate reform targets when contemplating institutional solutions to reduce the democratic deficit.

In the final contribution to this section, Christopher Lord suggests a double shift, first from the focus on political institutions emblematic of the previous contributions to the inclusion of a broader set of societal stakeholders and, second, from an emphasis on electoral channels and bargaining to deliberation. Lord sets out with the claim that even though the EU is a decentered polity, that is, a polity which "is not centered on a single menu of policy, nor on a single institutional method . . . ; nor . . . does it have clear boundaries with contiguous systems, political social or economic," (Lord, chapter 6) this does not imply that the EU is unsuited to parliamentary politics. Lord argues that postparliamentary forms of representation such as stakeholder networks are more suited to a de-centered polity since those affected will vary from policy to policy and hence sector-specific networks rather than fixed-composition parliaments should represent policy addressees. However, even postparliamentary solutions to the question of representation presuppose the very parliamentary politics they are intended to replace since there has to be a body which answers the following questions: Who guarantees equal access to those affected by political decisions? Who decides on the criteria by which postparliamentary mechanisms of representation, such as stakeholder networks, are governed? Lord shifts back to parliamentarism and sides with Habermas when he argues that for decisions to be converted into legitimate law they should have to pass at some point through "sluice gates" of parliament, that is, that part of the public sphere that is procedurally structured and capable of taking decisions which affect society as a whole according to fair procedures and deliberative standards. Lord argues that "[a]s long as rulemaking contains such a point there is no reason why proposals should not originate in "autonomous and spontaneous" sub-systems of civil society" (Lord, chapter 6).

The Public Sphere and Civil Society: Prerequisites for Democratically Legitimate Rule Making

Christopher Lord's contribution has already alluded to the concept of the public sphere and the role of civil society, both of which are at the heart of the ensuing contributions. Klaus Eder and Hans-Jörg Trenz argue that institutional mechanisms and structures such as parliaments, political parties, and elections are insufficient mechanisms for the democratization of the EU polity. For a polity such as the EU where the constituent parts (the member state polities) are already democratic, the question of democratic legitimacy emerges in a new light: Can the EU actually avoid democratization? The authors argue that political communication and deliberation trigger collective learning processes which are crucial to develop a common European identity. It is in this context that the authors introduce the concept of "public space" as a crucial mechanism for democratization. Public spaces are "arena[s] of communication in which those who govern and those who are subject to governance . . . gather and express particular interests, concerns and expectations . . . The public space . . . initiates a process in which political decision-making is mediated through public opinion and collective will-formation." (Eder and Trenz, chapter 7) By analyzing the coverage of the quality press in different EU member states, the authors provide empirical evidence to bolster the argument that political communication triggers a process of Europeanization and thus contributes to the creation of a European public space, a necessary prerequisite for the democratization of the EU.

Donatella della Porta's chapter is also located at the civil society– and deliberation–centered ends of our first two dimensions of democracy. She argues that, historically, social protest movements have played a crucial role in the democratization of the modern system of states by pushing for civil, political, and social rights and by constituting a critical public sphere. While the nation-state used to be the only point of reference for social movements, the growing importance of the EU level in affecting the welfare of socioeconomic actors has produced a situation in which social movement actors have come to discover the European level as a target for political demands. By implication, della Porta shows by means of induction that social protest movements have adapted their strategies to use different paths to voice their concerns to affect national and EU-level decisions.

Democracy and Political Participation

Participatory democracy has become a buzz-word in the Brussels orbit; it assumes a prominent place in the Commission's White Paper on Governance and in the Constitutional Treaty which devoted a special article to the principle of participatory democracy. Part of the motivation that drives political advocacy for and action towards participatory democracy at the EU-level is the belief that increasing the opportunities for popular participation is paramount to counter-steer what Robert Dahl coined the "fundamental democratic dilemma": The dilemma between, on the one hand, achieving effective and efficient government for the people by supranational problem-solving and, on the other hand, the concomitant reduction of government by the people by making it more difficult for citizens to raise their voice via traditional parliamentary channels has triggered calls for expanding the opportunities for discussion, citizen participation, and influence.[92] Others, however, argue that participation by all those "relevant" actors who are affected by a particular decision is itself crucial to generate system effectiveness and hence contributes to the polity's overall level of legitimacy.[93] This is where Hubert Heinelt's chapter takes off. He argues that the sovereignty of the state and the capacity of the people to shape their fortunes democratically via binding decisions issued by representative bodies are limited; consequently, participation and effective policy making cannot rely merely on government backed by the state but on governance. Governance is seen as a mode of problem solving which reaches beyond the hierarchical authority of the state into the societal realm, emphasizing forms of social interaction and decision making through mutual accommodation by means of deliberation and exchanges of reasoned arguments instead of preference aggregation (through voting), bargaining, or hierarchical direction. In chapter 9, Heinelt introduces different dimensions of governance which correlate with particular "worlds of democratic action" which are prejudiced towards particular forms of democratic

participation (voting/bargaining and deliberation/arguing) as well as particular models of democracy (deliberative democracy versus liberal democracy). Heinelt's approach is characterized by an instrumentalist view on participation, that is, participation is considered a means to improve the
effectiveness and legitimacy of political decisions.

Michael Greven's contribution points at the contested nature of the concept of participatory democracy in democratic theory. In the late 1960s and
1970s, the concept was employed as a critique of democratic elitism. Today,
participatory governance is conceived of as a functional contribution to effective and efficient governance and policy-making and derives its legitimacy
primarily from its perceived instrumental value to promote the effectiveness
and legitimacy of governance solutions. In this perspective, Greven criticizes
the prevailing scholarship on participatory democracy for its instrumentalism and functionalism since the right to participate depends on the possession of a particular quality or resource which is relevant to the problem at
hand. Greven ends on a cautionary note, maintaining that the present dominant discourse on participatory governance constitutes—what he calls—"Be-
griffspolitik", an "active concept-policy" (Greven, chapter 10) which promotes
a technocratic perspective of authoritative problem solving which is "stimulated not by accident but by more technocratic than democratic institutions
like the World Bank, the European Commission, and hegemonic factions of
policy-oriented political scientists" (Greven, chapter 10).

Beate Kohler-Koch reflects on the latest concepts and strategies that have
been propagated by EU institutions, above all by the Commission, to enhance
efficient and democratic governance by putting state-society relations on a
new footing. European and national associations have been, from the very beginning of European integration, important collective actors in representing
interests and giving input to EU policy formulation. As intermediary organizations they provide an infrastructure for a European transnational civil society and successively integrate different national political spaces. The contribution explores the democratic potential of a strengthening of civil society
organizations and their wider involvement in EU affairs from the perspective
of liberal, deliberative, and participatory democracy. The Commission has revised its consultation regime in a way to support a more pluralistic representation of interests and to give prominence to arguing instead of bargaining.
Nevertheless, it is open to debate whether the new regime will work in favor
of a more equal representation of interests and can improve the discursive
quality of policy formulation. First, it is doubtful whether procedural reforms
can overcome the institutional impediments of the EU polity and the national
self-reference of European societies. Second, notwithstanding the dedication
to improve democratic input legitimacy, EU institutions pursue their own

agenda. For the sake of high-quality performance, the Commission is dependent on expert advice and has to invest its scarce resources of time and manpower where it yields the greatest benefit. Associations, on their part, have to live up to the functional demands of the EU system with further market strategies and oligarchic tendencies within organizations. Thus, EU associations have structural difficulties to act as schools of democracy. Nevertheless, the normative discourse and the more inclusive consultation strategies have given general interests a stronger voice and have strengthened the legitimacy of arguing over bargaining. Policy formulation and decision making at the EU level has become more transparent and it has attracted more public attention. This may build up over time not so much as the result of the intentional strategies but because of unintended consequences due to the dynamics of raising expectations concerning the political responsiveness of the EU.

Deliberative Democracy

The deliberative turn in contemporary democratic theory is represented by the final set of contributions in this volume. In his chapter, Rainer Schmalz-Bruns asks how the EU polity should be designed in order to meet the normative standards set by a deliberative understanding of democracy. Since deliberative democracy does not prejudice a particular organizational principle and hence does not offer ready-made prescriptions about the design of democratic institutions, it suggests that institutions—to meet the standard of deliberative democracy—should foster those principles that enable individuals to exercise their right to justification and to improve the epistemic quality of political decisions. Schmalz-Bruns argues that a deliberative democratic approach offers an attractive alternative to dominant approaches in the literature for which the democratic shortfall of the EU constitutes a seemingly inescapable dilemma: For the EU to become a standard democracy "it must become recognizably like the modern state or federation and will therefore not only face the danger of the growing alienation of its citizens . . . but will have to give up its polycentricity and postsovereignty; or, if it is to be a novel form of democracy without sovereignty and hierarchy, then it must give up the standard requirement that its polity constitutes a determinate and sovereign *demos*." (Schmalz-Bruns, chapter 12) For deliberative democrats a demos is not based on a cultural community but is constituted by a "reflexively integrated moral (and legal) community, where the sovereignty of dispersed *demoi* is invested into an order of internally deliberative institution" (Schmalz-Bruns, chapter 12) For the EU, this implies that legally circumscribed forms of reflexivity which are visible and accessible to all must be built into the system. Schmalz-Bruns stresses that this form of deliberative democratization cannot do without a state, that is to say, a hierarchical form of self-intervention, since a system of governance—to be considered democratic—has to possess an organized capacity to act.

Christian Joerges's chapter is not about deliberative democracy in the sense outlined above, but points to a particular quality of EU law. Joerges argues that EU law is a species of conflict of laws which resolves conflicts between states by taking recourse to principles which are acceptable to all national polities concerned. Joerges maintains that the law, thus conceived, can be a response to the observation that "nationally organized constitutional states are becoming increasingly incapable of acting democratically. They cannot include all those who will be affected by their decisions in the electoral process, and vice versa, citizens cannot influence the behavior of those political actors who are making decisions on their behalf" (Joerges, chapter 13). As a consequence, Joerges promotes the normative argument that the extra-territorial effects and burdens which one state inadvertently imposes onto neighboring states in a globalized and interdependent world cannot be justified by taking recourse to domestic democratic processes. For Joerges the supremacy of EU law coincides with a call "for the identification of rules and principles to ensure the co-existence of different constituencies and the compatibility of these constituencies' objectives with the common concerns they share" (Joerges, chapter 13). Joerges argues normatively by claiming that EU law should structure political deliberation in a way that meets these requirements and empirically by positing that EU law has fulfilled this role by civilizing "national idiosyncrasies, with good reasons and considerable de facto success" (Joerges, chapter 13).

Notes

For comments and earlier versions of this chapter we wish to thank John Eric Fossum, Christoph Humrich, Katja Rüb, Frank Schimmelfennig, Anne Elizabeth Stie, and Guido Schwellnus. We also gratefully acknowledge research and editing assistance provided by Christian Fäth, Stefan-Fabian Lutz, Jens Schmidt, Julia Schneider, and Angelika Weiske. Special thanks go to Laurence Lessard-Phillips who language-edited the entire book manuscript. We gratefully acknowledge financial assistance and logistical support by the Mannheim Center for European Social Research (MZES).

1. Majone 1998, 6.
2. Richardson and Jordan (1979) introduced the term to characterize the policy process in the UK stressing informal relationships between different actors in the policy process rather than solely the formal institutions of government and their rela-

tionships. See Anderson and Burns, 1996, for a discussion about the decline of parliamentary democracy in Europe and the increasing importance and potential for non-parliamentary forms of interest representation in the EU and its Member-State polities.

3. See Gerstenberg 1997, 352.
4. See, for instance, Dryzek 2000.
5. See, for instance, Hix 1998.
6. See, for instance, Eriksen et al. 2003 and Eriksen and Fossum 2004.
7. See Majone 1996.
8. See Majone 2000; 2002.
9. See Ipsen 1972.
10. See Mestmäcker 1994.
11. Moravcsik 2002, 605.
12. Moravcsik 2002, 605.
13. Moravcsik 2002, 607.
14. Moravcsik 2002, 613.
15. Moravcsik 2002, 622.
16. Dahl 1998, 115.
17. Dahl 1998, 115.
18. Dahl 1998, 116. See also Follesdal and Hix 2005, 18–22.
19. See Weiler et al. 1995.
20. Kielmansegg 2003, 57. See Scharpf 1999 for a similar argument.
21. Kielmansegg employs the term "belastbare Identität", which is translated by Cederman 2001, 154 with identity "strong enough to carry the weight of democratic politics".
22. See Lepsius 1999, Cederman 2001, and Seidendorf 2005 for a somewhat more positive assessment of the EU's capacity to develop a collective identity.
23. Follesdal and Hix 2005, 17. See also Hix 1998.
24. See Hix 2002.
25. See Hooghe and Marks 2001; Peters and Pierre 2004; Bache and Flinders 2004.
26. Marks and Hooghe 2003, 233.
27. Kohler-Koch 1998, 15–16.
28. Benz 2003, 88.
29. Benz 2003, 101.
30. Hooghe and Marks 2003, 237.
31. Schmitter 2002, 55.
32. See Kohler-Koch 1999.
33. For detailed information, see the GOVDATA database provided by the Network of Excellence CONNEX ("Connecting Excellence on European Governance") funded under the 6th Framework Program for Research (www.connex-network.org).
34. See Héritier 1999, 275.
35. Swyngedouw et al. 2002, 128.
36. Papadopoulos 2006, 13.
37. Peters and Pierre 2004, 86–88.

38. See Rhodes 2000, 77.
39. See Stoker 2003, 10.
40. Peters and Pierre 2004, 88.
41. See, for instance, Pharr and Putnam 2000; Cain et al. 2003; Dalton 2004.
42. See Dalton et al. 2003.
43. Warren 2001, 226.
44. See Burns 2000.
45. See Burns 2000. Fossum 2005, 24 offers an overview of how analysts have invented a terminology to depict the less definite relation between territory and identity.
46. See Commission 2001a, 11-18.
47. Commission 2001a, 3.
48. Commission 2001a, 4.
49. See European Commission 2001a, 15.
50. See, for instance, Joerges et al. 2001.
51. See Carter and Stokes 2002, 2, 3.
52. See Majone 1998, 6.
53. See Höreth 1999 for an overview.
54. See, for example, Dahl 1989; Gutman 1993; Held 1995, 2002; Post 2006.
55. For an overview see Held 2002, chapter 9.
56. See Dahl 1989, 105; Pettit 1997.
57. Post 2006, 25.
58. Post 2006, 26.
59. See Held 2002, 300.
60. Post 2006, 29.
61. See Gosepath 2001.
62. Post 2006, 31.
63. See Gosepath 2001; Kolm 1993; Arneson 1993.
64. See Gutmann 1993, 414.
65. See Gutmann 1993, 418.
66. Habermas 1997, 288 (authors' translation).
67. See Habermas 1994, 533.
68. See, for example, Vilmar 1973.
69. See Schmidt 2000, 257–259.
70. See Dahl 1989.
71. Dahl 1989, 153–162.
72. See Lijphart 1984, 1999.
73. Michelman cited in Habermas 1997, 282-283.
74. Riker 1982, 6.
75. See also Riker 1982.
76. See Dahl 1989, 170.
77. Warren 1992, 8.
78. Downs 1957, 27–28.
79. See March and Olsen 1989, 1998.
80. See, for example, Waltz 1979; Grieco 1988.

81. See, for example, Schweller 1994; Mearsheimer 1995.
82. See, for example, Keohane and Nye 1977; Keohane, 1984.
83. See Scharpf 2004.
84. Fearon and Wendt 2002, 57.
85. March and Olsen 1995, 6.
86. March and Olsen 1995, 154.
87. See March and Olsen 1989, 23.
88. Habermas 1981, 385.
89. Risse 2000, 10.
90. Dryzek 2000, 170 (emphasis added).
91. See, for example, Cain et al. 2001.
92. See Dahl 1994.
93. See Gbikpi and Grote 2002, 26.

I

DEMOCRACY: THE CONSTITUTIONAL PRINCIPLE OF THE EU

2

A Disputed Idea Becomes Law: Remarks on European Democracy as a Legal Principle

Armin von Bogdandy

Eᴜʀᴏᴘᴇᴀɴ ꜱᴏᴄɪᴀʟ ꜱᴄɪᴇɴᴄᴇꜱ have dealt impressively with the issue of democracy in European integration. This chapter will not retrace the development of the current debate nor enrich it with further suggestions. Instead, this chapter presents several elements of European positive law, which together can be considered the debate's result in terms of positive law. Certainly, this concrete result will, in turn, be shaped further by the waves of future debate. But the debate will have changed: waves break differently on the open sea than they do against solid rock. This solid rock is binding law.

Development and Basic Features

In order to understand the current law, it is important to remember that until the 1990s it was widely held that the supranational authority did not legally require democratic legitimacy beyond the general requirements established for an international organization.[1] Hence, for over thirty years, legal science focused not on the principle of democracy, but rather on the rule of law.

The thesis that the Community should have its own democratic legitimacy began to develop as a political request of some and not as a legal principle that the Community had to respect in order to be legal under its members' constitutions.[2] After 1990, however, a rapid development took place which followed two different, albeit connected paths: one, based on civil rights thinking, focusing on Union citizenship,[3] and another, based on institutional thinking, oriented at the legitimacy of the Union's organizational set-up.

The development from political demand for an independent democratic legitimacy to legal principle has been arduous. Tellingly, even the act of 20 September 1976 concerning the election of the representatives of the European Parliament by direct universal suffrage does not contain the term "democracy."[4] Beginning in the 1980s, the ECJ very cautiously began to use the concept of democracy as a legal principle.[5] The Treaty of Maastricht then employed this term, although it mentions its role on the supranational level only in the fifth recital of the Preamble. With Article F of the EU Treaty in the Maastricht version democracy found its way into a treaty text—yet not as a basis for the Union, but rather with a view to the Member States' political systems. The leap was not made until the Treaty of Amsterdam whose Article 6 EU then laid down that the principle of democracy also applies to the Union. External provisions buttress this internal constitutional development. Of particular importance is Article 3, Protocol No. 1 to the ECHR (European Convention of Human Rights) in its recent interpretation by the Strasbourg Court,[6] as well as—albeit less clearly—national provisions such as the amended Article 23(1) of the German Basic Law.[7]

The Convention's draft of the Constitutional Treaty tried to make another leap which, however, almost certainly would have failed. In selecting democracy as the theme of the introductory quotation,[8] the Convention's draft declared democracy as the highest value of the Union. This primacy, though, arose not solely from the prominent placement. The quotation comes from Pericles' funeral oration for the soldiers who died in the Peloponnesian War, in which "speech democracy" is elevated as the value that even justifies sacrifice of human lives.[9] To suggest democracy as the Union's primary value is risky. Certainly, most Union citizens would place high value on democracy, yet the discourse of democracy in the introduction seemingly intimated that the Union—at least as the Convention's draft would have it—exists for the purpose of realizing democratic ideals. Many citizens, however, may—rightly—believe that democracy's status in the Union is not fully satisfactory. Moreover, considering the institutional alterations, the Constitutional Treaty is unlikely to fully mend the often lamented democratic deficit. Thus, there is a difference between the discourse of the law as reflected in the most prominent declaration of the Convention's draft and the everyday experience of Union citizens. Fortunately, the Intergovernmental Conference (IGC) deleted the reference to Thucydides' narrative in the final version of the Constitutional Treaty. With the more classical approach of extending the codecision procedure to more fields of EU action and the adoption of the more innovative—yet still not fully convincing—articles on the democratic life of the Union,[10] the IGC thus took steps which could prove more successful than the overambitious Convention draft.

As it is stated in Article 6 EU, "democracy" carries no definition. On the European level, the meaning of the principle of democracy is yet to be determined. Nothing better depicts the uncertainties of how to understand the unional principle of democracy than Part I Title VI and Part II Title V of the Constitutional Treaty. Under the headings "The Democratic Life of the Union" and "Citizens' Rights" respectively, a number of seemingly unconnected provisions are amassed; it will require a singular intellectual effort to reconstruct them as a meaningful whole.[11]

However, such innovative scholarship is needed anyway. More than for any other constitutional principle, it is beyond question that the principle of democracy requires a specific concretization for the European Union and that any analogy to nation-state institutions must be carefully argued. A remarkably complex interdisciplinary discussion on European democracy has developed on the basis of this insight.[12]

From the perspective of a European doctrine of principles,[13] that is, a systematic exposition of the most essential legal norms of the European legal order, the preliminary question of the possibility of democracy at the Union level can be neglected.[14] Firstly, a doctrine of principles that belongs to the realm of political sociology barely touches this question. More importantly, the Union's constitutional law has normatively, and thus for a doctrine of principles decisively answered the question in Article 6(1) EU: democracy is a constitutional principle of the Union.

A European doctrine of principles must define the unional principle of democracy. The easier part of that exercise is to discard inappropriate understandings, which are prominent in numerous national legal discourses concerning the concretization of the principle of democracy. This is particularly true for the theory, which understands democracy in a substantive sense as the rule of "the people" in the German sense of a *Volk*. Such an understanding implies empirical bases that scarcely emerge at the European level. It would also be difficult to square with manifold provisions of the current treaties[15] although the substitution of the word "peoples" with "citizens" in the Constitutional Treaty might point to a shift in this conception in Articles I-1(1), I-20(2) and I-46(2) CT-IGC. Of course it is possible to proceed formally and conceive *das Volk* as the sum of all Union citizens.[16] However, this strategy that essentially concretizes the principle of democracy would create severe strains on other central Union principles, in particular Articles 1(2) and 6(3) EU and Article 189 EC. These norms suggest that the principle of democracy within the context of the Union must be concretized independently from the problematic concept of European "people."[17]

As an alternative, the individual's opportunities to participate come into the foreground. Peter M. Huber conceives the European principle of democracy as giving the individual a sufficiently effective opportunity to influence the basic decisions of European policy through unional as well as national procedures. The European principle of democracy thus contains an optimization requirement insofar as its objectives encompass the full utilization of possibilities to participate at both levels.[18] This understanding of democracy does not necessarily require breaking with understandings developed under the national constitutions, but correlates with the civil rights understanding of democracy. The concretization of the principle of democracy finds confirmation in the legal concept of Union citizenship.[19]

However, the unional principle of democracy would be misunderstood if it placed only the individual Union citizen at center stage. The Union does not negate the democratic organization of citizens in and by the Member States.[20] Thus, alongside the Union citizens, the Member States' democratically organized peoples[21] are to be active in the Union's decision-making process as organized associations. A concretization strategy should build on these two textual elements: the current treaties speak on the one hand of the peoples of the Member States and on the other hand of the Union's citizens insofar as the principle of democracy is at issue.[22]

The central elements, which determine the Union's principle of democracy at this first level, are thus named. The Union is based on a dual structure of legitimacy[23]: the totality of the Union's citizens, and the peoples of the European Union organized by their respective Member States' constitutions.

At the conceptual level, the understanding of the unional principle of democracy suggests an abandoning of the conception of democracy as the self-determination of a people. However, the Constitutional Treaty depicts the Union as such an instrument of self-determination.[24] This conception becomes implausible since the peoples of the Member States no longer exercise such self-determination (if they ever did). In addition, conceptions that consider democracy as an instrument of individual self-determination[25] do not have much of a chance for success within the Union context. On all levels the civil rights and control-oriented conceptions of democracy seem more appropriate.[26]

The Principle of Democracy and the Institutional Structure

In almost all understandings of democracy, the most important element lies in the choice of the political personnel through free elections by the citizens. There is no reason why this should be different for the Union. Elections provide two lines of democratic legitimacy for the Union's organizational structure. The European Parliament, which is based on elections by the totality of the Union's citizens, and the European Council as well as the Council, whose legitimacy is based on the Member States' democratically organized peoples, institutionally represent these lines respectively. In the current constitutional situation, the line of legitimacy from the national parliaments, as shown in particular by Article 48 EU as well as the preponderance of the Council and the European Council in the Union's procedures is clearly dominant. The Constitutional Treaty increases the relative weight of the European Parliament (EP) without, however, equalizing the two lines of democratic legitimacy.

It is doubtful that a principle of dual legitimacy as a concretization of the principle of democracy could be formulated at all since the codecision of the EP has by no means been incorporated into all areas of competence, nor do all important personnel decisions require its approval and other institutions are not answerable to it for all acts. Nevertheless, there is broad consensus that the EP's current scope of competences already permits the assumption of a principle of dual legitimacy.[27] The decision concerning appointments to the Commission and thus the "political motor of integration" is based on dual legitimacy pursuant to Article 214 EC[28] as is not only the greater part of the legislative process pursuant to Article 251 EC[29], but also the budget according to Article 272 EC[30] and the decision on accepting a new member under Article 49 EU.[31]

Yet, in view of the current legal situation, the principle can only be understood as meaning that the democratic legitimacy of Union acts can be derived by way of the Council and the EP. The European principle of democracy does not, however, specify which institution in any concrete case must take a concrete decision.[32] The legitimacy of any specific act is a question of procedure, based on the relevant competence: for such sectoral regulation, the principle of democracy can promote stability but cannot modify procedure itself.[33] The demand to expand parliamentary powers remains in the political sphere; it can scarcely be based on the Union's principle of democracy.[34]

If the legal impact of the principle of democracy is limited, its implications are enormous. A transnational parliament can confer democratic legitimacy although it does not represent a people. Moreover, a governmental institution (the Council) is also able to do so. This contrasts sharply with national constitutional law, where such decisions are usually considered democratically problematic.[35] Moreover, in Germany the participation of the governments of the *Länder* in the federal political process through the Federal Council is rarely acknowledged as having a role in conferring democratic legitimacy on federal law.[36] The idea of a unitary people is too strong.[37]

In Member States' constitutional law the principle of democracy is usually further concretized by the Parliament's specific position in the overall constitutional structure. At this point, European democracy remains hazy.

One encounters an open situation, displaying this principle's lesser degree of development.

Some aspects should be briefly highlighted. One concern is whether and to what extent the system of European government is a parliamentary one.[38] Applied to the Union, this concerns the relationship between the EP and the Commission. Legally the EP's control over the Commission's composition is, in certain respects, greater than that of the French National Assembly over the French government.[39] Yet, whereas a semiparliamentarian system of government has been realized on the weak French basis, nothing of the sort has occurred on the European level. It is quite conceivable that the Union's constitutive plurality prevents such a system from developing. Thus, the congressional model is also being discussed as an option for the EP.[40] It appears to be an empirically, constitutionally, and politically open question as to what form the European parliamentary system will finally take.[41]

The Parliament's lack of a right to legislative initiative may also become characteristic. It gives support to a conception grounded in the realistic parliamentary theories of the twentieth century.[42] The lack of a right to legislative initiative can be construed in such a way that a society gives up the understanding of legislation as self-legislation, dear to important strands of democratic thinking.[43] The EP's whole organization may be understood instead as a safeguard against the governing bureaucracy becoming overly autonomous.[44] This conception points to a sober understanding of the principle of democracy but may have good prospects for that very reason. This fluidity shows that the ECJ has been wise not to use the principle of democracy for far-reaching developments of the law in the interinstitutional area, since, in contrast to the principle of the rule of law, sufficiently concretized and agreed strategies are still missing.

Transparency, Participation, Deliberation, and Flexibility

The principle of democracy, whether understood as an opportunity to participate, as a check on governmental abuse, or as self-determination of the citizens, confronts greater challenges under the Union's organizational set-up than it does within the nation-state context. Greater private freedom in the Union is bought at the cost of less democratic self-determination. Contrasted with the nation-state, the Union's sheer size and constitutive diversity, the physical distance of the central institutions from most of the Union's citizens, and the complexity of its Constitution, which can only be modestly reduced, are some of the factors that place greater restrictions on the realization of the principle of democracy by way of electing representative institutions. In light of this insight, further strategies for the realization of the principle of democracy have received far greater attention than within the national context. This is especially true of transparency, participation of those affected, deliberation, and flexibility.

Sometimes the discussion concerning these concretizing strategies appears to be carried by the hope that they might compensate for the Union's democratic deficit. However, such considerations can only be useful in the political realm, but not in the legal context. There are no criteria as to how a deficit in electoral legitimacy could be legally offset.[45] Yet the following two concepts establish a new strategy for the realization of the principle of democracy.[46]

The transparency of governmental action—its comprehensibility and the possibility of attributing accountability—is only peripherally associated with the principle of democracy in the German domestic context.[47] European constitutional law places itself at the forefront of constitutional development when it requires that decisions be "taken as openly as possible," that is, transparently. The Amsterdam Treaty first declared this, placing it prominently in Article 1(2) EU. The specific democratic meaning of transparency in European law was already found in the 17th Declaration to the Maastricht Treaty on the right to obtain information, which states that the decision-making procedure's transparency strengthens the institutions' democratic character. Article I-50 CT-IGC confirms this understanding.

Transparency requires knowledge of the motives of decision makers. From the beginning, community law has recognized a duty to provide reasons for legislative acts,[48] which is something that is hardly known in national legal orders.[49] Of course this duty was first conceived primarily from the perspective of the rule of law,[50] and yet its relevance for the principle of democracy has meanwhile come to enjoy general acknowledgement.[51] Access to documents, which now also enjoys the dignity of being laid down in Article 255 EC, is also of great importance to the realization of transparency. It has further become the subject of a considerable body of case law,[52] which is slowly eroding the still powerful "tradition of secretiveness."[53] A further aspect is the openness of the Council's voting record on legislative measures.[54] The Constitutional Treaty develops these elements further with its provisions on the transparency of the institutions' proceedings and the access of the individual to the institutions' documents in Articles I-50, II-102, II-I399 CT-IGC.[55]

The second complex concerns forms of political participation beyond elections. Popular consultations appear as an obvious instrument, and referenda have occasionally been used to legitimatize national decisions on European issues (such as accession to the Union or the ratification of amending treaties). To extend such instruments to the European level has been proposed for some time[56] and the citizens' initiative figures among the innovations of the Constitutional Treaty.[57] At this moment, however, it is very difficult to evaluate the possible importance of such strategies as a way to invigorate the democratic principle.

Whereas the Union has no experience with popular consultations, it has much experience in allowing special interests to intervene in the political process. Comparative research between the Union and the independent regulatory agencies under the U.S. Constitution has indicated that such participation of interested and affected parties may be a further avenue in the realization of the democratic principle.[58] Article I-47(1)–(3) CTI-GC is based on this understanding, while such inclusion is still waiting to be generally recognized as a strategy for the realization of the principle of democracy at the nation-state level.[59] There is, however, no principle in primary law that gives a right to affected parties to participate in the legislative process.[60] However, there are secondary legal provisions, which are understood in this light.[61] This concretization of the principle of democracy requires much further elaboration.

An interesting development in this regard is the use of the so-called convention method for the creation of fundamental European law, as was the case with the Charter of Fundamental Rights and the Constitutional Treaty. The instrument of the Convention allows for the inclusion of interested parties and experts in the law-making process.[62] Article 443(2) CT-IGC even introduces a compulsory Convention for the revision of the Constitutional Treaty. With respect to all such forms of political participation, the issue of how to guarantee political equality is still unanswered, as is the question of how to avoid political gridlock or the so-called agency capture by strong, organized groups.

A most important strategy to strengthen democracy at the supranational level is to increase the flexibility of the Union. Flexibility was introduced as a general strategy by the Treaty of Amsterdam and considerably expanded by the Treaty of Nice[63] and the Constitutional Treaty.[64] The flexibility provision allows a democratic national majority to shape a given national situation without frustrating the will of the European majority. However, difficult questions remain to be resolved such as competitive equality in the internal market[65] and the possibility of leaving the Union, as foreseen in Article I-60 CT-IGC, which upholds the prospect of national self-determination as an important aspect of democracy.[66]

Conclusion

The preceding considerations demonstrate that the legal principle of democracy is only slowly taking form at the European level, building on some established conceptions while introducing a number of innovative accentuations and far-reaching modifications. For example, in national constitutional law political equality of all citizens is a core element of democracy that greatly influences the organizational set-up.[67] By contrast, the Union's constitutional set-up must give diversity similar and important instruments of expression.[68] This explains and probably justifies some limitations placed on the principle of political equality.[69]

The most important conceptual modification of established national constitutional doctrine concerns political unity, which most scholars consider as a fundamental basis for democracy in the constitutional state (even in the federal variant). The Union lacks such political unity, since it comprises discrete, nationally organized peoples and, thus, structurally related minorities.[70] This finds its constitutional expression *inter alia* in the guarantee of respect for the Member States' identity, the lack of will to found a state, the want of a comprehensive community of solidarity and defense,[71] as well as the central role of the Council and the European Council in the decision-making process.

By establishing democracy as a legal principle of the European Union, a disputed idea has become law. Accordingly, the debate should progress. As this contribution should have shown, the law urgently requires a redefinition and this will be realized with further debate. This debate, however, takes place in a nascent archipelago where successful navigation requires different skills than in the high seas.

Notes

1. Randelzhofer 1994, 40.

2. That, by contrast, was the case with the rule of law and fundamental rights (see Kaiser 1966, 33). There is thus a striking parallel to the constitutional developments of the nineteenth century; see Böckenförde 1992, 143.

3. This path will not be presented here. See Kadelbach 2006.

4. Act concerning the election of the representatives of the Parliament by direct universal suffrage, OJ L 278, 8.10.1976, 1.

5. The principle has been used very carefully and above all to strengthen existing provisions; see especially Case 138/79, *Roquette Frères v. Council* [1980] ECR 3333, para 33; Case C-300/89, *Commission v. Council* [1991] ECR I-2867, para 20; Case C-65/93, *Parliament v. Council* [1995] ECR I-643, para 21; Case C-21/94, *Parliament v. Council* [1995] ECR I-1827, para 17; Case C-392/95, *Parliament v. Council* [1997] ECR I-3213, para 14. But see the CFI judgement Case T-135/96, *UEAPME v. Council* [1998] ECR II-2335, para 89, that interprets the principle of democracy with greater liberty. See Britz and Schmidt 1999, 481; Langenbucher 2002, 265–286.

6. ECHR, *Matthews v. United Kingdom*, Rep 1999-I 251; see Ress 1999, 226; Bröhmer 1999, 197–217. In the judgement the ECHR determined that the European

Parliament has to be considered as a "legislature" in the sense of Article 3 Protocol No.1 to the ECHR. Hence, people of Gibraltar cannot be deprived of their democratic right to participate in European Parliamentary elections.

7. Article 23(1) German Basic Law concerning the openness to European integration reads, "(1) To realize a unified Europe, Germany participates in the development of the European Union which is bound to democratic rule of law, social and federal principles as well as the principle of subsidiarity and provides a protection of fundamental rights essentially equivalent to that of this Constitution. The federation can, for this purpose and with the consent of the Senate, delegate sovereign powers. Article 79(2) & (3) is applicable for the foundation of the European Union as well as for changes in its contractual basis and comparable regulations by which the content of this Constitution is changed or amended or by which such changes or amendments are authorized." On similar provisions in other constitutions see Grabenwarter, 2006 and Pernice 1998.

8. The text reads as follows, "Our Constitution . . . is called a democracy because power is in the hands not of a minority but of the greatest number."

9. Thucydides 1954, II, 42 and II, 44. The idea that the readiness to make sacrifices is a key element to a collective identity is often found in U.S.-American constitutional theory. For the viewpoint of a leading proponent of the "cultural study of law," see Kahn 2000, 8; and also Haltern 2006.

10. Arts. I-45 *et seq* CT-IGC CT-IGC refers to the signed Constitutional Treaty in its document version of August 6, 2004, also referred to as CIG 87/04.

11. For the first comprehensive effort, see Peters 2004, 37.

12. For the identification of sixty-four positions on the European democracy problem, see Schimmelfennig 1996.

13. See von Bogdandy 2006.

14. See Kielmansegg 1996; Offe 1998; Scharpf 1999b, 672; Grimm 1995, 282; Fuchs 2000, 222. For a contrary position, see Zuleeg 1999, 11; Habermas 2001b.

15. E.g. Articles 1(2) EU, 189 EC.

16. Augustin 2000, 110.

17. For a detailed analysis, see Dellavalle 1993, 217.

18. Huber 1999.

19. Article 17 EC.

20. Article 17(1) EC.

21. Articles 1(2) and 6(3) EU, Article 189 EC.

22. The Constitutional Treaty alters this picture: although "peoples" remains a constitutional concept, the Constitutional Treaty always uses the term "citizens" in the context of democracy. This should not, however, alter the concept of dual legitimacy, as already expressed in Article I-1(1) CT-IGC.

23. On the model of dual legitimacy, see Peters 2004; Oeter 2006; Dann 2006.

24. This is underlined by the third recital of the Preamble (fourth recital of the Convention's draft) which states that the peoples of Europe are determined, "united ever more closely, to forge a common destiny."

25. Frankenberg 2002, 148, leans in this direction. See also Habermas 1992, 532; Pernice 2000, 160.

26. Augustin 2000, 246, 319, 388; Wallrabenstein 1999, 138. The dichotomies used herein are developed in Von Bogdandy 2004.

27. Decisions of the German Constitutional Court (Entscheidungen des Bundesverfassungsgerichts) 89, 155 at 184.

28. Article I 27 CT-IGC.

29. Article III 396 CT-IGC.

30. Articles I-56, II-I404 CT-IGC.

31. Article I-58(2) CT-IGC.

32. This notwithstanding the political demand that, at least in those areas in which the Council decides by majority decision, the Parliament should be involved by way of the codecision procedure.

33. The principle of democracy is thus not a criterion for the horizontal distribution of competences; see Case C-300/89, *Commission of the European Communities v. Council of the European Communities* [1991], paras 20 *et seq*; but see Advocate General Tesauro, *ibid*, I-2892 *et seq*.

34. However, the approach taken by the Court of First Instance in its judgement in Case T-353/00, *Le Pen v Parliament* [2003] ECR II-1729, paras 90 *et seq*, and the ECJ in its judgment in Case 208/03 P, *Le Pen v Parliament* [2005] ECR I-6051, paras 50 *et seq*, is too cautious in that it rejected an autonomous, extensive right of Parliament to verify the vacancy of the seat of one of its members as not having separate legal effects. The reasoning is based on the state of Community law after the 1976 Act. The principle of democracy enshrined in Article 6(1) EU could and should have been of more significance in this regard. See Nettesheim 2003, 954.

35. On the discussion, see Von Bogdandy 2000b, 108 and Ipsen 1993, 425. On the controversial democratic legitimacy of the German Federal Council, see Jekewitz 2002; Bothe 2002. See Bauer 1998 for a contrary position.

36. For the relevant discussion, see Hanebeck 2004, 119 *et seq*, 279 *et seq*, 312 *et seq*.

37. Similarly, see Böckenförde 1992.

38. See Dann 2006.

39. According to Article 8(1) of the French Constitution, the President nominates the Prime Minister; the Prime Minister's dependence on Parliament results from Article 49 in conjunction with the obligation to resign according to Article 50. The parliamentary competences contained in Article 214 EC are to some extent greater, yet the two thirds quorum required for a motion of censure according to Article 201 EC is too high to establish a parliamentary system of government.

40. Coultrap 1999, 107–135.

41. On the issue of consociational democracy as a possible understanding, see A. Peters 2004; Oeter 2006; and Dann 2006.

42. A. Peters 2001, 639; Schmidt, *Demokratietheorien* 1995, 115.

43. See Frankenberg 1997, 80; Verhoeven 2002, 34.

44. For more detail, see Dann 2006.

45. Klein 1981, 661; Britz and Schmidt 1999, 490.

46. On the duty to provide reasons, see Müller-Ibold 1990, 53. On transparency, see Lübbe-Wolff 2000, 278. On participation, see Curtin 1997, 53.

47. Expressly so in Lübbe-Wolff 2000, 276.

48. Article 190 EEC Treaty, now Article 253 EC; Article I-38[2] CT-IGC.

49. For a comparison, see von Bogdandy 2000b, 440.

50. Scheffler 1974, 44, 66.

51. A. Peters 2004, 63; A. Peters 2001, 268.

52. Case C-349/99 P, *Commission v. Arbeitsgemeinschaft Deutscher Tierzüchter* [1999] ECR I-6467; Cases C-174/98 P and C-189/98 P, *Netherlands et al v. Commission* [2000] ECR I-1; Case C-41/00 P, *Interporc v. Commission* [2003] ECR I-2125, para 39; Case T-309/97, *The Bavarian Lager Company v. Commission* [1999] ECR II-3217; Case T-92/98, *Interporc Im- und Export v. Commission* [1999] ECR II-3521; see Kadelbach 2001, 186.

53. Committee of Independent Experts 1999, para 7.6.3.

54. Article 207(3)(2) EC; in detail, Sobotta 2001, 144, 198; Commission 2001a, 15.

55. In detail, see Peters 2004, 64.

56. Abromeit 1998a, 80; Zürn 1996, 49.

57. Article I-47(4) CT-IGC.

58. Pathbreaking, Majone 1996b, 284, 291. The Commission has displayed considerable interest; see Commission 2001a, 13.

59. For a comparison, see Von Bogdandy 2000b, 67, 391.

60. Case T-521/93, *Atlanta et al v. Council and Commission* [1996] ECR II-1707, paras 70 *et seq*; Case C-104/97 P, *Atlanta v. Council and Commission* [1999] ECR I-6983; see Peers 2001, 605.

61. Commission 2001a, 19; see also Scharpf 2001a.

62. In detail, see Scharpf 2001a, 45.

63. Articles 40 *et seq*, 43 *et seq* EU, Articles 11 *et seq* EC.

64. Articles I-44, III-416 CT-IGC.

65. Wouters 2001, 301.

66. Nicotra 2003, 447.

67. See Hesse 1999, 125, 130.

68. On this relationship, Frankenberg 2002; Schmitt 1993, 388.

69. However, the redefinition and emasculation of democratic equality in Article I-45 CT-IGC can hardly be considered satisfactory. The question remains as to what the fundamental idea of democracy is: equality, self-governance, qualified participation by the norm's addressee, or elite competition?

70. Lepsius 2000.

71. See, however, Articles I-41, I-43 CT-IGC.

A COMMENT ON VON BOGDANDY

Ulrich Haltern

Armin von Bogdandy's enlightening paper on the legal dimension of European democracy is remarkable in both its hermeneutic reach and its subtle criticism. Clearly in command of the various discourses on European democracy, Von Bogdandy admirably succeeds in making clear-cut distinctions between law, social sciences, and political sciences. This, in itself, is a task not easily performed. He also lays out the path of the law, or its genealogy, with regard to European democracy. As he makes clear, his contribution is part of a larger project on what he calls a "European doctrine of principles," and lawyers, I am sure, are eagerly expecting his fully fledged exposition of a European *Prinzipienlehre*. It will doubtlessly display the virtues that sustain Von Bogdandy's position as one of our leading legal academics, and will repay our closest attention.

For longer than I care to acknowledge I have been toiling in the all-too-fertile vineyards of European democracy discourse myself. Increasingly, much of legal writing in the field of European democracy has left me strangely untouched—as if it did not have much to do with European citizens at all. At the same time, I have found political science studies on European democracy incisive and illuminating, but also oddly detached. Wondering why, I have come to believe that much of the writing in the field of European democracy, as thoughtful and rewarding as it is, misses important points. I am now convinced that legal studies, above all, are in need of a new, and different, approach. I will try and explain the problems I have by starting with Von Bogdandy's piece. I will then sketch a different approach which, for want of a better word, I will call a cultural study of law and democracy.

I.

Von Bogdandy's inquiry—the one he calls a "European doctrine of principles"—is meant to be a "systematic exposition of the most essential legal norms of the

European legal order." As such, as Von Bogdandy acknowledges, it must "neglect the preliminary question of the possibility of democracy at the Union level." A European doctrine of principles has nothing to say about this open question, which, von Bogdandy maintains, "belongs to the realm of political sociology." Since Art. 6 (1) EU says there is democracy, there is democracy, at least as a constitutional principle.

This I find troubling, for a number of reasons, and while I do not want to quibble over Von Bogdandy's normative exegesis, it is my intention to take issue with his fundamental approach. "The true Europe," writes Philip Allott in his "The European Community Is Not the True European Community," "is palimpsest Europe, each layer present like the succeeding life-stages of a human being."[1] The same is true for European democracy in that its genealogy is rich and fragmented, and yet each layer is inseparable from the other. An approach that sets its mind to nothing but treaty provisions sees nothing but one single layer. How can we hope to understand a social phenomenon if we do not engage in phenomenology but in a "science of law"? The basic outline of Von Bogdandy's analytical script—in effect, Von Bogdandy does more than what his script says—reminds me of what Martin Shapiro twenty-five years ago described as "constitutional law without politics . . . the Community as a juristic idea; the written constitution as a sacred text; the professional commentary as a legal truth; the case law as the inevitable working out of the correct implications of the constitutional text; and the constitutional court as the disembodied voice of right reason and constitutional teleology."[2] To be sure, I do not mean to disparage doctrinal work. Quite to the contrary, doctrine is the first intellectual stratum of judicial developments. As such, it is neither intellectually empty nor without systemic significance. Joseph Weiler has made this point well: "[D]octrinal work is the foundation for all that came after. Clever archaeologists may, through flights of creative imagination, construct rich interpretive narratives from fragments of pottery, debris of buildings, remnants of documents. But someone must have dug the fragments up, exposed the debris, salvaged the remnants. The original doctrinal work is truly foundational."[3] Indeed, political science does construct narratives from fragments of legal doctrine. The question, though, is whether lawyers should acquiesce to such cruel division of labor, and whether political scientists really are better equipped for interpretation and narration.

It is my impression that legal academia (at least in Germany) has all too readily arranged itself with abandoning and ceding interpretive and narrative tasks to political science, political philosophy, and political sociology. Law has never been much of a theoretical discipline. There is remarkably little sensitivity to context. One of legal academia's main tasks, it seems, is to police the boundary between political and social developments on the one hand, and law on the other. Insulating itself from the discourses of other disciplines and society, law must fall out of touch with political and social processes. Law will be unable to take part in a societal discourse, and influence, or even guide it; moreover, it cannot hope to be taken seriously as an academic discipline by the humanities. This is particularly damaging in a field that evolves as fast and inconsistently as the European Union.[4]

II.

There is a deeper reason why I am unhappy with the state of legal studies. For the legal scholar, the role of law, and especially of the constitution, is to subject politics to higher norms of reason. Law expresses the reasonable ordering of the polity. This is the idea behind modern constitutionalism and constitutional decisions: reason itself constitutes the implicit constitution toward which every decision is reaching.[5] Legal scholars believe that if we cannot separate law from politics, we are facing a failure of the rule of law. Of course, interest groups may succeed in entrenching their interests in the law; but that, to the legal scholar, represents a deficiency which must be an object for reform.

For the legal scholar, then, the ideal of reason works within the object of the scholar's study. Reason is already there, and the scholar makes clear what it is that reason demands. It is his or her task to say "what the law is, and what it should be." Actually, since the constitution lays claim to reason within the polity, the distinction between what the law is and what it should be is narrow and almost disappears in the legal scholar's self-understanding. Reform is brought to law not from the outside, but is the internal development of the law itself.

Von Bogdandy's piece is replete with examples of precisely this self-understanding. It is not only his occasional remark that this or that provision is satisfactory or not, that this or that strategy should be expanded or not, that this or that point requires further elaboration. It is more the organizational structure of his belief. If reason works itself out from within the law itself, everything points toward objective, universal constitutionalism. Universal constitutionalism rests on two familiar and intertwined discourses, a doctrine of rights and a theory of political legitimacy. The former locates constitutionalism in a discourse on human rights, the latter in a discourse in the social contract tradition. Both discourses figure prominently in Von Bogdandy's thinking. Even though the rights argument is subtle in his present piece on democracy, Von Bogdandy has widely published on the question of fundamental rights in the Union (and has, to be sure, adopted a mildly critical stance).[6] The right to transparency is part of this discourse. The political legitimacy discourse in the social contract tradition is reflected in von Bogdandy's arguments on institutionalism, deliberation, and, above all, participation. Citizens who participate in the political process become part of the polity's governmental structure, develop "more confidence in the end result and in the Institutions which deliver policies"; indeed, the Union "will no longer be judged solely by its ability to remove barriers to trade or to complete an internal market; its legitimacy today depends on involvement and participation" (as the Commission's White Paper on Governance maintains). Participation signifies legitimacy because it reaffirms and authenticates the social contract. This belief is part and parcel not merely of global constitutionalism discourse, but of political science and political philosophy discourse as well.[7] I have my doubts, though, that this is the whole story.

III.

Social and political scientists have a different approach to law than legal scholars. This is particularly evident in their study of courts. One part of their inquiry is the institutional self-interest of courts. Courts want to be successful and will take measures that will legitimate their own judicial role, such as internal norms of consistency, self-citation, rationalization of jurisdiction, and so on. In addition, social and political scientists also explore the opportunities courts present to players to advance their own agendas. Interested individuals and groups will make use of courts when there is some advantage in doing so. To the political scientist, there is nothing about courts, or law, for that matter, that cannot be explained in the ordinary forms of social and political science inquiry. Courts may believe they speak a language of law instead of economics, and of rights instead of interests. Still, to political scientists, they are just another site for the contestation and construction of policy.

In contrast to legal constitutionalism, social and political science mostly locates reason not within the object they study, but in their own enterprise of study. The object they study—political practices of a community—responds to interests and power. Reason is what the social or political scientist brings to the conflicting interests that make politics. This is the reason of categorization and generalization. Reason is and must remain outside politics—something legal scholars would never accept. In the end, this is the fundamental split within the Enlightenment tradition: the locus of a practical science of politics.

I mention this for two reasons. First, Von Bogdandy's paper includes the social and political science approach to politics as well as it includes the legal approach. Von Bogdandy reveals himself as a legal academic who not only is informed by social and political science discourse, but as one who is able to engage in it, and put it to use. In this sense, his paper is an admirable example of what pure black-letter law is not: in full grasp of extra-legal arguments, and capable of coherently integrating them into legal thinking. Perhaps, legal academia is leaving the isolationist ghetto it has chosen for itself.

Second, despite all their differences, legal constitutionalism and political and social science have more in common than may be immediately apparent. Both are firmly within the Enlightenment tradition of understanding the political. That tradition is reflected by liberal political theory and distinguishes norms from meaning, and rules from identity. Modernity's larger problem, and its recurring debates, are about defining the reach of reason. The social contract tradition privileges reason, which is set against desire: reason must bring order to the chaotic character of (bodily) interests. Different forms of liberalism deploy different devices to filter interest from reason (take Rawls' veil of ignorance, or Habermas's ideal speech position), but all agree that the social contract can only be just if self-interest is transcended.

The conceptual matrix shared by scholars of law and political and social science, therefore, is binary. The political is determined through reason and interest. I believe this dichotomy is incomplete, and have argued, following Paul Kahn, to add a third element of political psychology, which is will.[8] In any case, both approaches—that of the political and social scientist and that of the legal scholar—miss much that is essential to law, and to democracy. They fail to understand how law is deeply embedded in beliefs about the rule of law: courts, for instance, construct and maintain an understanding of the polity as the expression of the rule of law. They also fail to understand law as a symbolic form. This is a dimension different from functional inquiries into norms and from interest and power studies. Democracy is about more than institutions, participation, deliberation, and flexibility. It is, too, about belonging to a community which may outlive ourselves, and about identity. The European Union has reached a stage where the symbolic dimension of community becomes the center of discourse, be it discourse about democracy, identity, the Constitutional Treaty, fundamental rights, or Union citizenship.

IV.

Europe has begun an urgent search for its own political imagination.[9] The Constitutional Treaty is but a very visible sign of this search. Europe is about to decide whether the political, for the Union, signifies the market, or humanity, or a self-narrative that reaches back to the symbolic arsenal of cultural mythology so well known from nation-state political rhetoric. We see this everywhere, not simply in the overused cultural artefacts of flag, anthem, Europe day, and Jean Monnet prizes, but also in documents such as the Charter of Fundamental Rights, the Treaty for a European Constitution, and, above all, the European Court's jurisprudence in the fields of human rights and Union citizenship. Partly, these artifacts and documents have proved unsuccessful in forging a political imagination.[10] Partly, however, there is much potential, especially in the Court's jurisprudence. The political has entered the European stage and will not easily go away. Today, we find ourselves in a legal, psychological, and discursive universe different from the one ten or fifteen years ago. European discourse is no longer attracted to the question of what we should do (for instance, with a view to the democratic deficit). It is now fascinated by the question of who we are. Europe's discursive nodal points are defined by contested notions of identity. Therefore, we will have to inquire what meaning we read into Union law, and how this act of reading and understanding interacts with our beliefs about ourselves, and our ends. No functional analysis can grasp this dimension of the law. An inquiry into our understanding of democracy must be part of this enterprise.

Von Bogdandy offers a glimpse of this dimension when he speaks of "self-determination of the people" and its ambiguous place in the Constitutional Treaty. Indeed, the question of political self-determination (sovereignty) is at the heart of the question of identity, and democracy. Democracy involves foundational commitments to both majority rule and nondomination.[11] Nondomination is an ever-present issue in the Union. Majority rule, while just as present, is much more difficult. What is it that leads a Danish citizen to accept a Council vote by the majority of Union members with the Danish representative outvoted? Majority rule, which is as foundational as it is contentious,[12] represents a great conundrum in the European Union, which assumes a constitution without a traditional political community defined and proposed by that constitution.[13] Does the Danish citizen accept the vote because national boundaries have ceased to play the constitutive role they used to play? Can we already talk about redrawn political boundaries? Or does she accept the vote because she has internalized a very high degree of tolerance for "the other", who is not part of "her" political community but whose opinion, and vote, she respects? Weiler calls this the "principle of constitutional tolerance" and interprets Brussels institutions and practices as enlightened practice: "Living the Kantian categorical imperative is most meaningful when it is extended to those who are unlike me."[14]

Any attempt to answer these questions needs to transcend arguments about institutions, transparency, and participation. One will need to read the origins of the political community, in this case the origins of the political in the European Union. However, social contract theory occludes the origins of the subject and assumes recognition of who is a subject. Similarly, sovereignty theory occludes the origins of the political community. The collective dimension of sovereignty becomes strangely invisible. Sovereignty theory in its traditional sense did not care about questions vexing theories of nationalism today. Did the nation precede the state, that is, was the task to draw state borders that were aligned with the nation? Or, as others think, would the nation form itself within borders of a state through the very process of political self-determination? Classical sovereignty theory is utterly uninterested in this divide between Romantic and Rationalist responses to nationhood and statehood.

Europe, however, has left the ballpark of classical sovereignty theory. With the effects of the Single European Act sinking in, and with the dawning of a genuinely political community after Maastricht and the Constitutional Treaty, myopic theories of sovereignty have become as outdated as dissatisfactory. European political integration, and European democracy, have opened the door to narratives of where we, as Europeans, are coming from, and who "we" are. Democracy in the Union is not suffering from a deficit because Brussels processes are too opaque. They are, of course, but that is not the point. The point, it seems to me, is that European democracy will not work—in that it will not lead to a vibrant transnational political life—unless European citizens understand, and are convinced of, the communal, collective dimension of a European political community. To convince them implies to work on a concept and praxis of self-determination that makes sense, and on a deeper theory of sovereignty.

V.

While it is beyond the bounds of this brief comment to map a theory of sovereignty, I will at least hint at some elements. Sovereignty is not merely a legal conception. Rather, it absorbs a whole universe of meaning and structures an entire worldview.[15] A cultural study of sovereignty involves looking at its genealogy. Sovereignty reaches back to the Church and traditional European sovereigns. The story of European political evolution is in substantial part a story of growing autonomy of the sovereign from the Church. Yet, it is wrong to merely think of this process as secularization. Rather, religious meaning migrated from the Church to the state: authority was sacralized. The meaning of the state was located in the being—the body—of the sovereign. The subject only realizes this political meaning by experiencing the self as part of the organic whole that is the sovereign corpus. Political identity, then, is not so much opposed to religious identity as a co-optation of that identity. Sovereignty expresses the participation of the finite in the sacred: even today we cannot speak of sovereignty without speaking of the deathless character of the state. To participate, then, means two things: mystical union, and following the law. The former act of participation is a deeply Catholic form; the latter, a Jewish form. Both forms pass into the Judaeo-Christian political tradition of the West. The Western political community is both, a participatory union of a people, and a nation under law.[16]

The European Union does not fit into this genealogy. This is precisely why we have so high hopes when it comes to European integration. Here is a polity which promises integration beyond sovereignty. We imagine the Union as a truly liberal order: a postpolitical order stripped of its attachment to a popular sovereign. The political, of course, is a contested domain and contingent upon the reality that surrounds it. We live in a European world of economic transactions, consumption, and markets—a world, that is, in which (in the words of the Schuman Declaration) "war becomes unthinkable." The political seems widely replaced by the market. Identity is as fluid as money-flows, citizenship becomes more a matter of consumption than of political rights and duties, and "the citizen-hero of the new Europe thus appears to be the Euro-consumer."[17] In such a world, with the political and the market increasingly being conflated, and "citizen" and "consumer" becoming essentially one and the same thing, it often seems there is little credible beneath or beyond the flat landscape of endless signification.[18] There is a flattening of identity and experience, an anemic political life—but still, this is progress, because we are leaving behind a heritage of sacrifice, collective sovereignty (with all its dangers), and calls *pro patria mori*.

Then again, things may quickly change. Political meanings are as contingent as any others: they can slip away with a slight change of perspective. As soon as the political enters the domain of sovereignty, ultimate values and ultimate meanings, it becomes incommensurable with the values of the market. That is one lesson of September 11, if we really did need a reminder. A slight change of perspective may yank us back onto a terrain where we distinguish between friends and enemies, believe in ultimate values, and crave for meaning that we derive from standing for some larger community which will outlive ourselves.

Disconcertingly, the Union is moving into this direction. It is turning toward collective identity and is searching for a genuinely political imagination. The Constitutional Treaty, the Court's citizenship jurisprudence, and the Commission's use of cultural artifacts attest to this. Such a turn is fraught with ambiguity. It is a turn towards mythical points of origin (take the signing of the Constitutional Treaty in the Sala degli Oriazi e Curiazi) which from the start runs into old demons.[19] It speaks the language of citizenship, rights, and universality,[20] and releases, amid all efficient bureaucracy, unspeakable remnants that make a cloudy and, possibly, demonic identity.[21] The arcane underside of the political drifts to the surface as soon as a polity turns to identity discourse, whether or not it is a transnational polity.

There is a profound temptation in awakening Europe's political imagination, and a great danger. On the one hand, aspiring to a world of deep politics, the Union would easily overcome the social legitimacy deficit and turn into a vibrant democracy. At the same time, it would enter the field of belonging, imagined authenticity, possibly of friends and enemies. The law would indeed be not about what we should do, but about who we are. On the other hand, Europe aspires just as much to a world of postpolitics, where we imagine ourselves as fluid, multiple, and fragmented. Here, the political looks like the market. This is the world of networks, a world stripped of sovereignty as well as of flesh and bodies.

The European model, if it is to be the second model, is not the model of the rest of the world, not even the American model. It is my suspicion, however, that the political will not simply go away, not even in Europe. Yugoslavia has taught us about the fragility of postpolitics; political rhetoric from Luxembourg will do little to rekindle our belief in the dawning of the age of postpolitics. Law in the Union may soon take on a meaning different from what it is today, and while this would lead to a vibrant political life, it is not difficult to spot the problems. In this light, maybe there is something to say for striving for civilization rather than eros.

The choice is not one to be made outside the law. On the contrary, it is closely connected to law and legal studies. Texts, above all legal texts, are a polity's memory, if you want the hard-disk storing authentic witness. In nation-states, some legal texts—constitutions—embody ideal historical meaning which links the present to the past, to some point of origin, like a revolution and the consecutive writing of a constitution. They construct an imaginative fabric that allows a state to inscribe its own identity into the identity of its citizens. They form a metaphysical and political deep structure that is largely ignored by theory but still has an important place in political practice.[22] Such texts constitute states as imagined communities and continue them over time. They can claim loyalty as their source of moral support because they are ours. To interpret a legal text, then, is to realize the ideal historical meaning, and to re-present the mythical point of origin of the polity. I do not see how legal scholars should be able to ignore this cultural dimension of law—especially when they write about democracy.

Notes

1. Allott 1991, 2499.
2. Shapiro 1980, 538.

3. Weiler 1997, 101.
4. Haltern 2005b.
5. Balkin 1997; Kahn 2003.
6. Von Bogdandy 2000a.
7. Habermas 1996a.
8. Kahn 2005; Haltern 2005a.
9. Ward 2001.
10. Haltern 2003.
11. Burt 1992.
12. Shapiro 2003.
13. Maduro 1998, 175.
14. Weiler 2000, 12.
15. Geertz 1973, 3–30.
16. Kahn 2005.
17. Shore 2000, 84; Urry 1995, 165.
18. Slater 1997.
19. Joerges and Ghaleigh 2003; Laughland 1998.
20. Rifkin 2004.
21. Haltern 2004.
22. Geertz 1983, 146.

II

WHAT FUTURE FOR PARLIAMENTARY DEMOCRACY IN THE EU?

3

Expanding National Parliamentary Control: Does It Enhance European Democracy?

Katrin Auel and Arthur Benz

Democratization through Parliamentarization?

The role of national parliaments is currently one of the most salient issues in the debate on democracy in the European Union (EU). From the 1970s onwards, it was the European Parliament (EP) which most prominently featured in institutional reform initiatives to create a democratic Europe. This changed in the mid-1990s when the 1996 Intergovernmental Conference (IGC) in Turin included not only the topic of an extension of the EP's powers, but also the participation of national parliaments as a means of democratizing the EU in the negotiation mandate for the Treaty of Amsterdam (see Rittberger's contribution to this volume). The revision of the Treaty on the European Union attracted greater attention to, interest in, and expectations of national parliaments of the EU Member States than any of the earlier revisions and extensions of the treaties. As a result, a legally binding "Protocol on the Role of National Parliaments in the European Union" was added to the treaty. Finally, the Treaty of Nice triggered an even broader debate on the role of national parliaments in the European political system, an issue the Convention on the Future of the EU then dedicated considerable effort to.

Following these developments in practical politics, political scientists became interested in the issue as well. Comparative studies have greatly contributed to our knowledge concerning the Europeanization of parliamentary institutions and procedures in the old Member States,[1] and in the new Member States similar studies have recently been completed or are under way.[2]

Nevertheless, the debate whether national parliaments can actually play an effective role in European policy-making or whether they are reduced to merely symbolic institutions is still ongoing. Existing studies have primarily focused on institutional changes and changes in formal proceedings, ignoring the changes in informal power structures. Researchers who realized the difficulties of parliamentary participation in the "two-level game" of European politic on the other hand, have not investigated the way in which parliamentary actors cope with the resulting practical difficulties.

In the following, we will argue that the actual power of national parliaments in the European multilevel system depends not only on their institutional rights to participate in and to scrutinize European policy-making but, more importantly, on the strategic use they make of these rights. The paper is divided in four parts. After a short outline of the normative and empirical justifications for the important role of national parliaments in the EU, we will discuss the challenges parliaments face in the European multilevel system. The third section will then provide empirical evidence on how national parliaments participate in EU policy-making and try to cope with these challenges, summarizing the findings of three case studies on national parliaments in the United Kingdom, Denmark, and Germany. Finally, we will sketch the implications of our study for adequately understanding the way in which democracy functions in multilevel governance.

The Importance of National Parliaments for a Democratic EU

From a normative point of view, the importance of national parliaments for a democratic Europe can be derived from the character of the EU polity. The democratic constitution of the EU is based on two pillars. One consists of the directly elected parliament representing the citizens of Europe, while the other consists of the representatives of the peoples of the Member States in the Council of the EU. As the main European legislative institution, the Council is neither accountable to nor controlled by the EP. This implies that democratic legitimacy of the EU requires the accountability of Council members to their national parliaments and, through them, to their national citizens.

This notion of a dual legitimacy has not only been confirmed by the German Constitutional Court, which argued in its decision on the Maastricht Treaty that the democratic legitimacy of the EU had to be guaranteed by national parliaments, but also by the Treaty establishing a Constitution for the EU. The Convention drafting the Constitutional Treaty dedicated considerable effort to the role of national parliaments by setting up a working group on this issue. In doing so, it acknowledged the legislative power of the Council, as well as the national basis of legitimacy of EU law. Beyond the fact that national parliaments were to be included in procedures designed to implement the subsidiarity principle, the Constitutional Treaty also proposed measures to make the parliamentary scrutiny of governmental policy-making in EU matters more effective.

However, while the democratic legitimacy of the EP is—at least in principle—accepted, the legitimacy derived from national parliaments is still under debate. Political scientists like Andrew Moravcsik argue that the process of European integration results not only in a transfer of legislative power from the national to the European level, but also from parliaments to the executive. Due to their direct involvement in European legislation, governments act as gatekeepers between the national political system and the European level and are able to control the flow of information, the coordination of divergent interests, the generation of ideas, and the handling of institutions.[3] Others have even diagnosed a general "erosion of parliamentary democracy" leading to a system of "post-parliamentary governance."[4] If these theories were correct, we would have to acknowledge that a deep gap exists between the normative demand for an involvement of national parliaments and the reality of European politics.

In fact, empirical studies on the role of national parliaments draw a different picture. They reveal strong efforts on the part of national parliaments to adjust institutions and procedures to the challenges of multilevel policy-making in the EU. Some scholars like Philip Norton[5] claim that European integration has led to a remarkable resilience of parliaments in European democracies, much stronger than their reaction to the much-debated general "decline of parliaments." Indeed there are good reasons for this assertion. While in domestic politics, parliaments have suffered from an incremental downgrading due to the decline of clear political cleavages and the increasing need for expertise in public policy. In European politics they are increasingly confronted with a visible structural change as their legislative competencies are explicitly transferred to a higher level. They have reacted to this obvious loss of power by implementing institutional reforms.

These institutional reforms aimed at solving two basic problems of executive-parliament relationships: the distribution of information and the balance of power. At the same time, however, they have created another and more difficult problem in coping with multilevel governance. In the next section, we will briefly discuss these institutional reforms and then outline the "second order problem" they generate, before providing evidence on strategies parliamentary actors have developed to deal with the latter.

Challenges for National Parliaments in a Two-Level Polity

Two problems between parliaments and the executive—information asymmetries and that of the imbalance of power—exist in each parliamentary system but are aggravated by European integration. In European policy-making, it is the executive which directly participates in decision-making while parliaments have no decision rights, only rights to control their national representative. Moreover, they have no direct insight either with regard to the substance of the agendas of European policies or on the positions of other Member States' governments.

During the process of European integration, national parliaments reacted to these problems through institutional reforms which varied from country to country given the different institutional settings and political cultures of national democracies. They modified but did not overhaul the existing parliamentary systems of individual Member States, following an existing path of development.[6] Despite these variations, the institutional reforms generally included the following. Firstly, parliaments set up rules endorsing their right to obtain comprehensive information on European issues from their government. While initially this right applied mainly to the so-called first pillar of the EU, in most national parliaments it has now been expanded to the second and third pillar. Secondly, in order to enhance their capacities to handle and process this information, all national parliaments have set up one or more special European Affairs committees. Thirdly, with regard to the problem of power, national parliaments extended their participation rights in the formulation of national preferences on European issues, as well as their power to scrutinize their government's behavior in the Council. This includes the right to draft resolutions on European issues before a final agreement is reached (the so-called scrutiny reserve).

For the purpose of this chapter, there is no need to go into the details of these reforms and the variations between Member States which are well documented in a number of publications.[7] Instead, we are interested in the practical consequences of these institutional changes, particularly those concerning parliamentary participation and scrutiny rights. While reducing information asymmetries is a general precondition for democratic processes in a parliamentary system, the powers claimed by national parliaments in European policy-making are not without complications. They produce a serious dilemma in practical politics.[8]

To put it very simply, an efficiency-accountability dilemma exists consisting of a choice between two unattractive alternatives. If a national parliament ties the hands of its government, the Council representative does not have enough leeway to negotiate with other Member State governments. In legal terms, national parliaments generally have the right to draft only nonbinding resolutions on European issues and yet, the government cannot simply ignore a public parliamentary statement. According to the basic norm of parliamentary systems, the government is bound to the will of the parliamentary majority. Governmental action is only legitimate if subject to parliamentary control and open for parliamentary rejection. Only then can it be guaranteed that the will of the electorate will actually be transformed into policy-making. Therefore, even a nonbinding resolution can have the detrimental effect of binding the government politically. If, however, parliament tries to avoid these effects by allowing its government to act autonomously, parliamentary involvement is reduced to a mere symbolic use of power, which undermines the legitimacy of European policy-making. Consequently, the democratic legitimacy of the Council depends not only on the rights and the real power of national parliaments, but also on the way parliaments handle this dilemma.

Parliamentary actors are quite aware of this problem. In the EU Member States, we can observe different strategies national parliaments apply in order to manage this dilemma. To demonstrate that these strategies reflect the institutional context of different parliamentary systems, we will present the case of three different types of parliamentary systems in Western European states, namely the United Kingdom, Denmark, and Germany.[9]

Coping with the Goal Conflict in the European Two-Level Games

The parliamentary systems of the United Kingdom, Denmark, and Germany represent three different types of parliamentary systems: The pure Westminster system, where agenda control is monopolized by the government ("fused parliamentarism with policy centralization"[10]); a system of a consensus democracy with a strong parliament, where the government—often formed by minority parties—controls the agenda in cooperation with groups in parliament; and a mixed system of majority democracy with executive-parliament cooperation, where the majority in parliament shares the power to control the agenda with the government, having thus considerable influence on the agenda.

Our comparative research on these three parliamentary systems reveals whether, and in which way, the strategies parliamentary actors develop to cope with the difficulties of the two-level game are influenced by the overall institutional context. Since we already knew from previous studies that the institutional adaptation of parliaments to European integration developed along different national paths, we had reasons to assume the strategies to cope with the challenges of European governance would vary accordingly.[11]

The British *House of Commons*

The British House of Commons focused its institutional reforms mainly on solving the information problems. It set up a committee system and a scrutiny procedure designed to improve the capacities of Parliament to supervise the policy-making of the government in European affairs. The scrutiny procedure includes a step-by-step selection of relevant information from the enormous amount of European documents. Firstly, European documents are transferred to the European Scrutiny Committee (ESC) whose task is

> to examine European Union documents and (a) to report its opinion on the legal and political importance of each such document and, where it considers appropriate, to report also on the reasons for its opinion and on any matters of principle, policy or law which may be affected; (b) to make recommendations for the further consideration of any such document pursuant to Standing Order No. 119 (European Standing Committees); and (c) to consider any issue arising upon any such document or group of documents, or related matters (Standing Order No. 143).

For this task, the Committee not only obtains information in the form of Explanatory Memoranda from the responsible department, but also has the right to ask for further information and to question the responsible minister. Documents considered important are then either deferred to one of the three European Standing Committees or, by a motion put down by the government,[12] to the Committee of the Whole House, which, of course, allows the government the possibility to avoid a plenary debate.[13]

As regards the problem of power, the British Parliament did take some steps to extend its rights of control against its government. According to Standing Order 119, the European Standing Committees have the possibility to debate a European decision as well as the respective governmental motion, and may decide to pass the government's motion, amend it, or even reject it altogether. To ensure that Parliament has the opportunity to deal with European matters before they are agreed upon at the European level, the House of Commons also implemented a "scrutiny reserve."[14] However, for the amendments to become effective, the committees must rely on the government, which tables the final motion on the Floor of the House.[15] On several occasions, the European Scrutiny Committee had demanded

> that, when a European Standing Committee has reported a resolution on a European Community Document, a Motion in the same form should be tabled when the document was taken "forthwith" in the House to complete the Scrutiny process. In other words, the Government should no longer be able to table a different Motion (perhaps even a Motion defeated in Standing Committee).[16]

In a later report it concluded "[at] present, the motion passed by the Committee has no practical effect [. . .]. It casts doubt on the value of serving in European Standing Committees if their decisions can simply be ignored, and undermines the credibility of the process."[17] The government, however, was not willing to accept explicit restrictions of its powers in European Affairs and made clear that motions tabled on the Floor of the House should "stand in the name of the Government, in a form with which it can agree."[18] In general, the House votes on the government motion without any further debate, a practice not unlike those in other national parliaments.

Thus, through a vote on the Floor of the House, Parliament does have the ability to defeat the government's motion. This power, however, has only rarely been applied. One may explain this with the de facto superiority of the government. However, if Parliament uses its power to politically bind the government, it reduces the negotiation power of the British government in the Council, which conflicts with the interests of the majority in Parliament. The opposition parties are in a better situation since they can strongly argue for the national interests without being held responsible for a failed national position in the negotiation processes at the European level. Indeed the pronounced confrontational party competition in the House of Commons is further intensified by a cleavage over European integration, with the Pro-European New Labour and the Euro-skeptic Conservative Party.[19] The Conservative Party is not only the institutional enemy of New Labour, but is also quite aggressively opposed to certain aspects of further European integration. This makes the situation of the majority even more difficult, because fierce party competition forces the majority, on the one hand, to loyally support its government's European policies, but, on the other hand, to demonstrate to the rather Euro-skeptic public that it strongly, and genuinely, defends national interests. Therefore, Members of Parliament (MPs) had to search for strategies to use their power without falling into the trap of this multilevel governance dilemma.

In this situation, Members of the British House of Commons make use of the institutional differentiation between the plenary and the committees in order to pursue their strategies. During the debates in the European Standing Committees and, above all, the European Scrutiny Committee, members of the majority group scrutinize the government's European policy by demanding full information on the negotiation situation in Brussels and the government's position. In addition, Ministers are regularly cited before the European Scrutiny Committee to question them on certain issues or to hold them accountable for incomplete information or breaches of the scrutiny reserve.

As this scrutiny takes place publicly,[20] Ministers are induced to take it seriously. Even without a binding mandate, Ministers have to explain how they integrate both European and national interests in their negotiation position. The fact that the government does indeed take the parliamentary scrutiny powers seriously is illustrated by the *Guide to Better European Regulation*, where the Cabinet Office reminded government officials that the information given to Parliament "should explain fully the policy and legal implications of a proposal for the UK and the reasons for supporting or opposing its provisions."[21] It must also be transmitted to Parliament in time, in order to spare the Minister responsible the embarrassment of having to appear before the ESC: "You should bear in mind that scrutiny committees that are not satisfied that they have been properly informed about any proposal have the option of inviting Ministers to give evidence on it."[22] These evidence sessions can be quite uncomfortable for the Ministers, as they generally have to face the Committee alone, that is, without a large staff, to answer questions unknown beforehand. Ministers are also quite often fiercely attacked by their own backbenchers: "Our job is to hunt them."[23] Even the opposition has to admit that the Labour members in the Committee "act as a group of parliamentarians, not as party members."[24]

These strategies allow Parliament to closely scrutinize the government's European policy-making and to hold the government publicly accountable. In the plenary, however, the majority supports its government according to the rules of the game played in the competitive parliamentary system. Debates on European issues are rare in the House and the Government has no problems to find support for its policy by its majority.

The Danish *Folketing*

The Danish case reveals a different form of participation by national parliaments in EU policy-making. In Denmark, reforms induced by European integration placed the European Affairs Committee in a strong position in European policy-making. Immediately after the accession to the European Community in 1973, a severe conflict erupted between Parliament—the *Folketing*—and the government over a European agreement, that the government could not explain to a satisfying degree.[25] As a result of the conflict, the *Folketing* enforced the provision that

> the Government shall consult the Market Relations Committee of the Folketing in questions relating to EC policy. . . . Prior to negotiations in the EC Council of Ministers on decisions of a wider scope, the Government submits an oral mandate for negotiation to the Market Relations Committee. If there is no majority against the mandate, the Government negotiates on this basis.[26]

In accordance with the Danish logic of "negative parliamentarism,"[27] the aim of this provision was to prevent the government from agreeing to a European decision that might not be supported by a majority in the *Folketing*.[28] This procedure entitles the Committee to formal veto rights vis-à-vis the government in European policy-making,[29] and "a government wanting to survive politically knows it will have to listen to the Committee"[30]. It goes without saying that the possibility of issuing a binding mandate causes the aforementioned dilemma. While the Danish case is often presented as a best practice example of strengthening the role of national parliaments and, thus, democracy in Europe, the implications for the effectiveness of European policy or the position of the Danish government are obvious. While the Parliament may be strong, a government whose hands are tied is weak in European policy-making. However, in practice, the European Affairs Committee learned to cope with this problem.

Mandates approved by the Danish Committee for European Affairs normally define no fixed governmental position in the Council. Instead, they outline a broad strategy that the government wants to pursue in Council negotiations, and provide rather flexible guidelines for its enactment. In ongoing consultations between the Committee and Denmark's representative in the Council, mandates may be revised if the negotiation situation calls for a change of strategy in order to find a compromise. Thus, instead of making only a single *ex ante* decision, the committee can monitor the processes of negotiations.

The success of this flexible adjustment strategy of binding mandates depends on several conditions. Firstly, party competition must not play a fundamental role in the debates of the Committee. As Denmark generally has minority governments, the opposition could otherwise completely obstruct the government's European negotiations efforts. Indeed, party competition generally does play a rather minor role in the Committee debates. Foreign and European policy-making in Denmark is traditionally based on a broad coalition between the four old parties[31] regardless of who is in government. Although different party views on certain political issues and decisions do play a role in the debates, these four parties focus mainly and strategically on what is achievable with which type of coalition in the Council. Thus, the Committee debates strategies rather than actual policy issues based on party political views. Secondly, the Committee must receive all relevant information not only on the European issue negotiated in the Council, but also on the negotiation position of other Member States' governments in order to be able to evaluate the options and constraints of the negotiation situation. Thirdly, and consequently, the cooperation between the parliamentary committee and the responsible Minister must be confidential, and this results in the Committee's debates not being publicized after the Committee meeting. Otherwise, the Danish negotiating position is known long beforehand, which may weaken considerably. In addition, confidentiality of the Committee's debates and results prevents party politics from gaining in importance and ensures an informal and consensual style of debate in the Committee.[32] Fourthly and most importantly, in order to maintain its veto power, the Committee must be willing to veto a policy of the government, or to even refuse to allow the government any negotiating mandate[33] if its own position is not sufficiently taken into consideration. Effective cooperation with the executive needs the shadow of the veto power of the Parliament. Indeed, in rare cases the *Folketing* refuses to give the Minister a mandate when it feels not properly informed by the government or not adequately included in European policy-making.

> If it comes up that the minister hasn't properly informed the committee, informed them too little or wrongly, he has to pay. . . . the worst thing you can do is trying to hide something. When it comes out that you have been trying to hide something, you are in big trouble.[34]

While the *Folketing* is a strong Parliament in terms of its real power, its strategies reveal some problems regarding the democratic quality and effectiveness of European policies. On the one hand, confidential cooperation between the executive and the Committee reduces the transparency of the parliamentary process to citizens. The mandating procedure requires confidentiality among the partners and therefore rules out public scrutiny in plenary sessions of Parliament. In addition, as the opposition generally takes part in the forming of a mandate,[35] it cannot critically scrutinize the government's policy-making in European affairs. On the other hand, the Danish representative in the Council is not always a very reliable negotiation partner, since it is not known whether, and in which way, the negotiation position will change as well as whether Parliament will finally accept the results. Thus, the often praised Danish example of participation of national parliaments in EU governance is not without flaws.

The German *Bundestag*

The German Parliament, the *Bundestag*, adjusted its institutional structure to European integration rather late. Until 1993, it had made several attempts to set up an effective European Affairs Committee, all of which failed due to the rivalry with the established standing committees.[36] In the course of the ratification of the Maastricht Treaty, the participation rights of the *Bundestag* (and the *Bundesrat*) were finally tied down constitutionally.[37] According to Article 23 of the German Basic Law (GBL), the *Bundestag* cooperates with the government in EU affairs. Parliament has to be comprehensively informed by the government and in time, that is, receive all relevant formal and informal documents as well as information on their content, the government's position, and the ongoing negotiation situation in Brussels. Article 23 also endows the *Bundestag* with a right to draft a resolution before the government agrees to a European decision. It clearly stipulates that the "federal government takes account of the Bundestag's resolution in the negotiations."[38]

As provided for in Article 45 GBL, a more powerful European Affairs Committee was finally set up in December 1994. Unlike most other committees, the establishment of the European Affairs Committee is constitutionally demanded and, thus, not subject to the Parliamentary Standing Orders. What is remarkable is that, in contrast to the procedures of other Member States' parliaments, the German European Affairs Committee is only responsible for matters related to the European treaties in general while all specific policies are, as in domestic politics, dealt with by the existing sectoral standing committees. As a rule, all committees hold closed sessions, but may, by decision, admit the public.

Members of Parliament know that they can require the government to follow their decided upon policy. However, they also are well aware of the problems that can arise in case of conflicts at the European level if they tie the hands of the responsible German representative. Therefore, a majority either completely abstains from drafting a parliamentary resolution or drafts it in close cooperation with the government, in order to strengthen its negotiation position in Brussels. Only in exceptional situations does the *Bundestag* use its powers against the government to effectively force it into adopting a parliamentary position.[39] At the same time, however, internal coordination within the majority parties offers opportunities for influencing the government beyond the drafting of formal resolutions. The most important coordination bodies in the *Bundestag* are the sectoral working groups of the parliamentary party groups, consisting of the party members sitting on the respective standing committees. This reliance on informal cooperation with the government is quite in accordance with the usual practice in legislation in the German parliamentary system.

How effective MPs are in influencing the government's negotiation position depends crucially on access to independent information. Here, one of the flaws of the German system becomes apparent[40]: MPs have to deal with the general problem of information overload, a problem which is aggravated by the fact that the *Bundestag* has no "filter committee" similar to the British European Scrutiny Committee. The fact that specific European policies have to be dealt with by the sectoral standing committees also means that European issues further add to the domestic workload. "It becomes increasingly difficult to deal with the mass of documents, to separate the important from the unimportant and to deal with all these issues in time."[41] Consequently, several MPs have built up interparliamentary networks, as well as contacts with European institutions. "In terms of transparency, much is still to be desired, so you have to get active as an MP to get the vital information, either through the government or through other sources."[42] In particular, members of the EP (MEPs), but also European Commission officials serve as a kind of burglar alarm to some German MPs by informing them on important Commission initiatives as early as possible. Building up interparliamentary networks with other national parliamentarians is also primarily used to access independent information, especially on the negotiation positions of other Member States, in order to help MPs evaluate the negotiation situations in the run-up to Council meetings.

However, contacts at the European level not only serve as information sources. A small but growing number of parliamentary "Euro-wizards" also try to influence European drafts directly through contacts with Commission officials, MEPs, and even other national MPs. "One example is, of course, the development of EU directives. There you have the possibility to influence this process by informally contacting commissioners or Commission officials that share our views. This has worked astonishingly well."[43]

This strategy of informal bothcooperation with and bypassing the government enables MPs to influence the government by formulating flexible positions as early as possible in the European policy process. However, the strategies have their flaws as well. The strategy of bypassing the government has no institutional basis and therefore depends completely on the initiative of individual MPs which only a small proportion of MPs are willing to take. As a result, it has not solved problems of information overload or the high workload of the special committees, nor, consequently, coordination problems between the European Affairs Committee and the special committees. Hence, parliamentary influence is increasing, but remains limited.

Worth mentioning in the German case is that the informal cooperation between the government and the majority does, of course, disadvantage the opposition. Therefore, networking with MPs from Member States where the respective sister party is in government is especially beneficial for opposition MPs in order to compensate the information head start of the government. "Quite interestingly, Austrian government members or colleagues again and again provided us with information that the German government had denied us."[44] At the same time, the opposition can use the channels of the *Bundesrat*, where the *Länder* governments not only have good contacts in Brussels, but also have access to the government with regard to European issues affecting the *Länder*.[45] As the majority of the votes in the *Bundesrat* are frequently controlled by the opposition, opposition MPs not only gain access to information. They also gain access to the informal preparation of European policies by cooperating with *Länder* governments from their own party, where they can also try to exert some direct influence.

As a consequence of these strategies, most cooperation between the Parliament and the government is transferred to internal, and therefore private, parliamentary party working groups. It takes place outside the formal proceedings and is not open to the public. The same is true for the cooperation of MPs with *Länder* governments or the direct but informal influence exerted by a few MPs at the European level, which are neither transparent nor subject to public scrutiny. The resulting opaqueness of the parliamentary process cannot be outbalanced by the formal debates in the committees either, because they sit in private as well. This may explain in part why debates in the plenary are more frequent in the *Bundestag* than is the case in the British or Danish parliaments.[46] Yet these debates, as well as the fact that Parliament can signal its veto power within them, mainly have a symbolic function.

Conclusion

This empirical study demonstrates that European integration does not inevitably turn national parliaments into powerless institutions in the European policy process as advocates of the deparliamentarization hypothesis have argued. Rather, it illustrates that a more nuanced analysis of the role of national parliaments in EU multilevel governance is needed, if we want to assess parliamentary strengths and weaknesses. Neither the improved access to information on European issues nor the mere extension of powers of parliaments in European affairs against their governments in European policy-making automatically lead to an improvement of democracy in the EU. It goes without saying that national parliaments do need information rights and institutional power vis-à-vis their government in European policy-making. However, in light of the problematic consequences of external interventions in the multilevel process, MPs have to use their rights strategically. Thus, when evaluating the effective role of national parliaments, one has to look beyond the formal institutions and account for the strategies that parliamentary actors develop to deal with information and power.

With regard to information, parliaments generally suffer less from too little information and more from information overload. The information asymmetry between Parliament and its government can be reduced if parliaments gain access to independent information concerning current and future developments at the European level, the negotiation position of other governments, as well as the negotiation behavior of their own government. Here, interparliamentary cooperation both with the EP and with parliaments from other Member States can be of great advantage. The greater problem they have to deal with is selecting the most important issues out of an enormous amount of documents. In this regard, a special committee responsible for filtering out important documents and providing information on their possible impact on domestic policies seems to be a very useful institution, as the British example demonstrates.

Concerning their participation rights, veto rights against a given government's European policy can have detrimental effects if they are not applied in an intelligent, strategic way as in the Danish case. Here, a strong Parliament has the best leverage on the government's negotiation position. Moreover, due to the frequent minority governments, the opposition could even determine the negotiation position. Yet, neither the governing nor the opposition parties exploit this power, because they are well aware of its negative impact on Denmark's strategic position in the Council negotiations. Instead, they cooperate with the government, provide it with flexible guidelines, and monitor the negotiations in Brussels. Thus, two issues are of considerable importance here. On the one hand, strategic use of power has to translate veto power into power to influence ongoing negotiations. As is revealed by the Danish, but also by the German case, cooperation with the government in committees or working groups provides the best opportunities for such influence, especially if cooperation takes place behind closed doors. On the other hand, this reduces the transparency of the parliamentary process. Consequently, the public is unable to receive sufficient information. Informal negotiations on mandates do provide parliamentary influence, but they also reduce the democratic quality of European policies in general, and can be risky in Member States where Euro-skepticism is widespread within society.

If we accept the notion of dual legitimacy generated by both the EP and the national parliaments as an adequate normative concept of democracy for European governance, strengthening these parliaments seems to provide the best way for reducing the democratic deficit. However, improved powers of national parliaments can quickly hamper European democracy by simply disturbing or even impeding European decisions instead of shaping them in a positive way. But, under the codecision procedure, the EP is able to directly influence policy contents by forcing the Council as a whole to adjust its decision proposal, the role of national parliaments is limited to influencing the negoti-ation position of only one negotiating partner in the Council. In the European negotiation system, however, governments representing the peoples of the Member States need sufficient discretion in order to arrive at decisions. Oth-erwise, governments are unable to negotiate compromises, which may, in the end, even block the European negotiation process. Hence, strengthening the mandating powers of national parliaments vis-à-vis their government does not necessarily contribute to more democracy in European policy-making. Rather, the quality of European democracy depends on the functional separa-tion of power and the interaction of the institutions forming the two-level polity of the EU. In this polity, the role of national parliaments consists of scrutinizing the government's policy-making, of holding the government ac-countable for its European policies, and of communicating European policies to their citizens. Moreover, national parliaments do need veto power, but they have to use it in a strategic way by intervening in European negotiations if the respective government significantly deviates from national preferences and if the parliament is unable to communicate European decisions to its citizens and achieve changes in line with national preferences.

It follows that multilevel democracy comes about in strategic interactions be-tween national and European institutions, among which the power to set the agenda, to make decisions, as well as to veto these decisions are distributed. By separating these powers, the European polity creates tensions between the insti-tutions holding them. If powers are used in an intelligent and strategic way, these tensions can induce processes of collective learning. During these processes, pref-erences of individual citizens, groups, nations, and their representatives are con-tinuously formulated and modified, not so much in processes of deliberation but rather in strategic interactions, that is, in mutual adjustments. Collective learn-ing is the real essence of the "intelligence of democracy."[47]

As intermediaries between the Council of Ministers, the EU's central leg-islative institution, and national communities of citizens, national parlia-ments play a crucial role in this process of democratic learning. Besides their function to formulate the will of the Member States' people, it is the parlia-ment's teaching function and its role as a scrutinizing and controlling inter-mediary between the government and civil society that contributes to Euro-pean democracy. Whether, and in which manner, a national parliament fulfils these functions and manages the challenges and the dilemmas inherent in Eu-ropean multilevel governance depends on the particular institutional settings of a national system of government. Therefore, apart from the general con-clusion formulated above, our comparative study reveals that, due to different institutional settings, each national parliament has to develop its own practice of participation within the EU.

Notes

1. Bergman and Damgard 2000; Kamann 1997; Finn Laursen 1995, 43–60; Maurer 2002; Maurer and Wessels 2001; Norton 1996; Smith 1996; Weber-Panariello 1995.
2. Agh 2004.
3. Moravcsik 1994.
4. Andersen and Burns 1996, 227–251.
5. Norton 1996.
6. Dimitrakopoulos 2001, 405–422.
7. For example, Maurer 2002; Maurer and Wessels 2001.
8. Auel and Benz 2004; Benz 2004, 875–900.
9. For an extended version, see Auel 2003, 259–280; Auel and Benz 2004.
10. Siaroff 2003, 454.
11. The following is based on evidence derived from sixty-one interviews with Members of the House of Commons, the *Folketing* and the Bundestag between June 2002 and April 2003.
12. "If the Government wishes to arrange a debate on the Floor, it must put down a Motion to defer the document and so bring it back to the Floor of the House" (UK Parliament 1996a, paragraph 7).
13. This has been a source of considerable conflict between the House of Commons and the government on several occasions (see UK Parliament 1996a).
14. The first resolution on the "Scrutiny reserve" had been adopted as early as 1980. The current "scrutiny reserve" is based on the resolution of November 18th, 1998 (Parliament 2001, Appendix 3): "(1) No Minister of the Crown should give agreement in the Council or in the European Council to any proposal for European Community legislation or for a common strategy, joint action or common position under Title V or a common position, framework decision, decision or convention under Title VI of the Treaty on European Union:—(a) which is still subject to scrutiny (that is, on which the European Scrutiny Committee has not completed its scrutiny) or (b) which is awaiting consideration by the House (that is, which has been recommended by the European Scrutiny Committee for consideration pursuant to Standing Order No. 119 (European Standing Committees) but in respect of which the House has not come to a Resolution)."
15. UK Parliament 2002b.
16. UK Parliament 1996a.
17. UK Parliament 2002a, paragraph 70. As early as 1991, the House of Commons' Procedure Committee criticized this rule as "a mockery of the scrutiny process and . . . a waste of the Standing Committee's time and effort" (cited from UK Parliament 1996c, 1996, paragraph 198).
18. UK Parliament 1996b, paragraph 12.
19. This is partly an effect of the new orientation of the New Labour Party. Against New Labour, which had discovered many of the former conservative issues of the market-oriented neoliberal agenda, "Europe" provided at least one issue on which to organize an election campaign. Accordingly, Conservative Party leader William Hague had closed the ranks of his party, deeply split on the European question since the sev-

enties, behind a rather Euro-skeptical stance. The development under the slogan "Britain in Europe, but not run by Europe" has also been pursued by the succeeding party leaders.

20. While the European Standing Committees sit in public, the ESC generally sits in private, but the public is admitted to the evidence sessions. In addition, the weekly reports of the ESC on the scrutiny of European documents are also published.

21. UK Government 1999, 20.

22. UK Government 1999, 20.

23. Interview by authors with majority MP, London, November 25, 2002.

24. Interview by authors with opposition MP, London, November 19, 2002.

25. Arter 1996, 111–123; Laursen 2001, 99–115.

26. The provision is not found in the constitution or even a law, but in the first Report of the Market Relations Committee of 29 March 1973. Nevertheless, all governments since 1973 have adhered to it. In practice, every Minister presents a mandate to the Committee before taking part in decisions in the Council of Ministers.

27. Laursen 2001, 99. According to Article 15 of the Danish Constitution, a government may remain in office as long as it does not have a majority in parliament against it.

28. Damgaard and Nørgaards 2000, 42.

29. Arter 1996; Laursen 1995.

30. Laursen 2001, 105.

31. The Conservatives (Konservative Folkeparti), the Liberals (Venstre), the Social-liberal Democrats (Radikale Venstre), and the Social Democrats (Socialdemokratiet i Danmark).

32. Nannestad 2003, 63.

33. If the Committee refuses to give the government any mandate, the government is in fact unable to agree to the negotiated European policy in any form.

34. Interview by authors with opposition MP and former Minister, 21 March 2003.

35. Statistics on the general voting behavior in the Committee (but not on the specific votes cast by the parties) published in 2003 revealed that more than 60 percent of the mandates had an all-party support and as many as 85 percent were opposed by only one party (interview by authors with the committee chairman).

36. Bila et. al., 1998.

37. Until the Maastricht Treaty, the ratification law on the Treaties of Rome had been the legal basis for the Bundestag's involvement in European legislation. The government was obliged to "keep the Bundestag and the Bundesrat informed on developments in the Council of the European Economic Community and the Council of the European Atomic Community" with the information to be given before a decision in the Council in those cases where "a decision has to be transposed into German law or is directly applicable in Germany."

38. Article 23 paragraph 3 clause 2 of the GBL.

39. For example, a conflict erupted between the government and parliament with regard to the European Convention. While Chancellor Schröder preferred a more executive-based Convention, the MPs demanded a stronger representation of national parliaments. After the European Affairs Committee had voted a respective resolution,

according to paragraph 93a of the *Bundestag*'s Standing Orders, on behalf of the plenary (Deutscher Bundestag 2002, 241 ff.), it formed alliances with other Member States' parliaments in order to enhance the pressure on the government. "That is something we used quite deliberately. This was about forcing the government to accept the parliamentary position" (interview by authors with majority MP, 2 July 2002).

40. Saalfeld 2003, 73–96.

41. Interview by authors with majority MP, 2 July 2002.

42. Interview by authors with majority MP, 26 June 2002.

43. Interview by authors with majority MP, 26 June 2002.

44. Interview by authors with opposition MP, 25 June 2002.

45. According to Article 23 GBL, the *Bundesrat* has the right to draft a resolution on EU matters, a resolution that is binding in matters touching core areas of *Länder* competencies.

46. Since 1986, however, a small number of European draft directives, which are considered especially important, are selected each year for debate on the Floor of the House in the Danish *Folketing* (Dahl, Næss, and Tangen 2001).

47. Lindblom 1965.

4

The European Parliament between Policy-Making and Control

Andreas Maurer

Situating the European Parliament in Flux

A KEY ELEMENT OF European democratic systems is that directly elected parliaments represent the citizens, aggregate their views and opinions, and act on their behalf in public policy-making. In this regard, the European Union's (EU) institutional design—pre- and postconvention and IGC 2003/2004—faces a multitude of questions as to how representative this system of multi-level governance is, in which way its quasi-executive branches—the Council, the European Council, and the Commission—are accountable to the citizens via directly legitimated bodies, how democratic the decision-making procedures between the Union's legislative authorities are, and how the European Parliament (EP) is able to (co-) steer the democratic governance in the EC/EU.

Arguing about the European Parliament and its potential to provide the European citizens a collective voice in the Union's policy cycles does not mean that parliamentarism and the parliamentarization of the EU's system[1] is the only way to bridge the gap between the citizens and the Union. One can easily assume that even with the entry into force of the Constitutional Treaty (CT, see CIG 87/04), many scholars and practitioners of European integration will continue to argue that focusing on the parliamentary input structures of the Union is only one of several ways in which governance "beyond the state"[2] might gain legitimacy. I therefore conceive the European Parliament and the cascade-like parliamentarization of the Union's decision-making system[3] as one among many essential tools for building a legitimate

European order. The EP constitutes one of the four core institutions of the EU. It is the only directly legitimated component of the EU's institutional set-up. The last five treaty reforms caused major implications for the European Parliament and its position vis-à-vis the other institutions, specifically the Council and the Commission. Also, the CT confirms Helen Wallace' analysis that the European Parliament was and still is "the largest net beneficiary of the institutional changes."[4]

This chapter tries to assess the dynamics of the European Parliament in operating according to a set of parliamentary functions. The overall question revolves around how the EP performs in adopting European legislation and in controlling the Union's quasi-executive branches. Do the rules provided by treaties, interinstitutional agreements, and similar bases matter for the EP as a "multifunctional organization"[5] and how do they relate to the repartition of workload within the European Parliament? In analyzing the European Parliament's practice during the past 1994–1999 and 1999–2004 legislatures, I propose to investigate the parliamentary implementation of the treaties and treaty amendments. In other terms, we will explore the real use of the different "constitutional offers" at hand.

Legal Offers and Exploitation—Methodological Clarification

Constitutional offers are defined as the EU's treaty provisions, a dynamic and evolving set of opportunity structures that provide parliamentarians with potential power to participate in the EU's policy-making process. I thus conceive the EU's primary law—the treaties and similar constitutional acts like interinstitutional agreements—as subsequent propositions to the EU institutions and the Member States for joint decision making and for delegating powers from one level to another. Evidently, the Union's constitutional bases do not dictate a clear nomenclature of procedures, actors to be involved, and policy fields to be applied.[6] Instead, the institutions have to choose—by application of one or more legal bases—whether an envisaged piece of legislation is subject to parliamentary scrutiny through consultation, for EP initiative reports or urgency resolutions, or if it has to be decided by qualified majority or unanimity; whether the legislation should be adopted in the format of a regulation, a directive, or another type; and whether referral should be made to the consultation, the cooperation, the assent, or the codecision procedure or without any participation of the European Parliament. In other words, different constitutionalized, procedural blueprints and interinstitutional rules compete for application.

To depict the European Parliament's development from a merely consultative assembly into a more powerful legislative chamber, I look at the realization of EU treaty-based provisions with regard to: the day-to-day utilization of different legislative procedures involving the European Parliament as a consultative body; the exploitation of different policy areas and respective legal bases which the treaties provide for adopting binding legislation; the workload of committees in the European Parliament; and the implications of procedures and institutional rules for Parliament's management. Several other developments illustrate the European Parliament's performance in the implementation of its scrutiny powers, *inter alia* its original scrutiny powers, the appointment and investiture of the European Commission and its role with regard to the nomination of the European Central Bank and other institutions, the possibilities to hold the EU's nonparliamentary institutions to account, and the proceedings and findings of the European Parliament's temporary Committees of Inquiry.

To capture the constitutionally based roles of the European Parliament, I distinguish and trace its different functions. Drawing on earlier works by Bourguignon-Wittke and others,[7] Grabitz and others,[8] Steppat,[9] Schmuck and Wessels,[10] and subsequent studies on the specific role of the European Parliament in a dynamic and evolving structure,[11] I define these functions as policy-making, controlling, elective, and system-developing.[12]

Policy-making is defined as the participation of the European Parliament in the EC/EU policy cycle in relation to the Council and the Commission. The function derives from Parliament's rights and obligations to (co-)negotiate and decide on European politics. The policy-making function thus reflects Parliament's capacity to participate in and to influence the preparation, adoption, implementation, and control of binding legislative acts.

The control function is defined through Parliament's rights and obligations to call other institutions of the Union to account. In addition to its traditional role in granting the budgetary discharge to the European Commission, the Parliament is involved in other, less spectacular scrutiny activities. It may put oral and written questions to the Commission and the Council, hear Commission officials and national ministers in parliamentary committees, hold public hearings, set up temporary committees of inquiry, and discuss the EU's performance with the Council's presidency.

The elective function covers Parliament's right to participate in the nomination and investiture of other EU institutions (the Commission, to appoint a European Ombudsman or Mediator). Thus, as studies previously carried out on the European Parliament considered the elective function only to a limited extent, this function has since been significantly developed.

Finally, the system-development function refers to the participation of the European Parliament in the development of the EU's constitutional system (such as institutional reforms and the division of competencies). Making full use of this function also relies on instruments such as the use of internally binding law such as the Rules of Procedure. Thus, the system-development function refers to Parliament's ability to present, promote, and defend proposals for institutional reform.

Time is a scarce resource. Different issues, agendas, parliamentary functions and roles compete for attention and define the relative, daily importance of EP functions and profiles of Members of the European Parliament (MEPs). Given the limits on time and resources of parliamentarians, the definition of certain priorities necessarily leads to other points on the agenda being treated as secondary. Hence, the European Parliament, its committees and its individual MEPs have to manage the allocation of their resources in order to fulfill the treaty-based duties according to a rather rigid time schedule. Each new EU treaty does not only bring new powers to the EP, but induces a revision of parliamentary tasks and functions in the light of time as a fixed constraint. To put it bluntly, during the 1970s, the EP could easily allow each individual member to act as freely as possible, because the EU's constitutional framework did not force the EP to deliver legislative amendments within a given time period. The introduction of the cooperation, the assent, and later on the codecision procedure thus terminated the EP's relative independence from the Commission's and the Council's work program. The substance of the policy-making function altered considerably and forced the EP to reallocate the time-schedule of its plenary and committee sessions in order to digest incoming legislative duties. Parliamentary efficiency became one of the favorite jingles of the EP. Kreppel's analysis on the evolution of the EP's rules of procedure underlines rightly the "most frequently cited reason for adopting a change, and often controversial changes were proposed in the name of greater efficiency."[13] Consequently, giving priority to a set of duties and resulting functions defines the set of duties to be treated as secondary issues and moves other parliamentary functions to the political backburner.

The Evolution of the European Parliament's Roles

The Luxembourg, Maastricht, Amsterdam, and Nice versions of the EU treaties, and again the recently finalized CT considerably alter the institutional balance among the EU's main actors.[14] The CT will have a major impact on the EP by increasing its formal powers in different ways. The modifications relate to areas where the codecision and the assent procedure apply, the simplification of the codecision procedure, the full recognition of Parliament within the field of home and judicial affairs, and the changes made to the procedure for the nomination of the President of the Commission and the other commissioners.

TABLE 4.1

Enumerative Procedural Empowerments: EP and Council Decision-Making Powers in the Constitutional Treaty, 2004

Decision-Making Modes in the Council / Participatory Rights of the EP	Unanimity	%	QMV	%	SMV	%	Specific Majorities > QMV	%	Rights of EU President	%	Sum	%
Autonomous Rights	1	0.33	3	0.99	0	0.00	0	0.00	0	0.00	4	1.32
Codecision	0	0.00	86	28.29	0	0.00	0	0.00	0	0.00	86	28.29
Assent	15	4.93	7	2.30	1	0.33	2	0.66	0	0.00	25	7.89
Consultation	28	9.21	23	7.57	4	1.32	0	0.00	0	0.00	55	16.78
Ex-Post-Information	7	2.30	10	3.29	0	0.00	0	0.00	5	1.64	22	7.24
No Participation	41	13.49	52	17.11	6	1.97	11	3.62	2	0.66	112	34.87
Sum	92	30.26	181	59.54	11	3.62	13	4.28	7	2.30	304	

Source: Author's calculation on the basis of the Constitutional Treaty, Doc. CIG 87/2/04.

Notes: QMV = Qualified Majority Voting; SMV= Simple Majority Voting (author's calculation).

The reforms realized with the adoption of the CT are constitutional follow-ups and adjustments to the Maastricht Treaty, and not a totally new conceptualization of the EU's paraconstitutional basis. Therefore, and in order to accelerate ideas about how the Parliament may develop in the next years, we should go one step below primary law and look into the exploitation of what has already been achieved. The CT reveals a tendency towards a multilevel polity where competencies are not only shared between the Members of the Council but also between the Council and the EP. In a retrospective view, Parliament's access to the decision-making system of the EC is the result of a slow but unrelenting process of treaty reforms. Hence, the relative proportion of Parliament's exclusion from the European policy-making process has diminished considerably. However, if we focus on the absolute rates of the treaty-based decision-making procedures, we have to recognize that the growth in consultation, cooperation and codecision procedures has been offset by an incessant increase in Parliament's nonparticipation.

The treaty reforms introduced and subsequently widened the scope of application of the codecision procedure both with respect to those policy areas which it had just introduced into the EC sphere and with respect to policy areas already covered by the cooperation procedure. The assent procedure was extended to new TEU provisions such as sanctions in the event of a serious and persistent breach of fundamental rights by a Member State. The IGCs from Luxembourg (1986) to Nice (2000) also confirmed a constant extension of consultation procedures for new policy areas such as in the field of home and judicial affairs as well as in social and employment policy. The introduction of a hierarchy of norms and procedures laid down in the CT[15] then resulted in a reduction of consultation and a switch from consultation to codecision. As a result of the last IGC processes, many core issues of European integration had been added to decision-making procedures, providing the European Parliament with considerable powers vis-à-vis the Council of Ministers and the European Commission. However, the European Parliament continues to be excluded from dynamic and costly policy areas such as tax harmonization[16] and trade policy.[17]

Apart from the extension of codecision, the Amsterdam Treaty simplified the procedure itself.[18] The simplification finally put Parliament on an equal footing with the Council in every stage of the procedure. Under the original codecision procedure, the Council could obstruct Parliament with a take-it-or-leave-it offer after unsuccessful conciliation.[19] The equalization of both legislative branches thus induced a more balanced set of veto powers. In more concrete terms, Codecision II (post-Amsterdam) had important effects for how the Parliament is perceived by the outside world: under the Maastricht rules, the Council could easily make the Parliament pay for the failure of a

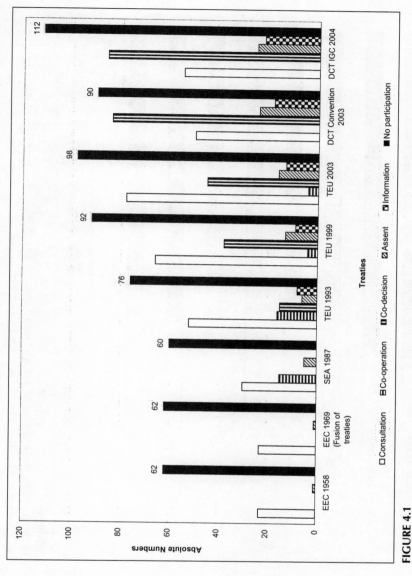

FIGURE 4.1

Decision-Making Powers of the EP and the Council (Absolute Numbers)

Source: Author's own calculation on the basis of the original EU treaties

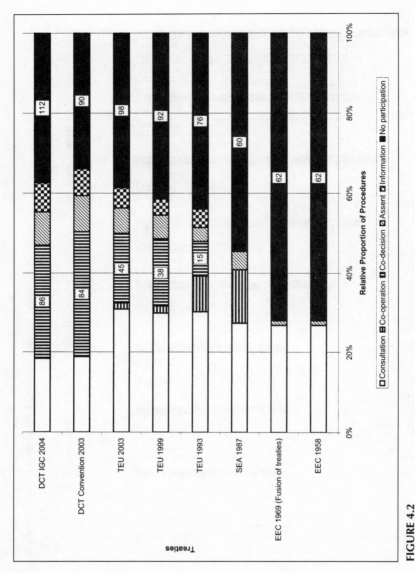

FIGURE 4.2
Decision-Making Powers of the EP and the Council (Relative, in Percent)

Source: Author's own calculation on the basis of the original EU treaties

draft legislative act. Since the entry into force of the Amsterdam Treaty, both Council and Parliament share the responsibility for the adoption as well as the failure of a proposed legislative act.

Sequential improvements for the European Parliament were also made with regard to its elective function.[20] The Maastricht Treaty granted the European Parliament the rights of consultation concerning the Member States' choice of the President of the European Commission; approval of the European Commission; and consultation on the appointment of the president, vice presidents and the members of the Board of the European Central Bank. The Amsterdam Treaty continued this trend. Not only had the Commission as a collegiate body, but also the President of the European Commission, become subject to a vote of approval by the European Parliament. The Nice Treaty confirmed these provisions and extended them towards a parliamentary election procedure. As a result, the Council, meeting in the composition of heads of state or government, must nominate the candidate it intends to appoint as President of the Commission with a qualified majority. After the president-designate receives the assent of the EP, the Council, again acting by a qualified majority and by common accord with the nominee for president can adopt the list of persons to be appointed as Members of the Commission. In the third phase of the nomination procedure, the EP has to give its assent to the President of the Commission and the other members of the Commission.

One should, however, not overestimate the implications for the practical political process. Heads of state and government are not forced to vote with a qualified majority. On the contrary, they are committed to take a consensual decision on the overall investiture package to avoid conflicts on the political level. On the other hand, the innovations made in Amsterdam and Nice may have far-reaching implications for the future style of governance in the Union. European political parties do not need a new treaty-based provision to decide to put up a top candidate for the Commission presidency. EU elections could become more alive and enriched through a kind of personalization of the Union's governing institutions. Provided that each of the European parties presents its contesting candidate for the post in question, not only the election campaign, but also the day-to-day life in Brussels and Strasbourg, could induce politicizing and mobilizing effects for the Union's citizenry.[21] However, assuming that the European parties would gain autonomy by introducing such a mechanism, national parties will not automatically adhere to the idea. Member State governments do not consent to the idea either, since the optional mechanism could restrict their autonomy in putting forward a candidate for the Commission's presidency.[22]

Serious deficits in the parliamentary dimension of the EU's legal constitution are as obvious as the achievements. With regard to the assent procedure, the EP failed to extend its power to cover all international agreements,[23] the decisions on the EC's own financial resources,[24] the extension of the authority of the institutions in pursuit of treaty objectives,[25] and, finally, the amendment of the TEU itself.[26] Moreover, some of the consultation procedures[27] give Parliament only a very limited power insofar as the Council may lay down a time limit for the EP's reaction. This in fact deprives the consultation procedure of its main impact for Parliament, namely to influence the Council's position by postponing its opinion. Moreover, the EP remains excluded from the so-called open method of coordination in the fields of economic, employment, and social policy. Amsterdam and Nice allow the Council to introduce closer cooperation between certain Member States by qualified majority.[28] The requests of the Member States concerned will be forwarded to the European Parliament. Yet neither the actual decision on closer cooperation nor the decision allowing a nonparticipating member to opt in requires any parliamentary involvement. As far as the CFSP area is concerned, the European Parliament's role remains restricted to ex-post information. Parliament's participation in shaping the substance of CFSP rests entirely at the discretion of the Member States' governments.

Exploitation I: Parliamentary Cogovernance in Practice

Both the cooperation and the codecision procedure had a considerable impact on the EP's involvement in the production of binding EC legislation.[29] Until July 2004 a total of 759 legislative proposals had been transmitted to the EP pursuant to the codecision procedure, of which 630 had been concluded. In 559 cases the Commission's initiatives resulted in binding legislation decided jointly by the EP and the Council. Seventy-one legislative proposals of the Commission failed. In sixty-three of these, the procedure lapsed because the Council was unable to adopt a common position and the Commission decided to withdraw its original proposal. Only four cases failed due to unsuccessful conciliation and another four cases failed after the EP voted against the agreement reached in the conciliation committee. Apart from these failures, the codecision procedure has led to satisfactory outcomes.[30]

Since 1996 nearly one quarter of EC legislation considered by the EP was adopted under the codecision procedure. The last three versions of the EU treaties strengthened the position and legislative role of Parliament regarding the internal market, including the areas of environment, consumer protection, transport, research, and education policy. Moreover, taking into account the total of legislation passed since 1986–1987 by adding together the percentages of both cooperation and codecision, their scope of application within Parliament had been significantly extended. However, if we take into

TABLE 4.2
Legislative Balance of the EP 1987–2003

			Activities of the EP							
	CON	COOP			COD					Assent
		Readings		*Passed*	Readings			*Passed*	*Failed or Withdrawn*	
Year		1	2		1	2	3			
1987	152	13	9	7						20
1988	131	45	45	44						14
1989	128	55	71	63						3
1990	159	70	49	56						2
1991	209	62	37	50						3
1992	243	70	66	62						11
1993	199	50	46	52	5	0	0	0	9	8
1994	168	33	21	21	18	34	8	23	3	11
1995	164	26	12	10	35	19	7	17	2	17
1996	164	31	34	25	34	37	9	31	0	8
1997	154	19	15	17	34	27	21	32	1	15
1998	215	38	24	24	41	43	11	38	1	4
1999	177	0	17	17	69	34	12	40	0	17
2000	113	0	0	0	60	53	18	63	11	14
2001	190	0	0	0	85	51	22	67	1	16
2002	136	0	0	0	90	56	20	77	0	4
2003	129	0	0	0	94	67	11	94	1	16

Source: Author's calculation on the basis of the Legislative Observatory and CELEX.
Notes: CON = Consultation; COOP = Cooperation; COD = Codecision.

account the overall output of binding legislation adopted either by the Council of Ministers or by the EP jointly with the Council, we should qualify this assessment: Hence, legislative acts concluded in 2003 pursuant to both the cooperation and codecision procedure represented only 39.3 percent of the total legislation adopted by the Council. However, before jumping to conclusions highlighting the relative failure of Parliament as a truly legislative chamber, we should take a closer look at the proportion between the Council's legislation and Parliament's involvement therein.

The overall EU legislative output consists mainly of three policy fields: agriculture and fisheries, trade, and customs policy. It is important to note the high percentage of Commission legislation authorized either by the treaty itself or the Council pursuant to its right to delegate executive competencies to the Commission in agriculture policy. In turn, the policy fields dealing with socioeconomic issues represent only 15 to 25 percent of the EC's production in binding law. If we concentrate on fields comprising the internal market such as industry, economic policy, environment and consumer protection, telecommunication and transport policy, the EP's legislative role becomes much more significant. Since most of the legislation in these fields requires cooperation or codecision, the participation of Parliament tends towards 75 percent. Hence a high proportion of the Council's output concerns nonlegislative acts, that is, executive or administrative acts, especially in the fields of agriculture, competition, trade, and customs policy. Neither the EP as such nor any of its component political groups has asked to participate in consultation or any other procedural rule when the Council deals as a price-fixing agency or when it confirms Member State nominations for one of its standing committees. If one concentrates exclusively on the Council's output in the fields of environment or consumer protection policy, the EP's participation through cooperation and codecision is much more significant (in 2003 around 82 percent).

Of the codecision procedures concluded up to the end of July 1999, 45.7 percent were based on Article 95 (harmonization measures concerning the internal market). For the 1999–2004 legislature, the exploitation of Article 95 declined toward 26 percent, while the use of the legal bases for environment, health, social, and transport policy augmented considerably, thus mirroring both the EP's new legislative powers and the increased importance attached to these policy fields.

If we take a closer look at the internal market measures passed under codecision, we identify nearly 80 percent of acts which were related to environmental and consumer protection policy. Being of a regulatory nature (definition of norms, restrictions, limits, etc.), the EU institutions based legislation on the general harmonization clause that Article 95 provides for. During the 1999–2004 legislature, 51 percent of the codecision procedures were based on new policy competencies incorporated into the Maastricht and Amsterdam treaties together with the codecision procedure (Education and Youth, Culture, Health, Consumer Protection, Trans European Networks, Data Protection). On the other hand, the exploitation of legal bases dealing with Title III ECT on the free movement of persons, services, and capital was less significant as 7.8 percent of all codecision procedures were based on one of these articles.

The increased referall to the codecision procedure has extensive effects on the functioning and internal management of the EP.[31] Given the time constraints imposed on the Parliament by the procedure and the concentration of its scope of application, Parliament had to adapt itself in several ways.

Similarly to what we can observe with regard to the scope of the procedure, codecision led to a structural concentration of workload in three permanent committees. Hence, the bulk of procedures during the 1994–1999 period touched the Committee on the Environment, Public Health, and

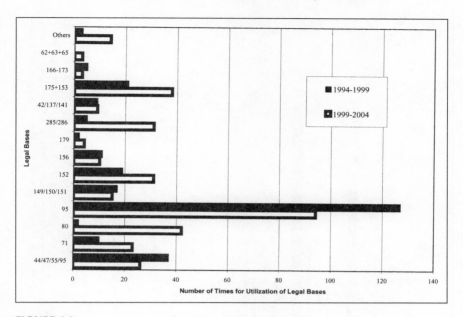

FIGURE 4.3
Exploitation of Legal Bases in Codecision 1994–2004
Source: Author's own calculation on the basis of the Legislative Observatory

Notes: Art. 40 = Free movement of workers; Art. 44 = Right of establishment; Art. 46 = Treatment of foreign nationals; Art. 47 = Mutual recognition of diplomas and provisions for the self-employed; Art. 55 = Services; Art. 71 = Transport policy; Art. 80 = Transport policy; Art. 95 = Internal market harmonization; Art. 137/138/141 = Social policy; Art. 149 = Education and Youth; Art. 150 = Vocational training; Art. 151 = Culture; Art. 152 = Incentive measures for public health; Art. 156 = Trans-European Network guidelines; Art. 166–173 = Multi-annual Framework Program for Research & Technology; Art. 175 = Environment programs; Art. 179 = Development policy; Art. 284 = Information policy; Art. 285–286 = Statistics and Data Protection.

Consumer Protection, the Committee on Economics, and the Committee on Legal Affairs. During the 1999–2004 period, the Committee on Regional Policy and Transport and the Committee on Trade, Industry, Energy, and Research Policy entered the club of the busiest legislative committees. The five committees concerned shared nearly 80.1 percent of all procedures concluded until July 2004.

The committees on Agriculture, on Fisheries, and on Civil Liberties were activitated by a relatively high amount of legislative consultation procedures. The Committee on Foreign Affairs digested the highest amount of assent procedures, and the two budgetary committees focused on both consultation and budgetary procedures. Only the committees on Employment and Social Affairs, on Constitutional Affairs, and on Womens' Rights and Equal Opportunities dealt merely with EU legislation.

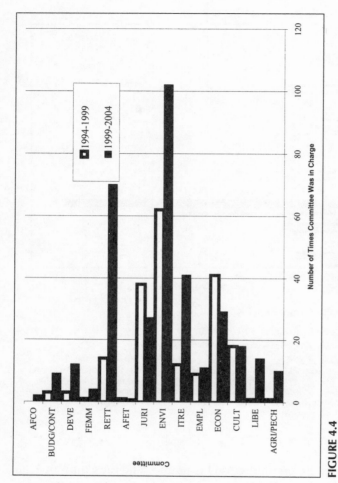

FIGURE 4.4

Exploitation of EP Committees in Codecision 1994–2004

Source: Author's own calculation on the basis of the Legislative Observatory

Notes: BUDG = Committee on Budgets; CONT = on Budgetary Control; LIBE = on Citizens' Freedoms and Rights, Justice and Home Affairs; ECON = on Economic and Monetary Affairs; JURI = on Legal Affairs and the Internal Market; EMPL = on Employment and Social Affairs, ITRE = on Industry, External Trade, RTD and Energy; ENVI = on the Environment, Public Health and Consumer Policy; AGRI = on Agriculture and Rural Development; PECH = on Fisheries; RETT = on Regional Policy, Transport and Tourism; CULT = on Culture, Youth, Education, the Media and Sport; AFCO = on Constitutional Affairs; FEMM = on Women's Rights and Equal Opportunities; AFET = on Foreign Affairs, Human Rights; DEVE = on Development and Cooperation

TABLE 4.3

Overall Exploitation of Codecision, Consultation, and Assent Procedures within the EP Committees 1994–2004

	AGRI/ PECH	LIBE	CULT	ECON	EMPL	ITRE	ENVI	JURI	AFET	RETT	FEMM	DEVE	BUDG CONT	AFCO
COD	15	10	33	71	20	50	175	73	2	78	5	12	12	2
CON	571	145	39	114	96	231	96	69	26	23	5	22	113	3
Assent	2	0	0	0	0	34	0	4	47	3	0	4	1	2
Sum	588	155	72	185	116	315	271	146	75	104	10	38	126	7

Source: Author's calculation on the basis of the Legislative Observatory.

Obviously, the extension of codecision confirms the ongoing dynamics of organizational concentration and functional differentiation-specialization within
the EP.[32] The rearrangement of Parliament's committee structure of April 1999
boosted these features to some extent. Both the new Committee on Legal Affairs
and the Internal Market (JURI) and the Committee on Industry, External Trade,
Research, and Energy (ITRE) took over the tasks related to codecision of the former three committees: Economic and Monetary Affairs and Industrial Policy;
Research, Technological Development, and Energy; Legal Affairs and Citizen
Rights. Therefore, concentration remained within the family of former legislative
committees. A challenge to the new Committee on Regional Policy, Transport,
and Tourism (RETT) was the fusing of two committee structures, which fulfilled
fairly different tasks. Whereas the bygone Committee on Regional Policy concentrated on a consultative role in distributive policy-making, the former Transport, and Tourism Committee acted under consultation, cooperation, and codecision and was involved in both the generation of some kind of European public
goods (Trans-European Networks) and regulatory policy-making. Therefore, the
fused Committee on Regional Policy, Transport, and Tourism developed a structure providing rather new cross-sectional views of Parliament. Since the Council
retained its sectional structure for regional and structural policy and transport
policy until 1999, the members of the Parliament's cross-cutting committee provided a more comprehensive perspective into the fragmented policies-actors
structure of the Council, the Committee of Permanent Representatives
(COREPER) and the related working group network.

Does Parliament Matter?

The powers and influence of the European Parliament in the European
Union's policy-making process are a matter of controversial dispute. Some
scholars argue that the European Parliament could be "regarded as a somewhat ineffective institution."[33] Others expand on this by suggesting that "it has
only very limited rights and no formal control of the executive,"[34] and that it
remains in "many, if not all, ways less esteemed and influential than most national parliaments."[35] In some opinions, MEPs are left with "more interest
than power."[36] Others argue that the European Parliament evolved towards
"the first chamber of a real legislature,"[37] as a "serious player in EU law making,"[38] and that it acts as an agenda-setting legislature[39] with significant impact on the EU's decision-making and policy processes.[40] Hence, through the
introduction and subsequent reform of the codecision procedure, the European Parliament gained more control in the legislative process (it can prevent
the adoption of legislation) and acquired more means of input into binding
EC legislation—the final legislative act requires Parliament's explicit approval.

Codecision had a considerable impact on the functional professionalization and policy field linked specialization of MEPs. Hence, the nature of EU legislation under codecision requires members to become experts in highly technical and complex issues. Expertise is not a new requisite for MEPs, however, and it is not exclusively relevant to the existence of the codecision procedure. Unlike other procedures, codecision provides much more room for maneuver, where Parliament and Council are obliged to settle technical issues of an immediate relevance for the EU's citizenry, face to face, and on an equal footing. If Parliament amends the Council's common position and the latter is not willing to accept the amended version, Parliament has the power to bargain with the Council on a joint compromise text. However, procedures and interinstitutional rules are not what the electorate is primarily interested in. Citizens do not vote on the basis of highly aggregated institutional settings, nor do they vote for an institution as a unitary body. On the contrary, electing the EP means selecting those parliamentarians who reflect the citizenry's wishes, interests, worries, and concerns. Elections are about people, parties, and cleavages.[41] The media are not interested in providing an account of how substance is being achieved. Public opinion too is oriented to daily or weekly news on who has ruled out whom, who is paying for what, who has achieved substance. In this context, MEPs are in an uncomfortable situation. The bulk of achievements is reached with overwhelming majorities, leaving apart the fact that Parliament is composed of political groups. Thus, the usual confrontation between left and right does not appear in the public realm. The net which frames deliberation and decision-making processes in the Union is highly complex. Since the lines of confrontation are interinstitutional instead of partisan based, they tend to depoliticize conflicts and substance.

Given that the expansion in formal powers confers MEPs with a heavier burden of responsibility, they must ensure that the culminated interests of the EU's citizenry are taken seriously. One method to measure the influence of Parliament is through an analysis of the track of parliamentary amendments and a comparison of the success rates of codecision with those of cooperation or consultation. The empirical evidence concerning the EP's relative success at different stages and readings of the procedures[42] does not confirm the prediction by Tsebelis and Garrett[43] who have argued that the introduction of codecision reduced the power of the EP.[44] Of the 86 joint texts agreed in conciliation during the 1999–2004 period, 17 percent corresponded to the Council's common position, 23 percent were closer to the EP's amendments adopted at its second reading, and 60 percent were genuine joint texts with EP amendments partly integrated into the final text.[45]

The EP does not simply propose amendments, but it approves the draft legislative texts at every stage of the procedure with Parliament's amendments.

Consequently, Parliament acts as a joint author alongside the Council or—
with regard to the first reading stage—the Commission during all phases of
codecision. Thus, a second way of measuring the degree of influence which
Parliament exerts on the substance of a legislative act dealt with under the
codecision procedure is to compare the final texts with the different drafts
prepared by the Council and/or the European Parliament. One can distinguish between four cases:

1. a final act corresponding to the Parliament's first reading which is defined as an act where the Council approves the EP's first reading draft
   without amending it;
2. a final act corresponding to the Parliament's second reading which is defined as an act where the Council approves the EP's second reading draft
   without amending it;
3. a final act corresponding to the Council's common position which is defined as an act where the European Parliament in its second reading approves the Council's common position without amending it;
4. a final act corresponding to the conciliation committee's joint compromise text which is defined as an act where the Council was not able to
   take over all parliamentary second reading amendments. In this case,
   conciliation becomes necessary and both the Parliament and Council
   produce a joint text subject to a third reading in both institutions.

During the 1994–1999 legislature, 73 successful pieces of legislation corresponded to the Council's common position, while only 31 were based on the
EP's second reading and 63 cases on the joint compromise text agreed between
Parliament and Council at the third reading stage. During the 1999–2004 legislature, 118 legal acts were adopted on the basis of the EP's first reading, while
91 grounded on the Council's common position, 93 on Parliament's second
reading, and 86 on the joint compromise between the two institutions.

However, we should not jump to conclusions in interpreting these figures as
a failure of the EP's influence. Firstly, even a legislative act which corresponds
to the Council's common position is an act concluded with Parliament's
agreement. Secondly, a legislative act corresponding to the common position
of the Council does not automatically represent a legislative act where Parliament had any influence. Hence, the Council in its common position incorporates parliamentary first reading amendments and consequently, the Parliament does not propose new amendments in the second reading stage.[46]

A third method to measure the EP's influence would be to analyze the substance of successful and unsuccessful parliamentary amendments. Of course,
the first two methods take no account of the relative political weight of

amendments, nor do they indicate the extent to which rejected amendments are eventually taken up in modified form in other, new proposals. Earnshaw and Judge note that it is not possible to "distinguish between 'substantive' amendments, designed to be accepted, and 'propagandistic' amendments, designed to advance an issue up the policy agenda of Council and Commission (without any realistic expectation of inclusion in the final directive)."[47] Therefore, quantitative success rates should not be overestimated. On the other hand, it has to be pointed out that, even if Parliament is exclusively successful in amending the recitals of a given draft proposal, the final act would still correspond to the EP's majority will. Being a joint act of the Council and the Parliament—the logic of the conciliation procedure means that the two co-legislators are condemned to finding an agreement—codecision leads to an equalization of these institutions. With the right to press the Council into conciliation or to reject the latter's common position, and thus the whole proposal, Parliament obtained real bargaining powers in order to change substantive issues within directives, regulations, and decisions.

Exploitation II: More Legislation Does Not Increase Parliamentary Scrutiny

Does the increase of Parliament's workload with regard to its policy-making function induce a change in attention in regard to its control function? Accountability is a key concept of Western democracies. It "can be seen as a precondition for other components of democratic rule: it is political responsibility that ensures that the terms on which political power is authorized are duly observed; and it is the need for power-holders to compete for re-election that gives them an incentive to be responsive to the public."[48] The EP's traditional instruments for holding other institutions to account—parliamentary questions—are oriented towards the single MEP and political groups. Questions are one of the "most free procedures in modern legislatures." They "give the individual MEP an excellent chance of promoting and defending those issues which he or she regards important."[49] In other terms, questions also enable MEPs to present or to defend their perceived constituency's interest. Given the observed characteristics of a legislative and specialist parliament regarding its policy-making function, questions can be regarded as a compensatory element for the individual and, with regard to the profile of MEPs, for the backbencher as well.

Due to the anticipated position and workload in EC legislation and thus to the expected restrictions on available plenary time, Parliament changed internal rules in 1993 to reorganise working mechanisms for executing its control function. Since then three kinds of questions are allowed. Written questions tabled by any MEP are the most popular of the procedures, since there are no

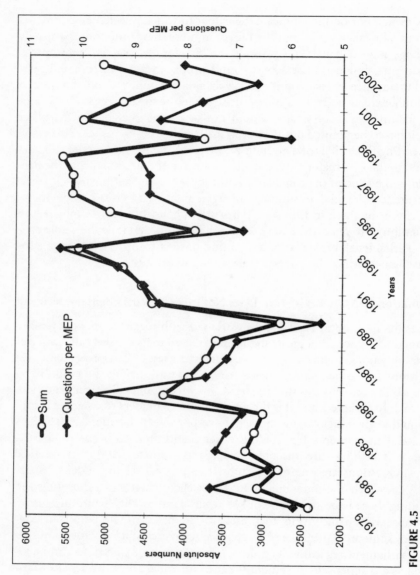

FIGURE 4.5
EP Questions 1979–2003

Source: Author's own calculation on the basis of the annual reports of the European Commission.

procedural constraints and members are free to decide when to submit a written question. Questions for oral answer (with debate) can only be tabled by a committee, a political group, or thirty-two MEPs. These questions are filtered by the Conference of Presidents who rule on their admissibility and order. The reply to these questions may be followed by the adoption of a resolution. Again, only a committee, a political group, or thirty-two MEPs may table such a resolution. Finally, questions in question time can be tabled by any MEP but the president rules on their admissibility and if they are in order.

The oscillation of all three types of questions during a parliamentary term does not follow a clear pattern except that of direct elections. MEPs increase the frequency with which they table questions prior to direct elections. However, since the entry into force of the Maastricht Treaty, the two types of oral questions have remained at approximate levels of 1000 and 250, respectively, per year. Moreover, questions for oral answer are at a very low level and—given the increase in number of MEPs since 1995 (626 in relation to 518 since 1986)—clearly in decline. In contrast, it seems that written questions enjoy a growing interest among MEPs. As regards the destination of questions since November 1993, we observe a slight but constant growth in questions to the Council of Ministers. This interest in the Council started to increase in the early 1990s, and has remained stable since the coming into force of the Maastricht Treaty. Consequently, the newly introduced types of question with regard to the second and third pillars have not had a significant impact on the operation of Parliament's questions. Overall, the most original instrument of the European Parliament's control vis-à-vis the Commission and the Council has lost its attractiveness.

Another possibility for scrutiny exists in article 193 ECT providing for the European Parliament to set up temporary committees of inquiry in order to investigate "alleged contraventions or maladministration in the implementation of Community law." Parliament started its first inquiry in early 1996 with an examination of the EC's transit system. In July 1996, the EP decided to set up a second committee on the BSE crisis which met thirty-one times during six months and presented its report in February 1997.[50] The two committees of inquiry were successful in various ways. In spite of the lack of a judicial sanction mechanism designed to oblige witnesses to tell the truth, the two committees recorded the evidence and made it available to the general public. In doing so, the EP ensured that witnesses would be held to account by a wide audience outside the Parliament. The BSE committee encouraged and enjoyed a significant press and media coverage.[51]

Due to a conditional threat of a possible motion of censure,[52] there was a direct and visible impact of the committees' work on the investigated institutions, namely the Commission. In its resolution of 19 February 1997, Parliament warned the Commission that if the recommendations of the BSE committee were not carried out within a reasonable deadline and in any event by November 1997, a motion of censure would be tabled. The threat of voting a motion of censure was a novelty for the European Union. It showed how the right of inquiry can be combined with other powers at Parliament's disposal. And Parliament's work mattered: within the European Commission, the responsibilities of the directorate general responsible for consumer affairs were widely expanded. In turn, the prestigious, but highly criticized director general for agriculture was obliged to hand over seven scientific, veterinary, and food committees as well as a special unit which evaluated public health risks. Most important perhaps was that the BSE inquiry also had a considerable impact on the outcome of the 1996–1997 IGC. It led to a fundamental change of the legal basis for EC legislation in the field of veterinary medicine. Article 152.4b ECT as amended by the Amsterdam Treaty held that "by way of derogation from Article 37, measures in the veterinary and phytosanitary fields which have as their direct objective the protection of public health" are to be decided pursuant to the codecision procedure. The two committees of inquiry proved to be an effective additional means for the European Parliament's supervisory powers. The European Parliament demonstrated "its traditional pugnacious assertiveness of its rights and its ingenuity in exploiting constitutional grey areas."[53] Article 6 of the interinstitutional agreement holds that the rules "may be revised as from the end of the current term of the European Parliament in the light of experience." Given the two "testcases" of the BSE and the Transit Committee, future negotiations between the institutions may focus on a sanction mechanism for Member States that refuse to cooperate in an inquiry. However, given the Council's—that is, the Member States'—reluctance during the original negotiations on the agreement, the Parliament is not likely to gain additional powers.

Exploitation III: More Legislation Equals Less Individualised MEP Work

Own initiative and urgency resolutions are an indicator for measuring the interest of MEPs in using different nonlegislative scrutiny instruments offered to the EP. Initiative reports and resolutions reflect awareness and interest of individual MEPs in making an issue public to the outside world— toward the Union's citizenry but also toward the Council and the Commission. Given the historical lack of parliamentary powers in relation to participation in binding EC legislation, MEPs and political groups referred to the opportunity of own initiatives or urgency resolutions to give evidence of their general interests, their attention paid to a given issue, or of their willingness to shape the policy agenda. For political groups, initiative resolutions are one of the core instruments which allow them to present their original point of view on a given issue. Even if own initiatives do not result in the adoption of new regulatory or distributive legislation, they allow MEPs and political groups to prove of their collective—denationalized—interest in EU politics. Hence, in contrast to codecision, where action against the Council (amendments to or rejection of its common position) requires the approval of an absolute majority (during the 1999–2004 legislature at least 314 votes), own initiative resolutions pass with the simple majority of votes cast. Accordingly, whereas codecision condemns the two major political groups—the Party of European Socialists and the European Peoples Party—to reach agreement on parliamentary amendments which in consequence move the left-right cleavage apart from the agenda, own initiatives and similar resolutions provide each political group the opportunity to present their original socioeconomic argument before the public. A major consequence of the shift towards EP legislative power and its effective execution is a strong decrease in the number of nonlegislative resolutions, own initiative reports (inviting the Commission to forward legislative initiatives), and resolutions after statements or urgencies. The number of these activities fell sharply from 2.41 per MEP in 1979 to 0.15 per MEP in 2003.

Figure 4.6 shows the evolution of parliamentary initiative and urgency resolutions between 1979 and 2003. What becomes observable is that the evolution of the total number of initiatives and urgencies correlate with the constitutional setting and development of the Community/Union over time. In this regard, the growth from 1984 to 1986 reflects Parliament's activity in relation to European Political Cooperation and—more importantly—to its attempts in evolving the prior EEC into the European Union. The introduction of the cooperation and the assent procedure (Single European Act) then resulted in a continuous decrease of own initiatives. Only the debates on the Maastricht Treaty reversed this trend. However, since the entry into force of Maastricht, the usage of initiatives is again declining continuously and dramatically. Moreover, if we take into account the growth of Parliament due to the enlargement of the EU to include Spain and Portugal in 1985 and Finland, Sweden, and Austria in 1995, we observe a significant decrease in resolutions per MEP from 1984 to 1985 and from 1994 to 1995 respectively. In other terms, the growth in number of MEPs did not result in an increase of non-legislative activity of Parliament.

Conclusion

Since 1993–1994 the codecision procedure has been implemented extensively. Clear focuses are observable in the areas of the internal market policy,

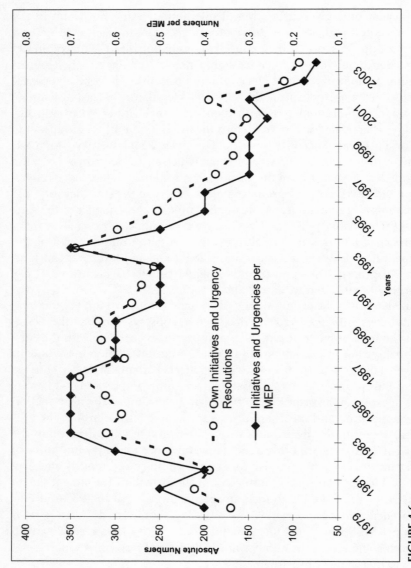

FIGURE 4.6
Initiative Reports and Urgency Resolutions 1979–2003

Source: Author's own calculation on the basis of the annual reports of the European Commission.

environmental policy, and parts of the EU's socioeconomic agenda. The empirical analysis points to a specific process of EU parliamentarization in these policy areas. On the other hand, the exploitation of the EP's policy-making function induced a specialization of MEPs and a segmentation of the EP into legislative and nonlegislative committees. MEPs active in policy-making become expert specialists in complicated matters. They present expertise and counterexpert's assessments to the Council's and the Commission's actors and argue about their political relevance and penetration into binding legislation. Indeed, this ability is also given by the consultation procedure. However, providing and battling for expertise and counterexpert's assessments was barely used due to the ineffectiveness of parliamentary amendments in this procedure.

Overall, the institutional *infinalité* of the EU treaties helped the EP to strengthen its sphere of influence because it did not have to integrate itself into the stiff corset of a representative's chamber whose majority is obliged to the loyalty to the Commission or the Council. Differently, the simple absence of an institutional hierarchy otherwise usual in the EU Member States between government and parliament permitted the EP to adapt its potential as a co-legislating and power-limiting institution. The inclusion of the EP into the EU's legislative procedures had no negative effects on the efficiency of the whole decision-making system. On the contrary, the power extensions of the EP in its policy-making function led altogether to more efficient decision-making sequences, although the potential for interinstitutional conflict has increased between Council and EP.[54]

The increase of formal legislative powers of the EP induced a considerable shift of emphasis from the control function to the policy-making function, because policy-making claims more and more time and personnel resources. Under this point of view the investigation could prove that the parliamentary calendar downgrades the more original functions of the EP in the area of its control function through questions, initiatives, and urgency resolutions. Consequently, the possibilities of MEPs for mediating citizens' or constituency concerns are significantly reduced. This development should be considered as but one important reason for the low attraction of the EP with the EU's citizens. The policy-making function is not evolving as an incentive for the EU citizens to vote for the EP, because the possibility of party political aggregation of voters' interests within the EP remains complicated in phases of the EU's decision-making processes in which the EP can exercise its power vis-à-vis the Council.

The biggest mediation problem of the EP exists in a decisive rule of the EU treaties. The EP needs more than 50 percent of the votes for adopting amendments in the legislative area. Neither of both big political groups manages this majority. Also in the sixth legislative period, the two groups are dependant on at least three further groups if they do not want to decide as a grand coalition. The treaty-based threshold constraints let the EP appear as a closed actor who is not able to transcend competing voters' interests into the day-to-day work. Both the treaty constraints and the EP's practice thus provoke a structural competition and communication deficit.

One of the essential challenges for the EP's future development follows from this mixed balance of the EP's functions. Another increase in legislative power will not help to legitimize the increase of the EP's importance if the processes of interest articulation, interest mediation, and interest penetration still run exclusively between institutions that can only be perceived as single actors in the abstract. An essential step in reinforcing linkages between the EP and citizens could be made through a more open and self-confident use of the available conflicts of interests within Parliament as well as within the European political parties and other transnational aggregates of the civil society. The EP should start to use its potential as an arena and public space in order to assist the construction of transnational communication structures.

Notes

1. Fischer 2000; Napolitano 2002.
2. Jachtenfuchs and Kohler-Koch 1996.
3. Maurer and Wessels 2001; Maurer 2002.
4. Wallace 1996, 63.
5. Judge and Earnshaw 2003, 24.
6. Hofmann 2003.
7. Bourgignon-Wittke et al. 1985, 39–60.
8. Grabitz et.al. 1988.
9. Steppat 1988, 5–35.
10. Schmuck and Wessels 1989.
11. Maurer 1996; Wessels 1996.
12. Maurer 2002, 86–88.
13. Kreppel 2002a, 104.
14. Huber 2003, 574–599; Jacobs 2003; Nickel 2003, 501–509; Scelo 2002, 578–582; Schoo 2004, 63–74.
15. Articles I-33 to I-37 C.
16. Article 93 ECT.
17. Article 133 EC.
18. Maurer 2003b, 228–230.
19. Garrett 1995, 289–308; Tsebelis and Garret 1997, 74–92.
20. Article 214TEC.

21. Padoa-Schioppa 1998; Hix 1995, 525–554. The idea of creating a politicized linkage between the Commission and the Parliament is not as new as it seems; see Jacqué 1989, 217–225.

22. Nickel 1998.

23. Articles 133, 300 and 301 ECT

24. Article 269 ECT

25. Implied powers, Article 308 ECT

26. Article 48 TEU

27. E.g., Article 39 TEU

28. Búrca de 2003, 814–839.

29. Crombez 1997, 97–121 and Crombez 2000, 363–381.

30. Of the 348 approved acts, 236 cases were reached without convening the conciliation committee out of which 157 were approved by Parliament without amending the common position of the Council. In the remaining 79 cases the Council accepted all of the second reading amendments proposed by the EP. And 112 common positions were subject to conciliation and joint compromise texts of both the Parliament and the Council.

31. Shackleton 2000, 325–342 and Maurer 2002.

32. Bowler and Farrell 1995, 219–243 and Farrell and Héritier 2004.

33. Nugent 1994, 174.

34. Leggewie, 2002/2003, 3–4.

35. Church and Phinnemore 1994, 253.

36. Peterson and Bomberg 1999, 45.

37. Duff 1995, 253.

38. Scully 2000, 235.

39. Tsebelis 1994, 128–142; Burns 2002; Farrell and Héritier 2004.

40. Kreppel 2002a, 1.

41. Hix 2001, 663–688.

42. Maurer 1998, 42, partly reproduced in Hix 1999, 97.

43. Tsebelis and Garrett 1997, 74–92.

44. On the criticism against Tsebelis and Garrett see Moser 1996, 56–62; Scully, 1997a, 233–252; Scully 1997c, 58–73; and Scully 1997b, 93–103.

45. European Parliament 2004, 14.

46. Hubschmid and Moser 1997, 225–242.

47. Earnshaw and Judge 1996, 102.

48. Lord 1998, 80.

49. Raunio 1996, 357.

50. The transit regime of the EC is a system whereby goods coming into the EC are exempted from tax until they reach their country of destination inside the EC or cease to be liable on leaving the EC's territory.

51. Shackleton 1997.

52. Shackleton, "The European Parliament's New Committees," 11.

53. Lord 1998.

54. Westlake 1997, 23.

A COMMENT ON AUEL, BENZ, AND MAURER

Rudy B. Andeweg

Parliamentarization versus the Democratic Deficit

There are those who doubt that European integration has resulted in a democratic deficit,[1] and there are those who, while acknowledging the existence of such a deficit, see no role for parliaments in remedying that situation.[2] However, the dominant approach to democratic legitimacy in the EU is that a parliamentarization of EU decision making is an important part of the solution. Within this dominant strategy, authors and politicians who are inclined to see the EU developing into a supranational political system stress the importance of the European Parliament as the crucial link in the chain of delegation and accountability from citizens to EU policy-making institutions. A clear example of this line of thinking can be found in German Foreign Minister Joschka Fischer's famous speech at Humboldt University in 2000 in which he called for a "full parliamentarization" of the EU itself. Others, who continue to see the EU as a predominantly intergovernmental system, emphasize the role of the national parliaments of the Member States as the most important mechanism linking the citizens to the EU. A good example of this view can be found in British Prime Minister Blair's reaction to Fischer's Humboldt speech: "The primary sources of democratic accountability in Europe are the directly elected and representative institutions of the nations of Europe, national parliaments and governments."[3]

Depending on their view of European integration in general, individual authors and individual governments may prefer to strengthen either the European Parliament or the national parliaments, but in practice we see that both the European parliament and the Member States' parliaments have received more powers with regard to EU policy-making. With the establishment of European Affairs Committees, procedures to ensure that information is relayed to parliaments in time, and de facto veto rights in some Member States, national parliaments have started to fight back.[4] In this volume, Katrin Auel and Arthur Benz focus on the growing involvement of national parliaments in EU policy-making, comparing the British, Danish, and German experiences in this respect. Meanwhile, the European Parliament evolved from an appointed into a directly elected institution, from having powers only of consultation, via cooperation and assent, to powers of codecision in some areas, and from having no involvement in the composition of the Commission to asserting new rights with regard to the investiture and censure of the Commission. In this volume Andreas Maurer traces these changes and analyzes their impact. In this way, the two chapters in this volume are important contributions to our understanding of the effects of the two strands of the strategy to reduce the EU's democratic deficit by strengthening parliamentary powers.

In my reaction to these two contributions I shall concentrate not on the relative merits of parliamentarization at either the national or European level, but on what these two approaches have in common, as well as on the core question of whether the currently dominant strategy of parliamentarization can result in a higher level of legitimacy for the European Union at all. To this end I make four observations: two about the approach taken by Maurer and Auel and Benz (and indeed by most academics and politicians when discussing parliamentarization), and two about the current role of parliaments within the EU as depicted in both chapters.

Parliaments as Constitutional Institutions Rather Than Political Arenas

In a seminal paper, Nelson Polsby has made a distinction between parliaments as "transformative institutions," as political actors able to transform public policy, and parliaments as "arenas" that do not affect public policy as unitary actors, but that provide a venue for outside actors (ministers, MPs, political parties) to meet, debate, and fight over the content of public policy.[5] Both Maurer, and Auel and Benz, use parliament as their unit of analysis and analyze changes in the position and powers of national parliaments and the European Parliament. In short, they treat parliaments as institutions, implicitly assuming that these parliaments are actors in their own right. Only occasionally do these chapters discuss how new rights and procedures affect the opportunities of parties or MPs to influence EU policy. However, parliaments that can be classified as transformative institutions are relatively rare; Polsby mentions the U.S. Congress, and one may well argue that even the American legislature has changed in the direction of an arena since Polsby published his analysis in 1975. Most parliaments in parliamentary systems of government clearly fall into the category of arenas in which the perpetual struggle between political parties is played out. It is for that reason that Anthony King has warned against the "two-body image" in discussions of executive-legislative relations in England, Germany, and France.[6]

Of the parliaments discussed by Auel and Benz, only the Danish *Folketing* approaches Polsby's ideal type of a transformative institution, because the regular occurrence of minority governments reduces the salience of the struggle between government and opposition and opens up opportunities for ad-hoc coalitions on individual issues. The symbiotic relationship between government and parliamentary majority in the UK and in Germany, however, turns any discussion of the powers of "the" parliament vis-à-vis "the" government into a rather formalistic exercise in constitutional law rather than political science.

There are interesting parallels between the European Parliament and the U.S. Congress—also because of the absence of a strong political relationship between the parliamentary majority and an executive; occasionally the European Parliament indeed does display an institution-like homogeneity, but research has also shown a growing cohesiveness of the parliamentary parties within the European Parliament, which is more likely to be found in a political arena. Towards the end of his chapter, Maurer acknowledges the problem when he writes that "[a]nother increase in legislative power will not help to legitimize the increase of the EP's importance if the processes of interest articulation, interest mediation and interest penetration still run exclusively between institutions that can only be perceived as single actors in the abstract." (Maurer, this volume, chapter 4).

Executive-Legislative Relations Rather Than Political Representation

The reason why parliamentarization is considered such an important remedy to the lack of EU legitimacy is that parliaments provide the crucial linkage between civil society and government (or, at the EU level, between civil society and Commission and/or Council): Members of Parliament (MPs) and parties in parliaments maintain relations with both civil society and government. Curiously, however, the two sets of relations are dealt with in two separate bodies of literature. The literature on political representation studies the interactions between MPs and parties on the one hand and civil society on the other hand, whereas the literature on executive-legislative relations focuses on the interactions between MPs and parties on the one hand and government ministers on the other hand. This bifurcation in the study of parliaments is deplorable because it is precisely the combination of the two relations that may generate legitimacy.

The chapters by Auel and Benz, and Maurer, are illustrative of this general problem. Auel and Benz discuss how Europeanization of policy-making may have contributed to a weakening of national parliaments relative to national governments, and how national parliaments have reclaimed some of the powers through institutional reform. Auel and Benz seem to take the incorporation of European issues in the process of political representation for granted when they assert that "[g]overnmental action is only legitimate if subject to parliamentary control and open for parliamentary rejection. Only then can it be guaranteed that the will of the electorate will actually be transformed into policy-making" (Auel and Benz, this volume, chapter 3). However, strengthening parliamentary control over EU policy-making alone does not guarantee that the will of the electorate with regard to EU issues is translated into policies.

Likewise, Maurer documents what he calls the "cascade-like parliamentarization of the Union's decision-making system": the gradual strengthening of the European Parliament vis-à-vis Commission and Council in EU policy-making. He does not look into the extent to which the European Parliament represents the will of the European citizenry on European affairs; this is taken for granted: "Electing the EP means selecting those which reflect the citizenry wishes, interests, worries and concerns" (Maurer, this volume, chapter 4). However, as we shall see momentarily, Maurer does show how the increase in the European Parliament's policy-making powers has steered MEPs away from activities that provide better opportunities for mediating citizens' or constituency concerns.

One may well wonder whether the greater problem with regard to democratic legitimacy in the EU is the lack of powers of the European Parliament and national parliaments with regard to EU policy-making, or the lack of European content in the relationship of these parliaments with civil society. When it comes to European affairs, the content of political representation in the EU seems disconnected from the content of executive-legislative relations in the EU, depriving European citizens from a meaningful influence over European policy.

Mandate Rather Than Accountability

If we accept for the moment the emphasis on executive-legislative relations rather than on political representation, there are two ways in which parliaments can exert their power over governments: through "ex ante controls" (in the jargon of principal-agent theory) or mandating procedures, and through "ex post controls" or accountability procedures. The parliamentarization of EU policy-making consists primarily of the strengthening of ex ante controls.

Auel and Benz point out that national parliaments have obtained rights to receive information on European issues from their governments, that they have set up European affairs committees to process this information, and that "scrutiny reserves" have been introduced in many Member States. At first sight, this would seem to amount to a strengthening of ex post rather than ex ante controls, but this is misleading. With, possibly, an exception for the UK, the information rights do not consist of governments accounting for their actions in the working groups, COREPER, or Councils of Ministers, but of early warning mechanisms alerting parliaments to new Commission proposals on which a position may have to be taken in the near future. Similarly, the scrutiny reserve is not an accountability mechanism, but a mandating mechanism for parliament to influence the government's position on EU issues in advance.

At the EU level, the European Parliament has obtained more powers to influence future policy, whereas accountability mechanisms have not been expanded to the same extent. There is now a provision for setting up committees of inquiry (but they have been used only twice so far). With regard to parliamentary questions, new rules were introduced in 1993 to limit the number of questions asked. Maurer shows that accountability mechanisms are now used less frequently by the European Parliament: "The increase of formal legislative powers of the EP induced a considerable shift of emphasis from the control function to the policy-making function, because policy-making claims more and more time and personnel resources" (Maurer, this volume, chapter 4).

In general, parliamentary systems of government rely more on ex ante than on ex post controls,[7] and given the predominance of that type of regime within the European Union, it is perhaps not surprising that parliamentarization of EU policy-making relies primarily on strengthening ex ante controls. However, precisely with regard to EU policy-making it is doubtful whether ex ante controls are able to democratize the system. Fritz Scharpf, for example, has argued that the preconditions for input-oriented legitimacy (giving a mandate to a majority) are simply not met: "Given the historical, linguistic, cultural, ethnic, and institutional diversity of its member states, there is no question that the Union is very far from having achieved the thick collective identity that we have come to take for granted in national democracies—and in its absence, institutional reforms will not greatly increase the input-oriented legitimacy of decisions taken by majority rule."[8] It would make more sense, Scharpf implies, to invest in output-oriented legitimacy (accountability).

In addition to this theoretical argument, the chapters by Auel and Benz and by Maurer also provide empirical evidence that investing in ex ante controls may not contribute to solving the democratic deficit. The central point in the chapter by Auel and Benz is the dilemma faced by MPs when they use the scrutiny reserve or mandating procedure. Through this procedure national parliaments can influence the negotiation position of their government in the Council, but by doing so they also restrict their government's room for maneuver to defend the national interest in those negotiations. What is in the interest of national citizens—a strong national parliament weakening their government's position in Brussels, or a weak national parliament, leaving their government with a strong position in EU negotiations? As Auel and Benz conclude, "Hence, strengthening the mandating powers of national parliaments vis-à-vis their government does not necessarily contribute to more democracy in European policy-making" (Auel and Benz, this volume, chapter 3). At the EU level, Maurer suggests that the strengthened policy-making role of the European Parliament also does not strengthen democracy: "The policy-making function is not evolving as an incentive for the EU citizens to vote for the EP, because the possibility of party political aggregation of voters' interests within the EP remains complicated in those phases of the EU's decision-making processes in which the EP can exercise its power vis-à-vis the Council" (Maurer, this volume, chapter 4), while the shift away from the control function may further weaken democratic legitimacy as, "[c]onsequently, the possibilities of MEPs for mediating citizens' or constituency concerns are significantly reduced" (Maurer, this volume, chapter 4).

Depoliticization

Perhaps the most striking similarity between Auel and Benz's chapter on the national parliaments and Maurer's chapter on the European Parliament is that both chapters provide evidence that parliamentarization has led to a (further) depoliticization of decision-making on EU issues. In the Danish *Folketing*, Auel and Benz observe how the mandating procedure forces parliamentary actors to downplay political differences and to focus on questions of negotiation strategy. "Indeed, party competition generally does play a rather minor role in the [European Affairs] Committee debates"; "Thus, the Committee debates strategies rather than actual policy issues based on party political views"; "In addition, confidentiality of the Committee's debates and results prevents party politics from gaining in importance and ensures the informal and consensual style of debate in Committee" (Auel and Benz, this volume, chapter 3). In Germany, MPs of the governing majority in the *Bundestag* cooperate closely with the government on European issues, but opposition MPs also have influence as opposition parties frequently control the *Bundesrat*: "As a consequence of these strategies, most cooperation between the Parliament and the government is transferred to internal and therefore private parliamentary party working groups. It takes place outside the formal proceedings and is not open to the public" (Auel and Benz, this volume, chapter 3). The lack of party political differences over European affairs is also evident in Germany: According to a study of voting behavior in the *Bundestag* European Affairs Committee, "more than 60% of the mandates had an all-party support" (Auel and Benz, this volume, chapter 3). A partial exception is the UK. In the British House of Commons, Auel and Benz observe strong party competition over European integration in plenary sessions, but a less partisan atmosphere appears to prevail in the European Scrutiny Committee: "Even the opposition has to admit that the Labour members in the committee 'act as a group of parliamentarians, not as party members'" (Auel and Benz, this volume, chapter 3).

At the EU level, the introduction of the codecision procedure has contributed to depoliticization. As Maurer concludes, "The nature of EU legislation under codecision requires Members to become experts in highly technical and complex issues" (Maurer, this volume, chapter 4). Moreover, the strengthening of the European Parliament's legislative power has led to a strong decrease in the number of nonlegislative resolutions, own initiative reports, and resolutions after statements or urgencies, which often were more politicized, "whereas co-decision condemns the two major political groups—the Party of European Socialists and the European Peoples Party—to reach agreement on parliamentary amendments [because of the absolute majority requirement] which in consequence moves the left-right cleavage apart from the agenda" (Maurer, this volume, chapter 4). It is this consensual, depoliticized nature of EU policy-making that may well contribute to a perception among citizens that European integration is a conspiracy of the elites, which renders the EU particularly vulnerable to populist revolt.

Conclusion

The parliamentarization of EU policy-making, whether at the national or at the European level, has primarily resulted in giving parliaments as such more rights to influence policy ex ante. The provisions for accountability and for political representation on EU issues have not been strengthened, at least not to the same extent. The analyses by Maurer and by Auel and Benz can be interpreted to indicate that this strategy is unlikely to remedy the European democratic deficit. Parliamentarization can only increase the EU's legitimacy if the European Parliament and/or national parliaments do translate the views of citizens into European policy. Future institutional engineers are well advised to search for reforms that increase the European content of political representation, that emphasize ex post accountability rather than ex ante mandates, and above all, that politicize EU policy-making. If the EU's citizens continue to have every reason to doubt that they are offered real and meaningful choices with regard to European affairs, parliamentarization is doomed to fail.

Notes

1. See, for example, Moravcik 2002, 603–624.
2. See, for example, Andersen and Burns 1996, 227–251.
3. As quoted in Crum 2003, 375–95. Crum also distinguishes a third approach, the French vision of the EU as "a federation of nation-states" which leads to strengthening the links between the European Parliament and the national parliaments.
4. Raunio and Hix 2000, 142–68.
5. Polsby 1975, 277–96.
6. King 1976, 11–36. Also see Andeweg and Nijzink 1995, 152–178.
7. See Strøm 2003, 55–106.
8. Scharpf 1999a, 9.

5

Constructing Parliamentary Democracy in the European Union: How Did It Happen?

Berthold Rittberger

THIS CHAPTER SETS OUT by pointing at a paradox. Despite the flourishing of the literature on the EU's democratic credentials, we still lack a systematic explanation for why the EU's institutional structure displays the imprints of the model of parliamentary democracy, a characteristic feature for national democratic political systems but much less so for international institutions. Not only does the EU's institutional structure comprise a directly elected parliamentary organ—the European Parliament—with appointment, control, budgetary, and legislative powers, but also in the more recent past, the role of national parliaments in EU decision making has been enhanced, culminating in the adoption of a subsidiarity control mechanism in the Treaty establishing a Constitution for Europe (TCE) signed by the EU member states in October 2004. In this chapter I will aim at answering the question of why Member States have gradually enhanced the powers of the European Parliament and, albeit less so, of national parliaments. The focus of this study will be on the period following the adoption of the Single European Act (SEA) although reference will be made to previous instances of the European Parliament's empowerment.

This chapter proceeds as follows: In the ensuing section, I will ask under what conditions policy-makers will be inclined to project the model of parliamentary democracy onto the EU level, thereby leaving an imprint on its institutional set-up either by empowering the European Parliament and/or strengthening the role of national parliaments in EU policy-making. In the sections that follow, theoretical propositions will be elaborated and subjected to empirical testing.

Why Empower the European Parliament and National Parliaments?

Concerns about the democratic credentials of the EU abound; this section will ask under what conditions policy-makers from the EU Member States take recourse to the model of parliamentary democracy as a guiding principle for institutional design and reform. Why have policy-makers from the national governments of EU Member States continuously employed the model of parliamentary democracy as a blueprint for institutional reform since the early days of supranational integration which is reflected in the successive empowerment of the European Parliament in EU decision making and, as of more recent origin, the augmenting role attributed to national parliaments?

The Model of Parliamentary Democracy and Institutional Reform in the EU

Since the early days of European integration in the 1950s, the then Common Assembly of the European Coal and Steel Community (ECSC) has undergone a remarkable journey from merely a supervisory body to twin arm of the budgetary authority to colegislator. Long gone are the days when the European Parliament was qualified as inconsequential "talking shop" and compared to assemblies of international organizations, all of which were considered "innocent of legislative power."[1] One indicator for the increasingly potent role of the European Parliament in EU policy-making lies in the observation that some scholars compare the European Parliament with its domestic counterparts.[2] Some even refer to the European Parliament as "one of the world's more powerful elected chambers."[3] The gradual empowerment of the European Parliament, however, is not the only mark which the model of parliamentary democracy has left on the EU's organizational surface: Since the 1990s, policy-makers increasingly contemplate endowing national parliaments with a more prominent role in EU policy-making. Article I-11(3) TCE has endowed national parliaments with the power to scrutinize Commission proposals and assess their compatibility with the principle of subsidiarity. Tables 5.1 and 5.2 offer an overview of those instances of treaty reform which have led to changes in the role and competencies of the European Parliament and of national parliaments in EU policy-making.

How can we explain the gradual empowerment of the European Parliament and, as of more recently, the augmentation of national parliaments' role in EU policy-making? I argue that what triggers Member States' decisions to enhance the powers of the European Parliament and of national parliaments is the perceived salience of decisions to pool and delegate sovereignty from the domestic to the European level. Salience can be defined as the perceived discrepancy

TABLE 5.1

Parliamentary Democracy in the EU: The EP Path

	Control of the Commission	Appointment of the Commission	Budgetary Powers	Legislative Powers
1951(ECSC Treaty)	Censure vote against High Authority (Art. 24 ECSC)	—	—	—
1957 (EEC and EAEC Treaties)	Censure vote against Commission (Art. 144 EEC)	—	Consultation and nonbinding amendments (Art. 203 EEC)	Consultation (Art. 137 EEC, Art. 107 EAEC); 18 instances in EEC and 11 in EAEC
1970 (Treaty of Luxembourg)	—	—	Right of amendment, EP may reject entire budget (Art. 203 EEC)	—
1975 (Treaty of Brussels)	—	—	EP may reject entire budget; EP with sole right to grant discharge (Art. 205a EEC)	—
1986 (SEA)	—	—	—	Cooperation procedure (Art. 189c EEC); assent procedure

(continued)

TABLE 5.1
Parliamentary Democracy in the EU: The EP Path (*continued*)

	Control of the Commission	Appointment of the Commission	Budgetary Powers	Legislative Powers
1991 (Maastricht Treaty)	—	Consultation on nominee for Commission President CP; College of Commissioners: vote of approval (Art. 158 TEU); synchronization of EP's and Commission's terms	—	Introduction of codecision procedure (Art. 189b TEU), extension of other procedures
1997 (Treaty of Amsterdam)	—	Nominee for CP to be approved by EP; College of Commissioners: vote of approval (Art. 214 ECT)	—	Reform and extension of codecision procedure (Art. 251 ECT)
2000 (Nice Treaty)	—	—	—	Extension of codecision procedure (Art. 251 ECT)
2004 (Treaty establishing a Constitution for Europe)	—	Nominee for CP to be elected by EP; in proposing a CP Member States have to take into account the elections to the EP (Art. I-27, 1)	Reform of annual budgetary procedure (compulsory-non-compulsory expenditure distinction removed, Art. III-310); constitutionalization of multi-annual financial framework (Art. I-54 and III-308)	Codecision to become "ordinary legislative procedure" (Art. I-34, 1 and Art. III-396); extension to new policy areas

TABLE 5.2
Parliamentary Democracy in the EU: The National Parliament Path

	Role/Competencies of National Parliaments	*Legal/Treaty Base*
1991 (Maastricht Treaty signed)	National parliaments to receive Commission proposals in "good time" for information and examination	"Declaration on the Role of National Parliaments in the European Union" (No. 13)
	Representatives from national parliaments and EP encouraged to discuss "main features" of the EU	"Declaration on the Conference of the Parliaments" (No. 14)
1997 (Treaty of Amsterdam signed)	Information for national parliaments; six-week period between Commission proposal submitted to national parliaments and Council adoption of a position	
	COSAC (Conference of European Affairs Committees) to examine legislative proposals and make "contributions" relating to fundamental rights, subsidiarity, establishment of an area of freedom, security, and justice	"Protocol on the Role of National Parliaments in the European Union"
2000 (Nice Treaty signed)	*Inter alia* calls upon role of national parliaments in the EU architecture to be debated	"Declaration on the Future of the Union" (No. 23)
2004 (Treaty establishing a Constitution for Europe signed)	Information for national parliaments; fixed six-week period between Commission proposal submitted to national parliaments and the Council adopting a position	"Protocol on the Role of National Parliaments in the European Union"
	"Subsidiarity" control by national parliaments on Commission proposals; initiation of infringement proceedings before the ECJ (national governments on behalf of national parliaments)	Art. I-11(3) and annexed "Protocol on the Application of the Principles of Subsidiarity and Proportionality"

between "ought" and "is": The more a proposed or implemented step of EU integration (such as transfers of sovereignty) is perceived to curb the competencies of national parliaments, the more salient the democratic deficit of European integration becomes and the stronger is the normative pressure on EU actors to redress the situation by offering democratic compensation by either strengthening the European Parliament or national parliaments.[4]

As soon as the six prospective Member States of the ECSC took the decision to delegate sovereignty to the quasi-executive supranational high authority in 1954 the question about its democratic accountability was raised: Since the key motivations for the Member States to create a supranational high authority was to ensure its independence from Member State governments' interventions in the policy-making process, the question as to who should hold it to account was answered by the Member States by creating of a supranational parliamentary assembly which was endowed with powers of executive scrutiny and control.[5]

Similarly, the planned attempts to introduce an own resources system for the Community finances in the mid- and late 1960s led the Member State governments to ponder over the question as to who should be entitled to take decisions about Community expenditure: the Member States, the European Parliament, both jointly? Even though the first attempt to create an own resources system in the mid-1960s failed after the French "empty chair" decision which left Community business paralyzed until January 1966, the question about how the European Parliament should be associated with spending decisions was already raised in this context by the Member States, most notably the Benelux countries, Germany and Italy. During the negotiations leading to the adoption of the Treaty of Luxembourg in 1970, the same Member State governments pressed for the European Parliament to acquire budgetary powers as a consequence of the creation of an own resources system. These governments argued that with an own resources system in place at the Community level, national parliaments are partially stripped of one of their traditional roles, their role to approve budgetary expenditures. Consequently, it was considered appropriate that there had to be some guarantee of parliamentary involvement in deciding on the expenditure of own resources.

In the mid-1980s, the decision of the Member State governments to transfer sovereignty to the Community level by adopting qualified majority voting (QMV) in the Council of Ministers as a result of the negotiations leading to the SEA increased the perceived salience of the democratic deficit of decision making since the adoption of QMV was perceived to aggravate the marginalization of national parliaments in exercising control and influence over EU decision making. As a result, the Member States decided that the European Parliament had to be given a more prominent role in the legislative decision-making process that exceeded mere consultation.

From these sketches we can derive a more general expectation: The transfer of sovereignty from the domestic to the supranational level poses a threat to domestic procedural mechanisms through which democratic participation and accountability can be granted. Transfers of sovereignty thus increase the perceived salience of the democratic deficit. How do Member States respond to this challenge? Research has shown that Member States respond by projecting domestically established procedures for democratic participation and accountability onto the EU level. This is not surprising: Searching for novel solutions for how to best respond to the democratic challenges posed by transfers of sovereignty to a supranational organization, policy-makers are inclined to employ cognitive shortcuts.[6] Shortcuts are helpful heuristics in decision-making situations. They are parsimonious cognitive models which are linked to internalized categories of traditional thinking and hence offer familiar solutions to problems framed as being familiar: "An institutional model that combines well-known features of the national systems of democracy will be taken up more easily than complex constructions of associate or deliberate democracy."[7] The use of shortcuts can thus be described as prototype matching[8]: Policy-makers activate solutions that match "surface indicators: [R]epresentation is linked to parliament, political control to increasing parliamentary powers."[9]

However, this does *not* automatically imply that Member States will offer the same answer as to how the model of parliamentary democracy should be translated into actual institutional design choices. The shortcuts activated may very well differ across different groups of actors. I label these shortcuts or cues which actors adopt to translate the model of parliamentary democracy into prescriptions for action legitimation strategies by which I mean those institutional reform proposals derived from alternative legitimating beliefs. Legitimating beliefs are defined as "normative orders in which specific constructions of the legitimacy of a political system are (re)produced through the ascription of purpose and meaning."[10] Legitimating beliefs reflect national histories as well as economic and political organizing principles which themselves are reflected in the constitutions and political systems of individual EU Member States. Scholars have demonstrated that actors holding different legitimating beliefs offer different responses to the question about the degree to which national parliaments and/or the European Parliament should be given a role in influencing and controlling EU decision-making processes.[11] Based on extensive empirical research, Markus Jachtenfuchs and collaborators have developed a set of analytically distinct legitimating beliefs: Federal State, Intergovernmental Cooperation, Economic Community, and Network Governance.[12]

Conditional upon which legitimating beliefs policy-makers hold, alternative solutions as to how Member State governments are likely to respond to the transfer of sovereignty problem will be proposed. For example, Member State governments who view the empowerment of the European Parliament critically, such as the proponents of an Intergovernmental Cooperation legitimating belief have—for long—stressed the negative repercussions of European integration on the status and role of national parliaments and press for solutions to the democratic deficit at the domestic level. Conversely, those Member State governments who hold a Federal State legitimating belief consider the empowerment of the European Parliament as the key to alleviate the perceived democratic deficit.[13] In this context, I distinguish between a European Parliament route and a National Parliament route as alternative legitimation strategies which are derived from the Federal State and Intergovernmental Cooperation legitimating belief respectively; as will be demonstrated below, policy-makers pursue these legitimation strategies with a view to alleviate the perceived democratic legitimacy deficit that results from their own decisions to transfer sovereignty to the supranational level.

Proposition I. Transfers of sovereignty are perceived by policy-makers to undermine domestic procedures of democratic accountability and participation. In order to find an appropriate response to these challenges, policy-makers take recourse to the model of "parliamentary democracy" from which they derive legitimation strategies as more concrete cues for institutional design and reform choices.

The Relative Success of Alternative Legitimation Strategies

Having advanced an argument about when and why Member State governments perceive the EU's democratic legitimacy deficit as salient and how they intend to alleviate it, we now need to shed light on the determinants of success of the two different legitimation strategies, the European Parliament and the National Parliament routes (see tables 5.1 and 5.2). Why have concerns about national parliaments—until the 1990s—not been translated into institutional reform solutions at the EU level? Once the Member State governments decided to walk down the National Parliament-route, why did they do so only fairly reluctantly which is reflected in the limited scope of competencies attributed to national parliaments in EU policy-making (predominantly informational rights)? Can we theoretically deduce determinants for the relative success of alternative legitimation strategies?

Which factors determine whether a rule, norm, or—in the case at hand—a legitimation strategy exercises a strong or weak compliance pull on Member

States' behavior? Why do actors follow some rules and not others? Thomas Franck has argued that the higher the legitimacy of a rule, the stronger its compliance pull. The degree to which an international rule "will exert a strong pull on states to comply" depends on four observable characteristics: determinacy, symbolic validation, coherence, and adherence to a norm hierarchy.[14] To the extent that the relevant legitimation strategy possesses these properties, actors are likely to follow its prescriptions. In the ensuing paragraphs, I focus specifically on two dimensions of legitimacy: determinacy and coherence.[15]

Coherence refers to a rule's "connectedness, both internally (among the several parts and purposes of the rule) and externally (between one rule and other rules, through shared principles)."[16] A rule gains legitimacy when it is applied both consistently (when "likes are treated alike") and coherently (when distinctions in the treatment of "likes" can be justified by referring to a commonly accepted principle).[17] According to Florini, "[A] new norm acquires legitimacy within the rule community when it is itself a reasonable behavioral response to environmental conditions facing the members of the community and when it 'fits' coherently with other prevailing norms accepted by the members of the community."[18] Existing rules can thus provide a hospitable environment for a particular legitimation strategy and increase its legitimacy.

Determinacy refers to a rule's textual clarity: According to Franck, "Rules which are perceived to have a high degree of determinacy—that is, readily ascertainable normative content—would seem to have a better chance of actually regulating conduct in the real world than those which are less determinate."[19] A legitimation strategy is determinate if it offers clear behavioral prescriptions (the "Do's") or prohibitions (the "Don'ts") and hence "a rule is more likely to be perceived as legitimate when its contents are relatively transparent, when the content can be determined with comparative ease and certainty. . . . [A] rule's determinacy may be ascertained either from its text or from the application of the text in specific disputes by a legitimate clarifying process."[20]

If determinacy and coherence are thus key to explain the differential success of the European Parliament and national parliament legitimation strategies, what would we expect with regard to the determinacy and coherence of the two legitimation strategies? Based on the observation that the European Parliament has benefited more than national parliaments from Member States' decisions to firmly imprint parliamentary democracy on the EU's institutional structure, we would expect the European Parliament legitimation strategy to score higher overall in coherence and determinacy than the national parliament legitimation strategy. However, given the more prominent role attributed to national parliaments in the recent past, we would also expect that the determinacy and

coherence of the national parliament legitimation strategy has improved relative to the European Parliament legitimation strategy over time.

> *Proposition II.* The higher the determinacy and coherence of a specific legitima-
> tion strategy, the more likely it is that this legitimation strategy will influence in-
> stitutional reform and design decisions among policy makers.

In the ensuing empirical analysis I will proceed as follows. First, I will ask
whether transfers of sovereignty increased the perceived salience of the democratic deficit among policy-makers (Proposition I). Hence, I would expect
policy makers to react to instances of sovereignty transfers (as a result of treaty
reforms) by employing legitimation strategies which, in turn, guide the search
for institutional solutions to the perceived challenges posed by transfers of
sovereignty. Secondly, I will test the plausibility of the proposition that the relative degree of determinacy and coherence of our two legitimation strategies
affects their relative success in influencing institutional reform and design decisions (Proposition II).

The Relative Success of Different Legitimation Strategies

I have argued above that in the run-up to the SEA, Member State governments
responded to the introduction of QMV by voicing concerns about the increasing marginalization of national parliaments in exercising control and influence
over EU decision making. With the introduction of QMV, ever more policy
decisions would be taken at the EU level. Did Member State governments in
subsequent treaty reforms equally share a concern about the looming democratic legitimacy deficit triggered by the pooling of sovereignty?

During the negotiations leading to the adoption of the Maastricht Treaty,
the prospective extension of QMV prompted national governments and domestic political parties to activate the "link" established in the negotiations
leading to the adoption of the SEA. According to this "link," the extension of
QMV to new policy areas goes hand in hand with legislative involvement of
the European Parliament (in all areas where QMV applies). This link which
became a guiding principle for future treaty reform and possessed a high degree of determinacy as it offered a clear behavioral prescription: Once the
scope of application for QMV is extended, legislative involvement of the European Parliament must follow suit.

All political parties in Germany unequivocally supported an extension of
the European Parliament's legislative powers. The major political parties in
the *Bundestag* demanded that "[i]n the course of the development of the Eu-

ropean Community towards a European Union, the democratic deficit shall be eliminated in particular by strengthening the European Parliament's legislative and control powers."[21] Claims of a similar nature were voiced in other parts of the Community. The Belgian government complained about an increasing democratic shortfall if further transfers of sovereignty were not accompanied by increasing the European Parliament's legislative powers.[22] The Dutch government was equally concerned about the lack of democratic "flanking" mechanisms as the integration processes advanced. It contended that any "transfer of powers to a supranational authority must . . . be accompanied by guarantees of sufficient democratic control at this level."[23] Even governments which, traditionally, displayed a skeptic attitude toward the democratic legitimacy leverage provided by a more resourceful European Parliament, did not dispute the logic that transfers of sovereignty could not "go alone." The Danish government remarked in a memorandum which was approved by the *Folketing*'s Common Market Committee on 4 October 1990 that "[g]reater Community integration calls for a strengthening of the democratic process" and concluded that "the influence of both national parliaments and the European Parliament should be strengthened."[24] The British government was somewhat more critical about the potential of the European Parliament's capacity to alleviate the legitimacy deficit, yet with one exception: As long as the European Parliament directed its focus on scrutinizing the Commission, the British government welcomed an enhanced role of the European Parliament since this would constitute another institutional check on the Commission and not undermine the power of the Member States.[25]

Following Maastricht, the IGCs leading to the adoption of the Amsterdam and Nice treaties did not see serious efforts by Member State governments to dispute the link between extending QMV and including the European Parliament in the legislative process.[26] However, disagreement continued to be pungent regarding the scope of the European Parliament's influence and the scope with which QMV should be extended to new policy areas. In Nice, for instance, the extension of QMV to policy areas hitherto governed by the unanimity rule was sparse and thus was the extension of the codecision procedure and of the European Parliament's legislative powers.[27] In the light of the imminent enlargement, Declaration No. 23 attached to the Nice Treaty, called upon the Member States to launch an encompassing debate about the future of the EU which should, among other things, eventually produce "a simplification of the Treaties with a view to making them clearer and better understood without changing their meaning."[28] Following the European Council meeting at Laeken of December 2001 and the establishment of the European Convention which was to be endowed with this task, a working group on "Simplification" (Working Group IX) was instituted which set itself the twin objective of making the European system of governance more transparent and more comprehensible.[29] With respect to the simplification and reform of legislative procedures, the report issued by the working group stipulated that the co-decision procedure should "become the general rule for the adoption of legislative acts."[30] The Draft Treaty establishing a Constitution for Europe (DTC) and the ensuing IGC which resulted in the signing of the Treaty establishing a Constitution for Europe (TCE) implemented the working group's recommendation: Article I-34(1) TCE stipulates that what was hitherto known as the codecision procedure becomes the "ordinary legislative procedure." The logic inherent in the "QMV equals European Parliament legislative involvement" formula had thus not only gained a largely uncontested status in the post-SEA era; this formula also offered a clear behavioral prescription regarding its implementation: "If you extend QMV, you have to allow for parliamentary participation in the legislative process." It can hence be concluded that the European Parliament legitimation strategy possessed a high degree of determinacy in the period under scrutiny.[31]

The success of the European Parliament legitimation strategy cannot be attributed merely to its high degree of determinacy. The coherence of the European Parliament legitimation strategy with its normative environment played an equally important role in accounting for its relative success vis-à-vis the national parliament legitimation strategy. In the mid-1980s the European Parliament legitimation strategy did not face a particularly hospitable normative environment. During the IGC leading to the adoption of the SEA, most of the Member States saw one of the key conditions to successfully implement the single-market program in augmenting the efficiency of decision making by introducing QMV. The call for greater parliamentary involvement in legislative decision making, motivated by democratic legitimacy concerns, ran counter to the efficiency objective. Including another potential veto point in the legislative process could not easily be squared with the efficiency postulate. Thus, while democratic legitimacy concerns clashed with efficiency concerns in the period leading to the adoption of the SEA, the situation reversed remarkably in the mid-1990s. During the Amsterdam IGC, efficiency-based arguments were actually used to support the reform of the Maastricht version of the codecision procedure, calling for a scrapping of that part of the third reading of the legislative procedure whereby the Council could reaffirm its common position confronting the European Parliament with a take-it-or-leave-it proposal. This simplification of the procedure, formalized in the Amsterdam Treaty, implied an increase in the European Parliament's influence over legislation while, at the same time, achieving the efficiency objective! Similarly, the convention process called for a simplification of the existing plethora of legal instruments. This development played into the hands of the

European Parliament: The decision to reduce the number of legal instruments and applying codecision as "ordinary legislative procedure"[32] for the passage of laws and framework laws did not only serve calls for enhanced efficiency but also served those who called for more democratic legitimacy. In sum, although the efficiency norm was "hostile" to an increase in the European Parliament's legislative powers at first, this situation reversed in the mid-1990s once the European Parliament's legislative powers were firmly enshrined in the treaties. Since then the coherence of the European Parliament legitimation strategy with its normative environment became an additional factor conducive for its success.

To analyze the relative success of the national parliament route, I will distinguish between three phases characterized by different degrees and combinations of determinacy and coherence. In the first phase, the pre-Maastricht era, the national parliament legitimation strategy had not left its imprint on institutional design in the treaties. At subsequent IGCs, several declarations and one protocol have been added to the treaties (see table 5.2) primarily aimed at improving the information national parliaments receive with respect to EU legislative initiatives (second phase). The third phase captures the proceedings of the convention process. As a result of the adoption of the TCE, national parliaments were, *inter alia*, endowed with a subsidiarity control mechanism and the right to initiate infringement proceedings before the ECJ.[33]

First Phase: Pre-Maastricht

How can we explain that the issue of the involvement of national parliaments in EU decision making cropped up only in the early 1990s, making its way into the Maastricht Treaty as Declaration No. 13 on the "Role of National Parliaments in the European Union" and as Declaration No. 14 on the "Conference of the Parliaments"? Although discussions about the role of national parliaments in legitimizing EU decision making in the era of QMV have not materialized in terms of a treaty article or even a declaration annexed to the SEA, Member States expressed, nonetheless, concerns that the role of national parliaments in affecting EU decision making was fading. Although countries like Denmark and the United Kingdom were firm proponents of the belief that democratic legitimacy is vested in the domestic parliament and cannot be provided by the European Parliament, the national parliament legitimation strategy did not leave its mark on the SEA. Why? The explanation for its absence lies in the low degree of determinacy and coherence in this period. At the advent of the signing of the SEA, Member State governments had difficulties foreseeing the impact of the introduction of

QMV on the role of national parliaments in EU policy-making. Even though there was a sense that the pooling of sovereignty would come to the detriment of national parliaments, the governments who publicly expressed most worries about this development did not articulate a clear-cut strategy as to how the potential weakening of the national parliaments' powers could be counteracted (apart from resisting the transfer of legislative powers to the European Parliament). Some domestic parliamentarians even viewed this as part of a strategy on behalf of their governments to further weaken the national parliaments.[34] Domestic conditions regarding the strength of national parliaments in scrutinizing their executives' European endeavors also vary substantially.[35] The Danish Parliament, for example, could rely on an effective parliamentary control mechanism over the government on European policy issues which was exercised by the powerful European Affairs Committee of the *Folketing*.[36] Given this variation and the fact that there was no prior experience with regard to the repercussions of QMV on the workings of domestic parliaments and, consequently, no clear prescription as to how national parliaments should be connected to European decision-making, the determinacy of the national parliament legitimation strategy assumes a low value in this period. Additionally, there were no Community norms around which could have potentially bolstered the success of the national parliament legitimation strategy. In sum, the impact of the national parliament route on institutional design decisions remained negligible.

Second Phase: Maastricht and Post-Maastricht

The entry into force of the Maastricht and Amsterdam treaties in 1993 and 1999 respectively was accompanied by transfers of national sovereignty through the extension of QMV. Member State governments voiced concerns about the consequences of pooling through the extension of QMV for processes of democratic accountability and interest representation. In this context, the roles of the European Parliament and of national parliaments in EU decision making were mentioned as significant themes for discussion at the IGCs under the banner of democratic legitimacy.[37] While the national parliament legitimation strategy had not left its imprint on the SEA, the Maastricht Treaty explicitly acknowledged the role of national parliaments in EU decision making in two annexed declarations, one calling for improving the information received by national parliaments on legislative initiatives[38] and the other encouraging national parliaments to contribute to substantive policy issues.[39] Furthermore, the Amsterdam Treaty annexed a protocol on the "Role of National Parliaments in the European Union" which specified some of the provisions of the Maastricht Declaration No. 13. These formal treaty changes have to be qualified as being very modest in scope. They were chiefly about improving information for national parliaments regarding EU legislative initiatives which they could employ to improve the scrutiny process vis-à-vis their national governments. Nevertheless, even a modest increase in the success of the national parliament legitimation strategy has to be accounted for. The answer lies in a modest change in the determinacy of the national parliament legitimation strategy. Analyzing statements and memoranda outlining the positions of Member State governments during the IGCs leading to the adoption of the Maastricht and Amsterdam treaties, it strikes the analyst how little agreement there was among the Member State governments as to how national parliaments should be involved in EU decision making in order bring Europe closer to the citizens. The responses offered by Member States vary substantially and can be distinguished according to the degree to which unilateral or joint solutions for the strengthening of national parliaments are sought:

1. Improvement of domestic scrutiny procedures vis-à-vis national governments by improving the information flow from the EU to the domestic level (unilateral action).
2. Improvement of scrutiny procedures vis-à-vis national governments by drawing on forums such as a conference of European Affairs Committees, the so-called COSAC (joint coordination).[40]
3. Instituting a (second) chamber at the European level constituted of national MPs with roles other than merely scrutiny.

With regard to the first issue—the upgrading of domestic scrutiny procedures vis-à-vis national governments by improving the information flow from the EU to the domestic level—there was widespread agreement among the Member State governments to improve domestic scrutiny procedures. In the run-up to Maastricht, the British government issued a statement which stipulated that the role of national parliaments in scrutinizing EC legislation should be increased. It emphasized, however, that the modalities regarding the increasing of their role should be "a matter for member states, not for the Community. . . . We would welcome if national parliaments in other states were to increase their own role in scrutinizing EC legislation."[41] A Danish government memorandum echoed the British government's position stipulating that "a considerable part of what is known as democratic shortfall is attributable to the fact that not all national parliaments have an adequate say in the decisions taken at Community level."[42] It was also the Danish government in the preparation for the IGC leading to the adoption of the Amsterdam Treaty which stressed that national parliaments should be enabled to play a more prominent role in EU decision making via their national governments by obtaining timely information on EU-level legislative initiatives.[43] The Spanish government equally argued that the main role of national parliaments "in relation to EU decisions should concern the monitoring and control exercised by each member state parliament on the actions of its government in the Council, and that it is up to each member state, not the Union, to determine how this activity should be exercised."[44] To fulfill this role properly, the Spanish government called for the European institutions, the Commission in particular, to supply national parliaments with all the requisite information. With a view to the second category (joint action) and third category (second chamber), both the Maastricht and Amsterdam IGCs saw selective support for closer cooperation between national parliaments and their MPs in weakly institutionalized forums such as COSAC and a conference of parliaments, modeled on the idea of the *Assizes*.[45] The question as to whether a second chamber of national parliamentarians should be instituted alongside the European Parliament was even more controversial.[46] In the run-up to Maastricht, proposals were brought forward for a congress of national parliamentarians, which was later modified to being a conference of national parliamentarians and MEPs. This proposal gained initial support from the United Kingdom, Portugal, Spain, and Greece.[47] In a debate in the French National Assembly, the French Minister for European Affairs, Elisabeth Guigou, laid out the core function of such a congress: Its role should be to discuss "themes of common interest and issue an opinion on the broad orientations of the Union."[48] While even among the supporters of a second chamber there was no uniform view as to what exact role and competencies it should be endowed with, other governments expressly opposed the idea. Regarding measures for cooperation between national parliaments which were of a less formal and institutionalized nature, such as COSAC, there was disagreement as to its exact role and status. In the run-up to Amsterdam, the Spanish government opposed a formalization of the COSAC structure arguing that "closer links with the national parliaments should not lead to the creation of a new institution or permanent body with its own staff and premises, or of a second chamber of national MPs."[49] The Spanish government expressed its opposition to a regular convening of a conference of parliaments as laid down in Declaration No. 14 annexed to the Maastricht Treaty given their lack of success. Other Member State governments, such as Austria, called for a consolidation of COSAC, yet they expressed stark opposition to any proposals establishing a second chamber. What can be concluded from the above with reference to the determinacy and coherence of the national parliament legitimation strategy? While all three proposals to enhance the role of domestic MPs display a high degree of determinacy—proposals for unilateral action (improving information) and joint action (COSAC) and even the issue of a second chamber offered clear behavioral prescriptions. Yet, only proposals to improve the information for national parliaments met with unanimous support. With respect to improving the role of joint coordination mechanisms, such as COSAC, or even the creation of a congress or second chamber, there was partial support at "best" (COSAC) and almost unanimous opposition at "worst" (second chamber). Partial support for joint coordination mechanisms was mirrored in the relatively widespread support for improving the informal role of COSAC and in the equally widespread opposition to formalize COSAC. Only a small number of Member State governments supported a more enhanced role for COSAC in particular in certain policy areas (such as subsidiarity, justice and home affairs, own resources, enlargement, and general CFSP guidelines). How can we account for the lack of acceptance of those proposals which envisaged a strengthening of national MPs by endowing them with a more potent role in EU decision making within COSAC or even by erecting a second chamber?

It has been argued that the legitimacy of a particular legitimation strategy also depends on its coherence, "which is to say, its connectedness, both internally (among the several parts and purposes of the rule) and externally (between one rule and other rules, through shared principles)."[50] Did proposals for empowering institutionalized *fora* for national MPs or for creating a second chamber display high levels of coherence? A rule is coherent when it relates to other rules of the same system in a principled fashion and when, in applying a rule, cases which are conceptually alike will be treated alike.[51] Did the proposals for enhancing the role of national MPs relate to other rules in a principled fashion, that is, did the proposals accord with those principles which to uphold was considered key by the Member State governments in this context?

Raunio[52] argues that proposals to strengthen domestic MPs in a congress of national MPs or even to introduce a second chamber faced serious principled opposition by a majority of member states: First, it was argued that introducing an additional institution on the European level "would work against making the EU political system more transparent and understandable. Regardless of what the precise function of that second chamber would have been, a colegislator with the Council and the European Parliament, or a watchdog of the subsidiarity principle, its introduction would make the EU system more complex."[53] These proposals thus appeared unreasonable and hard to justify in light of one of the underlying purposes of institutional reform: promoting the transparency of EU decision making! Secondly, these proposals also threatened to upset the relationship "between the legislative and executive organs, as national MPs—who at the national level control their governments in EU matters—would simultaneously become directly involved in shaping EU legislation. In terms of its composition, it is hard to understand how the decisions of such a body would differ from those of the Council"[54] since the composition of each national delegation in a congress or second chamber would probably reflect the strength of the parties in the domestic parliament which would imply that the position of each national delegation would be identical to that of its national government. Third, there was also a widespread fear that by empowering domestic MPs the powers of the European Parliament would be hampered, a scenario which was, for instance, tacitly favored by the French government.[55] Since the European Parliament's role in granting democratic legitimacy to EU policy-making is considered foundational by the vast majority of Member State governments, there was no principled justification or argument on offer which legitimately permitted an actor to square the quest for more democratic legitimacy of EU policy-making with a reduction in the powers of the European Parliament. There remains the proposal to enhance the informational rights of national MPs in EU affairs. This proposal met with little resistance, not only because it involved no "sovereignty costs" for national governments but because the proposal was not in conflict with other proposals and rules which could have hampered its coherence. However, once proposals were advanced to reform domestic scrutiny procedures, the "overwhelming majority, if not all, of member states resisted reforms that would have given the Union a say about how national parliaments should organize their scrutiny of government in EU affairs."[56] Proposals of this type did not resonate at all with domestic constitutional principles. The Amsterdam Treaty even makes explicit that the scrutiny by individual national parliaments of their own government in relation to the activities of the Union is a matter for the particular constitutional organization and practice of each Member State.

Third Phase: The Convention Process

Only a few years after the adoption of the Amsterdam Treaty the German Minister for Foreign Affairs, Joschka Fischer, delivered a speech at the Humboldt University in May 2000, which triggered a vibrant debate among major European political leaders, featuring prominent figures such as Tony Blair and Jacques Chirac. One of the recurrent issues was the question of how the role of national parliaments in EU decision making could be enhanced. Political leaders voiced strong support for an additional body, "a second chamber in Brussels."[57] There was, however, widespread disagreement regarding the features of said second chamber, the major being "[w]hether what is proposed is a second chamber with specific powers, or what might perhaps be better described as a community or committee of parliaments, coming together to perform specific tasks, but mainly advising rather than deciding."[58] During the convention, the issue of a congress or second chamber was taken up, expressly favored by the President of the Convention, Giscard d'Estaing himself. Among the convention members there was considerable disagreement not only as to its desirability but also among the proponents of the congress idea as to how its exact role and competencies should be defined.[59] The convention process, however, brought about substantial change in the role exercised by national parliaments. By instituting an "early warning mechanism" with respect to guarding the subsidiarity principle, national parliaments were attributed a substantially new role. Although the convention members quarreled over the modalities of how national parliaments should be permitted to intervene when they objected to a Commission legislative proposal on subsidiarity grounds ("yellow" or "red card"), there was widespread agreement among the members about the general idea that national parliaments should not only be better informed about the legislative intentions of the EU, but that they should also be able to express their objections where legislative proposals were considered to run counter to the principle of subsidiarity.[60] These measures also found their way into the TCE adopted by the Member State governments in October 2004.[61]

To explain the introduction of the "early warning mechanism," which can be triggered by national parliaments, we have to take a closer look at the coherence of the national parliament legitimation strategy since the determinacy of the different proposals remains unaltered (see previous section). The question about the delineation of the EU's competences—which was becoming an ever more fervently debated theme following the adoption of the Nice Treaty and the "Declaration on the Future of the Union"—made subsidiarity a guiding principle of institutional reform. This debate proved to be extremely conducive for the success of the national parliament legitimation strategy. The principle of subsidiarity has been "a fixture in the political and constitutional debate"[62] since it was first espoused in the Maastricht Treaty and further specified at Amsterdam in the "Protocol on the application of the principles of subsidiarity and proportionality."[63] In Declaration No. 23 of the Nice Treaty, the Member State governments explicitly recognized "the need to improve and to monitor the democratic legitimacy and transparency of the Union and its institutions, in order to bring them closer to the citizens of the member states."[64] For this purpose, they called for a broad debate about the future of the EU which should address, *inter alia*, the following questions: How can "a more precise delimitation of powers between the European Union and the Member States, reflecting the principle of subsidiarity" be established and monitored? What role should national parliaments play in the "European architecture"?[65] At its December meeting in Laeken in

2001, the European Council adopted a "Declaration on the Future of the European Union" committing the EU to become more democratic, transparent, and effective. The declaration laid down sixty questions targeting different themes concerning the future of the EU, such as the division and definition of powers, the simplification of the treaties, the EU's institutional setting, and the move toward a constitution for Europe. It also foresaw the convening of a convention to examine these questions and themes. It was early in the convention phase that two working groups were established to deal with the principle of subsidiarity (Working Group I) and the role of national parliaments (Working Group IV) in order to meet some of the demands of the Laeken mandate. While both themes, the role of subsidiarity and of national parliaments in organizing and legitimizing EU governance, had been on the Member States' EU reform agendas since the early nineties, policy-makers had not established a nexus between subsidiarity and national parliaments until the convening of the convention.[66] The working group on subsidiarity was guided by the assumption that the application and monitoring of subsidiarity should and could be improved upon. In its final report, the group proposed to the convention that national parliaments should be given an important role in monitoring the compliance of legislative initiatives with the principle of subsidiarity via an "early warning system" (*ex ante* control). Furthermore, the working group stipulated that the convention should adopt a provision to allow appeals to the European Court of Justice against violations of subsidiarity (*ex post* control).[67] The group was not shy to stress "the innovative and bold nature" of its proposals.[68] The working group on national parliaments "reinforced the main findings of the subsidiarity working group by underlining that national parliaments should play a key role in monitoring the principle of subsidiarity."[69] The IGC leading to the adoption of the TCE signed in October 2004 in Rome by the heads of government adopted these provisions largely unaltered in the "Protocol on the application of the principles of subsidiarity and proportionality."

The elevation of the subsidiarity principle to a guiding norm in the discussion about delineation of the levels at which policies and competencies shall be allocated proved to be a "hospitable" context for the national parliament legitimation strategy. I have already argued that Member State politicians held that national parliaments were a key to strengthen the democratic legitimacy of the EU by bringing it "closer to the citizens." It was thus seen as a logical and widely accepted argument that the political institutions that were seen to have suffered most from ever more transfers of sovereignty to the European level—national parliaments—should be entitled to have a say regarding the application of the principle of subsidiarity, putting, if

TABLE 5.3
Summary—Legitimation Strategies and Their Success

	European Parliament Route	National Parliament Route		
		Pre-Maastricht (1st Phase)	*Maastricht and Post-Maastricht (2nd Phase)*	*Convention Process (3rd Phase)*
Determinacy (simplicity and clarity of prescription)	*medium/high:* the formula "QMV=EP-legislative involvement" gains uncontested status; continuing disagreement about the degree of EP involvement (SEA, Maastricht, Amsterdam)	*low:* the post-SEA phase poses the first (and hitherto unknown) challenge to national parliaments legislative prerogatives	*medium/high:* proposals to enhance role of domestic MPs/ national parliaments offer relatively clear behavioral prescriptions (e.g., improving information mechanisms, instituting a second chamber)	*medium/high:* national parliaments are viewed as potential guardians of the subsidiarity principle via ex ante and ex post controls; differences as to additional roles of NPs in EU decision making persist

(continued)

TABLE 5.3
Summary—Legitimation Strategies and Their Success (continued)

	European Parliament Route	National Parliament Route		
		Pre-Maastricht (1st Phase)	*Maastricht and Post-Maastricht (2nd Phase)*	*Convention Process (3rd Phase)*
Coherence ("fit" with the normative environment)	*low* (SEA): efficiency norm (introduction of QMV) conflicts with EP participation in legislative process	*medium/high* (since Amsterdam): simplification of the treaties (norms of transparency and efficiency) conducive for EP legitimation strategy	—	*low*: transparency principle and central role of the EP in granting democratic legitimacy conflict with proposals to enhance role domestic MPs institute a second chamber	*high*: convention/TCE specifies application of subsidiarity principle and calls for national parliaments to monitor its application
Overall impact	**Medium/high**	**Low**	**Medium**	**Medium/high**

deemed necessary, a brake on the appropriation of policy-making competencies by the Commission. Since Maastricht, the subsidiarity norm had thus itself undergone a process of specification, which—in the convention process—found its expression in a concrete proposal for institutional reform, most notably in the establishment of a clearer delineation of competences between the national and the EU level, but also in the introduction of an *ex ante* subsidiarity control mechanism to be exercised by national parliaments. Given its concrete mandate (to tackle the question of subsidiarity and devise a role for national parliaments) and broad participation, the convention thus succeeded in increasing the determinacy of the subsidiarity norm which had hitherto been too vague to have led to concrete and mutually accepted institutional design or reform proposals. Consequently, this development had positive repercussions on the national parliament route by improving its coherence with the subsidiarity norm.

Conclusion

In this chapter I have argued that the often lamented democratic legitimacy deficit is not merely a concept or construct which besets academics and media commentary, but a state which policy-makers perceive as problematic once they decide to transfer sovereignty to the EU level which raises salience of the perceived legitimacy deficit. European integration which is reflected in Member States' decisions to transfer sovereignty triggers a democratic spillover process: Once integration looms, normative pressure is generated to counter the threat which policy-makers in the EU associate with integration, namely that further integration undermines domestic democratic process and institutions. In turn, policy-makers have continued to respond to these challenges by projecting the model of parliamentary democracy onto the European level. I have argued furthermore that these projections were not uniform. It has been shown that politicians came to consider both national parliaments and the European Parliament as potential reform targets when contemplating institutional solutions to alleviate the democratic legitimacy deficit. Yet, it has also been shown that institutional reforms to alleviate the legitimacy deficit are strongly biased towards the European Parliament route as the dominant legitimation strategy. Nevertheless, national parliaments have caught up since the early nineties and have since been considered to fulfill an ever more important role in legitimizing EU governance.

Notes

1. Hovey 1966, vii.
2. Scully 2000; Bergman and Raunio 2001.
3. Hix et al. 2003, 192.
4. See Rittberger and Schimmelfennig 2005. The ensuing paragraphs draw from Rittberger 2003, 2005.
5. The French delegation to the ECSC negotiations argued that "the High Authority is a body that partially fuses states' sovereignty and, from a democratic point of view, its existence therefore cannot be envisaged without the inclusion of a control body. It is for this reason that the French initiators of the plan have thought of a parliamentary control organ comprised of the members of the different national legislatures . . . The High Authority has to be accountable to the assembly. If the assembly is not satisfied with the way the High Authority fulfils its duties, it shall censure the High Authority." (Historical Archives of the European Communities, AA/PA.SFSO–53, 22 June 1950, author's translation).
6. See Kohler-Koch 2000, 517.
7. Kohler-Koch 2000, 517.
8. Kohler-Koch 2000, 521.
9. Kohler-Koch 2000, 521.
10. Jachtenfuchs et al. 1998, 413.
11. Katz 2001; Jachtenfuchs 2002; Rittberger 2003, 2005.
12. See Jachtenfuchs et al. 1998.
13. See Jachtenfuchs et al. 1998; Jachtenfuchs 1999.
14. Franck 1990, 49.
15. Both the International Relations literature and the Comparative Politics literature analyze the compliance pull of norms by referring to their properties and characteristics (in the IR-literature, see, for instance, Florini 1996; Legro 1997; Finnemore and Sikkink 1998; Keck and Sikkink 1998; Risse et al. 1999; and Schimmelfennig 2003; in the CP literature, see, among others, Hall 1989, 1993; Jacobson 1995; McNamara 1998; and Blyth 2002).
16. Franck 1990, 180.
17. see Franck 1990, 144.
18. Florini 1996, 376–377.
19. Franck 1990, 52.
20. Franck 1990, 64.
21. Deutscher Bundestag, Drucksache 11/7729 of 23 August 1990, author's translation.
22. See Corbett 1992, 121.
23. Corbett 1992, 127.
24. Corbett 1992, 160.
25. Douglas Hurd, the Secretary of State of Foreign and Commonwealth Affairs, emphasized before the Select Committee on the European Communities of the House of Lords that the "European Parliament could play a larger role . . . as a financial watchdog. . . . We would like to see [the MEPs] looking more closely at anti-fraud measures, value

for money and for the financial control of the Commission to be more directly responsible to them" (House of Lords 1990, 211). John Major also shared this view outlining the government's negotiating aims which included *inter alia*, "more power for the European Parliament to control the Commission and investigate fraud" (Major 1999, 274).

26. For instance, the Benelux governments issued a memorandum in which they explicitly acknowledged the link between the application of QMV and legislative co-decision for the European Parliament (European Parliament 1996, 20). Similarly, a Spanish government document on the IGC foresaw that "there will be considerable scope for progress through an extension of the field of application of the codecision procedure; this concept should . . . logically be viewed in close relation to majority decision-making" (European Parliament 1996, 47).

27. During the IGC leading to the adoption of the Nice Treaty, codecision and parliamentary involvement was a lesser concern. The treaty provided for six new cases of codecision. Yet, among the new cases under QMV, three legislative ones remained outside the codecision procedure: financial regulations, internal measures for the implementation of cooperation agreements, as well as the Structural Funds and the Cohesion Fund. Since these policies are particularly important issues on account of their major budgetary implications, some Member States resisted the call for codecision in these areas. The European Parliament bemoaned that "in refusing even to consider switching matters already subject to qualified-majority voting to the codecision procedure, the [IGC] was rejecting a basic institutional principle on which significant progress had been made at Amsterdam: as a general rule, codecision should accompany qualified-majority voting in matters of a legislative nature" (European Parliament 2001, 28).

28. Treaty of Nice, 'Declaration on the Future of the Union' (No. 23, paragraph 5).

29. See European Convention, CONV 424/02. All Convention documents (CONV) can be accessed through the European Convention website european-convention.eu.int (last accessed 16 June 2006).

30. See European Convention, CONV 424/02, p. 15.

31. Interestingly, some commentators refer to this formula as a "technical" one, ignoring its underlying normative logic: The recommendation by the working group that QMV and codecision should go hand in hand "transformed the debate over the group's reports from the technical to the political and drew the plenary into discussion as to whether the EU should retain unanimity at all" (Norman 2003, 102).

32. Article I-34(1) TCE.

33. See Raunio (2004) for an excellent discussion and assessment of the implications of the competencies conferred on national parliaments by the convention.

34. See also Wolf 1999. For example, many British MPs argued that the introduction of QMV constituted a serious threat to national parliamentary sovereignty. To mention just one example, Michael Knowles, a pro-Europe Conservative MP, voiced disapprovingly that "[t]his House is effectively chopped off from the European Parliament, and that is no accident. The Select Committee [of the House of Commons on European Legislation] therefore cannot act effectively. Indeed, it is designed not to act effectively. Yet any suggestion that its mandate should be widened is constantly resisted by the Executive because that would shrink the powers of the Executive" (Hansard Parliamentary Debates, House of Commons, 5 December 1985, 356). The government sought to downplay this concern. Only when directly confronted with a question by

Robert Jackson, Conservative MP, did Foreign Secretary Geoffrey Howe try to give assurances that national parliamentary sovereignty would not be undermined by the outcomes of the SEA (see Hansard Parliamentary Debates, House of Commons, 23 April 1986, 323).

35. See Auel and Benz in this volume.

36. Malcolm Rifkin, Minister of State in the Foreign and Commonwealth Office stated before the House of Lords Select Committee on the European Communities, "I think there are a number of countries, perhaps even a majority of countries, which would have the gravest of reservations about increased powers for the European Parliament and their improvement to the conciliation procedure. . . . I'm conscious that when Danish ministers are negotiating within the Council of Ministers they have to refer back to their own national parliament if they wish to change their negotiating mandate. There is a much tighter control as regards the relationship between the Danish Parliament and the Danish Minister than exists between other national parliaments and ministers in other Member States. Anything that directly or indirectly seems to affect the powers of the Danish Parliament vis-à-vis the European Parliament is treated with much more sensitivity and is much more controversial than is the case in other countries" (House of Lords 1985, 48).

37. In an exchange with Ted Rowlands, Labour MP, Douglas Hurd, Secretary of State for Foreign and Commonwealth Affairs, indicated that both legitimation strategies had supporters among the EU Member States: While Rowlands argued that the "Spaniards, French, Italians and even the Germans did not see sovereignty in terms of national parliamentary institutional powers and, in fact, there was great willingness to forsake a lot of national parliamentary power to bridge the European parliamentary deficit," Douglas Hurd replied, "I think we do think more clearly and strongly in terms of national parliamentary sovereignty than probably any other Member States. The Danes, of course, have a sovereignty system which puts a big accent on it" (House of Commons 1990a, 13).

38. Declaration No. 13.

39. Declaration No. 14.

40. In the original COSAC stands for Conférence des organes spécialisés dans les affaires communautaires et européennes des parlements de l'Union européenne (Conference of Community and European Affairs Committees of Parliaments of the European Union).

41. House of Commons 1990b, 6.

42. Corbett 1992, 160.

43. European Parliament 1996, 24.

44. European Parliament 1996, 60

45. The *Assizes* are based on an idea expressed by French President Mitterrand which he expressed in 1989 in a speech to the European Parliament: "Why should," he asked, "the European Parliament not organise assizes on the future of the Community in which, alongside your Assembly, delegations from national parliaments, the Commission, and the governments would participate?" (Mitterrand quoted in Corbett 1998, 296) The European Parliament quickly conceived of the Assizes as a possibility for a joint parliamentary preparation of the IGC leading to the Maastricht Treaty (see Corbett 1998, 296).

46. The idea of instituting a second chamber has been voiced by French politicians with Laurent Fabius (then President of the French National Assembly) or President Mitterrand advocating the creation of a second chamber in 1989 and 1990 respectively.

47. Corbett 1992, 61.

48. See *Le Monde*, 21 June 1991.

49. European Parliament 1996, 60.

50. Franck 1990, 180.

51. Franck 1990, 143.

52. Raunio 2004.

53. Raunio 2004, 8.

54. Raunio 2004, 8.

55. Raunio 2004, 7.

56. Raunio 2004, 6.

57. Norman 2003, 97; House of Lords 2001.

58. House of Lords 2001.

59. European Convention, debate of 28 October 2002.

60. European Convention, debate of 18 March 2003.

61. See the "Protocol on the application of the principles of subsidiarity and proportionality" annexed to the TCE.

62. Sypris 2002, 13.

63. The Edinburgh European Council of December 1992 defined the basic principles underlying subsidiarity and laid down guidelines for interpreting Article 5 (ex Article 3b), which enshrined subsidiarity in the EU Treaty. In Article 5 ECT it reads, "In areas which do not fall within its exclusive competence, the Community shall take action, in accordance with the principle of subsidiarity, only if and insofar as the objectives of the proposed action cannot be sufficiently achieved by the Member States and can therefore, by reason of the scale or effects of the proposed action, be better achieved by the Community." See also Große Hüttmann 1996 for an overview of the subsididarity principle in the EU.

64. Treaty of Nice, Declaration on the Future of the Union (No. 23, paragraph 6).

65. Treaty of Nice, Declaration on the Future of the Union (No. 23, paragraph 5).

66. The French government tried to establish such a connection calling on national parliaments to monitor the appropriate application of the subsidiarity principle. Addressing the French National Assembly on 3 February 1994, then French Minister for Foreign Affairs, Alain Juppé, expressed his hope that national parliaments would be empowered to challenge EU legislation on the grounds that the subsidiarity was violated (European Parliament 1996, 66).

67. See European Convention, CONV 286/02.

68. See European Convention, CONV 286/02, p. 5.

69. Norman 2003, 98. See also European Convention, CONV 353/02.

6

Parliamentary Representation in a Decentered Polity

Christopher Lord

THIS CHAPTER TAKES SERIOUSLY the claim that the EU is a decentered polity but disputes the contention that the Union is unsuited to parliamentary politics. The first section discusses what is meant by the claim that the EU is a decentered polity; the second considers obstacles to the Union's parliamentarization; the third argues that attempts to propose nonparliamentary forms of representation for the EU only collapse back into the parliamentary politics they are supposed to replace; the fourth argues on both normative and empirical grounds that parliamentary politics need not be incompatible with a Union of decentered structures and identities; the fifth concludes.

The EU as a Decentered Polity

To say that the EU is a decentered polity is not to suggest that it is decentralized. Rather, it is to claim there is no single center from which power is exercised over the many policy outputs of the Union, and there is no single organizing principle by which its various institutions interact. As Philippe Schmitter has put it, the Union is really a "plurality of polities at different levels of aggregation."[1] For her part, Heidrun Abromeit unpacks the complexity of the contemporary EU as something that is

> characterised by (1) various levels (community, member states, subnational units) as well as (2) various dimensions (territorial and "functional") of policy making; that combines (3) highly complex formal (institutionalised) as well as

(4) equally complex informal ways of decision-making; that binds together, furthermore, (5) actors of varying degrees of "europeanisation," acting (6) in policy areas of different degrees of europeanisation and (7) with different numbers of participants, agreeing policies (8) under different decision rules. And perhaps this long list of complexities is not complete.[2]

The following paragraphs argue that the Union has developed into a markedly decentered and dispersed polity through the interaction of four processes: declining uniformity in its policy scope; a growth in the number and variety of institutional methods that enjoy formal authorization by its treaties; a hollowing out, in turn, of each of those authorized procedures by new and informal methods of governance which are themselves varied in nature; and an increasing blurring of the boundaries between the Euro-polity and a variety of contiguous entities including its own Member States, and private social and economic systems. The next section of the chapter will then add a further consideration: the EU is no more centered on an agreed and developed sense of political identity than on uniform policies and structures.

The Decline of a Uniform Acquis Communautaire

Leading actors in the early European Community sought a single body of policies (or *acquis communautaire*) that would apply uniformally throughout the territory of the EC. The first president of the European Commission, Walter Hallstein, wrote of the impossibility of achieving certain core objectives, such as free exchange of goods and services, without common disciplines covering a range of policies.[3] In contrast, the modern Union increasingly resembles a policy patchwork. In some cases particular Member States have options to participate they have yet to exercise (UK and Denmark on monetary union). In others, they have obligations to participate that have proved difficult to fulfil (Sweden on monetary union). In still others, they can opt into a policy on a piecemeal basis without being obliged to participate in it overall (UK and Ireland on Schengen). Across the range of Union policy, citizens may experience the same decision differently on the ground, depending on whether the local implementing authority decides to gold-plate it or introduce gaps or delays to its implementation.[4]

More broadly, the Union is increasingly developing the institutional technologies that allow it to integrate flexibly, without all Member States signing up for the same policies at the same time. The present fashion for open methods of coordination works on the assumption that coordinated diversity in national approaches may be Pareto superior to "one-size-fits-all solutions," where national preferences are far apart, where the marginal costs and benefits of particular options are very different for Member States who start off from different points in their previous policy development, or where there are benefits to be had from retaining an element of competition between national policies and models. Constructive abstention in the CFSP demonstrates another possibility: a minority of Member States may consent to the adoption of a Union policy provided they are not themselves bound by it. On top of all this, the Nice Treaty introduced a general flexibility provision that the Constitutional Treaty now seeks to extend to a general system of accelerators and breaks that particular Member States can employ to go faster or slower than the rest.

The Declining Relative Importance of a Single Community Method

In addition to proclaiming a need for a uniform *acquis communautaire*, many leading actors in the early European Community also attempted a more or less standard method of making decisions. Although the meaning of the "Community method" has changed over the years, its supporters were for the most part able to insist until the 1980s that only policies conforming to it could be included in the treaties. Thus one reason why the British Prime Minister, John Major, claimed that the Maastricht European Council had been "game, set and match" for UK negotiators was that the TEU broke the monopoly of the Community method on policies with formal treaty authority.[5] This had two effects: first, the rules that make it procedurally hard to change the treaties once they have been agreed to could now be used to entrench institutional methods other than the Community method; and, second, it accordingly became harder to sustain the expectation that in the long run all policies would converge on the one Community method of decision making.

Indeed, treaty changes since the 1980s have simultaneously elaborated the "political systemness"[6] of those areas of Union policy-making that are well stratified into a political system (notably through the development of legislative codecision), and reduced their relative weight in the Union's overall institutional order. They have done this by proliferating a number of less structured processes "beyond the Community method." Examples are the Common Foreign and Security Policy, Justice and Home Affairs, and even forms of macro-economic policy coordination that, though nominally a part of pillar one, hardly follow the Community method *strictu sensu*. Even in the case of policies where the formal decision rules seem to resemble the standard Community method, it can be a struggle to keep the real locus of decision making within the formal rules of the political system. Thus legislative powers assigned to the Council or Parliament under the treaties, are, in the European Parliament's assessment, often arrogated *de facto* by comitology committees.[7] To give another example, attempts by Commission reformers to enforce uniform standards of public administration constantly run up against the need for a slender bureaucracy to subcontract its functions and configure itself somewhat differently in relation to each problem it has to solve and each network of collaborators whose cooperation it needs. It is to the impact of changes in informal governance methods for the further decentering of the Euro-polity that the analysis now turns.

Hollowing Out: The Decline of Institutional Hierarchy and the Decentering Logic of Network Governance

In spite of their variety, most institutional methods that have been formally authorized by the treaty presuppose some fairly well-defined locus of control. Thus the Community method presupposes that the Commission can exercise oversight, bring infringement proceedings in the ECJ, and be held responsible to the EP no matter where, in practice, implementation occurs on the ground. The second and third pillars, for their part, presuppose that the European Council can exercise general policy direction. Yet these hierarchies of control may be hollowed out or decentered in practice by more informal modes of decision making.[8] Social complexity often requires decision-making to be devolved to experts and the informal policy networks and epistemic communities by which they pool their expertise. Such networks operate behind the formal rules and institutional demarcations of the EU's political system.[9] They are also intrinsically heterogeneous. By assumption they will expand to the point at which they include all actors needed for the delivery of the goals of the others,[10] and that, of course, is likely to vary from one policy area to another. Thus to a decentering of the Euro-polity caused by a growth in the number of formally authorized institutional methods has to be added the impact of sector by sector variation in informal patterns of decision making.

The Decline of Institutional Boundaries

Using the geometric analogy that an object needs a defined perimeter if it is to have a defined center, a final sense in which the EU is decentered is that it is often difficult to distinguish boundaries between its activities and those of contiguous political and social systems. Wolfgang Wessels[11] has questioned the boundaries between Member State and Union institutions by documenting how often national and EU-based actors fuse their policy instruments. The heavy reliance of Union decisions on policy networks challenges a further boundary relationship, namely that between the Union as a public body, and the many private actors who are empowered by the *de facto* devolution of much EU policy framing and implementation to consultations with stake-holder groups. The Union may not have collapsed into private-interest governance, but the networks in which so much of its policy are framed involve an implicit bargain between public and private actors in which the latter trade their cooperation in the realization of policy for the benefits of a pan-European regulatory framework and a measure of public legitimation at that level. Such an erosion of boundaries between government and private actors is hardly unfamiliar to the hollowed-out states to be found on the domestic political scene.[12] Yet there is a difference between the infusion of existing states with new governance methods and their adoption *ab novo* in a non-state political system. While a substantial residue of administrative hierarchy and uniform application of law will be present in the first case, it is questionable how far the second has ever had those qualities.

In sum, then, reasons for considering the Union a decentered polity are that it is not centered on a single menu of policy, nor on a single institutional method either formal or informal; nor, indeed, does it have clear boundaries with contiguous systems—political, social, or economic. Even many who would be uncomfortable with the term "postmodern polity" would probably agree that the dispersed and decentered nature of the Union is an important component of what makes it a nonstate polity. The classic characteristics of "stateness" are, arguably, no longer to be found in their entirety at the national or European level, but have, instead, been partially displaced to a hybrid of the two, with the EU enjoying primacy of laws over a significant but far from ex-haustive area of competence, while Member States more or less retain the mo-nopoly of legitimate violence that ultimately lies behind enforcement.

Nonstate + Postnational = Postparliamentary?

Jo Shaw argues that "conventional parliamentary approaches to democracy represent inappropriate attempts to offer legitimate anchorage" to a polity that has a "deeply ambiguous relationship" to notions "of stateness and related questions of nation, demos and ethnos."[13] As this quotation suggests, there are two different reasons for doubting the suitability of the Union for parliamen-tary politics: one which points to its nonstateness, the other that is more con-cerned that the EU does not appear to have a "people" with an agreed and well-defined political identity among themselves or with the Union itself. There may, of course, be causal connections between nonstatehood and prob-lematic identity formation. Yet each presents different difficulties for parlia-mentary representation at Union level, as this section will explain, albeit with the help of stylized arguments, rather than views that can be attributed to any particular author.

First it should be noted that parliamentary politics are taken here to mean the delivery of the defining attributes of democratic rule—public control with political equality[14]—through a representative body. The controlling powers of the representative body can be various. They might, for example, include the power to make and break the executive of the political system, or the power to withhold essential resources such as finance or legislative authority. Political equality, for its part, is usually institutionalized by electing the representative body on the principle of "one person, one vote." In most parliamentary systems, mass political parties then complete the linkage between the exercise of public control by a representative body and the casting of votes by politically equal citizens. Mass parties clarify who the public can reasonably hold responsible for governing performance and who not, usually by dividing those who compete for power into supporters and opponents of incumbent officeholders.[15] By presenting alternative programs of government they also go some way towards interacting with voters in a way that allows values and resources to be allocated and traded off across policies, and not just within them.

Claim 1: The EU Is Unsuited to Parliamentary Politics Because It Is Not Centered on a State-Like Political System

Those making this claim might argue that the three main enabling conditions for parliamentary democracy—the willingness of citizens to participate in elections, the development of political parties that offer any two voters more or less the same choice wherever they are geographically located in the political system, and parliaments that can ultimately control all public decisions—are more likely to develop in state-like polities that have a clear locus of sovereignty, administrative hierarchy, and a system of law that is uniformly enforced. Even allowing that liberal-democratic states will by definition leave large areas of personal and social autonomy, it is the knowledge that states have the ultimate legitimate power to regulate all other relations in society[16] that underscores to the citizen the importance of taking part in elections. The importance of having a share in the power of the state is also an incentive for political parties to compete efficiently. This, in turn, helps citizens make choices. Parties eager to maximize votes will distill complexity into simplicity,[17] and, in one way or another, fish for support throughout the political systems in a way that allows any two voters, however unknown to one another, to coordinate their choices by the simple device of voting for the same or related parties.[18]

*Claim 2: The EU Is Unsuited to Parliamentary Politics
Because It Is Not Centered on a Demos*

The EU is, arguably, not just a nonstate polity. It is also a postnational one. This further compounds the difficulties of applying parliamentary politics. As Richard Katz puts it, "The EU is not sufficiently like a nation-state for the popular sovereignty model to be applied."[19] Given low levels of "community" there is apparently little to ground the notion of a popular sovereignty exercised through parliamentary procedures at European level. Overly aggressive claims to represent a Union-level parliamentary majority are at best only likely to be met with bafflement along the lines of "a majority of what? A majority of whom? Not a majority of anything that I can recognize as a single people and feel myself to be a part of." Once again, Heidrun Abromeit puts the point well:

> Representative institutions and parliamentary majority rule work well and provide for the democratic legitimation of government only under the condition that they are based on a collective entity called the "people" or the "nation", united by a common language, a common culture, common traditions. Such a "collective identity" is lacking in Europe, and will be lacking for a long time to come. Where it is absent no "public opinion" can emerge; and without public opinion, representative government lacks basis and substance. Parliamentary debates and decisions will then be miles apart from the wishes and demands of the populace; that is, they are pointless or mere symbolism.[20]

Under such conditions, a strong form of parliamentary politics at Union level would in all likelihood only be a source of political tension. The majority opinion of a European Parliament would inevitably conflict at least some of the time with the strongly held majority opinion of at least some democratically elected governments and parliaments at national level.[21]

Given that it is by no means clear whether national or European-level majorities would be viewed as the more legitimate in the case of conflict between the two—beyond the certainty that different people would give different answers to this question—it is unsurprising that a great many Union procedures are aimed at avoiding just such a clash of majorities. Decision rules require a high level of consensus on both the Council and EP sides of codecision. Indeed, the Council, for its part, prefers to decide by consensus, even where qualified majority voting is available to it,[22] while the structure of codecision encourages the EP to make only "moderate"[23] demands in relation to the median preferences of governments represented on the Council.

These, however, are all factors that limit the development of parliamentarism at Union level at the same time as they enable it by moderating the risk of it clashing with democratic majorities in particular Member States. They mean European elections are likely to involve low stakes and have little mobilizing force. The stakes are limited to an opportunity to choose one half of one branch of government,[24] since, of course, the EP is only one part of the EU's legislature, and it has only weak powers to shape the EU's executive.[25] The mobilizing force of the elections is arguably then further dampened by arrangements that encourage the Parliament to decide matters consensually within itself and in its relationship with other institutions, while, for the most part, using its powers to change policy outcomes by only small increments.[26] This is not an environment in which parties can easily simplify choice by dividing into government and opposition; nor is it one in which they can strongly articulate themselves by bundling too many issues together at any one time from across the range of public choice and then emphasizing their connection to ideological differences.

Of course, it might be objected to all the foregoing that multinational and even multilingual polities often have strong forms of parliamentary politics. Yet at this point the Union runs up against a further difficulty. As long as we hold with Jean-Marc Ferry[27] that the Union ought to have a "double normative reference" point in its Member States (or at least its national democracies) and in individual citizens, proportionality in the representation of citizens has to give way to some degree to parity in the representation of the states. Thus even in the case of the EP—which comes the closest of all EU institutions to proportional representation of citizens—the ratio of MEPs to citizens varies by a factor of ten across Member States. It is, moreover, hard to see how that ratio could ever be improved in the direction of greater political equality without abandoning the principle that Member States should be units of representation in the EP. Each Member State, after all, has to be given a minimum of seats if it is to hold a meaningful European election and have a reasonable prospect of representing a diversity of political parties in the EP.[28]

Towards a Substitute Parliamentarism?

The last two sections argued that the Union is a decentered and dispersed polity. The resulting nonstate polity creates difficulties for any attempt to apply parliamentary politics to the EU. These difficulties interact with others attributable to the Union's postnational character. Yet, as we will now see, the legitimating and democratizing qualities of parliamentary politics are not easily dispensed with. The result is that the most thoughtful proposals for nonparliamentary forms of representation at EU level have to find some means of mimicking the benefits of parliamentary politics.

One benefit of parliamentary politics is their holistic character. In other words they provide a site for lawmaking in which all problems can be comprehended in relation to all others. This, as we have seen, is important if representatives are to influence trade-offs of value across the range of public policy, and control the externalities and cumulative unintended consequences associated with individual actions. As Jürgen Habermas puts it, the decentered society or polity that does not also have some means of recentering decisions and managing connections between them is in a sense self-defeating: "It can no longer benefit" from its own "complexity" and "differentiation:"[29] "Each sub-system becomes insensitive to the costs it generates for other systems. There is no longer any point where problems relevant for the reproduction of society as a whole can be perceived and dealt with" and "[b]ecause they are specialized for functional co-ordination, corporatist structures are no match cognitively for accumulating problems."[30]

But the need for there to be some point in a representative process that can consider the whole range of considerations that go into public policy-making is much more than functional. This is because legitimate lawmaking needs to be able to answer three questions at once: a) How can we reconcile competing interests under conditions of procedural fairness? b) How can we decide "who we are and seriously want to be?" c) How can "we act in accordance with principles of justice?"[31] Thus, as Habermas further argues, the legislator needs to be a body that can consider the full range of reasons—pragmatic and technical, ethical and to do with identity, moral and to do with rights—for acting in one way rather than another. Moreover, lawmaking and executive control then have to be unified. Only if the legislator can follow through with executive control is "legitimate power" differentiated from "mere administration."[32]

Another benefit of parliamentary politics lies in their amenability to institutionalize political equality and deliberative ideals. A well-structured system of parliamentary politics ultimately ties representatives into a structure of political competition in which their policy and office goals are arbitrated according to the principle of "one person, one vote." It is only through such a reweighting of the dice that the political system attains an element of autonomy in which it is able to produce outcomes that differ from those which would prevail under a given—and usually unequal—distribution of power in society. Moreover, only bodies that can find some means of institutionalizing political equality are likely to be able to proceduralize deliberative ideals, given that the latter include equal access of all points of view to a public arena. As is often argued, even measures that have been agreed to by impeccable democratic procedures are likely to be seen as forms of arbitrary domination,[33] if they are not also accompanied by a public forum that allows all those who would have preferred alternative outcomes to see for themselves that their views have been argued and reasons given for setting them aside.[34]

If, then, it is hard to manage without the synoptic character of parliamentarism, and its capacity to institutionalize political equality and deliberative standards, can these features at least be mimicked by proposals for postparliamentary forms of representation in Union institutions? A good test is provided by proceduralization, since this is probably the most analytically sophisticated and self-conscious attempt yet to respond to the decentered character of the EU's polity with proposals for postparliamentary forms of representation. As set out in publications sponsored by the former Forward Studies Unit (FSU) of the European Commission,[35] proceduralization takes parliamentarism to be where representatives "formulate broad policies in legislative chambers, oversee their detailed implementation by bureaucratic departments" and "impose a particular understanding of the problem and the means to resolve it." It questions whether this—or, indeed, the application of any single "method"[36]—is still equal to the demands of "legitimate rule production" in decentered societies, which, it argues, increasingly require that methods of decision making should themselves be bargained and deliberated on a case-by-case basis with those who are likely to be affected by each set of rules. Since those affected will vary from one policy to another, it is specific stakeholder networks, rather than fixed composition parliaments, which should represent policy addressees, and take on the task of shaping decisions and methods of taking them.

As a first step in assessing how far they succeed in presenting an alternative to parliamentarism, it is important to note that advocates of proceduralization assume a continued role for an EU public authority in regulating stakeholder networks. It is not hard to see why they need to make that assumption. As Mancur Olson[37] argues in relation to collective action in general, only those for whom the marginal return exceeds the marginal cost of organizing to influence a policy process will do so, and this favors special or concentrated interests over public and diffuse ones. Likewise, the literature on the form of representation preferred by proceduralization reminds us that networks in their self-organized form are likely to be confined to actors who are both veto- and power-holders. This follows from the prediction that self-organized networks will expand to the point at which they include all those who are needed for the delivery of the goals of the other participants, and no further.[38] Any hope that networks of this kind might voluntarily include the powerless, subsidize the participation of those for whom the marginal cost of self-organization is greater than the marginal return, accept the higher transaction costs of a membership that is larger than the minimum needed to achieve their own goals, and equalize resources needed for fair deliberation by providing as a public good knowledge that has been acquired at private cost, would have to contend with the contrary temptation to secure incumbency advantage by cartelizing the benefits of public policy in a manner that favors insiders over outsiders.

Thus the FSU publications suggest that the EU-level public authority should referee stakeholder networks in the following ways to ensure they have the representative qualities that merely self-organizing networks are likely to lack:

- to guarantee equal access to all those affected by a decision to the stake-holder networks;
- to equalize the material and cognitive resources available to different stakeholders;
- to ensure any one policy is evaluated from the point of view of all others;
- to encourage collective learning and the substitution of public reason for purely private preference formation.[39]

Obvious question to ask of any EU-level public authority that might be designated with a role of regulating stakeholder networks are, first, who then, should guard the guardians? And, second, who is to decide the criteria by which the networks are to be regulated? After all, the regulatory roles listed in the previous paragraph presuppose criteria for who is entitled to access and participation in, and in what numbers; criteria for transparency and publicity; criteria for fairness and equality of opportunity and resources; criteria for deciding what is the force of the better argument; and criteria for what it is to meet deliberative standards such as good reason giving, and public reasoning.

If the public authority is to referee stakeholder networks, lay down criteria for their representativeness, and maybe even appoint lay members to them, is it to be left to do all of this of its own volition, or in a way that can ultimately be controlled by the public? Unless the latter, it is unclear in what sense the use of stakeholder networks would allow citizens to remain actors at all, let alone consider themselves as authoring their own laws. Any person designated to speak for the diffuse and unorganized public interest in stakeholder networks or any rules requiring the stakeholder network to consider alternative interpretations of the diffuse public interest on a basis of equality and deliberative fairness, would not be designated "by" citizens but "for" them. They would not be based on citizens' own judgements but on some paternalistic interpretation of what the needs and values of citizens are. Instead of an administration that is programmed by a process of representation, the process of representation would be programmed by the administration. Even, therefore, if stakeholder networks could be made to simulate the qualities of representative institutions, it is by no means clear that the latter can be dispensed with as a source of authorization and control.

Bringing Parliamentarism Back

At this point the analysis would seem to have reached an impasse: a decentered polity seems unsuited to parliamentary politics; yet, attempts to tailor postparliamentary solutions to the EU's decentered polity presuppose the very parliamentary politics they are intended to replace. The time has come to question the assumption that parliamentarianism really is incompatible with a decentered nonstate polity. Classic accounts such as John Stuart Mill's *Representative Government* offer reassurance. In Mill's view, the representative body needs some measure of "ultimate control" over all public decisions "in their entirety," yet that can and should be a control of "last resort."[40] As long as the parliamentary authority has a control of last resort over all those who make public decisions, there is no reason of principle why executive power should be structured into a single administrative hierarchy rather than dispersed across agencies or even, in more contexts, across stakeholder networks that are regulated by different public bodies. The only difficulty may be the practical one that the cost of parliamentary monitoring may rise with complexity in patterns of delegation in the making of public policy, though, in some ways, the deconstruction of often opaque administrative hierarchies into agencies and networks with specialized responsibilities can also add to visibility.

Habermas makes the further point that parliamentary politics are not incompatible with the social and cognitive complexity that often drives the fragmentation of policy-making into specialized agencies and networks in the first place. He reminds us that all that is needed for proposals to be converted into legitimate lawmaking is that they should "at some point" pass through the "sluice gates" of that part of the public sphere that is procedurally structured with what we have taken here to be the attributes of parliamentarism, namely an ability to take decisions affecting society as a whole according to fair procedures and deliberative standards. As long as rulemaking contains such a point there is no reason why proposals should not originate in autonomous and spontaneous subsystems of civil society. In other words, far from presupposing a top-down approach to lawmaking, the representative qualities of parliamentary politics can be achieved by filtering bottom-up initiatives.

Moreover, the notion that members of a decentered society and polity of dispersed activities and weak identities can at some moment accept the re-centering of decisions needed to pass them through the sluice gates of parliamentary structures is, in Habermas's view, easier to imagine once we stop thinking about popular sovereignty as something that needs to be vested in a fixed demos (he uses the term "macro-subject"!) and conceive it instead as a property of the rules of democratic discourse themselves. Thus he writes:

> The discourse theory of democracy corresponds to the image of a decentred society . . . a society in which the political public sphere has been differentiated as an arena for the perception, identification and treatment of problems affecting the whole. Once one gives up the philosophy of the subject, one needs neither to concentrate sovereignty in the people nor to banish it in anonymous constitutional structures and powers. The "self" of the self-organising legal community disappears in the subjectless forms of communication that regulate the flow of discursive opinion- and will-formation. Popular sovereignty retreats into democratic procedures.[41]

Given that Habermas views those "sovereign democratic procedures" as following automatically from a proper understanding of what it is to adopt democracy as a decision-rule, it would be entirely coherent for members of a group to see the act of agreeing to parliamentary procedures with fair deliberative standards as in and of itself establishing the binding force of those procedures, regardless of how little members of the group otherwise identify with one another, or of how fixed or flexible they may otherwise be in coming together across policies to regulate aspects of their lives in common.

The foregoing insights from political theory tell us that the standards of parliamentary government are not in principle incompatible with a decentered polity. However, several of the doubts reviewed in the second section about the capacity of the EU to develop a parliamentary dimension to its decentered polity are based on empirical claims that can be debated with the help of evidence from the EU's post-1979 experience with a directly elected European Parliament. Although that experience has neither tested all possible ways in which parliamentary politics could be applied to the European arena, nor developed any one approach in a manner that has delivered more than a "semi-parliamentary" European Union,[42] the following paragraphs argue it offers sufficient evidence to help with the assessment of at least three claims that a Union of decentered structures and identities is unsuited to parliamentary politics.

One claim that can be assessed empirically is that in a polity as decentered as the EU, parliamentary elections are unlikely to confer legitimacy through participation. As is well known, less than half of voters participated in the last two European elections (49.6 percent in 1999 and 44.5 in 2004). Moreover, participation has declined in an inverse relationship to the empowerment of the EP by treaty changes since the mid-1980s, and to its own efforts to elaborate a model of parliamentary politics through its internal politics and procedures.[43] As seen, abstention may well be causally linked to the decentered power structure of the EU polity. Since European elections are not centered on a simultaneous choice of both a government and a parliament, but are, in contrast, fought over the comparatively narrow terrain of just one half of the EU's legislature,[44] it is perhaps unsurprising that they do not motivate voters or parties to the same degree as national general elections. What is less clear, however, is that low participation in EP elections saps public support for an elected parliament at Union level. Not only is participation in Union elections in line with some other systems of divided government (notably the United States), but, the legitimacy of legislative elections in such systems may depend less on voter mobilization *per se* than on opportunities to constrain power-holders, and, arguably, it is not the level of participation that determines the representativeness of those who exercise checks and balances, but the absence of marked differences in the willingness of different kinds of voter to participate.

Also open to empirical assessment is the claim that public acceptance of a parliament with strong powers is unlikely in a polity that is not centered on a well-defined demos. In answer to this doubt, it should be noted that the question of whether a polity has a sufficient identity to sustain representative politics is one that always needs to be tested against the specific representative institutions it is proposed it should use. After all, some forms of representation are designed to cope precisely with low or even nonexistent feelings of community. Needless to say there is not much evidence that (reliably) connects feelings of identity with the European Union to specific options for its institutional development. However, table 6.1 sets out some of the few tentative indicators that are available of public acceptance of different options for collective decision making at Union level, both in terms of scope (the number of policies subject to joint decision at both levels of government) and method (the degree of majoritarianism). Questions 4–6, for example, demonstrate that around two-thirds of the public would prefer a Commission President to be chosen either by the EP or citizens themselves, even though that solution would be significantly majoritarian in allowing a simple (parliamentary or electoral) majority to allocate a key position of executive power. Now it may just be that respondents were not fully aware of the implications of their answers. However, an alternative possibility is that there is an underlying coherence to the answers in the table that confirms that even in a political system like the EU with a relatively low sense of community, the use of parliamentary or other majorities to make key appointments would be acceptable, provided those officeholders then had to operate under decision rules requiring consensus with other institutions. The EU's political system offers much scope for such solutions.

TABLE 6.1
Public Identification with the EU

	EU15	Aus	Bel	Den	Fin	Fr	Ger	Gr	Ire	It	Lux	Neth	P	Sp	Swe	UK
A. ACCEPTANCE OF JOINT DECISION MAKING																
1. Number of issue areas (max 27) where majority accept joint decision making	19	13	19	12	10	17	20	16	14	23	20	17	21	27	9	10
B. ACCEPTANCE OF MAJORITY DECISIONS																
2. Member States should retain vetoes to preserve essential national interests	50	67	45	71	62	51	51	69	57	51	68	50	44	38	60	47
3. States should drop vetoes to make EU more efficient	25	16	33	18	27	28	30	12	15	25	17	32	15	23	26	19
4. The president of the Commission should be selected by heads of govt.	14	16	11	22	22	16	13	14	23	15	18	14	21	13	18	10
5. EP should elect president of the Commission	32	31	35	40	35	26	38	35	21	37	30	39	18	25	39	24
6. Citizens should elect president of the Commission	34	32	36	25	29	41	33	31	28	32	42	31	29	36		

Source: Eurobarometer, no. 57, 2002.

The final claim we will assess is that the EU's polity has failed to produce a form of parliamentary politics centered on choices relevant to the Union itself. The suggestion here is that the European Parliament struggles to provide "value added" to the representation of the public, since its voting alignments replicate the left-right cleavage structure of national politics while giving less attention to the development of new dimensions of choice specific to the European Union. In particular, issues of more or less European integration are comparatively unimportant in explaining the voting behavior of MEPs. A difficulty, however, with this argument is that it is by no means clear why left-right preferences should not be considered European issues, given that the Union is so heavily involved with socioeconomic regulation. In any case, the EU political system does not so much suppress the supranational-intergovernmental cleavage as allow it to be addressed on a national-territorial basis through the treaty formation process. For the EP to concentrate on pro-anti integration preferences, rather than left-right ones, would not improve representation. It would mean giving up a focus that corresponds to the Parliament's powers for one where another body, the European Council, makes the key choices. Indeed, the left-right character of the EP has led some to question how far there is a disconnect at all between the electoral and parliamentary levels of EU party politics. Herman Schmitt and Jacques Thomassen[45] have shown that MEPs line up in the same order along a left-right dimension of political choice as those who vote for them. Although I argue elsewhere that this is far from sufficient to overcome all the deficiencies in the EP's electoral linkage back to the citizen, it at least ensures a resemblance of represented and representatives along one key dimension of choice.[46]

Conclusion

In questioning whether stakeholder networks should be advocated as an alternative to parliamentary politics, I do not seek to deny that stakeholder networks may well have representative qualities that parliamentary politics lack. While the latter emphasize political equality and general allocations of value across the range of public policy, the former acknowledge that those with intense interests in a particular policy may have a legitimate interest in being intimately consulted on its development. Moreover, provided they do not become cartels of those with insider advantage, stakeholder networks are more likely to focus on Pareto-improving than redistributive outcomes. A need to proceed by consensus gives them an incentive to search for decisions that leave the overwhelming majority of their members at least as well off as before, while shared expertise in the policy in question reduces the search costs in the discovery of such solutions. Indeed, Adrienne Héritier argues that where networks are made up of well-informed but mutually suspicious actors, they can be unusually demanding forms of reciprocal accountability between different categories of policy-maker.[47]

If, however, stakeholder networks have representative qualities that parliamentary politics lack, the converse is also true. This chapter has identified those qualities as a capacity to comprehend diverse interpretations of the diffuse public interest[48] and use them to make defensible allocations of value across the range of public policy using procedures that ensure political equality and equal access. It has further argued that stakeholder networks cannot be used to simulate such representative qualities without presupposing some form of authorization and control by the very parliamentary politics that some of their advocates seek to replace. Such an objection, of course, only applies to proposals to use stakeholders' networks as substitutes, rather than complements, for parliamentary politics. An understanding of how best to represent the public at Union level would benefit greatly from further normative reflection and empirical research into how best to integrate the contributions of parliamentary politics and stakeholder networks.

Notes

1. Schmitter 2001.
2. Abromeit 1998a, 8.
3. Hallstein 1970, 28.
4. Richardson 1996.
5. Forster 1999, 160, 175.
6. Quermonne1994; Hix 1999.
7. European Parliament, 1998.
8. Rhodes 1996.
9. Kohler-Koch 1996.
10. Peterson 1995.
11. Wessels 1998.
12. Rhodes 1996.
13. Shaw 1999, 581, 584.
14. Beetham 1994, 27–8; Weale 1999, 14.
15. Ranney 1962.
16. Beetham 1991.
17. Schattschneider 1960.
18. Cox 1997.
19. Katz 2001, 58.
20. Abromeit 1998a, 33.
21. Dehousse 1995.

22. Matilla and Lane 2001.
23. Kreppel 2000.
24. Blondel et al 1998.
25. Lord 2004, 140–2.
26. Kreppel 2000.
27. Ferry 2000.
28. European Parliament 2000.
29. Habermas 1996a, 342–3.
30. Habermas 1996a, 52.
31. Habermas 1996a, 181.
32. Habermas 1996a, 134.
33. Pettit 1997.
34. Mill 1972 [1861], 239–40; Dewey 1927; Eriksen and Fossum 2000b.
35. Commission 1997; De Schutter, Lebessis and Paterson 2001.
36. De Schutter et al 2001, 18.
37. Olson 1965.
38. Peterson 1995.
39. Commission 1997; De Schutter et al 2001.
40. See Mill 1972 [1861], 228.
41. See Habermas 1996a, 301.
42. Magnette 1999.
43. Corbett et al, 2003; Judge and Earnshaw 2003.
44. Blondel et al 1998, 250–3.
45. Schmitt and Thomassen 2000.
46. Lord 2004.
47. Héritier 1999.
48. Pollack 1997.

A COMMENT ON RITTBERGER AND LORD

Deirdre Curtin

One of the most extraordinary features in the evolution of the European Union as an international organization is the manner in which the European Parliament has incrementally over the years acquired stature and powers. Given that the Member States have from the very beginning, in the classic tradition of public international law, been the "masters of the Treaties," it can be considered surprising that at the very time they transferred executive and legislative powers to the European domain and, in a certain sense, were liberated from the (parliamentary) constraints that applied at the national levels, they set about, almost gratuitously it seems, building a parliamentary system at the European level. The reasons why Member State governments went down this parliamentary road at the European level are not entirely clear.

Until fairly recently the European project has been considered an elite project with government ministers and civil servants, both European and national, as the dominant actors. Why should Member States have strengthened an autonomous actor on the European political stage which could only, in the long run, be destined to become their rival? Was it strategic in the sense of a ploy to weaken in the long term the supranational Commission? Or were there other factors which led to the institution of a system of parliamentary democracy at the European level itself rather than just linking the European enterprise more firmly with the already prevailing system of parliamentary democracy in all of the Member States?

Berthold Rittberger in his chapter in this book systematically argues that the choice made by the governments to strengthen the European Parliament cannot be explained by strategic motives but rather reflects a deep-rooted form of institutional mimetism. In other words, the political culture of European leaders leads them to the belief that if they do transfer salient competences out of the national domain and into the European domain, then they must offer democratic compensation for the fact that they are *de facto* reducing the role of national parliaments over such salient issue areas. At the same time it does not follow that Member States will model the European parliamentary level very precisely on the national level when it comes to specific institutional design choices. But it does give them an overall legitimation strategy that they can use to respond to critics.

His key argument is to the effect that the European Parliament legitimation strategy can be ascribed both to its determinacy (its link in particular with the move to QMV) and its coherence (across fora and actors). There is certainly force to his arguments and to his empirical examples. One can read the gradual (from IGC to IGC) evolution of the increase in legislative powers of the European Parliament as the result of a grand legitimation strategy by the governments to silence the critics. However, this is only part of the story. The very same governments have at the same time been involved in a strategy that cordons off whole areas of activity from any effective parliamentary input, much less control.

In a sense it can be said that via the mechanism of tying more codecision to an increase in QMV, the Member State governments have engaged in a strategy of deflecting attention away from other glaring instances of executive dominance not embedded in any system of parliamentary democracy. Rittberger's reading of the European Parliament legitimation strategy culminated in a sense in the provisions of the Constitutional Treaty where the governments (on the prompting of the Convention on the Future of Europe) effectively introduced a clearer distinction between in particular the Union legislative power and what is in fact the Union executive power. The Union legislative power is now defined and in principle takes place in codecision with the European Parliament. The executive power is however not defined, or at least only in terms of what it is not: it is not the legislature and does not adopt legislative acts; it adopts nonlegislative acts.

What is the significance of this fact? I would argue that the Member States' grand European Parliament legitimation strategy was also premised on ensuring that the European Commission as effectively the executive of the EU was subject to mechanisms of executive accountability at the level of the EU itself. At the same time as the Member States increased the European Parliament's role in legislation, they also increased certain accountability mechanisms fitting within an understanding of parliamentary democracy and which enhanced significantly the role of the European Parliament vis-à-vis the European Commission. The underlying premise for this aspect of the overall legitimation strategy is that the European Commission as the EU executive needed to be embedded in a relationship with parliament in this fashion (however imperfect that might be).

In recent years the Commission has built on the fact that the legislative power has become much more clearly defined at the EU level (and involving both the Council and the European Parliament) as well as its own self-perception, underpinned by institutional facts and practices, to argue that it must once and for all be recognized as effectively the executive power in the EU. It developed this thinking further in the Convention on the Future of Europe which ultimately drafted the Draft Constitutional Treaty. It lost this battle, the executive role of the Council and indeed the European Council being not only maintained but actually re-enforced in the final text which emerged.

The scope and nature of executive power is difficult to define in substantive terms. One approach is to identify a core set of tasks that are commonly undertaken by the executive branch of government across various political systems. The executive will usually plan the overall priorities and agenda for legislation. It will normally have principal responsibility for foreign affairs and defense. The executive will have an important say in the structure and allocation of the budget. It will also have responsibility for the effective implementation of agreed upon policy initiatives and legislation that has been enacted. The executive can generally be said to have two types of power: political, the leadership of society through the proposal of policy and legislation (agenda setting and initiative of measures) and administrative, the implementation of law, the distribution of public revenues, and the passing of secondary and tertiary rules and regulations. On this definition it is clear that the Council of Ministers also exercises executive powers and not only in the sense of implementing powers, especially with regard to the newer policy areas since the Treaty of Maastricht. Moreover, the executive map of the Council reveals the hybrid nature of the institution with a strong and growing internal administrative structure (the increasingly important and powerful Secretariat-General as well as its policy directorates) but also an increasingly extensive external administrative structure, composed of various Union agencies which are for the most part set up under the auspices of the Council of Ministers. In a sense what comes through at this level is the fundamentally non-majoritarian nature of many executive and operational tasks carried out in a relatively autonomous fashion at the European level.

In terms of agenda-setting it is clear that the European Council has as a matter of practice in recent years acquired a very preeminent role, displacing to a considerable extent the centrality of the Commission's tasks in that regard. The conclusions of European Council summits effectively set the agenda for the various institutions, both the Commission and the Council of Ministers. The Commission has in particular come to terms with this changed reality by negotiating an annual legislative program with its legislative partners, the Council of Ministers and the European Parliament. Moreover, the Council of Ministers has itself acquired since the provisions of the Treaty of Maastricht a not insignificant power of initiative in the newer policy areas.

In terms of implementation and application of legislative instruments it is clear that not only has the Commission's power to adopt these measures been decentered considerably by the role and power of the comitology committees composed of national civil servants but also that other actors have taken over aspects of such tasks. This includes not only the specific tasks of agencies in certain technical areas of regulation but also the increasingly significant role of the Secretariat-General of the Council of Ministers, of certain high-level committees acting under the auspices of the Council, as well as the role of certain quite autonomous Union agencies.

This evolution of the executive powers of the Council of Ministers dates since the implementation of the Treaty of Maastricht and forms the flip side of the development of more codecision in an increasing range of legislative matters. The EP legitimation strategy has deflected attention away from the fact that while Member State governments were on the one hand sharing increasingly their legislative power, they were at the same time developing rather extensive pockets of executive power which basically managed to subsist outside of any framework of parliamentary democracy.

If one now turns to the second legitimation strategy of Member States according to Rittberger, that involving increasing the role of the national parliaments, then one can in fact find support for the subterfuge involved. Rittberger documents the empirical evolution of what he terms the national parliament legitimation strategy which only in the second phase, post Maastricht, left a (weak) imprint on institutional design in the treaties. The third phase resulted most significantly in their endowment with a subsidiarity control mechanism. This is an enhanced (albeit logistically complex) window of opportunity for the national parliaments to intervene in the early stages of the legislative process to object to a Commission legislative proposal. In other words, it is focused both on the adoption of legislation and the Commission's role in that regard as agenda setter. In many ways it highlights how much the EU political system is not premised on a fully-fledged system of parliamentary democracy as we know from the Member States but rather on a very muddled attempt to include some institutional design elements which give some role to parliaments, both European and national, but without any holistic view of how and where many decisions that matter are taken at the EU level. Despite the various legitimation strategies by the governments we are left with a very plural executive not embedded in a system of parliamentary democracy. Moreover, the system of checks and balances is very weak. As Hamilton put it more than two centuries ago, "One of the weightiest objections to a plurality in the executive is that it tends to conceal faults and destroy responsibility."

Christopher Lord in his piece takes seriously the claim that the EU has developed over the years in a fragmentary and decentered fashion and provides examples at different levels of this empirical fact. In many ways it fits in with the reading that has been given above of the evolving plurality and dispersion of executive power. Indeed, he would add the further decentering logic of not only plethoras of committees, expert and otherwise, and agencies but also of network governance as more broadly understood. This leads us away from the formal quest for government to a much more inclusive understanding of governance. The use of the term governance has become very fashionable in the context of the EU. The problem is that talking about governance as opposed to government facilitates a certain tendency towards concealing the locus of governing authority and the relationship with the citizens in a democratic polity. If governance is so decentered and fragmentary, then how can parliamentary politics play a role?

Christopher Lord argues eloquently and convincingly that one should in effect not throw out the baby of parliamentary politics with the bathwater. In his view the legitimating and democratizing politics are not easily dispensed with, especially the fact that parliamentary politics enable a holistic view to be taken of the various problems at issue in a given political system. There is certainly considerable force in this argument that only parliaments can consider the whole range of considerations that go into public policy-making. He ties this in too with the need to unify lawmaking and executive control "Only if the legislator can follow through with executive control is legitimate power differentiated from mere administration."

The problem in the EU context is precisely the fact that the legislator can only very imperfectly and very incompletely follow through with mechanisms of executive control and that there is as yet little recognition of this fact. While not disputing the overall thrust of Lord's paper that we need not to exclude the development of further parliamentary politics at the EU level, I do query how parliamentary politics can get to grips with the very scattered nature of executive activity at the EU level in the short and medium term. The evolution of the European Union towards a full-scale parliamentary democracy with the Council being gradually weakened to the benefit of the directly elected European Parliament is extremely unlikely. The more likely scenario is a muddling through with the complex mixtures of supranational and intergovernmental power centers that we have at present, with visible and invisible centers of power and with imperfect democratic legitimation and accountability.

One strategy would be to accept the imperfect status quo, fairly far removed from our traditional notions of government imprisoned in closed institutions and the province of professional politicians, and attempt to operationalize the application of principles of good governance right across the spectrum of executive activity as we find it. The principles of good governance formulated by the Commission in its White paper on Governance in 2001 (openness, participation, accountability, effectiveness, and coherence) could be revamped and deepened and applied right across the spectrum of

EU executive activity. Moreover, this could be done even in the event of the nonratification of the text of the constitutional treaty. It would of course not solve the issue of parliamentary democracy at the EU level, but it could at the very least facilitate control of the executive by various actors, including parliaments, and put the spotlight where the evolving centers of power have come to lie in the complex and fragmented EU polity.

III

THE PUBLIC SPHERE AND CIVIL SOCIETY: PREREQUISITES FOR DEMOCRATICALLY LEGITIMATE RULE MAKING

7

Prerequisites of Transnational Democracy and Mechanisms for Sustaining It: The Case of the European Union

Klaus Eder and Hans-Jörg Trenz

The Democratic Deficit of the EU Revisited

MOST OF THE DEBATE regarding the European democratic deficit concerns the normative desirability and viability of a European democracy. On a more elementary level, however, the taken-for-granted assumption that we need to establish democratic procedures at the European level can be contested. Apart from the unclear normative status of a European democracy, good arguments exist that support the view that democracy interferes with the functional requirements of complex steering systems like the European Union (EU). As a consequence, it is argued that this puts at risk the major achievement of European integration in terms of its regulatory capacities and efficient and rational policy outcomes.[1]

Putting aside normative questions concerning the shape and contents of a European democracy, we must clarify mechanisms of democratization beyond the nation-state. We must reconsider the role and functions of democracy in the complex multilayered system of EU governance. This will lead to an understanding of democracy as an organizing principle and as a pushing factor of European political integration. As we will attempt to demonstrate, democratic procedures in a complex multilayered and polycentric governmental arrangement like the EU are unavoidable and may be even more necessary than ever before.

In a recent paper,[2] we argued that a functional necessity to base complex social order on democratic procedures exists. Based in democratic functionalism, this theory predicts that the utter quantity of political communication increases along with the complexity of societies. The decisive argument is that the unfolding of political communication binds actors and institutions involved in the force of arguments and counterarguments. This increases the reflexivity and multiperspectivity of their communication, thus triggering collective learning processes. When such collective learning processes are unavoidable within this novel form of transnational governance, we can conclude that the EU requires even more democracy than the nation-state if it is to survive. This functional necessity of democracy becomes a catalyst for institutional change and reform. European integration is linked to unintended processes of democratization which go beyond its willful constitutional design—which does not imply that it will succeed more easily.

This functionalist perspective suffers from deficiencies of functionalist arguments. It omits the mechanisms of this functional relationship. However, it forces us to reconsider what may be called the classic approach in explanation of democratization for the provision of an inquiry into the prerequisites of democracy. This approach—canonized in the political sociology of Seymour Martin Lipset[3] and extended by authors like Robert D. Putnam[4]—looks for the necessary, and possibly sufficient, conditions that trigger or block processes of democratization thus explaining the democratic performance of nation-states.

The crux with this approach is that it does not really grasp the dynamics of how previously democratized societies generate different configurations of prerequisites in the course of their democratization. Identifying the configuration of historically specific democracy prerequisites leads to an explanation of why democratization did arise within a given historical context. However, such an explanation becomes tautological when processes of democratization are triggered in already democratized societies. We therefore need a dynamic perspective in order to account for democratization as soon as a series of such democratic prerequisites are taken for granted. Following this, further inquiry is required into how democratization takes place. Thus, the "why question" generates a black box, which encompasses the following: What pushes the transformation of, for example, a market economy into a democratized polity? This is the question relating to the mechanisms of democratization. If prerequisites are taken for granted, then we have to ask what turns these prerequisites into mechanisms of democratization.[5]

Applied to Europe, such a perspective seems obvious, given that prerequisites of democracy are found everywhere in Europe. The democratization *of* Europe is beginning at a time when the transition to democracy within Europe has only recently been concluded.[6] The nation-states comprised within the current democratization of the EU are consolidated democracies. Under such conditions, transitology, the offspring of the search for prerequisites, no longer provides adequate input into a theory of democratization. Therefore, we have to turn to the question of how the existing prerequisites of consolidated democracies are transformed into mechanisms for democratizing the EU. In this case, it is the "how question" for which we seek an answer.

The Public Space as the Prerequisite for
Democracy and as the Arena of Democratization

The question of how to conceive mechanisms of democratization has not yet found an analytical focus. We are instead confronted with a series of dispersed debates on the role of elite competition; veto-power games; arenas of negotiation, deliberation, and representation; the mobilization of collective actors and interest groups; and so forth. In the following, we propose to reconsider the role of public spaces as the focal point for furthering the debate on democratization. A "public space" is defined as an arena of communication in which those who govern and those who are subject to governance in a given legally constituted polity gather and express particular interests, concerns, and expectations that interfere with political decision making. The public space thus initiates a process in which political decision making is mediated through public opinion and collective will formation. In this sense a public space provides a mechanism of democratization. The way in which it distributes chances of access, arenas of debates, and links to the institutionalized system of political decision making finally indicates a polity's degree of democratization.[7]

The debate on whether a public space exists or can exist at the transnational level of political communication is divided around different normative conceptions concerning the role of the public space and its contributions to democracy. This informs empirical research on the issue.[8] In its simplest version, the argument states that since there is no public space, there can be no democracy in Europe. In a more refined version, it is acknowledged that the quality of political communication that has developed over the last two hundred years within the nation-state is hard to supersede. Based on a historically grown common political language, a quality newspaper culture, and an effective national political socialization in the schooling system, the requisites of functioning public spheres are rendered in a way that cannot be matched by transnational cultures of political communication.

Our own empirical research has shown, instead, that public communication and discourse in the EU has a greater impact than expected, given common sense perception and description in Europe. Certainly, this does not unfold as normative theories would claim as necessary. So we find a rudimentary European public space as a prerequisite of transnational democracy, yet we can still claim that there is no democracy in Europe. The difference here lies in the fact that the democratic deficit of the EU is now seen through the eyes of the emerging European public space. We thus presuppose that, as a functional consequence of the prerequisite of a European public space, democratization of the EU will ensue. Yet, we do not know how this proceeds.

Focusing on this "how question," the empirical observation of an expanding European public space allows us to view emerging forms of political communication in Europe as a mechanism of democratization. In what follows, we will discuss how this mechanism influences the taken-for-granted prerequisites of democracy in the Member States and beyond. We thus describe a) new institutional arrangements that b) increase political communication which c) coincide with new forms of organized collective action and interest representation, finally d) introducing processes of collective will formation.

Prerequisites of Democracy and Mechanisms of Democratization in the EU: Institutional Arrangements

A multilevel system of democratic nation-states is provided with a central prerequisite of democracy, namely existing democratic arrangements and procedures at a lower level of aggregation. Thus, the question is whether the emergent supranational level can avoid democratization if its constituting parts are already democratized. The institutional structure of the EU is in fact organized in a manner which favors enlightened administration in search of ways to establish a system of good governance. In its White Paper, the Commission has committed itself to such an institutional self-description of good governance, conceived as democratic government without its representative element. The EU would thus steer towards a novel mode of democratic governance contingent on alternative channels of preference aggregation, or deliberation, in horizontal interactions among a multitude of actors and institutions.

In such horizontal institutional settings like comitology, there is no fixed place for the people in Europe. Collective decision makers are neither located above the people nor can the people be identified amongst them. From a deliberative point of view, only people who reasonably agree or disagree with reasonable decision makers are recognized. From an institutional perspective, such an unclear status of the people—and of democracy—is perceived as insufficient. Therefore, the institutional reform process aims at strengthening those elements that increase the visibility of the people's presence and participation in the multilevel governance system.[9] These representative or direct links back to the people have remained, so far, rather weak or purely symbolic, although the convention process has clearly led to their revival. The constitutionalization of the EU reflects this new departure of political institutions in search for the will of the people.

It appears that the European integration process cannot do without a symbolic representation of the will of the people built into new institutional settings and procedures of deepened integration. However, as the debate on the shape and contents of a European constitution has shown, classical arrangements, such as political parties, parliamentary assemblies, or other representative bodies, no longer provide sufficient mechanisms of democratization in terms of representing the will of the people. New institutional arrangements have therefore used a more direct form of addressing the constituting publics of Europe. They have developed forms of what can be called multilevel communication governance, which works to expand traditional forms of top-down communication management to an interactive mode of communication between networking actors and constituting publics.

European multilevel communications governance builds on the normative premises of public sphere and democracy.[10] It thus replaces the classic mechanism of democratization that seems to survive the test of transnationalization, the mechanism built into the form and structure of a public sphere. European multilevel communications governance further relies on mass media communication, which—contrary to the general wisdom—regularly crosses national frontiers. New institutional arrangements thus foster diffuse forms of transnational political communication on levels below and above national arenas. This provides a prerequisite for European democracy, as well as a mechanism for the EU's democratization. Before turning to the effects of enhanced European political communication on collective action and will formation, we will present some empirical data concerning the degree of Europeanization of political communication in quality newspapers.

The Diffusion of Political Communication in the EU

On the basis of a quantitative survey of European news coverage in quality newspapers, the thesis of a persisting communication deficit in the EU can no longer be upheld.[11] Instead, we observe the differentiation of a highly Europeanized media subsystem constituted of quality newspapers penetrated by the effects of resonance of European political communication. Resonance has been measured, firstly, in quantitative terms as the total share of European political communication in the national media. One out of three political articles in a European quality paper makes political reference to Europe, and one out of five directly reports about at least one European issue. The amount and density of European political communication within the geographic area of the EU is also clearly demarcated from outside. As revealed by our control sample, the *New York Times* makes three times fewer references to European political issues and uses, on average, six times less European rhetoric than European newspapers.

Secondly, the structuring of resonance has been measured with regard to the convergence of issues and the reciprocity of communication. There is a common universe of issues and debates which determines the visibility of the political Europe in the single Member States. Moreover, there is a constant generation of European-wide attention for particular events and issues of common relevance, such as the common currency, the process of Eastern enlargement, the common foreign and security policy, the institutional reform of the EU, or the European Convention. Successful strategies of transnational media agenda setting are applied not only by national governments, but also by highly prominent supranational institutional actors such as the Commission's president, single commissioners, the European Central Bank president, or the High Representative of the Common Foreign and Security Policy.[12]

Thirdly, the structuring of resonance of European political communication in the national media has been measured in terms of interpretative frames and the spread of rhetorical patterns that make sense of the common European political universe of meaning. As expected, the great bulk of European issues are framed in instrumental terms (85 percent, as compared to 38 percent in normative terms and 27 percent in identitarian terms with only minor differences between news-papers and countries examined).[13] We further observe the spread of reflexive rhetoric concerning Europe in either of the following forms: a rhetoric containing generalizing statements or a rhetoric containing comparative statements.[14] These different cases represent the impact of European models of appropriateness on national and subnational actors when particular policy outcomes are measured and contextualized and political goals and interests are redefined.

Our quantitative survey delimits Europe as a space of political communication that supersedes the existing regional and national spaces through the effects of transnational resonance. The resonance of European political communication is measured in terms of the unifying effects of transnational agenda setting through European actors and institutions. This is done in terms of the parallel coverage of the same issues and events and the shared relevance in debating and interpreting these issues and events. We thus find an expanding European public space in co-evolution with the expansion of European governance. Such a public space cannot be called democratic as such.

It works as a prerequisite of European democracy which, under certain conditions, can set off mechanisms of democratization. In the following, two of these democratizing mechanisms, as possible effects of the expansion of a European public space, will be looked at: first, the constitution of collective actors as carriers of a European democracy, and second, the constitution of a European collective will as the outcome of European democratic practice.

The New Interorganizational System of Collective Action and Interest Formation

The European public space is not only peopled with a silent public, but also with an increasing number of collective actors. With a voice in Europe, these actors comprise more than just the functionaries in Brussels and the national representatives in European bargaining. Rather, they constitute an open interorganizational field that is continuously expanding and setting its own institutional rules. To understand the dynamics of organized collective action in the EU, it is not sufficient to analyze single actors' strategies of mobilization and interest aggregation. The European polity that is characterized by contentious politics cannot be understood without reference to its constituting parts. The emerging political field of contention and claims making is embedded in a social environment which shapes the interactive dynamics, attitudes, and rules of behavior within the field.[15] Here we identify the constituting dynamics of a European polity, which takes its own normative infrastructure as a basis for institutional expansion and polity building. Weiler[16] called this the real European invention to build a polity on a set of normative rules that reproduces itself through continuous addition of further procedural rules. It is this positivization of constitutional rules that allows us to speak of reflexive institutionalization as a mechanism of democratization.

Claimants, who are in turn volatile collective actors, populate the open interorganizational field of collective action. They respond less and less to fixed and organized forms of claims making and interest representation within one polity (for example, through protest in the form of a social movement), but become engaged in all kinds of contentious politics at different levels of political aggregation.[17] The term "movement advocacy coalition" (MAC) has been introduced to describe these loose interorganizational forms expanding into the transnational realm.[18] MACs foster the increasing isomorphism among collective actors in Europe on particular issues, even without stable and direct interorganizational links between the Member States. They are held together by some form of political activism which is grounded in shared concerns and attempt to produce some ideas concerning their possible solutions. Since such groups and networks no longer follow the pattern of organizing themselves as social protest movements, we prefer to describe them as loose and shifting interorganizational links of claims makers with particular shared concerns such as environmentalism, antiracism, gender issues, or minority rights.

Similarly to other transnational governance arrangements, the EU offers various institutional access points for such interorganizational fields of activism. These access points have come to the attention of political theorists because they maximize one particular mechanism of democratization: deliberation. They reduce deficits in the participatory dimension by developing a specific interorganizational culture of interested collective actors behaving as partners of governance. They further facilitate a particular communicative logic of impartial justification and reason giving, which qualifies them as strong publics, imbued with decision-making power.[19] Examples discussed in the literature include comitology, the European Parliament committees, and the two conventions.[20]

We are not interested in the quality of deliberation as such or in its possible impact on EU decision making, but rather in two social side effects of relevance in the explanation of the democratizing dynamics within the EU polity. First, deliberative institutional designs such as strong publics rely on interorganizational communication and networking calling attention to other internal publics of the EU. They thus facilitate the emergence of what may be called "interorganizational publics of European governance"—generally conceived as expert publics, epistemic communities, and other interested parties. Related to the emerging civil society sector of EU claims making and contention, these interorganizational publics may be considered as learning entities that increase their chances of participation and voice in the European polity. This is not done through individual interest representation but through the definition of a common good linking them to institutional decision making.

Second, strong and interorganizational publics need an external audience in order to validate their representative claims. The deliberative mechanism reiterates specific normative expectations and attitudes extending beyond the interorganizational field, thereby opening the interorganizational publics to a shared public space of diffuse attention and interests. Reflecting on its own normative deficits, particular institutional settings emerge that are specialized to deal with normative expectations that are raised in the process of polity building. The convention drafting a European constitution is so far the most outstanding experience of that kind. It develops high deliberative capacities in order to design the future institutional structures of the EU. Currently, it faces the so-far unknown urgency to link these deliberative capacities with the will of the people. At this point, we require a second mediatization of European political communication. We require not only the media as an amplifier of selected political communication, but also in its more active role of enhancing the Europeans' collective will.

The Formation of a Political Will: The Constitutional Debate as a Process of Collective Learning in Europe

From Formal Representation to Mediatized Representation

Constitution making in the EU has become emblematic in its search for mechanisms linking European institution and polity building to the will of the people. For the first time, the convention process initiated in May 2002 has claimed to represent—or better, to constitute—such a will of the European people. It has done so in drafting a constitutional treaty that must be signed by the governments and that also must pass referenda in many Member States. Democratic procedures constitutionalizing the EU polity thus resemble procedures of constitution making in existing nation-states. In the EU's case, however, the proof that democratic procedures are at work is not a sufficient legitimating mechanism. The idea that democratic procedures automatically lead to the expression of the will of the people becomes questionable.

From a sociological point of view, the expression of the will of the people is always linked to claims of representation of collective actors and their general visibility and credibility for a general public. From a normative point of view, this insight is transformed into the search for good procedures and best practice in order to validate such claims of representation. We follow a different path by identifying, primarily, new mechanisms through which such claims of representation are raised and defended in the course of European constitution building. As we will attempt to demonstrate, such claims for representation create a new kind of transnational resonance, transforming the multiple voices of the European people into a single voice which cannot be dismissed by European decision makers.

The convention process was designed according to the classical model of people's representatives freely deliberating on the institutional design and decision-making procedures of their polity. The historical experience has also shown that such constitutional deliberations need additional mechanisms for legitimating their activities. Constitutional debates must involve larger constituencies than those comprised by the interorganizational contention of constitution makers. The question that arises is how far the constitutional process can also successfully claim to represent the will of the people through mediatized chains of representation.

In the theater of democracy, we generally assume that there is one central arena where various players compete for the attention of the public. However, the theater metaphor is misleading in the sense that the performance on the political stage is only rarely linked to the direct approval or disapproval of the public in attendance. The political theater relies on the mediatized representation of its performance. This does not necessarily imply a loss in the expressive capacities of the play. On the contrary, the mass media allows the introduction of a decisive new stylistic element that makes up the democratic theater of modern nation-states. The media performance generally includes representative publics as parts in the play.[21] Representative publics raise the people's voice within the game, not outside the game or after the game's conclusion. They do not play the role of actors but act in the name of the public they claim to represent. It is through such representative publics that the political theater is turned into a democratic theater.

The European framework calls for a further change of this theater metaphor. The European play is given in many theater houses at the same time, and in front of different publics. There is, however, an overarching institutional arrangement that assures a certain degree of standardization of the single performances. In addition, fixed players appear on all stages. To the extent that the same players enter different stages to participate in the same play, they also have to adapt to the preferences and expectations of different publics. At the same time, the European democratic performance connects formerly fragmented publics which are increasingly becoming aware of each other. They become a European public, which pays attention to the performance on an additional overarching stage made up of representative publics watching what occurs on the front stage. The European people thus turn into observers of the representative publics, who evaluate and criticize the European democratic performance for their part.

If we are to analyze the convention process as a meta-arena of democratic performance, we must understand how players in the European political game become representative publics who raise their voice for the European people. We assume that it is not the convention as such, but its capacity to generate representative publics that accounts for processes of collective will formation in the EU. In what follows we identify 1) the mass media as a representative European public that raises the voice of the people—this is the function of commentaries in the media—and 2) the prominent governmental actors (as representative European publics) who often leave their role as national representatives to speak in the name of a European public.

Media as Representative of European Publics

As a representative of the European public, the quality press has not only been developing its own criteria for the publication of political news about the EU, but has also engaged itself in public opinion formation processes at the European level. The quality press is not simply the passive mediator of European political communication, facilitating autonomous opinion and will formation processes of the public. By shaping and structuring public opinion overtly, newspapers must be analyzed in their most active role as political actors and campaigners. This last role is of particular importance for overcoming the segmentary fragmentation of public spheres resulting from the selective amplification of political communication within nationally biased media systems.

In the convention process, the mass media has stepped forward in its more active and independent role as an advocate pushing for the European integration.[22] The quality press can no longer be held responsible for preserving the national bias and sometimes even for spreading hostile and anti-European attitudes among the public. Against this general wisdom, the quality press has become a dynamic forerunner of European integration, promoting the deepening and the constitutionalization of the EU. In short, quality newspapers raise the European voice against the undecided, hesitant, and particularistic attitudes of national governments and sometimes even against the Euro-skepticism of their own readers.

Governments as Representative of European Publics

A perception of governments acting in the capacity of European representative publics may not be expected, especially given the commonly held understanding that governments in international relations act as unique legitimate representatives of their national publics. In the European framework, this representative function of governments takes a new meaning. The institutionalization of multilevel governance arrangements with plural commitments of all the actors involved leads to a role differentiation for governments as a) autonomous entities (state sovereignty), b) national representatives (popular sovereignty), and c) European representatives (sovereignty of the supranational entity).

In this new constellation the legitimacy of governments as the masters of the treaty relies on the legitimacy of the EU as a whole. Governments are more dependent than any other actor, such as the Commission, on their capacity to build legitimacy. To do so, the masters might be compelled to speak with different voices and not with the national public's single voice. Their role differentiation leads to a change in the appearance of governments: The government as a whole is no meaningful entity in European politics. Instead, single governmental representatives step forward to raise the voice of the European people—although, as in the case of the Fischer Humboldt speech, they might be forced to do so as private beings—while others within the same government might continue to defend national sovereignty.

Governments as the masters of the treaty have committed themselves to a conception of European sovereignty that compels them to appear as European representative publics. In this role, governmental representatives, and not, for example, representatives of European institutions, have called successfully for the constitutionalization of Europe. There is a long tradition of solemn discourses and declarations by the heads of states, in which they exhort European integration.[23] Their European attitude is measured against the exemplary "lives and teachings of the European saints"—the founding fathers of the EU.[24] This creates an expectation of progressive Europeanism against the mainly functional attitude of the European bureaucrats—the latter perceived not as the masters but as the servants of Europe.

The constitutionalization of the EU was introduced by such rituals which compelled all heads of state to take the role of a representative public of the EU. The numerous solemn speeches of 2000 resemble a kind of creed in which the heads of state avowed their firm belief in the glorious future of Europe. The higher morality of Europe is evoked in such speeches, sometimes in delimitation to the outside world, sometimes in delimitation to the nationalist histories of certain nations, and sometimes expressing faith in a better future and a world of greater justice. Here we find the core elements of a European narrative that point to a further mechanism of democratization of the EU.

The Story of European Integration: From the Representation of the Collective Will of the Europeans to the Collective Representation of Europe

Narratives of a shared memory, a collective fate, and a future destiny are seen as essential ingredients for evolving democratic practices. In this context, the question has been raised whether the European integration process, in order to become democratic, needs a similar strong identity kit that is generally attributed to the nation-state or whether a weak and supplementary identity will be sufficient. Obviously, there is no definite or scientific answer to this question, as many critics or promoters of the project of European democratization would prefer. From an analytical point of view we can only observe the self-reflexivity of public discourse in which Europeans negotiate their collective identities. We can observe how Europeans deliberate and reflect their own unity in diversity and the particular semantic forms and narratives that emanate from this. Again, the mass media serve as a focal point for such debates on the European collective self-understanding.

A content analysis of editorials in opinion-leading newspapers concerning the future and the constitutionalization of the EU in 2000 revealed a surprisingly high degree of reciprocity of the underlying ideas and concepts of the public discourse concerning Europe. A common narrative plot emerges, based a) on shared memories of a glorious past, b) on the same diagnosis of the present crisis, and c) on the identification of shared values and principles for shaping the future. As we have argued elsewhere, the parallel account of the past, present, and future of European integration points to a fundamental consensus concerning the unity of political Europe, given the diversity of its elements.[25] In raising the European voice, media discourse creates discursive representations of this unity that are used less for the creation of condensed images of the collectivity than for the denotation of an ongoing process of collective will formation.[26]

Moving from the treatment of the collective representations of Europe as fixed images and symbols to a new paradigm of semantic self-ascriptions of the European polity points to a changing practice of collective identity formation. In contrast to the symbolic repertoire of the nation, the semantic used for representation of European integration remains highly flexible, open, and comprehensive. The mass media looks at the unity of the political Europe and, at the same time, at its own contingency and constructedness. This is what we identify as the major difference between the traditional identity discourse within the nation-state and European semantic representations. The media's view concerning Europe's political unity is based on a second-order observation. Unlike traditional identity discourses, which repress the contingency of underlying concepts, the semantics of the self-description of European society unfold through an observation of multiple practices of identity formation within the European political space. In doing so, the quality press constitutes a European second-order observer who builds a new semantic of unity from the reflexive view on the diversity of units.[27]

Europe's political society forms the core of this discursive practice of self-ascription. Its genuinely political character consists in imagining the unity of society as a collective of self-determination and governance. Self-governance thus becomes the major identity marker of the political Europe. The belief in governance as the fundamental *leitmotif* of European integration is constantly repeated in the media. It implies a political community that expresses its neutrality towards the plurality of ideological and religious thoughts and societal beliefs, including the supremacy of politics over the market and the belief in the governance of society. It is also a political community held together by the principal affirmation of building supranational institutions and the subsequent delegation of powers to those institutions.

The reflection of this model of self-governance is the process of reflecting Europe's unity and diversity. "Unity in diversity" is an old mythic element, and a recurrent theme of European religious, philosophical, and political thought. As such, there is already a collective historical European experience in dealing with unity in diversity. There are ready-made semantics that can be applied by media discourse. More than a mythos, the concordia discors[28] and discordia concors[29] remain an open paradox. The debate concerning the future of Europe is filled with such paradoxes. Newspaper editorials are the arena where these viewpoints may be heard.[30]

From a traditional perspective, it might be hard to accept the reality that substance does not suffice, and that a recurrent discursive practice is required to defend the unity of Europe. However, this is not the case for the quality newspapers who commonly refer to Europe as the "open institutional construction site,"[31] the "Flickenteppich" (patchwork carpet),[32] "the eternal god Janus,"[33] or the "creuset multiculturel et multireligieux."[34] Over time, newspapers have become quite acquainted with this strange construction and have developed their own vocabulary for designating the paradoxes of the unity of Europe and expressing their astonishment that "despite all, it works" (*ça marche, malgré tout*)[35]:

The contingency of the European integration project as a "compromise of compromises"[36] must be constantly renegotiated. Its success, as well as its permanent failures, are thus becoming the last resort of collective identity formation. For the self-imagination of the political society of Europe, such a bizarre construction also has clear advantages. Europeans who wish to find each other together within a political community must learn to love the paradoxes which they find themselves in, and not simply as members of single nations. The search for the *finalité* of European integration that is achieved through constitutionalization is itself one of these paradoxes. And Europeans who observe this never-ending game through the media are gradually acquainting themselves with the idea that the EU's genetic laboratories are apparently trying to invent the "eggs producing wool-milk-pig" (*Eier legende Wollmilchsau*).[37]

The central function of newspaper editorials concerning the EU consists in allowing for the imagination of the European society as a collective of political self-determination. In unfolding the paradox of the unity in diversity of the EU, newspapers apply a second-order view concerning the contingent and constructed character of traditional identities. Beyond collective identities, such a discursive practice results in a lasting and unfinished process of self-description of the Euroepan political society. It remains to be seen whether, and to what extent, this collective practice of identification is turned into a different collective practice of democracy.

The EU as a Case of Reflexive Democratization or of Postdemocratization?

How does the unfolding of public communication and collective representation within European governance relate to democracy? The issue of democracy in the EU is certainly not a question of the application of adequate procedural rules (in the sense of one man/woman—one vote). If we restrict democracy to the right principles, we would have to identify a democratic deficit within the EU, compared to the smooth functioning and taken-for-granted reality of such procedural rules within the nation-state.

It has often been observed that European integration proceeds in a democratizing fashion, which in itself is not, and some would say cannot, be democratic.[38] European integration has contributed, without a doubt, to the democratic consolidation of European postwar societies. Only recently has it been discovered that the EU might also have negative effects on the functioning of democracy within its Member States. The concern with democracy in the EU emerges out of a similar concern in the Member States. This is what we refer to as the reflexivity of European democracy. Reflexive democratization proceeds in a communicative practice of searching collective expressions for the justification of European governance. As has been seen, the semantic representation of the unity of Europe is immediately linked to the representation of the Europeans' collective will. The unity in diversity of Europe is represented in a political society in search of the expression of a collective will. In the European framework of diversity of already existing and consolidated democracies, such a process does not straightforwardly lead to the emergence of a new democratic unit—a European demos. It leads, however, to the perception of a free-floating collective will of the European people as a by-product of ongoing communication and contention regarding European governance.

Presently, there is no alternative to the collective project of democracy beyond the nation-state. It is reflexive democratization and not postdemocratization that has to solve the riddle of a second-order democratization of already democratized societies. The present constitutionalization of the EU implies that the reflexivity of European governance becomes part of the collective experience of Europeans. This does not necessarily produce a popular consensus. Inherent in such an undertaking is the risk of initiating a process of democratization against the collective will of the Europeans. Yet, even this worst-case scenario could only become manifest through collective representations of people feeling affected by a European second-order democracy. The new protective movement against a democratically constituted EU might bring about the failure of particular attempts of democracy in Europe, like a European constitution. However, this would only be an additional contribution to the EU's reflexive democratization.

Notes

1. In the postnational situation, the regulatory state (Majone 1994, 77–101) poses a challenge to the claim that supranational institution building needs a democratic basis, according to the nation-state model.

2. Trenz and Eder 2004, 5–25.

3. Lipset 1994, 1–22.

4. Putnam 1993; Putnam 2000.

5. With regard to the argument for mechanisms substituting the variable-oriented explanation, see Hedström and Swedberg 1998; and McAdam, Tarrow, and Tilly 2001. Mechanisms are seen to provide a microsociological foundation of the explanation of macro processes.

6. Schmitter 2003, 70–85.

7. The theoretical background for seeing the public space as a mechanism of democratization can be found in the tradition of enlightenment thought, a tradition that has been reconstructed systematically by Jürgen Habermas.

8. Gerhards (2001, 145–158) argues that there is none. Eder and Kantner (2000, 306–331) and Eder and Trenz (2003, 111–134) argue that there is something—at least a lot of political communication. From our perspective, it is useless to continue a debate that has reduced the empirical issue to contradictory descriptions of reality. One makes the empirical conclusions allowed by his theory.

9. Reform process aims, first of all, at creating a greater role for European, national, or regional parliaments (see Maurer, Auel, and Benz as well as Rittberger in this volume) and the European Court of Justice, and finally generating some direct access points to the administration in the form of the social and civic dialogue, public hearings, or complaints to the ombudsman (see Heinelt in this volume).

10. The core normative principles of good governance, as enumerated in the Commission's White Paper, can be easily translated into core principles of the network system of communication governance (Commission 2001a, 15ff). The principal task consists in making European networks representative and inclusive through widening the circle of networked European actors—or citizens—thus enhancing communication on European issues. At the same time, the network model offers opportunities for decentralization and subsidiarity. It turns the top-down process into a bottom-up process, therefore enhancing communication and debates on European issues both at the subnational and local level.

11. This empirical research is based on a representative sample of European or Europeanized political news coverage in 2000, which includes the following newspapers: *Frankfurter Allgemeine Zeitung, Süddeutsche Zeitung* (Germany), *Le Monde, Libération* (France), *Guardian, Times* (UK), *La Repubblica, La Stampa* (Italy), *Die Presse, Der Standard* (Austria), *El Pais* (Spain), *New York Times* (USA). For further details see Trenz 2004a.

12. Our survey also allows us to identify the losers of this media attention game. There is a clear media bias towards institutional and governmental actors and away from civil society. From the institutional perspective, the low media salience of the European Parliament, national parliaments, and other noninstitutional actors has given rise to increasing efforts of public relations and image politics, hence increasing the news values of European actors, issues, and events.

13. Typical issues linked to interest negotiations among the Europeans are institutional reform, competition policy, and the debate on the Euro. Only a few articles refer to purely normative or identitarian framings (e.g. the *Charta of Fundamental Rights* or the struggle for a European identity). Instead, 45 percent of the articles use multiple

framings, raising issues in the context of interests and/or values and/or identities. The Haider case, institutional reform, and Eastern enlargement are examples of this multiple framing practice, thus indicating the increasing relevance of conflicting debates on European issues.

14. A generalizing use is made by pointing to the unity and commonness of a problem beyond the particularity and diversity of its elements, namely unemployment as a European problem, a tragedy with European dimensions. Comparative statements refer to the effects of standardization, which are linked to Europe: "Our national achievements in education are far behind European standards."

15. Eder and Trenz 2003.

16. Weiler 1999.

17. Eder 2001, 45–75; Trenz 2001, 87–98.

18. Keck and Sikkink 1998.

19. Eriksen and Fossum 2002.

20. Eriksen, Joerges, and Neyer 2003; Eriksen, Fossum, and Menéndez 2004.

21. Think, for instance, of a talk show where a media public observes, among others, the reactions of the audience, which—in contrast to the attendance in a parliamentary assembly—is allowed to intervene, and thus becomes part of the game. Think also of the Wagner festival in Bayreuth, where the selected public that enters the theater becomes an attraction for the television public. In this case, the representative public makes its own and independent performance, whereas most parts of the general public would not be interested in the real opera performance. Physical nonpresence does not exclude the outside public from evaluating the performance. However, they only have to rely on what the participating critics—if there are any—tell them or what they can see or read in the mass media.

22. Maurer 2003a; Trenz 2004b.

23. Petersson and Hellström 2003, 235–252.

24. Milward 1992, 318ff.

25. Trenz 2004b .

26. Soysal 2002, 265–284.

27. This is a rather paradoxical result: The self-reflexive view on the contingency of unity can only be expressed as the unity of Europe's political society.

28. Unity in diversity.

29. Diversity of units.

30. Here, the role of intellectuals must be highlighted not only as one of the major sources used by the journalists but also as the guest authors of many editorials. For a recent example see the Habermas-Derrida initiative for relaunching a critical European public sphere (Habermas and Derrida 2003 or Muschg 2003).

31. *La Repubblica*, July 4 2000, 7.

32. *Frankfurter Allgemeine Zeitung*, May 5 2000, 7.

33. *Le Monde* September 12, 2000, 21.

34. *Libération*, October 6, 2000, 10.

35. *La Repubblica*, October 19, 2000, 16.

36. *La Repubblica*, October 19, 2000, 16.

37. *Standard*, September 15, 2000.

38. Schmitter 2003.

A COMMENT ON EDER AND TRENZ

Lars-Erik Cederman

Eder's and Trenz's democratic functionalism takes a very optimistic, post-nationalist approach to the democratization of the European Union, which argues that the EU is actually in the process of democratizing itself, thanks to the Constitutional Convention and other factors.[1] Although I argue elsewhere[2] that studies of democratization need to account for both the internal and external dimensions of this process, here I will focus on the internal aspects that are most relevant to Eder's and Trenz's contribution.

For starters, their functionalist research program improves on the existing literature in at least three ways: in its emphasis on dynamic processes rather than static conditions; its attention to the vertical dimension of integration, which previous studies' focus on horizontal networks has neglected; and in its empirical pragmatic approach, which is a clear step forward from the existing literature's highly normative orientation.

Dynamic Macro Processes

Most of the research in this area is concerned with the static conditions of democratic governance. Here, the debate has revolved around the applicability of abstract principles as well as descriptive questions such as whether the EU was or was not democratic at a particular point in history. Such scholarship often focuses on specific policy areas or concerns specific institutional provisions, such as the accountability of the Commission to the European Parliament.

In a welcome development, Eder and Trenz propose that we should instead look at the problem of democratization from a dynamic macro perspective. This signals a return to the focus on processes of classical integration theory, and indeed, the authors refer explicitly to Deutsch and Haas. With the slow progress of the European integration process in the 1970s, Deutsch and Haas's integration theory has attracted relatively little attention in recent years. Ironically enough, their theorizing may be more relevant than ever, now that the EU has entered its explicit polity-building mode.

Vertical Dimension

Eder's and Trenz's chapter also provides a needed complement to the prevailing emphasis on horizontal exchange processes within transnational policy-making networks, be it among committees, NGOs, or other actors. They rightly point out that current theorizing in this area fails to articulate mechanisms that create the conditions for broader popular participation to emerge. This is a step forward, and not only compared to the bulk of the recent literature on networks that tends to adopt this concept uncritically.

Empirical Pragmatism

Too much research about the democratic deficit has focused on normative reasoning at the expense of actual empirical developments. It would be unfortunate if social scientists were to get stuck in preconceived normative schemes while the integration train steams out of the station. In response to this problem, Eder and Trenz try to frame normative issues in as flexible a way as possible. For example, they offer a detailed study of newspaper articles in the European quality press as a way to gauge the viability of a European public sphere.

Critique

Now for the bad news: While Eder and Trenz are moving in the right direction, they have gone either too far or not far enough. Let's look at the three points in reverse order.

Too Normatively Pragmatic

In their desire to avoid prejudicing their analysis in normative terms, Eder and Trenz appear to have lost sight of important normative principles, and this threatens to dilute the very meaning of democracy in their analysis. In short, this implies throwing the democratic baby out with the normative bath water. It is thus no wonder that they are less nervous about the democratic deficit than many other observers.

By refusing to pinpoint what they really mean by democracy, they are weakening the power of their analysis. Their subjective criterion seems particularly slippery. It depends on a process of reflexive democratization, which consolidates a nascent European public space by creating opportunities for European collective actors to assert themselves, which in turn paves the way for

Europeans to imagine themselves as a political community. This scenario makes the democratization of Europe look practically inevitable, since it even manages to transform resistance into building blocks of democracy. Although this is an appealing prognosis, the content of the democracy that this process is geared to produce deserves closer scrutiny. Of course, there will always be a debate about what democracy means, and as Eder and Trenz point out, such debates will themselves contribute to overcoming the deficit, but there has to be some minimal standard, a threshold below which we should be talking about some other concept than democracy.

This is not the place to list candidates for such necessary conditions—political theorists have worked on this at least a couple of millennia. It seems more important to highlight what they leave out. In contrast to both procedural and substantive definitions of democracy, Eder's and Trenz's conceptualization lacks the criterion of popular involvement or participation. Even where they mention the masses, they figure as a source of resonance rather than as agents. Ultimately, too much flexibility leads to complacency that could hide real problems. Obviously there is no single definition that all can agree on, but this shouldn't imply that anything goes.

Vertical Dimension Too Vague

Let me now return to the pitfalls contained in the second strength of this paper: namely their recognition that the horizontal dimension doesn't suffice in studies of the democratic deficit.

This time, I want more rather than less: Eder's and Trenz's story about vertical integration remains somewhat vague and incomplete. In particular, the institutional mechanisms are not clearly articulated. For example, they suggest that practically any type of communication would do. Moreover, although they highlight the EU's constitutional debate, I searched in vain for a broader set of institutions and procedures that would be capable of driving their postulated collective learning process. In particular, especially in view of the constitution's importance for the long-term development of the Union, I would have expected them to analyze the contents of the constitutional draft—and not just the fact that various political actors fight over it.

Instead, Eder and Trenz refer to a self-correcting dynamic that allegedly spontaneously engenders democracy. In fact, such a belief in an autopilot process strongly resembles the classical functionalist theory of David Mitrany,[3] which Haas revised. Mitrany thought that the demand for efficiency and welfare would bring about political structures more or less automatically. In contrast to that account, Haas's[4] neofunctionalist elaboration clearly out-

lined a number of mechanisms that he believed would lead to a shift in identities, through a so-called spillover process. In its current form, Eder's and
Trenz's theory of democratic functionalism looks more like Mitrany's auto-
matic process than Haas's contingent spillover hypothesis, because it remains
quite vague about the actors and the institutions involved. As Trenz and Eder
have themselves pointed out, functionalist theories without a clear specification of the mechanisms behind them run the risk of degenerating into teleo-
logical tautologies.[5] Thus, here there's more work to be done!

Of course, the fact that the EU has acknowledged that it suffers from weak
legitimacy is a step in the right direction, but that alone hardly represents a solution to the democratic deficit. Quite on the contrary, some of the PR remedies invoked by the Commission may actually make the situation worse by in-
citing a type of resistance that can be very dangerous in the European context,
if it provokes an already apathetic citizenry to abstain from voting in European elections and to withdraw even further from the fragile European public sphere. Where might more precise institutional mechanisms be found? To
find out, we return to the historical process of integration.

Historical Dimension Needs to Be Highlighted

I have already praised Eder's and Trenz's theory of democratic functionalism for its efforts to tease out a dynamic logic that has been obscured by other
contributions to the debate. It probably doesn't come as a surprise that I want
them to try even harder. Indeed, my criticism is that the dynamics of the theory could be rendered more explicit by drawing on historical sociology. But at
the same time, it is not hard to see why Eder and Trenz are reluctant to look
into the rearview mirror of history. Like most postnationalists, they reject
anything that smacks of demos, that is, a European *Volk*. And it is true that this
type of reasoning can easily degenerate into an essentialist interpretation of
democracy along the lines of the German Constitutional Court's infamous
Maastricht decision.[6]

Nevertheless, I would submit that their position is much too cautious. It is
possible to learn from Europe's historical processes of state formation and nation building without necessarily subscribing to the demos thesis. Here I
adopt McAdam, Tilly, and Tarrow's[7] position that comparisons should not be
made at the level of outcomes, but rather at the level of mechanisms. Instead
of dismissing this or that author as a proponent of the demos thesis, we need
to do a better job at critically evaluating the mechanisms that brought about
a public sphere at the national level, and then explore how these might be
transplanted or transcended at the European level.

Regardless of whether or not one believes that the criteria for democratic governance should be radically reframed, anyone engaged in a project of European-level identity formation should consider the institutional mechanisms that are currently operating at the national level. This is precisely the weakness of postnational schemes of democracy, such as those proposed by Habermas[8] and Held,[9] and indeed by Eder and Trenz. As one of the foremost experts on these issues, Craig Calhoun, recently put it, cosmopolitanism rests on "inadequate sociological foundations," even in the EU, where these foundations are probably strongest.

Calhoun's diagnosis is right on target: What is missing from these postnationalist perspectives is an account of political socialization, and Eder's and Trenz's version of democratic functionalism is no exception. The vertical component of their theory incorporates the citizenry, but ultimately it treats it as a relatively passive source of resonance. In any case, participation requires a minimum of knowledge and engagement that does not emerge out of thin air. As generations of nationalists have experienced, identity politics requires hard, institutional work.

But what are the mechanisms that should be highlighted? Without assuming what should, or could, be done at the European level, it is helpful to glance at the macro-sociological literature on nationalism and nation building, including the work of Gellner, Deutsch, Rokkan, and Flora.[10] This immediately puts the spotlight on the usual suspects, such as the media, educational institutions, and language politics. This is not the place for me to elaborate on these topics. Instead, I will content myself with a few hints.

1. In Europe, schools and universities remain the main factories of politically aware citizens. Far from being limited to teaching professional skills, state-run mass education helps young citizens understand the rules of the polity and their rights and obligations as citizens.[11]

2. Overlapping with education, there is the issue of language. Any polity requires a language regime and a minimum level of linguistic coordination to support political communication. The traditional nationalist model has been one single high language, but as the Swiss case illustrates, other arrangements are also possible.[12]

3. In addition, despite recent enthusiasm for the Internet, without traditional mass media, political interest groups, and parties there can be no structured public discourse involving large numbers of people. Following in the footsteps of Benedict Anderson, Trenz and his colleagues rightly point out that simultaneity in terms of issue coverage is an important factor in this context. But it is far from sufficient. To adopt their metaphor, a symphonic composition certainly requires that the musi-

cians be on the same page, but it also demands an intricate weave of exchanges that allows the instruments to blend in with each other. In contrast, Jürgen Gerhards has documented how national media establishments, including institutions for the education of journalists, remain profoundly nationally segregated.[13] Here we still have a set of parallel orchestras, possibly all of which are playing Beethoven, but which are doing so from separate concert houses.

The crux is that all these institutions are incredibly weak at the European level. This is hardly surprising since, as Tobias Theiler has shown, the identity-conferring policies of the EU have so far been effectively blocked by its Member States. Theiler demonstrates that educational policy remains limited to mostly horizontal exchanges and vocational training, and that it has failed to achieve a truly European dimension.[14]

Within this context, it is troublesome that the problem of Europe's weak political socialization has failed to elicit any serious remedial efforts. In particular, this applies to the Constitutional Treaty. On the other hand, it is true that the former German President von Weizsaecker wrote an open letter[15] to the Constitutional Convention, cosigned by Delors and many other prominent Europeans, urging it to take the cultural dimension seriously. But even before being massaged by the European Council, the draft did not propose anything to create the institutional preconditions for a strengthened participatory infrastructure. This is a squandered opportunity, because contrary to what Eder's and Trenz's functionalist automatism implies, institutional mechanisms are necessary to effect change at the mass level. It is not enough for a handful of intellectuals and academics to debate the problem.

Notes

1. On postnationalist approaches to democratization, see Cederman 2001a, 139–74.
2. Cederman 2001b.
3. Mitrany 1943.
4. Haas 1958.
5. Trenz and Eder 2004, 5–25.
6. Bundesverfassungsgerichtsentschiedung of 12 October 1993, 2 BvR 2134/92 and 2 BvR 2159/92 (1994) 89 *Entscheidungen des Bundesverfassungsgerichts* 155–213.
7. McAdam, Tarrow, and Tilly 2001.
8. Habermas 1998d.
9. Held 1995.
10. Gellner 1983; Deutsch 1953; Flora 1999; Flora 2000, 151–66.

11. Theiler 2001, 115–40; Theiler 2004.

12. Kraus 2000, 138–63.

13. Gerhards 1993, 96–110.

14. Theiler 2004.

15. "Der Stellenwert von Kultur und Bildung innerhalb der neuen europäischen Verfassung—Ein Appell," signed by Richard von Weizsäcker, Jacques Delors, Ingvar Carlsson, Garret Fitzgerald, and Wim Kok, Arpad Goencz Princess Margriet of the Netherlands, published in several major European newspapers on April 3, 2003.

8

The Europeanization of Protest: A Typology and Empirical Evidence

Donatella della Porta

PROTEST USUALLY ADDRESSES the national level of government. Historically, a new repertoire of collective action—of which main features survived until today—developed together with the nation-state.[1] Social movements organized petitions and demonstrations on press freedom, religious freedom, and electoral rights.[2] The labor movement, in alliance with socialist parties, struggled for social rights—democracy—developed when the "masses entered history."[3] Indeed, Charles Tilly[4] noticed the existence of "a broad correspondence between democratization and social movements [;] the maps of full-fledged institutions and social movements overlap greatly." During the last two centuries, "social movements generally flourished and spread where further democratization was occurring and receded when authoritarian regime curtailed democracy." By pushing for the enfranchisement and the recognition of associational rights, social movements contributed to democratization. Using protest as a main resource, social movements have been important players in the emergence and evolution of the nation-state, mobilizing for civil, political, and social rights. At the national level, social movements constituted a critical public sphere, subjecting the public decisions of the elected representatives to what Bertrand Manin[5] called the "test of the discussion."

The nation-state is no longer the exclusive point of reference for social movements: sub- and, especially, supranational levels have been added and have become increasingly important, above all through the process of European integration.[6] The Europeanization of protest could indeed increase the transparency (and therefore public accountability) of European governance.

Moreover, the European level could emerge as an additional lever for public interest groups, offering channels of access (or at least *voice*) to those actors weaker at home. Faced with a European governance that is no longer working under conditions of "permissive consensus,"[7] European social movements could contribute to the development of a European identity "from below."[8]

But are social movements able to adapt to multilevel governance, performing their functions as critical public spheres? Are they able to represent general interests, balancing the pressures from strong specific interests? Notwithstanding the relevant functions that social movements could play for the democratization of European governance, studies into the effects of the construction of European institutions on social movements and protest—and vice versa—are still in their infancy. In fact, the first analyses in this area have closely reproduced the debate on Europe, as it has unwound in other areas of the social sciences with two contrasting images of the Union: the intergovernmentalism of the realist approach or transnationalism with institutional overtones. As Stefano Bartolini[9] has observed, the results that scholars from different schools rely upon depend largely on the institutions, the policies, the sector, or the process they study. Studying the intergovernmental conferences and their outcomes, one concludes that these tend to be intergovernmental; their supranationalism comes to light when studying the sentences of the Court of Justice. In parallel, in the studies concerning protest, the emerging images are often influenced by empirically observed objects. Thus, research with regard to protests in single states offers a realist intergovernmental image of the dominant role of the nation-state, which remains the target of most protest. Research on protest events, collected mainly from newspaper sources, all stress the paucity of protests targeting European institutions directly, both in general,[10] and in specific fields such as migrant rights[11] or environmental protection.[12] Research on the activities of public interest groups in the European institutions points, instead, to the emergence of a new polity and the creation of a new politics.

The studies on collective action seemed, in a simplistic reading of its early results, to expect that protest at the European level had to reproduce the national pattern, as indicated in figure 8.1, while national actors were expected to act at the national level, transnational European actors were expected to form at the EU level.

Taking the recent trends of the expansion of competences of EU institutions into account, the analyses of protest and social movements have now begun to address multilevel strategies of protest. As I shall argue in this chapter, protest in fact manifests itself according to different paths. Social movement organizations, as well as other actors using protest seem to adapt their strategies so as to address the various territorial levels of government simultaneously. To do

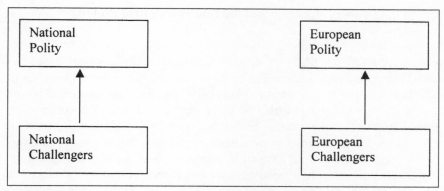

FIGURE 8.1
Europeanization of Collective Action: The Nation-State Model

this, they have developed strategies of "crossed influence," which are used as pressure at the national level in order to change decisions at the European level, or as pressure at the European level in order to change national decisions. In the next two sections, I shall analyze the characteristics of two types of crossed mobilization: (a) mobilization at the national level to change decisions at the European level (section 2); and (b) the use of the European level as a source of resources for modifying national decisions (section 3).[13] It is, however, necessary to add that (c) the construction of community institutions, as with the policies chosen by the EU, are increasingly the object of lively responses by loose networks of local, national, and transnational actors (section 4). I shall argue, however, that both domesticated and Europeanized protest carry the potential to generate transnational effects—leading to social mobilization and a nascent public sphere—which, in turn, holds the potential to increase the democratic quality of the EU.

I shall discuss these three paths of the Europeanization of protest, presenting some novel empirical findings. In particular, in my analysis on the emergence of European movements, I shall refer to the results of a survey conducted at the First European Social Forum (ESF), a transnational meeting of the movement for global justice held in Florence in November 2002. During the ESF, the Gruppo di Ricerca sull'Azione Collettiva in Europa (GRACE) interviewed 2384 activists.[14] The semistructured questionnaires have been condcuted face-to-face, with a random sampling of participants in various events at the Fortezza da Basso, where the forum took place.[15] The empirical insights gained from this survey are helpful in the laying of a foundation for further theoretical reflection on the nexus between protest, social movements, and democratization of EU governance.

Two-Level Games and the Domestication of Protest

As mentioned above, research has indicated that concerns about EU decisions have been expressed principally at the national level, where elected political institutions are supposed to be more accountable to the citizen-elector. The low presence of protest at the European level has been explained by the political opportunities available at other territorial levels of government.[16] Research on social movements has in fact stressed that protest grows when grievances, resources, and opportunities are present, that is, when protesters believe their actions could have an impact upon decision makers.[17] Furthering this hypothesis, the limited number of protests geared to influence the EU institutions could be explained by the undeniable deficit in representative democracy, as well as the weakness of a European public sphere. However, if protesters could generate disagreements and criticisms, they would find it difficult to mobilize against an unaccountable and opaque target. As for the former, not only are the areas of responsibility of the European Parliament still rather limited, but its electoral legitimacy is effectively undermined by low participation rates in elections, the absence of European programs and parties, as well as the secondary role that Europe plays for many Euro-deputies.[18] The Council is composed of ministers of member governments, electorally responsible to citizens, but who, in fact, have rarely been given a specific mandate on EU issues. Additionally, with the conjunct decision making adopted for most issues in the first pillar, the Commission has gone beyond the power of an intergovernmental institution[19] without an adaptation of the mechanisms of accountability. The technocratic nature of many decisions and the complexity of the decision-making process have added yet more competences to the EU's bureaucracy.

Besides the weak electoral accountability of EU representative political institutions, the difficulties in building a European public sphere must be emphasized. The Europeanization of the public sphere has usually been considered a delicate issue, in terms of the flimsiness of the process[20] and the lack of research on the topic.[21] If more recent research pointed to more complex results, which revealed an increasing Europeanization of national public discourses,[22] the participation of civil society actors in the mass-mediatic debate on Europe remained limited.[23]

Since protest grows when institutions are accountable to the electorate, the relative inaccessibility of the supranational level to protest and the weakness of the European public sphere explain why social movements continue to predominantly target national governments. In particular, movements that want to pressure the EU in favor of national interests (in direct competition with other national interests represented in the EU) might well choose a two-level game strategy.[24] This would help to push the national governments that, in turn, may attempt to negotiate better arrangements at supranational levels. In their analysis of protest in Europe,[25] Doug Imig and Sidney Tarrow[26] observed that most EU related events (406 out of 490) were cases of domestication. In particular, domestication characterizes many instances of mobilizations of European farmers.[27] As indicated in figure 8.2, this is protest against EU decisions, but organized at the national level, where domestic actors target their national governments in order to push them to address the EU institutions.

Such a path of mobilization may be seen as proof of the persistent relevance of the nation-state as a target for protest, as well as the permanent weakness of the EU institutions. Without denying the tendency of protest to address national governments, I shall suggest that national protests against EU-induced policies show a potential for the transnationalization of protest and the emergence of a transnational public sphere. While it is true that social movements are better able to organize and pressure decision makers via disruptive actions at the national level, the effects of national protests do not stop at national boundaries. In fact, a more careful look shows the rise, in the course of these protest campaigns, of innovations both in the organizational structure and in the frames of the protest, with the development of European networks and European identities.

The campaigns of dairy farmers against EU milk quotas in Italy during the mid-1990s[28] are an illustration of the potential for the Europeanization of protest. For the protesting dairy producers, the most relevant political actor was the national government, which was expected to protect its farmers. The protesters were asking whether "any authority in our national government concretely [looked] after the interests of producers—together with those of

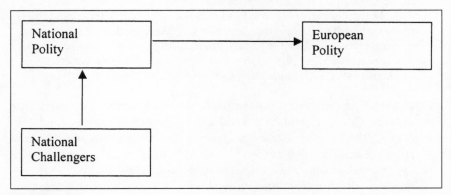

FIGURE 8.2
Domestication of Collective Action

the consumers—in a world dominated by globalization and, before that, by Europe."[29] The movement against fines on milk quotas led, however, to a new organizational structure of representation, with a form of direct democracy coming out of the traditions of past social movements. Specific EU policies as well as their implementation were criticized; even an image of European agriculture characterized as "high quality" as opposed to merely profit-orientated was developed. However, this new actor did not criticize the European integration process itself.

First of all, the policy of the government, accused of unfair and clientelistic management of the quotas, and the very representative value of the traditional parties and unions came under discussion. Indeed, spontaneous committees developed above all in areas of Catholic white subcultures (in particular, the provinces of Padua and Verona). Many activists were disappointed members of Coldiretti, an organization that represented farmers' interests, which had also been close to the DC (Democrazia Cristiana). Trust in these organizations had collapsed with the emergence of the corruption scandals of the early 1990s. As an older activist explained, "Those of my age believed in the unions. We were all proper members, active and a lot of us . . . lent a hand in local politics as well. But after *Mani Pulite* (Clean Hands) we all left."[30] The activists soon came to believe that the political institutions and the unions were incapable of understanding the farmers' claims and channeling them into the decision-making processes. "You could ask for a regional assessor for a meeting, but they wouldn't come. The ones from the union found face to face encounters hard going and after a couple of times they hadn't the courage to go through it again."[31] The protesters indeed moved beyond the traditional structures of agricultural interests representation. As an activist explains,

> at the beginning we had meetings with eight or ten dairy farmers at someone's house. The fines had already arrived and some had paid up. . . . we began spontaneously, a bunch of guys in their thirties. It was only after that we found there were similar groups that met in Crema, thanks to friends from other provinces. And so we decided to see whether they had perhaps decided to do something or even whether we could do something together.[32]

In the statute of one of the organizations founded during the protest, the Spontaneous Committee of Milk Producers (*Comitati Spontanei Produttori Latte*—or COBAS), direct democracy, with a decentralized structure organized around assemblies that are open to all with no reliance on official membership, emerged as one of the inspirations of the movement.

Along with the construction of a new organizational structure, attention was moreover paid to the definition of the collective identity of European farmers. The point of reference of the movement focused on the small and medium dairy farms, and above all, dynamic ones. At that time, the protestors were not the losers of Europeanization:

> The determined dairy farmers who initiated protest were essentially from thriving farms with long productive histories, recently inherited from the most dynamic members of the family. In most cases, a corporate agreement existed between brothers and/or cousins. Self-defined as traditional or historic, the farmers had invested hundreds of millions or even billions [of Lira] in the hope of being able to take on international competition in an efficient manner in the early 1990s.[33]

In most cases, these farmers belonged to a new generation of farmers, characterized as young and well-educated. The protestors proposed agricultural policies that were both critical of protectionism and neoliberalism, framing both as an adaptation to Europeanization and globalization. They asked for "appropriate state and community control and promotion of the quality, cleanliness and freshness of the products, especially when covered by marks with a protected origin"[34]. This would allow the modernization of dairy farms as well as protecting "the environmental and qualitative peculiarity of productions."[35] In case the liberalization of the markets led to price competition, the mobilized farmers had proposed a protection of product quality, binding tradition to innovation. For this reason, in the beginnings of the movement, emphasis was placed on moving away from the image of the poor and ignorant *contadino* (small farmer). "We acted so as to detract from the image of what some wanted us to be. 'They are peasants, they don't know how to speak, look how they dress.' We began by producing a stimulus in order to show others who we really were, what we did and what we were saying."[36]

If the protest campaign against the milk quotas tended to remain mainly national, this indicates the limits of domestication, which in fact only works to the extent that the national governments retain large autonomous power, as well as for actors that are better protected at the national rather than the supranational level. The organization of a march of Italian farmers in Brussels confirms the perception of the need to also address the EU level. In fact, the Italian farmers developed contacts with colleagues from other European countries, where globalization and Europeanization had also created new collective demands. Along with these new demands, new organizational strategies and identity discourses arose in connection with production in the primary sector. The march in Brussels, as well as the mobilization of European farmers against WTO-supported policies, indicates the capacity of collective actors that emerge and act mainly at the domestic level to overcome national borders, and frames their concerns within a broader social agenda.[37] Especially after the shift in agricultural policies (with Agenda 2000) from subsidies to

market liberalization and WTO-supported policies of competition, the Confédération Paysanne Européenne mobilized at the EU level against what it defined as neoliberal stances.[38] It developed a European identity while criticizing
the specific policies of scaling down regulations on the use of hormones, genetically modified organisms, pesticides, and the like.[39]

The Search for EU Alliances: An Externalization of Protest?

Domestication is therefore often the strategy that allows protestors to overcome the weak democratic accountability of EU institutions, meanwhile
producing European structures and frames. In other cases, organized interests look at the EU as an additional arena for the mobilization of resources
that may then be used at the national level. In this case, there is a strategy of
externalization[40]—defined as the mobilization of national bodies targeting
the EU in an attempt to put pressure on their own governments. As figure
8.3 indicates, in this case actors who are feeling weak at home try to mobilize allies at the supranational level: protest addresses the EU institutions in
order to push them to intervene in domestic affairs. This strategy has been
used, above all, by movements that tend to ally supranationally and have in
fact appealed to the kinds of discourse and identity legitimized at the European level. This is the case, for instance, of environmental campaigns,[41] as
well as of the Euro-strike in 1997 of Spanish, French, and Belgian workers,
accusing Renault of having disregarded the right to consultation with the
workers' representative, demanded by European legislation.[42]

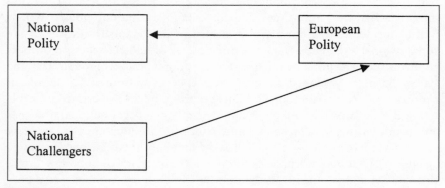

FIGURE 8.3
Externalization of Protest

For social movement organizations, exercising influence on the EU level is not a simple task, as other organizations emerged as more effective than social movements in organizing and influencing EU institutions. First of all, business organizations found it much easier to go European than labor organizations. In 2002, the official register of the Commission included 709 organizations in industry, the services, professions, and agriculture and only 149 diffuse and other interests (e.g. artisans and consumers).[43] Moreover, in contrast to business organizations, movements active at the EU level—such as the Platform of the European Social NGOs; European Anti-Poverty Network; Human Rights Contact Group; European Migrant Forum; United (against racism); and European Network of Women—are usually loose and poorly staffed networks. EU level environmental movement organizations are, for the most part, little more than transnational alliances of different national groups. Although they are successful in raising issues and concerns, they have only very limited resources.[44] Inclusion has also been selective. Only the organizations that adapt to the rules of the game obtain routine access to EU institutions, though usually of an informal nature.[45] Moreover, the more important EU institutions become, the more structured and less accessible they seem to be for weakly organized interests.[46]

Nevertheless, certain changes in the European institutions have facilitated access by movement organizations. First of all, if the development of the EC towards the creation of a common market explains the dominance of producers' interests, the progression of market-making legislation (from the Commission, the Council, but also the Court) was also concomitant with an increase in demand for market-correcting policies—evident in the mobilizations of consumers, environmentalists, and so on. Moreover, in recent times, the debate about good governance and the democratic deficit induced the Commission to reflect on the involvement of civil society, starting with Delors and the social dialogue, and, especially after Maastricht, to go shopping for broader social acceptance of EU policies (White Paper on Governance) as well as for allies in the power play with the Council. In fact, (some) social movement organizations have recently been granted increasing participation in return for expertise and legitimacy. The Commission has biannual meetings with all NGOs involved in the social platform and also holds weekly meetings with the environmental Group of 8 and various groups of experts. The largest environmental groups of the so-called gang of four—Greenpeace, WWF, Friends of the Earth, and the European Environmental Bureau—have close relationships with the Commission's Directorate General for Environment (ex DG XI), which provides financial support to all but Greenpeace.[47] So strong was the support of the European Union (especially on behalf of ex DG V, the Directorate General for Employment, Social Affairs, and Equal Opportunities) for the European Trade Union Confederation that the Europeanization of trade unions has been described as "a story of interactions between European institutions seeking to stimulate Euro-level interest representation, a small number of unionists who perceived Europe as important, and the growing significance of European integration itself."[48] The European Parliament has worked as a main channel of access to various organizations, especially in areas where parliamentary committees are more active and relations of movement organizations with the Commission more difficult. With a view to regionalist movements, Liesebth Hooghe[49] observes the increasing power of the Committee of Regions. Feminists, environmentalists, and unions have also been able to obtain favorable decisions from the Court of Justice, especially with the increasing competence of the EU on environmental and social policies.[50]

Bearing the aforementioned limits in mind, one effect of protest externalization has been the creation of supranational organizational structures and identities. In fact, the European arena offered representatives of different EU countries the opportunity to meet each other, build organizational networks, coordinate activity, and construct supranational discourses. Hence, growing interaction can help facilitate the development of a common European identity.

The Emergence of European Movements?

The domestication and externalization of protest seem therefore to have facilitated the rise of conflicts directly linked to the characteristics of the European Union, increasingly expressed through unconventional forms of protest involving loosely structured networks of European activists. The objectives of these protests tend to be more and more general, with the participation of national and supranational actors turning simultaneously to various governmental levels. As indicated in figure 8.4, protest targets different levels of governance and involves loose networks of national (often local) and transnational groups.

More and more, Europeanized protest addresses the lack of concerns at the EU level for social equality. Since its origins, the EU has been a reaction to the weakening of the European nation-state in certain key areas, from the military defense of its frontiers to the expansion of markets. As Bartolini[51] puts it, the process of territorial de-differentiation at the base of European integration was fuelled by the evidences of the intolerable consequences of historical rivalry between the European states as well as the growing risks of an economic marginalization of Europe in the world economy. The deepening of this process demands, however, the creation of cultural identity and citizenship that can sustain the social sharing of risks and legitimate political decisions.[52] The EU's launch of campaigns on general ethical issues such as gen-

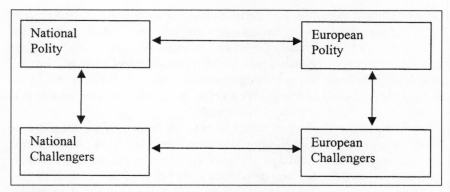

FIGURE 8.4
European Social Movements

der equality, anti-racism, and human rights,[53] are evidence of the search for a moral basis for collective, European identity. Such a moral basis could potentially become an equivalent to what the nation had represented in the construction of the state. One of the main instruments in the construction of the nation-state—citizens' rights—are, however, still weak at the EU level.

In fact, it is precisely against European economic and social policies that mobilizations are now beginning at the supranational level, with some early protests that, although rare, nevertheless represent an important signal of change.[54] The search for another Europe is best represented by the movement for globalization from below calling for various demonstrations against EU summits (for example, see Gothenburg 2001); and also organizing European Social Forums, as large assemblies of social movement organizations, the first of which was held in Florence in 2002, followed by one in Paris in 2003, one in London in 2004, and one in Athens in 2006. As I shall indicate, the protestors at the ESF expressed strong criticism of the forms of European integration, but no hostility to the building of supranational, European institutions and identities. They can therefore be seen as critical social capital for the emergence of a European polity.

The large success of the first ESF—with sixty thousand activists from all over Europe participating in three days of debate and between five hundred thousand and a one million activists in the closing march—was the result of networking between groups and individuals with, at least, partly different identities. The activists interviewed in Florence were well-grounded in a web of associations that ranged from Catholic to Green, from voluntary social workers to labor unions, from human rights to women's organizations: 41.5 percent of the participants are or have been members of NGOs, 31.8 percent of unions, 34.6 percent of parties, 52.7 percent of other movements, 57.5

percent of student groups, 32.1 percent of squats for the young, 19.3 percent of religious groups, 43.1 percent of environmental associations, 51.3 percent of charities, and 50.9 percent of sport and recreational associations.[55] In addition to a heterogeneous social base and multigenerational participation, the coming together of different ideologies was also indicative for the ESF. The attempt to keep these different groups together is a gamble for a movement that defines itself as "a movement of movements."

The multiform composition of the movement expresses itself in the differentiated attention to how globalization affects human rights, gender issues, immigrant conditions, peace, and ecology. However, the protestors converged in their demands for social justice and democracy from below as the dominant interpretative schemes, recomposing the fragments of distinct cultures. A multilevel public intervention able to reduce inequalities produced by the market and the search for a new democracy are the central themes of the emerging European movement. The first ESF presented itself as an important moment in the construction of a critical public sphere for the discussion of the European Convention and its limits. Together with the democratization of the European institutions, the activists demanded a charter of social rights, which exceeded the commitments outlined in the Treaty of Nice. The policies of the EU were criticized as essentially neoliberal, bringing about the privatization of public services and the flexibility of the labor market with a concomitant rise in work insecurity. Under the banner "another Europe is possible" various policies were demanded including taxation of capital and of financial transactions. There were also claims for public intervention in order to help the weakest social groups, as well as the strengthening of public services in sectors such as education and health. Although present in the event, the main parties of the Left and the union confederations were criticized for adopting neoliberal policies when holding office. In fact, the level of trust in public institutions tends to be low, with notable differences among the institutions. The scarce faith in political parties is also revealed in the answers to questions concerning party loyalty. With regard to ideology, the activists of the ESF in Florence located themselves mainly on the Left (45.7 percent), with an additional 29.7 percent on the far Left and 10.2 percent on the Center-Left. Their level of trust in national political institutions was very low: only 20.4 percent expressed trust in political parties, 6.1 percent in national governments, and 14.5 percent in national parliaments.

If we observe the goals and expectations of the ESF activists, the image of well-informed, networked, and committed but critical activists is confirmed. The movement against neoliberal globalization presents in fact a challenge and an opportunity for institution building at the European level. First of all, activists from different countries express a strong criticism of the actual politics and policies of the EU. As indicated in table 8.3, there is con-

TABLE 8.1A
The EU Attempts to Safeguard a Social Model That Is Different
from the Neoliberal One (all numbers are in percent)

	Italy	France	Germany	Spain	Great Britain	Total
Not at all	46.7	50.7	47.4	51.4	68.3	(53.7) 321
A little	43.7	35.8	43.6	38.5	26.1	(36.8) 220
Enough	8.9	8.2	7.7	6.4	4.2	(7.0) 42
Very much	0.7	5.2	1.3	3.7	1.4	(2.5) 15
Total number of respondents	135	134	78	109	142	598

Note: Cramer's V = 0.13 significant at 0.05 level.

TABLE 8.1B
The EU Mitigates Most of the Effects of
Neoliberal Globalization (all numbers are in percent)

	Italy	France	Germany	Spain	Great Britain	Total
Not at all	31.7	50.0	29.7	44.0	59.4	(44.4) 267
A little	51.1	27.9	48.6	40.4	21.7	(36.6) 220
Enough	15.1	13.2	14.9	10.1	5.6	(11.5) 69
Very much	2.2	8.8	6.8	5.5	13.3	(7.5) 45
Total number of respondents	139	136	74	109	143	601

Note: Cramer's V = 0.18 significant at 0.001 level.

TABLE 8.1C
The EU Strengthens Neoliberal Globalization (all numbers are in percent)

	Italy	France	Germany	Spain	Great Britain	Total
Not at all	3.6	3.0	2.4	1.5	6.1	(3.6) 22
A little	18.7	6.0	4.9	6.3	5.4	(8.6) 53
Enough	43.2	32.8	35.4	38.7	15.0	(32.3) 198
Very much	34.5	58.2	57.3	53.2	73.5	(55.5) 340
Total number of respondents	139	134	82	111	147	613

Note: Cramer's V = 0.19 significant at 0.001 level.

sensus among activists from different countries that the EU strengthens neo-liberal globalization; there is equally a shared mistrust in the capacity of the EU to mitigate the negative effects of globalization and to safeguard domestic social welfare models. Even if the Italians express a higher trust in the EU, and the British activists confirm their Euro-skepticism (followed by French and Spanish activists), the differences are still altogether minor. The

Table 8.2
How Much Do You Trust the EU? (all numbers are in percent)

	Italy	France	Germany	Spain	Great Britain	Total
Not at all	21.8	41.2	41.3	35.2	67.6	41.9
A little	56.3	46.3	48.8	54.6	29.0	46.3
Enough	19.0	10.3	10.0	9.3	2.8	10.3
Very much	2.8	2.2	—	0.9	0.7	1.5
Total number of respondents	142	136	80	108	145	611

Note: Cramer's V = 0.20 significant at 0.001 level.

data concerning trust in institutions (see table 8.2), confirms a deep criticism of the European institutions, with about half of the sample declaring a total mistrust in the EU, and a tiny minority expressing high trust.

The lack of trust in the EU has various sources. It can be traced back to the perceived democratic deficit, but also to EU economic and trade policies defined as neoliberalist in nature. The emphasis on free market and privatization, as well as the restrictive budgetary policies set by the Maastricht criteria are in fact stigmatized as jeopardizing welfare policies. The activists also criticize the European position on foreign policies as well as ecological issues, denouncing subordination to the USA.

We have to add, however, that the activists of the ESF express both a significant level of affective identification to Europe and a general support for the building of a European level of governance. First of all, about one half of the activists feel a sufficient or strong attachment to Europe. However, within the sample, there is less support from British and Spanish activists and more support from French, Germans, and Italians (see table 8.3). As for the potential intervention of multilevel governance institutions (see table 8.4b–d), the activists express little support for a strengthening of national governments but a

TABLE 8.3
To What Extent Do You Feel Attached to the EU? (all numbers are in percent)

	Italy	France	Germany	Spain	Great Britain	Total
Not at all	17.9	9.1	12.8	20.7	27.8	(18.2) 110
A little	29.3	31.8	29.5	49.5	31.9	(34.2) 207
Enough	45.7	43.9	37.2	28.8	26.4	(36.5) 221
Very much	7.1	15.2	20.5	0.9	13.9	(11.1) 67
Total number of respondents	140	132	78	111	144	605

Note: Cramer's V = 0.18 significant at 0.001 level.

TABLE 8.4A

In Your Opinion, to Achieve the Goals of the Movement Would It Be Necessary to Build New Institutions of World Governance? (all numbers in percent)

	Italy	France	Germany	Spain	Great Britain	Total
Not at all	24.1	15.3	31.3	11.4	21.3	(20.3) 123
A little	15.6	4.4	13.4	10.5	6.4	(9.7) 59
Enough	24.8	27.7	21.7	23.8	7.1	(20.8) 126
Very much	35.5	52.6	33.7	54.3	65.2	(49.3) 299
Total number of respondents	141	137	83	105	141	607

Note: Cramer's V = 0.18 significant at 0.001 level.

TABLE 8.4B

In Your Opinion, to Achieve the Goals of the Movement Would It Be Necessary to Strengthen the EU and/or Other International Supernational Institutions (Mercosur, Arab League, etc.)? (all numbers in percent)

	Italy	France	Germany	Spain	Great Britain	Total
Not at all	33.8	32.8	44.4	34.6	85.2	(47.5) 281
A little	28.1	18.0	22.2	28.0	5.6	(19.8) 117
Enough	27.3	25.4	14.8	25.2	4.9	(19.5) 115
Very much	10.8	23.8	18.5	12.1	4.2	(13.2) 78
Total number of respondents	140	123	81	107	142	591

Note: Cramer's V = 0.27 significant at 0.001 level.

TABLE 8.4C

In Your Opinion, to Achieve the Goals of the Movement Would It Be Necessary to Strengthen the United Nations (Giving Them Power to Make Binding Decisions)? (all numbers in percent)

	Italy	France	Germany	Spain	Great Britain	Total
Not at all	27.7	29.4	27.4	27.4	76.9	(39.1) 234
A little	18.4	12.7	14.2	14.2	7.0	(13.9) 83
Enough	29.8	26.2	31.1	31.1	6.3	(23.2) 139
Very much	24.1	31.7	27.4	27.4	9.8	(23.9) 123
Total number of respondents	141	126	83	106	143	599

Note: Cramer's V= 0.26 significant at 0.001 level.

TABLE 8.4D
In Your Opinion, to Achieve the Goals of the Movement Would It Be Necessary to Strengthen National Governments? (all numbers in percent)

	Italy	France	Germany	Spain	Great Britain	Total
Not at all	57.3	49.6	56.3	48.5	87.9	(61.4) 362
A little	26.6	18.7	27.5	25.2	4.3	(19.5) 115
Enough	14.0	20.3	11.3	15.5	5.7	(13.2) 78
Very much	2.1	11.4	5.0	10.7	2.1	(5.9) 35
Total number of respondents	143	123	80	103	141	590

Note: Cramer's V = 0.21 significant at 0.001 level.

strong interest in the construction of regional institutions. In this sense, they represent the social capital of committed citizens that, although critical, might represent an important source for the building of a European identity.

Although attachment to the EU, trust in the EU institutions, and agreement with the proposal of a strengthening of regional intergovernmental organizations (such as EU) are obviously correlated, there is, however, a high percentage of participants of the ESF that, although feeling attached to the EU or believing that EU level governance should be strengthened, do not trust EU institutions. We find that 67 percent of those who feel enough and 60 percent of those who feel very attached to Europe do not trust the EU (Cramer's V = 0.34 significant at 0.001 level); and similarly, 61 percent of those who agree enough and 54 percent of those who agree much with a strengthening of the EU level of governance do not trust the EU (Cramer's V = 0.41 significant at 0.001 level). Trust in the EU does not vary across either gender or educational level and is only weakly correlated with age.[56]

Whatever the outcome of the construction of a European-wide movement, the recent protests in favor of the welfare state mark the failure of the permissive consensus—or technocratic cover, as Hooghe and Marks[57] put it. Moreover, European integration produces increasing occasions for EU level protest. At the same time, however, similarly to the development of the nation-state, the presence of critical social capital may work as a challenge but also a resource for European institution and identity building.

Social Movements and Europeanization: Provisional Conclusions

In sum, there have been two ways of looking at the evolution of protest and European integration. On one hand, by way of observing protest as reported in the national press, several studies have emphasized the persistent targeting of national or even subnational levels of governance. From another direction, research on pressure groups has pointed to the mobilization of social movement organizations at the European level. As has been demonstrated in this chapter, the characteristics of Europeanization bent on the construction of a multilevel polity are reflected in the multilevel strategies on the part of social movements. In particular, this chapter has pointed at cases of domestication of collective action where the exercise of pressure on national governments is used to challenge EU policies. It has also been emphasized that externalization and protests at the EU level aim to change national policies. The former type of strategy is preferred by actors whose interests are traditionally vested in the nation-state and the latter by movement organizations addressing emerging cleavages. Both, however, aided in the creation of new structures and new frames for collective action. Indeed we noticed the emergence of a transnational movement addressing EU politics and policies.

Europeanization, therefore, has relevant consequences for social movements. Among others, a European social movement seems to be emerging in the guise of loose networks of organizations and individuals who increasingly organize common protest campaigns. It will be for future studies to determine to what extent the characteristics of the family of national social movements and domestic political opportunities reflect the characteristics of the movements for another Europe. However, it is possible to already delineate some elements of an emerging European movement, in which a set of organizations and discourses are interwoven in extremely flexible organizational structures, with identities that are tolerant of difference. Common denominators of such mobilizations that seem anything but a passing fad include demands for social rights and a democratization of European institutions, not least through the creation of a supranational, critical public sphere.

If multilevel mobilization presents the great challenge for European social movements, it also seems that the recent protests represent a challenge for EU integration. At the same time that the internal market was being liberalized, ever more and complex regulations as well as ever more powerful EU institutions emerged—although not comparable to those of the nation-states. Furthermore, the introduction of qualified-majority voting and the dominance of European laws in many areas are all elements that reinforce European institutions. However, they also make their democratic legitimization more problematic. Due to the weakness of a supranational public sphere, empowering the European Parliament is hardly an effective solution for the democratic accountability deficit from which the EU suffers. At the same time, functional interest representation, through mechanisms of consultation and dialogue, is not sufficient as a legitimation device, given the different organizational capacities (in particular at the supranational level) of the different actors. The search for output legitimization—at least in the technocratic sense of consensus obtained thanks to economic success—seems less and less credible when one bears in mind rising unemployment levels and economic inequalities across the EU.

By explicitly pointing to this failing and by attributing it to a political system that is hardly democratic and that relies on neoliberal policies, an emerging European social movement seems to have flagged one of the central problems of European integration. That problem is the weakness of a European identity that is able to carry out a similar function carried out by the nation in the construction of the nation-state. European social movements could indeed contribute to the building of a common identity: As with the nation-state, protest can stimulate citizens' integration, eventually contributing to institutional democratization and also legitimacy. Seen from this point of view, much will depend on the ability of EU institutions to construct civil, political, and social rights that can stand as the foundations of supranational citizenship.

Notes

1. Tilly 1984, 297–371.
2. Pizzorno 1996, 972.
3. Bendix 1964; Marshall 1992, 3–51.
4. Tilly 2004, 125.
5. Manin 1995.
6. Della Porta and Tarrow 2004.
7. Marks and Steenbergen 2004.
8. Della Porta 2006.
9. Bartolini 2002, 397.
10. For a comparative analysis, see Imig and Tarrow 2002, 195–223; for a review, see Della Porta and Tarrow 2004.
11. Giugni and Passy 2002, 433–460.
12. Rootes 2002, 377–404.
13. Parts 1 and 2 are a development of Della Porta 2003.
14. The survey was coordinated by Massimiliano Andretta and Lorenzo Mosca; Maria Fabbri was responsible for data inputting. I am grateful to Claudius Wagemann for his help with the analysis of the data.
15. We interviewed 1668 Italians, 126 French, 83 Germans, 106 Spanish, 143 British, and the remaining from other countries. The different size of country samples reflect the different share of national presence at the supranational meeting in Florence. However, when I used the sample to refer to the European movement in general, I weighted the responses in order to control for the oversampling of the Italian population. For the cross-national comparison, we have balanced the presence of Ital-

ians by extracting a casual subsample. Of the total number of interviewees, about half were born before 1977; 46 percent were women; 53 percent were students, 11 percent were unemployed or underemployed, 25 percent were dependent workers, and 7 percent were independent workers.

16. Della Porta and Kriesi 1999.

17. For a review, see Della Porta and Diani 1999.

18. Blondel, Sinnott, and Svensson 1998; Bardi and Ignazi 1999.

19. Scharpf 2002, 28.

20. Gerhards 1993, 96–110.

21. Le Torrec et. al. 2001.

22. See Eder and Trenz in this volume and Seidendorf 2003.

23. Della Porta and Caiani 2004.

24. See Putnam 1988.

25. The typology of Europeanized protest, proposed by Doug Imig and Sidney Tarrow, (2002) crosses over the national-international dimension both in terms of the actors of protest and their targets.

26. Imig and Tarrow 2002.

27. Bush and Imig 2001, 97–121.

28. In January 1997, the dairy farmers asked the government to suspend the collection of fines relating to the years 1994–1995 and 1995–1996 because of the irregularities committed by institutional organizations responsible for the matter, UNALAT and AIMA.

29. Cocca 2001, 191.

30. Cocca 2001, 159.

31. Cocca 2001, 69.

32. Cocca 2001, 64.

33. Cocca 2001, 145.

34. Cocca 2001, 188.

35. Cocca 2001, 189.

36. Cocca 2001, 193.

37. In a recent interview we carried out on the Europeanization of the public sphere (Della Porta, Donatella and Manuela Caiani, *Quale Europa?* Bologna, Il Mulino, 2006.), the speaker of the COBAS-latte stressed the importance of the European level for his organization and its support for an increased influence of the European institutions on agricultural policies.

38. Delorme 2002, 313–375.

39. On the discourse of the Confédération Paysanne, see Bové and Dufour 2000.

40. Chabanet 2002, 461–494.

41. Rootes 2002.

42. Lefébure and Lagneau 2002, 495–529.

43. These figures are taken from Eising and Kohler-Koch 2005a, 18. According to other sources, 67 percent of EU pressure groups represent sectors of economic interests, 9.6 percent the organised interests of professions, business, and labor, and only 23 percent public interests (Balme and Chabanet 2002, 59).

44. Rootes 2002, 382.

45. Marks and McAdam 1999; see Guiraudon 2001, 163–183, on migrant organizations.

46. Rootes 2002.

47. Rootes 2002.

48. Martin and Ross 2001, 57; see also Branch 2002, 279–312.

49. Hooghe 2002, 347–374.

50. Dehousse 1998; Balme and Chabanet 2002, 405–432.

51. Bartolini 2002.

52. Bartolini 2002.

53. Trenz 2002.

54. For instance, the European marches against unemployment in 1997 and 1999, see Chabanet, 2002, 461–494.

55. Andretta et. al., 2003.

56. Those who trust the EU (but not those who feel attached to Europe) tend to be slightly more trustful of political parties. In parallel, those who identify more strongly with the new global movements are more mistrustful of EU institutions, but feel only slightly less attached to Europe. Location at the extreme left has a stronger impact on trust and desire of a stronger EU than on feeling of attachment to the EU.

57. Hooghe and Marks 1995.

A COMMENT ON DELLA PORTA

Doug Imig

For years, the best answer to questions about the degree to which Europeans think about the European Union has appeared to be "not much." A range of studies have concluded that Europe is orthogonal to the concerns of most Europeans. This is particularly evident in studies of Eurobarometer data, where ordinary citizens demonstrate little understanding of the institutions and processes of the supranational state, and seem largely unconcerned with them.[1] Even in those arenas of social policy-making where the EU has been able to boast about high levels of public engagement and support (for example, on issues concerning the environment or on women's rights), it appears that that involvement has been largely invited, cajoled, induced, and heavily subsidized by the EU itself.[2]

But we should not equate this lack of interest in Europe with opposition. Even where citizens strongly prefer national to European policies and institutions—as in German allegiance to the Deutsche Mark—we do not find a concomitant anger toward European programs. (Those same Germans tend to like the Euro. Their equanimity has variously been explained as the product of the appealing design, or of the effective education campaign easing the introduction of the currency).[3] Researchers braced to study the protests accompanying introduction of the common currency were left with a story of a nonevent. Except for the grumbling of overworked French bank tellers, there was little organized opposition to the common currency at its introduction.

No wonder that observers have warned of the democratic deficit at the core of the EU,[4] and have grumbled that the supranational state is largely a contrivance of European financial interests. It is that unease with the public and democratic implications of the project of Europe that has motivated the quest for a European public sphere (the European Public Sphere project led by Donnatella della Porta, Ruud Koopmans, Paul Statham, and their collaborators).

That concern, in turn, has given particular significance to investigations of the Europeanization of protest. After all, we would reason, if the EU is the most developed supranational state in the world, then we would have good reason to expect that ordinary citizens increasingly would locate the source of their grievances within—and demand redress from—the institutions and programs of Europe rather than from individual national governments (with potentially profound implications for the traditional role of nation-states). In turn, Europeans should develop transnational, European organizations through which to express these grievances at the EU level. As Della Porta argues, historically "social movements have been important players in the emergence and evolution of the nation state . . . and the nation state is no longer the exclusive point of reference for social movements: sub- and especially supranational levels . . . have become increasingly important."[5]

In examining European protest, we begin to ascertain the ways in which Europe matters to Europeans. For example, Sidney Tarrow and I looked at protest within twelve member states over a fourteen-year period, and found that a small but growing share of all protest in those states concerned the institutions and policies of the EU.[6] Moreover, the evidence we examined suggested that the project of Europe actually does matter to ordinary people in ways that are specific and tangible.[7]

It was the austerity measures adopted by national governments seeking monetary union, for example, that led to the blockades and strikes of miners, machinists, and fishermen across the continent. And it was growing EU policy competence over agricultural policy that caused farmers to march through Brussels and to blockade the gates of Eurodisney (a ready proxy not only for European complicity, but also for American agribusiness and genetic modification).

As these examples suggest, during the 1980s and 1990s, the European project mattered in ways that involved the livelihood and well-being of ordinary people. Examining the issues that motivated a sample of nearly five hundred protest events explicitly targeting the EU and its policies, we find a marked clustering of protests around demands for protection against the neoliberal economic policies demanded by integration and monetary union.[8]

Given that Europeans perceived their grievances with the EU in local terms, it is logical that their responses were largely issue specific and located close to home as well. Protests were more likely to identify local rather than supranational targets, and the count and intensity of these events rose with key political events (including the development of the Maastricht and Amsterdam treaties), and followed the locus of decision making from the national to the supranational level and back again, as treaty development gave way to national implementation. Social actors also were inclined to turn first to their traditional repertoires of collective actions, which identified specific and local targets (leaving them on much less sure footing when making tentative forays against the EU itself. This was particularly evident in a higher level of violent

protests against the EU than against domestic targets during the earlier portions of our investigation.[9]

These findings led us to conclude that, at least in its early stages, protests
against European institutions and policies were much more likely to take the
form of the domestication of European issues rather than leading to the development of a truly European and transnational sphere of social movement
organizations and contentious political events. As Della Porta's essay makes
clear in examining the European Social Forum, the development of a transnational realm of European protest activity continues.[10]

Professor Della Porta is a key figure in the research on the Europeanization
of protest, and her essay for this volume is a welcome contribution that sheds
light on the ways in which social movement mobilization may increase the
EU's democratic quality. In particular, Della Porta tracks the emergence of
new, transnational, organizational forms. In the protest of Italian milk producers against fines, for example, producers banded together in organizations
that spoke to the traditions of social movements of the past, but which stood
distinct from the entrenched structures of earlier farmers' organizations and
unions and were designed to pressure their national government and the EU
more effectively.

The development of organizational structures capable of building and sustaining transnational mobilization is certainly a key to the development of a
European, or even of a global public. As Sidney Tarrow and his collaborators
have suggested, not all processes and mechanisms in the development of social movement campaigns are likely to have the same implications for the development of transnational movements.[11] In his ongoing examination of the
global justice movement, Tarrow has identified two key processes of scale
shift: diffusion, which is based on impersonal communication, and brokerage,
which is based on actors who bring together otherwise distinct groups.[12] Tarrow posits that diffusion will be more common than brokerage, but that brokerage will be more consequential in its impact, because "it is more likely to
identify common threads of interest and values between unconnected groups
and to produce sustained network ties among them."[13]

To this theoretical construct, Professor Della Porta offers tantalizing empirical insights, specifically concerning the events surrounding the European Social Forum. Della Porta identifies within the ESF a widespread European concern with the inequities inherent in European economic and social policies. In
this essay she presents some of the findings of surveys conducted with 2,384
of the some 60,000 activists who participated in the First European Social
Forum in Florence in November 2002.

This massive transnational movement event (and its successors) brought
together activists from all over Europe spanning associations and movements

that ranged from "Catholic to Green, from voluntary social workers to labor unions, from human-rights to women's organizations."[14] These activists were "well grounded in a web of associations," and spanned a "heterogeneous social base." They were multigenerational and had different ideologies.[15] The ESF appears to be a perfect example of scale shift through brokerage that Sidney Tarrow anticipates will have the power to leverage sustained transnational collective action. "If a global social movement is ever built, it will be through processes like a scale shift from the local to the national to the global level."[16]

Alongside the European dimensions of this event, it is the domestic, as well as the international and global dimensions of the European Social Forum that suggest a number of questions for further exploration. First, where should we place the European Social Forum along the continuum of transnational protest? At one level, this movement is certainly European, with activists banding together under the banner of "Another Europe," and arguing that the EU is complicit in the project of neoliberal globalization.[17] Certainly this is an ironic position: the project of Europe was ceded to neoliberal interests in part through the long silence of competing voices "from below."

But there is a further irony in that the ESF needs to be understood as not only a European but also as an international phenomenon in that its range of concerns spanned much of the global justice/anti-globalization agenda. In this sense, the advance of neoliberal globalization appears to provide a lightning rod for the formation of a collective European identity. As the survey data Della Porta presents amply attests, these activists largely concede the European project, and grumble instead over the effectiveness, trustworthiness, and ideology of the institutions of the EU in the face of globalization. Meanwhile, a number of observers have suggested that the organizations and networks that are sustaining the ESF are grounded within domestic rather than transnational political space, raising questions about the degree to which the ESF should be understood as transnational as opposed to being a much more traditional and domestic movement phenomenon.[18]

In sum, these findings suggest a provocative hypothesis: Organizations and networks such as those configured around the ESF may prove capable of sustaining a scale shift from the national to the transnational level. But perhaps it is the galvanizing potential of a shared antagonist—rather than the invitation to participate in a shared conversation about an alternative Europe—that sustains the process. Whether that antagonist is found in American multinationals aggressively campaigning for genetically modified foods or is found within the subversive forces of neoliberal globalization may be less important than that some external adversary is provoking European citizens to look beyond their immediate contexts and is causing them to consider the place of a unified Europe in the world.

Notes

1. Van Der Eijk and Franklin 2004; Marks and Steenbergen 2004.
2. Della Porta this volume; Rucht 2001; Helferrich and Kolb 2001.
3. Kaelberer 2004.
4. Schmitter 1996.
5. Della Porta, this volume, chapter 8.
6. Imig and Tarrow 2001.
7. Imig and Tarrow 2001, Trif and Imig 2003.
8. Imig 2004.
9. Imig and Tarrow 2001.
10. see also Norris, Walgrave, and Van Aelst 2003.
11. McAdam, Tarrow, and Tilly 2001; Tarrow 2005.
12. Tarrow 2005, 23.
13. Tarrow 2005, 23.
14. Della Porta, this volume, chapter 8.
15. Della Porta, this volume, chapter 8.
16. Tarrow 2005, 23.
17. Della Porta, this volume, chapter 8.
18. See Agrikoliansky, Sommier, and their collaborators 2005; Sommier 2003.

IV

DEMOCRACY AND
POLITICAL PARTICIPATION

9

Participatory Governance
and European Democracy

Hubert Heinelt

A BASIC CONSIDERATION in the ongoing debate on governance is that within modern societies the sphere of governance extends far beyond a state- or government-centered vision of policy-making. However, only from an abstract contractual point of view can one assume that the legitimation of a shift of competencies and power to particular governance arrangements to make and enforce societal binding decisions and answers to the questions of who should participate in them and how are developing from society endogenously, that is, without a political design by governmental institutions and respective forms of territorial interest mediation. In other words, the allocation or redistribution of power to certain governance arrangements is a political decision—or nondecision—of governmental institutions and forms of territorial interest intermediation. The same applies to the way participation is secured and decision rules are defined within governance arrangements. This is even more crucial considering that governmental institutions and forms of territorial interest intermediation, as well as interest intermediation within the EU polity and how they are functioning depends generally and particularly on the way the societally opened sphere of governance is structured and connected with governmental institutions and EU policy-making. This is not the least important for the democratic legitimacy of the EU.

The focus of this chapter is on democracy beyond the governmental structures in the sense of participatory governance. It starts from a summary of considerations which emphasize that governance of modern societies inevitably implies governance beyond governmental structures. Against this background, it is argued that it is a political task to turn the inevitability of governance into a participatory endeavor. Furthermore, different dimensions of governance (or governing orders) and connected forms of participation, as well as related models of democracy, will be highlighted. This will lead to a model of different worlds of democratic actions, which points to the importance of a complex and broad web of various forms of interest articulation and intermediation as well as decision making as characteristics of democratic political systems. Within such a web the concept of citizenship needs to be reconceptualized. It will be argued that the incremental and reflexive processes of identifying and recognizing actors who should participate are crucial in this respect. In starting to clarify such processes, the chapter will then look at the nascent debate concerning political capital. Finally, and against the background of the considerations developed in this contribution, some concluding remarks will be made with regards to how, especially within the EU multilevel system, actors possess the potential to participate in governing activities and affairs

The Inevitability of Governance

The manifold definitions of governance should not be presented and discussed here. This section will begin with some of the debate's main results:[1] Governance is seen as a fact, based on observations that the sphere of policy-making includes societal interactions not covered by the state or government-centered institutional structure of the political system. In this sense, policy-making is extended to society at large. This observation questions the traditional distinction in political theory between state and society. Consequently, participation in governing activities can no longer be perceived simply as a matter of being indirectly involved in governmental affairs through voting and through representation, but also through extended engagement in different forms of policy-making.

The creation of governance, or new forms of governance, beyond the governing activities of the state, is considered as closely related to actual transformations of the economic, social, cultural, and/or physical ways in which various aspects of collective life can be organized. This diagnosis is based on the following two observations. On the one hand, it is argued that system effectiveness[2] or governability can only be achieved through bargaining systems. This refers to global issues as well as to domestic ones, and it questions the sovereignty of the state and also the traditional forms of democratic citizen participation, that is, the vision of self-governing by mechanism of equal voting rights and accountable representation.

On the other hand, it is argued that societal interactions have become politicized in the sense that nearly everything impacts on or even concerns one's living and can become an issue of societally binding decisions, at least potentially. Regarding technological change, this is emphasized by Philip Frankenfeld's dictum: "To innovate is to legislate."[3] And what he highlights for technology also applies for other aspects of societal interactions and social change:

> Technology increases impacts of humans upon their world and upon other humans. . . . It creates power. It creates political communities or realms of common impact, often ex nihilo. Technology thus compels us to increase the reach and binding power of the politics and ethics through which we order human independence.[4]

One must realize that this is not a development of the last decade, namely the time in which the governance approach became dominant in the scholarly and political debates. On the contrary, it is a development that spans the last century. In this respect Michael Greven's[5] diagnosis is right that we are living in a *politische Gesellschaft*—a politicized society.[6]

What are the implications of such a diagnosis where (a) the sovereignty of the state and the abilities of people to influence their living democratically through societally binding decisions of representative bodies are limited and (b), at the same time, societal interactions are subordinated under the realms of binding decisions taken somewhere, somehow? To perceive these realms of accepting binding decisions as governance is important enough because they will be politicized. However, from a democratic point of view, this is only a first step. The next step should be to transform governance into participatory governance by enhancing the realm of democracy, that is, by bringing citizens back in.

To use Michael Greven's considerations as a point of reference, a fundamental politicization of society as such—or the ubiquity of governance—means nothing at all. It is well possible that the politicized society could assume a totalitarian or a democratic form. The latter is characterized by a multitude of forms of participation at various levels and, importantly, with real decisiveness. The former—far beyond the historical versions of totalitarianism—is characterized by forms of participation that are manipulated, guided, and extorted.[7] As Michael Greven argues,[8] this implies that the acceptance of a political system must not rely on mass mobilization as such or the dominance of majoritarian decisions. These (and especially a tyranny of the majority) can also be characteristics of modern totalitarianism. However, individual liberties and rights as means of participation in a broadened political sphere (*politischen Raum*) are making a difference. Specifically, the politicized society is the basis for a democratic society,[9] but it is a political task to turn the inevitability of governance into a dominant participatory form.

The Advantages of Participatory Governance

Participation is traditionally seen as a means to legitimize the decision-making procedures of the state. In addition, according to some traditions in democratic theory it is assumed that participation produces better results.[10] This is argued on several grounds. First of all, one basic normative assumption of democratic theory, starting from the idea of the natural rights of individuals, is that those who are affected by a decision shall be given a right to participate in the process leading to the outcome of that particular decision. Thus, even if the final decision is not based on their ideas, they have had the opportunity to make their argument heard. Secondly, participation by individuals with a broad range of interests, if undertaken in an open and free way, allows all participants to offer reasons for their position which aids in the elimination of egoistic and illogical positions.[11] Focusing on this reason (which can be classified a functional reason), one can summarize that participatory governance arrangements "would contribute in three distinctive ways to improving the quality of decision-making: (1) they enhance the opportunities for mutual accommodation through exchanges of reasoned arguments; (2) they serve to generate higher levels of trust among those who participate; (3) and this, in turn, allows them to introduce a longer time-horizon into their calculations since sacrifices and losses in the present can be more reliably recuperated in future decisions."[12]

Furthermore, it can be argued that against the background of societal complexity which makes "every practice . . . prone to failure, . . . governance [is] also likely to fail."[13] In the face of market, state, and governance failure and referring to Muecke[14] and Rorty,[15] Bob Jessop advises us to take the perspective of romantic ironists and to perceive participatory governance as a means of coping with the omnipresence of governing failures:

> In contrast to cynics, ironists act in "good faith" and seek to involve others in the process of policy-making, not for manipulative purposes but in order to bring about conditions for negotiated consent and self-reflexive learning. . . . [They] place self-organization at the heart of governance in preference to the anarchy of the market or the top-down command of more or less unaccountable rulers. In this sense self-reflexive and participatory forms of governance are performative— . . . they . . . become a self-reflexive means of coping with the failures, contradictions, dilemmas, and paradoxes that are an inevitable feature of life. In this sense participatory governance is a crucial means of

defining the objectives as well as objects of governance as well as of facilitating the co-realization of these objectives by reinforcing motivation and mobilizing capacities for self-reflection, self-regulation, and self-correction.[16]

Different Dimensions of Governance and the "Three Worlds of Democratic Actions"

Jessop places the often cited shift from government to governance in the context of the growing complexity and uncertainty—if not ignorance—of modern society. Like Kooiman[17] (see below) he uses the expression "meta-governance" to define the re-articulation[18] of different modes of societal co-ordination. These modes include[19] the ex post coordination through the anarchy of the market; ex ante coordination through imperative coordination by the state and hierarchy in all kinds of organizations as well as reflexive self-organization through ongoing negotiated consent in a corporatist order or horizontal networking.

In other words, "[Meta-governance] is the organization of the conditions for governance and involves the judicious mixing of market, hierarchy, and networks."[20] Jan Kooiman,[21] who distinguishes different governing orders, that is, first order, second order, and meta governing addresses the same topic with the expression meta governing.[22]

Meta governing can be linked to the formation of general or policy-specific images (or paradigms, *Leitbilder*, etc.). It is underpinned by communicative rationality based on dialogue or, more broadly on public deliberation. According to Kooiman, meta governing and the development of images imply a linguistic coding of problem definitions and patterns of action that are binding through ethical standards. In these kinds of interactions, participants can use their voice and influence the outcomes of debates by offering good reasons. For the development and creation of this kind of participation it is important to consider the distribution of voice-options and the conditions of being argumentatively influential.

First order governing is oriented towards operational actions or the "world of action"[23] with more or less narrow institutionally defined choice options.[24] This is the world of implementation and of administrative interest intermediation[25] where public administrations, their agents, and their supporters meet those addressed by a specific policy, or where policy addressees implement a program autonomously but related to influences on and by other actors.

Participation in this context means that those who are potentially affected by a policy must be involved in its implementation. Voice can again be an important element of such an engagement. But the importance of participation (by voice) in the context of first order governing is less related to ethics than effectiveness. This means that through participation the implementation of a program can be secured in line with policy objectives by taking the motives and concerns of the policy addressees into account. Furthermore, the willingness of policy addressees to comply can be secured by their participation. And finally, the knowledge necessary for achieving a given policy objective can be developed through participation. This underlines the importance of creating voice options as well as the circumstances and conditions under which specific actors can be influential.

However, there is another communication-based category of participation in the context of first order governing—namely bargaining. Bargaining rests on a specific kind of power which derives from exit options, the options of non-compliance or holding back relevant knowledge. This must be contrasted with debate-based forms of participation or with arguing, which can only be influential if good reasons can be put forward or if normatively more or less binding images are employed and developed at the meta governing level.

How do circumstances and conditions develop under which specific actors can be influential by voice or, more precisely, by arguing and/or bargaining? Only at first sight (if ever), does it seem plausible that they will totally develop endogenously in society or autonomously from politics. On the contrary, they are developed or established by political design and are related to certain statuses or features of citizenship. The political design of conditions under which specific actors can be influential by voice is more or less a task of what Jan Kooiman called second order governing.

Second order governing is geared towards institution building and the creation of policy instruments and/or programs. Effectiveness can be seen as a norm of second order governing as well just as in first order governing. By achieving effectiveness second order governing can acquire a specific kind of legitimacy, that is, output legitimacy. However, this kind of legitimacy is poor in a normative sense and insufficient when the sustenance and development of institutions—the political order—are concerned. It requires input legitimation through participation, and this form of participation relies on voice—arguing as well as bargaining—and on voting, that is, the equal right of all citizens to participate in systems of majoritarian decision making. In this context the traditional form of parliamentary participation is crucial for second order governing.

Due to the fact that second order governing is framed by meta governing, it can be indirectly influenced by the communicative rationality and the above-mentioned forms of debate-based participation. However, there are also options of a direct influence of debate-based participation, for instance, by different kinds of holders (see below) or even lobbying.

Against the background of this distinction between the three governing orders, it is possible to consider the interrelation between participatory governance and democracy, that is, between different forms (or common perceptions) of democracy (between the model of liberal and of deliberative democracy).[26]

- Liberal democracy stresses the individual's right to participate in general elections and, as a consequence, the aggregation of individual preferences to form guidelines for those in government and the option to make the latter accountable to the individual citizen. This form can be related to second order governing.
- Deliberative democracy puts emphasis on free, open, and public debate—and thus refers to the crucial element of participatory governance. This is important for meta governing as well as for first order governing. However, it has limited but not negligible significance for second order governing.

These considerations can be transformed in a model of "the three worlds of democratic actions"[27]: the world of meta-governance, the world of second order governing, and the world of first order governing (see figure 9.1). The

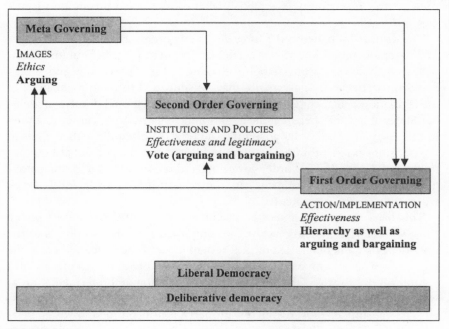

FIGURE 9.1
The Three Worlds of Democratic Actions

peculiarities of the different levels, as well as the linkages between them can only be sketched in this contribution. "One person—one vote" is only applicable in the world of second order governing, and the same applies for arguing in the world of meta governance. Besides the above-mentioned impact of meta governance in regard to framing second order governing (which is also true for 'framing' first order governing), second order governing is crucial in respect of creating conditions—and ways—of involvement in the world of first order governing, as well as in meta governance.

The democratic deficit attributed to the EU as well as to domestic policy-making is essentially an accountability deficit.[28] The necessity to solve it by placing emphasis on second order governing and voting by strengthening the ability of citizens as voters to express their preferences and concerns and to put pressure on their respective representatives should not be denied. However, the basic prerequisite for attaining accountability is through the transparency of policy-making and the public's ability to access information concerning the reasons and the reasoning behind why certain decisions have been taken in a particular context. Theoretically speaking, the black box where the input is converted into an output must be opened, either through extended forms of participation or through participatory governance. This presents the opportunity to establish what can be called throughput legitimation.[29]

The distinction between the three governing orders as well as the linkages to different forms of democratic participation can be quite helpful for an empirical analysis of European policy-making.[30] Meta governing and linked forms of participatory governance may be addressed through an analysis of the legislation debates at the EU level. Additionally, national debates in Member States about the specific policies and policy instruments can be analyzed in this regard. Second order governing can be scrutinized through analysis of the decisions on institutional settings and legal bases for policies at both national and EU levels. First order governing and related forms of participatory governance can be investigated on the operational—mostly local—level, where policies are implemented.

This brief attempt to show the usefulness of the outlined model of the three worlds of democratic actions for empirical analysis also points to the argument that a democratic political system is not to be conceived of as one regime "but as a composite of 'partial regimes'"[31] because it consists of a complex web of various forms of interest articulation and intermediation as well as decision making. This also means that in a democratic political system "citizenship, its most distinctive property, is not confined to voting periodically in elections. It can also be exercised by . . . joining associations or movements, petitioning authorities, engaging in 'unconventional' protest, and so forth."[32] However, this necessitates a redefinition, or reconceptualization, of the notion of citizenship.

From Citizens to Holders and Back

Participation based on citizenship is related to legal entitlement underpinned by the state, as the authority ultimately responsible and—because of the monopoly of power—capable of taking binding decisions. This is not only the case for the right to participate in elections. The same also applies to shareholders or owners whose legally secured property rights are the basis for their involvement, when specific collective decisions affect the private world of ownership. There can also be a legal entitlement for individuals to come together collectively and attain the legal (or licensed) status of a corporate actor involved in institutionalized forms of interest intermediation.

What do the assumptions about governance mean for the concept of citizenship? Since governing and the sphere of governance extend far beyond a state-centered vision of policy-making, citizenship-based answers to the question of who should participate seem to be insufficient. Against this background, Schmitter's reflections on holders, that is on "persons/organizations who could potentially be invited or allowed to participate [because] they possess some quality or resource that entitles them to participate"[33] are instructive. Based on the specific "quality or resource that entitles them to participate," Schmitter distinguishes specific holder categories (rights-holders, space-holders, knowledge-holders, share-holders, stake-holders, interest-holders, and status-holders).[34] Only one of them refers to "[r]ights that are attached to membership in a national political community and that presumably entitle all those having them to participate equally in all decisions made by that community. . . . In this case, the holders are usually called *citizens*."[35]

These distinctions can be very helpful in the empirical analysis because they enable researchers[36] (a) to classify governance arrangements according to the involvement of the different kinds of holders, (b) to identify changes in governance arrangements (for instance by marketization) as a result of shifts within the set of holders involved, and (c) to relate the effectiveness and legitimacy of policy processes to the participation of different holder categories.

However, Schmitter's answer to the question of who should participate is biased towards effectiveness because he concentrates on "the apposite criterion according to the substance of the problem that has to be solved or the conflict that has to be resolved."[37] In short, only those possessing some quality or resource to solve a specific problem or to resolve a specific conflict are entitled to participate. Based on Kooiman's reflections on the three governing orders—and the related model of the three worlds of democratic actions outlined above—this seems to be plausible for first order governing. However, second order governing and meta governing are also guided by standards other than effectiveness—namely legitimacy and ethics. Moreover, as will be shown at the end of this section, legitimacy and ethics play a role in first order governing as well. Legitimacy and ethics are important because the design of forms of participation and of entitlement is a political task in its purest sense, that is, a task based on an intentional and binding coordination of societal interactions.

To perceive the design of forms of participation and of entitlement as a political task and to relate it to standards of legitimacy and ethics is important, if it can be assumed that it is participatory governance that can bring democracy into the wider sphere of policy-making opened up by the shift from government to governance. This emphasizes the importance of the following question: How should the concept of citizenship be reframed in a way that the question of who should participate can be answered in a society in which governing extends far beyond a state-centered vision of policy-making?

To answer this question it is necessary to perceive citizenship within historical and dynamic conceptualizations, not simply within a static one.[38] This means that depending on changing societal conditions, one can (and should) imagine new forms of citizenship beyond the familiar civil, political, and social forms of citizenship. Consequently, the development of citizenship must be seen as a reflexive mechanism dealing with the negative consequences of societal change. As Roth argues, "[Due] to its dynamic character 'full citizenship' will never be reached but will remain always a goal.[39]

The way in which new forms of citizenship develop may be observed, for instance, in the cases of ecological and technological citizenship, but also for special statuses for ethnic groups or gender issues. What one can draw from the related political and scholarly debates is the following:

- New statuses develop incrementally and locally, that is, from the world of action, and not *a priori* by an authority ultimately responsible and capable of taking binding decisions.
- The relationship between a new status and the existing and constitutionally protected forms of civil, political, and social citizenship has to be clarified and determined. This is important because one cannot presume only positive feedbacks between the various types of citizenship.
- Unfortunately, there is not "one model of citizenship in the theory of democracy that can serve as a normative foundation."[40] "Therefore concepts aiming at a further democratization . . . by bringing the citizen back in will have to take into account that these efforts will have to address all the

differences and conflicts that already exist between liberal, communitarian, republican, and deliberative positions in democratic theory."[41]

- As an overall conceptual consequence one can argue that one should not construct new citizenships "apart from and unrelated to existing political 'polities.'" It is better to start "from existing democratically constituted and legitimated polities"[42] and the challenges "to existing democratic polities to introduce processes of a problem-oriented deliberation, in order to try to understand collectively what it means to be a 'citizen.'"[43] Whatever citizenship can mean, one aspect remains fundamental. Citizenship is based on a "status design" and is secured by the authority ultimately responsible for the political coordination of societal interaction, that is, the state.

This fundamental feature of citizenship can be related to Schmitter's holder concept in respect to the category of status holders. Particular holders have a status by being "recognised by the authorities ultimately responsible for decision and formally accorded the right to represent a designated social, economic or political category."[44] It can be argued that these holders have been recognized and formally accorded a specific right of representation because otherwise a particular policy runs the risk of losing or never acquiring legitimacy, or political and societal acceptance.[45] In this respect, the granting of a status addresses the effectiveness of a policy, not in a merely economic or technical sense, but in an essentially political way, that is, by addressing the issue of legitimacy. Usually, such a status is introduced in parallel to the politically defined and legally required procedures and contents of a specific policy. Such procedures and contents are crucial because the policy and the likelihood and/or credibility of its implementation are—in the shadow of (potential) political conflicts—politically and socially accepted only when the procedures and contents have been securely underpinned.

Maybe the term "ethics" is misleading because of its vagueness. According to Kooiman,[46] the term can be linked to images or paradigms. They are underpinned by communicative rationality which is concerned with what is good or bad, appropriate or inadequate for a whole society or for a specific sector of society. Provided such images have acquired the status of a shared "meaning system,"[47] they can have an influence on the answer to the question of political design for participatory governance. This is because such images influence the choice of the apposite criterion for identifying those who should participate based on the nature of the problem to be solved.

In summary, participation may be determined principally by effectiveness. Nevertheless, legitimacy plays a crucial role. To guarantee political and societal acceptance of political interventions, some actors are assigned a specific political status, permitting them to participate. Such a status implies bargaining power which can limit the discretion of other actors (for example, shareholders). Furthermore, particular images or common understandings are needed to agree on the apposite criterion for identifying those who should participate. Politically determined statuses and commonly developed images must be understood as elements for defining new citizenship, not just for defining holders. As mentioned above, such new statuses develop incrementally and locally. They are not simply constructed ex nihilo by an authority ultimately responsible and capable of taking such binding decisions.

Participation and Political Capital

These considerations on an incremental and reflexive process of identifying and recognizing actors who should participate can be linked to the nascent debate on political capital which reflects on (a) different resources permitting an integration in the political sphere and the achievement of political objectives as well as (b) the accumulation and mutual strengthening of such recourses.[48] Of course, legal entitlements are seen in this debate as crucial political resources, but emphasis is given to social networks and norms—not the least for making an effective use of the former. "Political capital, like social capital adheres in the relation between people."[49] The emphasis given to social networks and norms in this debate can be related to the considerations just outlined above insofar as social interactions and communication are crucial for developing and reproducing a common understanding of an apposite criterion for identifying those who should participate.

Furthermore, another issue links the consideration of an incremental and reflexive process of identifying and recognizing actors who should participate in the debate on political capital, namely the emphasis given to conflict as well as to consensus in the respective processes. Although it is stated in the debate on political capital that existing social capital can be used to create political capital,[50] it is also assumed that "it is quite possible, and very likely, that political capital may be acquired apart from social capital."[51] The main reason for this is that political capital can be based on and develop from confrontational or conflict strategies pursued by actors within closed social or policy networks—and not only from relations between amicably connected people, as usually assumed by proponents of the social capital approach.

Finally, the distinction between structural political capital and instrumental political capital drawn from concepts of political resources can be instructive.[52] Whereas instrumental political capital refers to "the resources which an actor, i.e. an individual or a group, can dispose of and use to influence policy formation processes and realize outcomes which are in the actor's perceived interest," structural political capital "refers to the structural variables of the political system which influence the possibilities of the diverse actors to accumulate instrumental political capital and condition the effectiveness of different types of instrumental political capital."[53] In accordance with our considerations, structural political capital, that is, structural variables of the political system, would include legal entitlement and legally fixed procedures and support schemes established by second order governing as well as shared images and meaning systems developed by meta governing through which political involvement should be mobilized and actors are endowed with opportunities to participate.[54] This formal empowerment has to be exploited by actors, and for doing so instrumental political capital is crucial which at least relies on relations between the actors enabling them to take advantage of certain endowments. Although instrumental political capital may play a crucial role in the sphere of first order governing, it is important for the other two worlds of democratic actions as well, that is, meta governing and second order governing.

Outlook: Towards a European Model of Democracy?

There is growing literature on the advantages, if not necessity of participatory governance in policy areas like planning, urban development, social inclusion, resource management, and so forth drawing on empirical cases all over the world.[55] However, there is some evidence that especially in the societies within the EU the shift from government to governance is complemented by a strengthening of participatory policy-making beyond the state and the core institutions of the EU. Especially within (or in some) sectoral European public spheres, one can observe processes of meta governing where images of good governance, which support and strengthen the participation of certain holders, are developed and reproduced. This is interlinked with a multitude of participatory practices in the sphere of first order governing. On the one hand, these practices rely more or less on different rules (if not statutes) set up by second order governing by the Member States. Furthermore, there is a substantial amount of evidence that these rules are spread by processes of policy transfer among the Member States. EU legislation supports such processes of spreading good (participatory) practice from one Member State to others. However, the EU has itself played a crucial role in designing participatory governance arrangements by creating and institutionally strengthening holders. This can be demonstrated by the rules governing the EU structural funds which have influenced governance arrangements. Furthermore, there is evidence in this policy field that participatory governance arrangements have contributed to the effectiveness of political interventions and of the legitimacy of EU policies in general.[56] However, differences are obvious not only between Member States but also between regions within a state which can be explained by differing structural political capital and instrumental political capital enabling actors to participate in the respective governance arrangements.

The same can be observed in the field of environmental policy within the EU. Especially in cases where policy instruments do not focus on certain contents but on the procedural framing of decision or policy-making, processes (like Environmental Impact Assessment/EIA and the Eco Management and Audit Scheme/EMAS) and holders received statuses to be informed, to be consulted, and to be actively involved in policy-making which reflects that new aspects of citizenship are evolving.[57] Respective rules set up by the EU, specified by domestic legislation, and adapted by and enforced at the operational level contributed to (a higher degree of) reflexivity in policy-making processes. However, this does not hold for all cases, and differences have been obvious, differences which can be explained again by variation in structural political capital and instrumental political capital accumulated by certain actors.

Notes

1. See Pierre 1999 and Pierre and Peters 2000 for an overview.
2. From the phrasing of Dahl 1994, 23–34.
3. Frankenfeld 1992, 460.
4. Frankenfeld 1992, 460–461.
5. Greven 1999.
6. A more direct translation, i.e. political society, seems inappropriate because the intellectual copyright for this term belongs to John Locke. Furthermore, the expression "politicized" seems to be more appropriate because it gives emphasis to an open process and not to a given status or the status quo.
7. Greven 1999, 140.
8. Greven 1999, 141–142.
9. See Greven 1999, 232.
10. For an overview, see Schmalz-Bruns 2002, 59–74; and Jessop 2002, 33–58.
11. In this context, Charles Lindblom (1965) developed an argument called the "intelligence of democracy."
12. Gbikpi and Grote 2002, 21.
13. Jessop 2002, 49.
14. Muecke 1970.
15. Rorty 1989.
16. Jessop 2002, 55.

17. Kooiman 2002 and Kooiman 2003, 170–187.
18. Jessop 2002, 49.
19. See Jessop 2002, 38f.
20. Jessop 2002, 49.
21. See note 18.
22. The following is based on Heinelt 2000, 2–5; see also Gbikpi and Grote 2002, 27–28 who used this source as well.
23. Kiser and Ostrom 1982, 179–222.
24. For the similar approach of the "three worlds of actions"—with a constitutional choice, collective choice, and operational choice level—see Kiser and Ostrom 1982 and Ostrom 1990, 50–55.
25. Heinelt 2002b, 97–120.
26. See Habermas 1992, 349–353; Habermas 1996b, 277–292; and Pierre and Peters 2000, 137–141.
27. To modify an expression of Kiser and Ostrom 1982.
28. Gbikpi and Grote 2002; for this debate see also Lord 2001, 641–61 or Majone 1998, 5–28.
29. Beside input and output legitimation; see Haus and Heinelt 2005, 14–15.
30. Heinelt 2002c, 15.
31. Schmitter 1993, 4.
32. Schmitter 1993, 4.
33. Schmitter 2002, 62.
34. Schmitter 2002, 62–63.
35. Schmitter 2002, 62.
36. Heinelt 2002c, 15.
37. Schmitter 2002, 63.
38. Like that of Marshall 1964.
39. Roth 2002, 79.
40. Saretzki 2002, 102.
41. Saretzki 2002, 102–103.
42. Saretzki 2002, 103.
43. Saretzki 2002, 103.
44. Schmitter 2002, 63.
45. This has been demonstrated empirically in Heinelt 2002a, 20–22.
46. Kooiman 2002, 76 ff.
47. Scott 1994, 70ff.
48. See Booth and Bayer Richard 1998, 780–800.
49. Fuchs, Minnite, and Shapiro 2000, 6.
50. Birner and Wittmer 2000.
51. Fuchs, Minnite, and Shapiro 2000, 6.
52. Birner and Wittmer 2000, 5–7.
53. Birner and Wittmer 2000, 6.
54. It should be mentioned that the debate on political capital can have a communitarian bias towards a pursuit of common interest and an achievement of shared political values (see Fuchs et al. 2000). But there are also other proponents emphasizing

that "there is also 'perverse political capital,' for example, in political systems which have institutions of repression" (Birner and Wittmer 2000, 6).

55. Any attempt to give an overview about this literature would be deficient. However, a few titles should be mentioned: Foley and Martin 2000, 479–491; Healey 1997; Fund and Erik Wright March 2001, 5–4; Grote and Gbikpi 2002; Heinelt et.al. 2002; Lovan, Murray, and Shaffer 2004; Haus and Heinelt 2005; Lowdes, Pratchett, and Stoker 2001, 205–222.

56. See Heinelt et.al. 2005, especially chapter 3.

57. See Heinelt et.al. 2001 and Heinelt and Smith 2003.

10

Some Considerations on Participation in Participatory Governance

Michael Th. Greven

The Political Concept of "Governance Arrangements"

OBSERVATIONS OF THE political science literature during the late 1960s and the early 1970s show prominent trends of themes related to participation. These trends initiated an enhancement of the typology for democratic regimes or at the least, theories of democracy. This is due largely to the fact that during and since the late 1960s and early 1970s, participatory democracy has been contrasted to representative democracy or other versions of democratic elitism.

After a long period during which the concept of "participation" had lost most of its relevance in public and scientific debates, a new concept, namely "participatory governance,"[1] has become a prominent topic in many publications—not least in the European Commission's White Paper on European Governance.[2] By no means are the elements of this topical concept self-explanatory or self-evident. Various definitions of "governance"and "governance arrangements" can be found in the political science literature. My aim is to raise some issues in the context of normative democratic theory, especially as far as the participation element of the topical concept is concerned. Hence, a very restricted version of the governance concept will be used, referring only to those governance arrangements where output affects nonparticipating and non-represented individuals and groups with a specific kind of authoritative allocation of values or regulation. As Renate Mayntz and Fritz W. Scharpf[3] have convincingly stated, one must distinguish between arrangements of "private self-regulation" of "internal problems of concerned groups" and sectors. This applies to private or public-private arrangements as well as to governance arrangements that have a regulatory binding or redistributive outcome for others who are not directly involved. The classical question emerging from the history of legitimate government regarding whether free citizens should obey arises in these circumstances for governance arrangements as well. Philippe C. Schmitter[4] answers this question convincingly when he states that "they [governments] have to root their legitimacy in distinctively political principles. . . . Just performing well will not be sufficient to ensure that their commands will be voluntarily obeyed." The accent of his statement seems to shift from legitimacy-based normative principles to mere functional obedience. This is a tendency frequently observed in the current discourse concerning participatory governance. In this chapter, I do not refer to what is referred to as "societal governance"[5] by Jan Kooiman,[6] or the fact that "many sectors in present-day societies largely govern themselves," but rather to the concept of political governance. Following this brief introduction of a restrictive, that is, political concept of governance I shall now focus on participation. It may be useful to start with a very brief summary and characterization of the first wave of discourse on participation.

Comparing Two Waves of Discourse on Participation: The Late Sixties and Early Seventies

The earlier discourse on participatory democracy focused on the participation of individual citizens within democratic frameworks, especially with a view to those participants who had been historically restricted by structural barriers or lack of social resources. Two prominent examples of such groups are workers and women. The increased participation of these groups within the public sphere was expected to result in less alienation.[7] Their subsequent emancipation—an almost forgotten keyword of those days—via self-determination[8] at the level of the individual and/or society at large[9] seemed to be at stake. One of the most analytically advanced publications of that time by Frieder Naschold summarizes a still convincing critique of democratic elitism,[10] the normative foundations of direct or participative democracy,[11] in the following way:

> As in classical theory of democracy, in empirical research participation also has to be conceptualised as instrumental as well as purposive in itself. Instrumental participation promotes the realization of individual interests which, even by a most benevolent elite group, cannot be appropriately perceived and fulfilled. But beyond the increased chance of satisfying individual material interests, partici-

pation [normatively] also has to be perceived as purpose in itself, which has to be seen in its therapeutical-paedogogical usefulness. Political participation offers the individual an *outside interest*[12] transcending mere private social existence and thus increases the meaningfulness of life.[13]

It should be noted that the instrumental dimension of participation in the above statement was perceived as such only in relation to the individual and his or her immediate gains. During this period, a reference to systemic or policy output effects of increased individual participation was presented in two very different versions. The most prominent version argued that increased individual participation on a mass level should not only lead to the democratization of the political system in a narrow sense, but also to all subsystems of society from families and education to the private sector and foreign policy-making. In this context, Fritz Vilmar argued for democratization as a strategy to bring about a gradual revolutionary system transformation of late capitalism and its class-based unjust rule structure into democratic socialism. Gradual regime change through massive and more or less permanent individual participation was thus explicitly meant as a functional equivalent and nonviolent alternative for a revolutionary strategy of elitist avant-gardes.[14] While the active majority of the Young Socialists in the governing SPD integrated participatory democracy in their *Doppelstrategie*,[15] the polemics of conservative authors such as Wilhelm Hennis and Helmut Schelsky perceived these processes as a real threat to individual liberties and representative democracy.

The intellectual and personal link between the two waves of the debate on participatory democracy can be seen in Fritz Scharpf's normative parallelization of participation and quality of policy outcomes as two equally important normative sources of legitimacy.[16] Scharpf already criticized the mere normative deductionism of theories of democracy, referring to empirical sociocultural traditions[17] focusing more on acceptance and satisfaction with policy output on the electorates' side than on participation. In logical and analytical terms this approach established a juncture between two different directions. One treated participatory input and satisfactory output as functional equivalents for legitimizing policies so that consequently a lack of participation could normatively be outbalanced by increased acceptance.[18] With a view to the other direction, participation could be connected to policy formation and output by the assumption that, given certain circumstances, participation would increase the problem-solving performance of policies and thus result in increased acceptance. This second line of argument had been developed in Naschold's study of democratic organizations—particularly political parties—but has now become related to the new field of policy research. This relation is the current linchpin for participatory governance. The shift from citizen participation (especially of those citizens affected by policy outcomes) to organizations, collective actors (like NGOs), and experts was already inherent. Coinciding with this change of the subjects of participation, the semantics and content of arguments changed from immediate interest representation of involved citizens to the increase of problem-solving capacity and the rationality of policy outputs. Jürgen Habermas's early philosophical theory of discourse as well as later deliberations by political scientists and policy research specialists fertilized the present prominence of deliberative democratic theory. This was conducted in the hope that increased participation under the specific rules of deliberative arrangements would also increase the rationality of policy outputs.

There are two essential shifts that occurred from the first to the present debate which can be summarized as follows: Firstly, participatory governance as it is employed presently refers to organized and/or collective actors without direct reference to individual citizens. Secondly, its main purpose and rationality is, as in, for instance, the prominent Commission's White Paper on European Governance,[19] to increase problem-solving capacity and, later, compliance and acceptance of policies and political regulation.

The first of a wave of debates on participation had in fact been a debate on the preferred structures and general aims of democracy from the individual citizen's perspective; it was also questioned whether it could be intensified and rendered more authentic as in the dominant Schumpeterian type of practice through individual and almost permanent participation. The claim for more participation questioned the traditional liberal split between the private and public spheres and institutions, between state and society, and culminated in the demand for the democratization of all life spheres. In its neo-Aristotelian version,[20] political participation was even perceived as the way of realizing humans' true destination as *zoon politicon*.

Currently, participatory governance also blurs the distinction between state and society and public or private action by various forms of public-private arrangements. However, it almost exclusively refers to those collective actors whose resources and cooperation are perceived as useful to compensate or overcome state—or market—failure in the provision of common goods or at least avoidance of common bads by cooperative action in governance arrangements.

While in the late 1960s and early 1970s participatory democracy had also been a strategy for some proponents to increase or unveil the conflict level of class or pluralistically divided societies, currently participatory governance, for the most part, presupposes a common perception of political and social problems, as well as the belief that cooperation leads to consensus and more rational policy outputs. What Robert Dahl called the "democratic dilemma," perceiving of "system effectiveness" and "citizen participation" as a kind of zero-sum game,[21] finds a theoretical pseudo-solution in recent approaches of participatory governance. This occurs by dropping the real citizens with their various and conflicting unlaundered preferences and replacing them, with nonelected and self-mandated collective actors.

Thus, beyond common terminology, the two waves of literature and discourse on participation have little in common. They also indicate two essentially different phases of modernization of democratic societies, both in their structural and material problems as well as in their perceptions. These two phases are not the result of voluntary decision making and action, but reflect objective and structural policy-making developments of recent years.[22] All those processes and developments which currently contribute to the "denationalization"[23] of governance especially seem to support what could be called the normative de-individualization of political participation. At supra- and international levels of politics out of functional reasons collective actors must play an almost exclusive role. Various kinds of collective and organized actors have always been present in national politics and policy formation. Among them political parties in normative and constitutional terms (depending on the political system) deserved normative priority and in some respects exclusiveness because their political participations rested on the notion of citizen equality, which was still viewed as the fundamental and ultimate source of democratic legitimacy and sovereignty of the people. While on the national level the participation of collective actors—other than political parties—had traditionally been perceived as an influence from outside the formal and legitimate democratic process of will formation and decision taking, in the present participatory governance discourse it also becomes genuine political participation which in tendency replaces citizen participation.

Some Problems of Participation in Participatory Governance

In what follows, a set of observations and clarifications of those analytical concepts which are frequently used in the present debate on the future of democracy will be outlined. Focussing on the literature concerning the EU system of governance, especially on participatory governance, does not imply that some of these problems are not also present at the national or subnational levels.

The first observation is more or less a methodological one—which also hints to my perception of the development of mainstream political science. While numerous recent contributions to the debate on democracy and democratic governance in the multilevel EU system of governance observe an ongoing and unprecedented fundamental process of changing conditions

and forms of policy formation, decision taking, policy implementation, and
acquisition of legitimation,[24] many contributions rarely inquire whether the
accumulative effect of all these changes may or may not in the end still result in some kind of democratic regime worthy of the label "democratic."
The contingent future of democracy seems to be taboo in political science.
As its inherent assumption suggests, in most cases this taboo is founded in
a lack of historical training or individual fantasy, restricting the possible
conceptualization and interpretation of empirical observations. Whatever
the kind and intensity of changes of principles, institutions, and practices of
present politics may be empirically observed, the tabooed perspective qualifies these changes *a priori* as changes within a democratic regime. In the
case of the EU as well as the world, these are perceived as steps of its democratization. In consequence it is seen as the original obligation and contribution of political scientists to provide the public discourse with the appropriate categorical changes and adjusted neologisms.

There are very few who imagine the possibility of evolutionary changes finally transcending or overcoming the historical regime form of democracy
and its fundamental normative principles. On the opposite hand, in order to
adjust the numerous empirical observations of *prima facie* undemocratic
phenomena with normative democratic theory, the latter becomes the target of numerous more or less radical reinterpretations and redefinitions, neologisms, and normative realignments. Simply put, the normative standards
become adjusted to the observed reality in order to reach the *a priori* pre-
tension that the object of observation still deserves the qualification of
"democratic" or "democracy." Klaus Dieter Wolf[25] provides us with one typical example, by arguing that in "any discussion about its [internationaliza-
tion of governance] re-democratization requires a set of appropriate normative criteria which must be compatible with the specific milieu in which
governance beyond the state takes place." This suggests that there is a specific milieu beyond which the democratic state restricts the search for appropriate and/or compatible normative criteria of democracy. It has usually
been the epistemic function of norms and normative criteria to provide the
basis for judgements on specific milieus, that is, empirical facts and circumstances, but this approach explicitly turns the relation between norms and
empirical realities at least partly upside-down.

Political science not only plays an important role in the process of "re-in-
terpreting the term democracy by drawing upon 'realistic' empirical observations"[26] but, at least in some debates in the field of democratic theory, it tends
to change its character from a normative evaluation of empirically observed
actual developments to an empirically based rediscription of normative concepts. In the first perspective, the final result of current changes may be the

observation of a fundamental regime change of former—more or less—democratic nation-states into—more or less—democratic supra- and transnational political regimes *sui generis* with a dedemocratizing impact on the existing nation-states. Referring to the same empirical observations, the second perspective[27] would redefine democracy or some of its traditional normative principles, and thus reach the conclusions that new forms and appearances of a posttraditional democracy are appearing.

The Ultimate Purpose of Participation and Participants in Participatory Governance

It is in this context that the new debate on participatory governance must be evaluated and discussed. If shifts of emphasis from the first to the second wave of debate on participation prove to be valid, then it indicates a fundamental and dramatic change in the normative as well as conceptual construction of democratic theory.

It seems as if the change from participation as intrinsic value for the individual citizen to a means for improved problem solving in complex governance arrangements deserves analytical and logical priority because the second shift from participation of citizens to participation of organized or collective actors and experts in various approaches only appears as its consequence. In the modern republican tradition of the late middle ages and relating these ideas to a specific, normative, and selective reception of the Athenian democracy, the democratic regime form had at first only been conceptualized as one type of organized and institutionalized system of rule among others. It was mainly characterized by two specific distinctions from other regime forms: the emphasis on political and legal equality of all citizens and on the fundamental equal right to participate in the political process. The latter is equated foremost as decision making on common laws. In representative systems this right was equated with voting equality. The Aristotelian system of six different regime forms and the negative normative evaluation of (classical) democracy is well remembered and remains influential. Modern democracy as a concept gained its positive normative connotations in political philosophy only when set in opposition to feudalism and absolutism. It foremost and originally referred to the question of the rationalist modern legitimacy of political rule- and lawmaking in the course of the French Revolution. As a consequence of the Christian interpretation and of stoic ideas, the notion of the individual as the bearer of natural rights gained more and more priority over the community; the new constitutional declarations started with the normative and logical primacy of the individual person and individual will and freedom (for example, human rights and the pursuit of happiness).[28] The fundamental legitimacy of all kinds and systems of rule and government was at stake. Against this background, the legitimacy of democratic or republican rule must remain problematic or even aporetic,[29] which is best observed in Jean-Jacques Rousseau's sophisticated and ambivalent construction of people's sovereignty and *volonté générale*, to which every citizen's personal will is contributing—as well as subdued to. But the argumentative construction of the fundamental contract, establishing what since has been called the "state" in continental modern political theory, serves only three original political aims: namely peace (i.e., absence of internal war), legal and political equality, and individual freedom—insofar as it does not interfere with the freedom of other citizens. These aims may be considered fundamental by all others, yet they do not legitimize any specific contents and purposes of policies. The right and opportunity of political participation was the procedural functional device through which this complex contract could be filled with political life.

What does this mean in our present context? Today, participation in participatory governance is perceived only as a functional contribution to good governance and policy-making and derives its legitimacy primarily from its value. Hence, the normative reference point is no longer the citizen with his or her preferences and opinions, but the presumed quality and rationality of the policy-making process or governance structure. It appears as if both normative reference points are compatible and not in tension or, even, in opposition to each other. This is the case in arguments like the aforementioned conceptualization of Frieder Naschold's theory of intraorganizational democracy. But organizations as voluntary communities of members cannot be used as an analogy of democratic political regimes as a whole, especially not where regimes and governance arrangements are concerned, in which membership is both uncertain and very often exclusive. A typical argument connects participatory governance with the normative concept of associative democracy,[30] thus assuming from the beginning that the participating actors in governance structures are representatives, "spokespersons"[31] of groups, organizations, and other types of collective actors. From a normative perspective three questions arise. The first one relates to the logics of collective action and asks whether the chances of participation in the sphere of associative democracy are at least as equally distributed as in those parts of democratic political decision making based on political equality—especially with regard to the election of candidates, voting in referenda, and democratic representation—which are derived from the OPOV-principle.[32] In many cases we know that the answer will be negative, given that the resources and opportunity structures of the pluralist system of interest and opinion mediation are selective, unbalanced, and more or less biased towards the resourceful individual as well as collective actors.

The second question relates to the kind of legitimacy of potential partici-pants in governance arrangements. It is very often assumed or implicitly pre-supposed that the rights of individuals and groups in a democratic order of an open society to express, organize, and pursue their interests and opinions already provide the specific kind of legitimacy required to participate in gov-ernance arrangements. This implies a categorical step away from the logics of the free public sphere of a democratic society, in which an individual is free to pursue his or her interests and express his or her opinion—be it as an in-dividual or through various kinds of collective action. While social inequal-ity of resources and power does prevail and is legitimate in the social sphere of the various publics of modern societies, the legitimacy of democratic pol-itics fundamentally and almost exclusively rests on the constitutionalized principles of legal but also political equality. Philippe C. Schmitter[33] states with reference to the multiple forms of collective actors of the civil society that "these organizations are not (and cannot be) democratically consti-tuted." This may be an exageration.[34] However, it is true that only the general accessibility of the democratic process by politically equal citizens provides legitimacy for the process leading to authoritative policy output. Since this equality is a political as well as a legal construct, it can only prevail in formal organizations and institutions—while the "informalization"[35] of governance arrangements is generally a threat to it.

The third problem is the typical principal-agent constellation. If, for nor-mative reasons, the citizens are the ultimate principles and all of civil society's actors their agents, how could the latter's pursuit of interests be controlled, es-pecially on a transnational level of governance? The proponents of participa-tory governance argue in favor of another and more selective way of recruit-ing potential participants in participatory governance. Two more or less representative examples deserve mention: Jürgen R. Grote and Bernard Gbikpi[36] express the opinion that "[regarding] the right to participate, per-sons/organizations should be entitled to participate depending on their pos-session of some quality or resource relevant to the substance of the problem that has to be solved." Thus, the right to participate is restricted and depen-dent on the possession of some quality and resources and not on the status as a citizen. Holders in a functional perspective[37] replace citizens in a normative perspective.

In light of all this, the following questions are worth asking. Who will make the decisions regarding the substance of the problem? In modern politics, is a problem always a problem for everybody, and is it the same for everybody? Which kind of qualities establishes the right to participate? Are the required re-sources for problem solving not dependent on the perception and framing of the problem at hand? How is it possible to guarantee the rights of participation in governance of those who disagree upon the definition of the problem and do not believe that governance is, in a particular case, necessary at all? While the democratic idea of the political process depends on the contingent articulation of the preferences of equal citizens—or their representatives—which inherently and incrementally leads to the construction of political problems and a possible agenda, the new approach of participatory governance rests on the very traditional premises of technocratic politics. In this framework, problems are given or defined by governance agencies and framed before the problem-solving process has even started.

Philippe C. Schmitter[38] has developed a detailed and sophisticated system of criteria which starts with the "logically prior notion of 'chartering' which rests on the presumption that a particular issue or policy arena is 'appropriate' for a governance arrangement." This appropriateness must be established by an authoritative decision before the establishment of a governance arrangement. It is not surprising that, according to Schmitter's[39] "principle of 'mandated authority,'" it is the Commission which would finally have to take this decision. Only two thoughts are worth mentioning at this point. Firstly, among all the institutions of the treaties, the Commission displays the widest gap between policy-making power and impact on the one hand and direct democratic legitimacy on the other. Secondly, agenda setting, combined with the institutional resources of chartering, staffing, and funding, are genuine resources of political power, as it can be empirically observed not only in the EU but elsewhere in the field of international organizations and institutions.

The statements above unveil that, implicit in this new approach, the political process is only perceived in the selective perspective of experts as a question of rational problem solving that could be performed better by experts than by anyone else. This is the traditional expertocratic approach of replacing citizens' democracy by technocracy. If the problem of power is considered at all, it is considered as a useful resource of governance or as an instrument of successful implementation and control.

Klaus Dieter Wolf has developed the idea that "formal authorization" to participate in governance structures, as a source of democratic legitimacy, could be analytically distinguished from what he calls "content based authorization". He mentions "expertise" or "morally based" authority or the act of "being an authority"[40] and proposes that these forms of authority should be valued as substitutes or equivalents of "formal authority." It is remarkable that this new approach has nothing to do with the argument for "output legitimacy" as in Fritz W. Scharpf's "complex democratic theory." Instead, he tries to find a source of legitimacy for the participation of collective actors or their representatives on the input side of the political process.

The same type of aforementioned questions arises when considering who is going to decide upon professional or moral authority especially in the case where more than one NGO exists in the same policy field. The problem of science-based authority and counselling is well researched and known as the experts' dilemma in public opinion formation.[41] Science-based expertise will usually be found with some authority taken on every position in actual conflicts. Scientific pluralism is no longer a problem just in the humanities. How, then, can the authority of science-based professionalism be established as one source of legitimacy for participation?

This discussion also raises the following issues. Is authority the same thing as public reputation? If more than one culture is concerned in governance structures—as it often appears to be in transnational governance—is its attributed authority or reputation stable and universal across cultural boundaries? Do the collective actors' claims and reputations for pursuing public goods really provide legitimacy in a pluralistic society where, very often with respect to the same policy problem, the claim is contested by competing collective actors?

Different Types of Decisions Require Different Types of Legitimacy

The last question can already be connected to a third group of problems inherent in concepts of participatory governance. In most cases, different types of political decisions are not distinguished in these approaches. In other cases, one possible type of decision is taken *pars pro toto* as typical for governance processes, leading to the same normative problems.

With respect to the functional necessities of government and participatory governance for societies or functional sectors, it is useful to distinguish between at least three different types of authoritative decisions: (1) allocation of public resources (including public infrastructures which, by their selective location, accessibility, and functional selectivity, are not always public goods in the strictest sense); (2) regulation of standards (rules in certain functional sectors, and technical norms); and (3) norm-setting in value disputes (as for instance the attribution of human dignity to unborn human life).[42] Even though in practice it is often disputed as to which category a decision demanded by certain proponents in the political process belongs, it seems as if most examples concerning participatory governance in the EU in the present context belong to the second category. This type of regulation in a functional or sectoral perspective seems to be the best fit to a notion of politics as rational problem-solving activity. Consequently, a discursive or at least negotiating type of

decision taking among the actors concerned[43] seems to be the most appropriate guarantee for a 'rational' decision and policy output.

But many decisions of this character have inherent allocative and sometimes also normative consequences for groups and individuals not participating or represented in the governance arrangement. Again the crucial question
relates to equality among citizens and the structural inequality of member-
ships in the civil society of voluntary associations. An example is found in
trade unions and business associations, as voluntary associations of workers
or professionals and employers in certain economic sectors. Since both are
voluntary associations they may represent a certain degree of membership on
both sides of this sector. This is not a problem if they negotiate a treaty for
their respective collective membership, because in a liberal civil society this
falls under the realm and jurisdiction of private law and the individual right
of free contracting property rights. But in the very moment when nonmem-
bers are affected by these private contracts a different form of legitimacy is required, which, on the normative base of liberal representative democracies,
can only be located in representative offices and institutions with legitimacy
derived on the basis of political equality. Citizenship in a democratic system is
not voluntary or optional[44] in the same manner as in civil society. As citizens
they are always affected by the policy output and norm-setting decisions of
parliaments or governments and, in the logic of democratic legitimacy, they
must accept and even obey these decisions for two reasons: First, in a formalized channel of interest expression on the input side of the political process,
they were regularly given the same chance of influence as all their cocitizens;
secondly, office holders in a democratic regime are themselves cocitizens with
equal rights and status elected to office just for a certain period of time. The
democratic system of government does not abandon the rule of persons upon
others, but given these two preconditions, it turns it normatively more acceptable and, to a certain degree, minimizes the risks of personal and permanent domination. Both conditions do not prevail in the realm of voluntary associations of civil society.

A Brief Outlook

The definition and understanding of democracy and democratic ways of
government are ultimately embedded in cultural self-perceptions and their
historical development. Currently, the discipline of political science tends to
neglect this evident cultural embeddedness but also the *a priori* historical
character of its concepts and contents. The dominant use of analytical con-

cepts in today's political science supports the impression that the professional discourse of political scientists should be strictly separated from other appearances of political thought. In the subdiscipline of the history of political ideas and theories, this artificial split has been questioned and criticized vehemently[45] and the consequences should be noticed also in current self-reflection of political thought.

Given this background, the present discourse on participatory governance whether with reference to global governance, the future of the European Union and its multilayer system of governments and governance arrangements, or within the nation-state, independent from the political or scientific background of the actor who expresses his or her views, represents and in many cases actively promotes an ongoing fundamental change of perceptions and normative justifications of politics. In this present rapid reformation, the common understanding and perception of concepts like "representative government," "democratic legitimacy," "citizen," "freedom, equality, and solidarity" are at stake in their traditional normative justification. The discourse concerning participatory governance, stimulated by more technocratic than democratic institutions like the World Bank, the European Commission, and hegemonic factions of policy-oriented political scientists, has recently been an important stream in this active concept-policy.[46] In part, the protagonists of this discourse may, without further reflection, believe in the seemingly democratic or republication promises of participation in participatory governance but evidently many of them, without recognizable scruples, already seem to have accepted the technocratic perspective of authoritative problem solving as residual of politics altogether.[47] A brief view into the history of politics—in the somewhat different case of the former socialist regimes of Eastern Europe, a view into a very present history—could at least help to irritate the illusion that technocratic or expertocratic regimes can be successful in the long run, both in their problem-solving capacity as well as in stabilizing their regimes. Politics always returns—the question is only whether the future will proceed with liberal democracy and individual freedom guaranteed against technocratic rule or something else.

Notes

1. Grote and Gbikpi 2002, 11–21.
2. Commission 2001a.
3. Mayntz and Scharpf 1995, 20–21.
4. Schmitter 2002b, 57.

5. It should be noted that the English concept "to govern" could be translated in German as "Regieren" (to govern) as well as "Steuern" (to steer). The first meaning should not be adopted for variations of societal governance for reasons of analytical clarification.

6. Kooiman 2002, 83.

7. Israel 1972.

8. Zimpel 1972.

9. Habermas 1961, 11–55.

10. Bachrach 1970.

11. These two concepts, at that time, had more or less been used as synonyms, while today the term "direct democracy" seems to be narrowed down in its meaning to plebiscitarian votes and referenda.

12. All quotations from German texts in this paper are my own translations.

13. Naschold 1969, 50f.

14. Vilmar 1973.

15. A mixed strategy of reformist parliamentarism and supposed anti-parliamentarian direct democracy.

16. Scharpf 1970.

17. Scharpf 1970, 7 and passim.

18. Interestingly enough, I never encountered the opposite proposition, where increased participation acts as a legitimatory balance to deficits in policy outputs.

19. Commission 2001a.

20. Arendt 1967.

21. Dahl 1994, 23–34.

22. Societies, in their reproduction through action and interaction, are permanently changing in many single aspects and never remain the same. Even if institutions and perceptions do not immediately reflect these changes, the distinction between two "phases" always remains the observer's construction. Also the objective and structural character of processes and developments rests, in epistemological terms, on the kind of perception and construction of reality by hegemonial social and political actors. This kind of knowledge opens the way for a deconstructivist critique of knowledge-based action paradigms dominant in current political and scientific discourse concerning governance, which is beyond the scope of this discussion.

23. Zürn 1998.

24. "Governance beyond the state . . . is primarily organized to the principle of functional differentiation. Governance without (world) government is basically composed of a system of sectoral regulations" (Wolf 2002, 38). It should also be noted that, in the history of national democracy, proposals for functional representation have been frequently made and sometimes practiced. For radical proposals of functional representation in "Spartenstaaten"—including the EU—see Burkhard Wehner (Wehner 1992).

25. Wolf 2002, 35.

26. Heinelt 2002b, 99.

27. Heidrun Abromeit (Abromeit 2002, 33 and passim) uses the term "affirmative reinterpretation" to characterize this kind of approach; if the facts do not fit the (nor-

mative) theory it seems easier to reformulate the latter so as to reach a normative verdict upon the former.

28. In this brief remark on contractualism, differences between the absolutist submission contract of Hobbes, the liberal trust-based version of Locke, and Rousseau's democratic version cannot be explained. The above mentioned *aporie* becomes evident only in the democratic version which today is more or less formed via human rights, the normative base of all recent versions of contractualism.

29. Siegfried Landshut, in a still brilliant reading from 1929, even calls Rousseau's approach a "theoretically violent solution" (Landshut 2004, 179).

30. Hirst 1994.

31. Schmitter 2002, 53.

32. OPOV (one person—one vote) is an abbreviation that was originally used by Claus Offe as "omov-principle" translated into the politically correct version; while there exist various forms of "representation" in religion, society, and politics, democratic representation strictly rests on the equality of those represented and the elected representatives.

33. Schmitter 2000, 34.

34. Since he explicitly included political parties in this statement—at least in the legal sense of the German law one has to oppose his judgment; in principle also member organizations of the civil society can in their internal structure be "democratically constituted."

35. As reference, see my previous paper focussing on the informalization of transnational government (Greven 2004).

36. Grote and Gbikpi 2002, 21.

37. Schmitter 2002, 62–64.

38. Schmitter 2002, 58.

39. Schmitter 2002, 61.

40. See table 3 in Wolf 2002, 199.

41. Nennen and Garbe 1996.

42. This type of decision has to rest on "democratic decisionism" (Greven 1999, 61–72) and not on any stronger version of "deliberative democracy" because remaining in the minority does not include also a judgment on the seemingly minor rationality of this minority. Therefore, the requirement for everybody to give good reasons for their position (Heinelt and Töller 2003, 11) tends to become illiberal.

43. Most authors like Schmitter use the term "affected"—but *de facto* the collective actors involved in governance arrangements very often represent more "concerned" than "affected" groups, because of the "crucial matter . . . [of] how affected actors are to be defined" (Schmitter 2002, 56, 57).

44. The exit option may today exist almost in every political system—since it is not symmetrically paired by a membership option in democratic regimes everywhere, citizenship cannot be taken as an analogy of optional membership in a liberal civil society.

45. K. Palonen's (Palonen 2003) book on Quentin Skinner and the collected works of the latter (Skinner 2002) could be used as an introduction.

46. "Begriffs-Politik" (politics with concepts) in the sense of Reinhardt Koselleck (Koselleck 1975).

47. One of the great scholars of political science and public law recently reminded us that in the aftermath of the Second World War, Nazi political elites all over Europe were deeply mistrusting the democratic process despite developing democratic systems. According to Helmut Ridder (Ridder 1995, 554–565) the early treaties on this background intentionally reserved important sectors of the economy to nondemocratic bodies of experts. For more than thirty years, no serious dispute about a democratic deficit of this technocratic regime appeared.

A COMMENT ON HEINELT AND GREVEN

Paul Magnette

The transformations of governance induced by the process of European integration are hardly original. That legislation can be passed outside the Parliament was already noticed by the first generation of pluralist theorists. In the years before and after the First World War, social scientists like Georges Gurvitch in France or Harold Laski in Britain studied in detail the negotiations between the social partners on the one hand, and the mushrooming of international organizations on the other hand, and concluded that this parallel change led to complex forms of multilevel governance—although they did not use the phrase. Neither are the normative implications of these changes really new. That decision-making processes involve a wide range of actors (well beyond the narrow circle of elected and accountable politicians), from experts and technocrats to trade unionists and lobbyists, and that this tends to blur the distinction between the private and public spheres, was also noticed by the authors of this generation. Some of them even endeavored, like the American philosopher John Dewey, to forge a new paradigm of democracy by dwelling on the democratic virtues of these innovative processes.

Still, the European Union has opened a new chapter in this unending discussion. Because it concentrates and accentuates long-term trends, it is often and rightly seen as a laboratory of political innovation. In the last twenty years or so, dozens of authors have undertaken to coin new concepts to capture its peculiar mode of governance, and to assess its democraticity (to speak like the EU Commission in its White Paper on European Governance). What these authors rarely do, however, is to discuss the normative foundations of these allegedly new forms of governance. With very few exceptions,[1] EU scholars tend to assume that the principles of democracy are the object of a wide consensus and that they do not deserve to be redebated. Paradoxically, even those who convincingly argue that the EU should not be seen as a state use the concepts formed within Western states to assess the EU's democratic quality.[2]

Michael Greven and Hubert Heinelt are right to draw our attention to this often neglected dimension of the current debate on democratic legitimacy in the EU. Indeed, the core concepts of democratic theory are challenged by the everyday functioning of the European Union. The Community method, combining the initiative of the Commission, the legislative work of the Council of Ministers and of the European Parliament, and the consultation of a wide range of *ad hoc* committees, makes it very difficult to decide who should be held accountable for the decisions taken on behalf of the EU. The very notion of accountability becomes problematic in this context, as was powerfully illustrated by the mad cow crisis in the end of the 1990s: Decisions can be taken, and eventually have terrible effects on public health, and the authors of those decisions cannot be identified and sanctioned. In view of such failures, one can be tempted to adhere to Robert Dahl's skeptical conclusion that "in practice, delegation might be so extensive as to move a political system beyond the democratic threshold."[3]

So-called new modes of governance only make the situation more intricate. When wide fields of market regulation are left to coregulation by stakeholders, when deregulation is prompted by the court's jurisprudence, or when wide ranges of organized interests are consulted upstream and downstream from the actual decision, one is entitled to wonder if the concept of representativeness still makes sense. The EU Commission itself, despite its efforts to guarantee a fair balance between the interests involved in the decision or consulted by the EU institutions, acknowledges that it is hard to agree on criteria defining an actor's representativeness. Beyond formal criteria, political inequalities also flow from deeper inequalities in the distribution of political capital and cognitive resources among organized interests.[4]

Greven and Heinelt are also right to draw our attention to the broader epistemological consequences of this situation. Faced with this kind of conceptual doubts, many authors argue that the EU forces us to revise our democratic concepts, without always measuring the risk of undermining the very concept of democracy. One such strategy consists of stressing the peculiar nature of the tasks fulfilled by the EU, and arguing that regulatory policies such as those made at the EU level do not call for representative politics but should rather leave more room to independent experts and impartial judges.[5] Yet, our two authors remind us that these distinctions are fragile—most regulatory policies do in fact have a distributive and/or normative effect—and that highlighting the efficiency of a given decision-making process does not exempt us from assessing its democratic quality, since the two aims (efficiency and democracy) ultimately have their own normative foundations.

An alternative revisionist strategy consists in showing that the EU praxis is in fact based on the same normative premises as representative democracy, and that it only differs in the way it implements them. If democracy is basically about submitting decisions to a fair process of open and public deliberation, as is nowadays widely assumed in political theory, then the EU, or some of its aspects, may be seen as an instance of deliberative democracy.[6] Some even argue that deliberation in the EU is, at least potentially, more open and more participatory than is usually the case in its Member States. To be sure, refusing to examine the democratic potentials of new institutions and procedures, on the pretext that democracy has been primarily represen- tative hitherto, would be a dogmatic option. Yet, one should not underesti- mate the risk of seeing the nature of democratic theory shifting from "a nor- mative evaluation of empirically observed actual developments to an empirically based re-description of normative concepts" to use Greven's words. Addressed to those scholars who plead for a creative interpretation of the EU as an original form of deliberative democracy, the critic would be un- fair. Charles Sabel or Christian Joerges, to name but two authors, have clearly indicated the epistemological status of their reconstruction: like Habermas's communicative rationality, their interpretation of the EU as a deliberative forum is a normative ideal-type, which is drawn from an empirical evalua- tion of the EU as it now stands, but which also aims at criticizing it on the grounds of the ideals it only imperfectly actualizes. However, many EU actors are less prudent: The debates generated by the preparation of the Commis- sion's White Paper on Governance published in 2001 have shown that the temptation to use a vague deliberative phraseology to legitimize their praxis is widespread within EU institutions.[7] True, the Commission and the Eco- nomic and Social Committee referred to the epistemic value of participatory practices in their reflections on governance and on the role civil society could play in the EU. Arguing that broadening the range of actors involved in the decision-making process tends to improve the quality of the decision, they seemed to echo Lindblom's claims; pleading for a constant evaluation of EU policies by experts and stakeholders, with a view to revise them permanently, they seemed to follow Dewey's argument in favor of democratic pragmatism. Still, contrary to Lindblom's and Dewey's claims, the Commission's view re- mains biased towards efficiency. The functionalist spirit of the origins, of which the EU never fully got rid, indeed encourages a shift from "participa- tion as intrinsic value for the individual citizen to a means for improved problem-solving in complex governance arrangements."[8]

Despite their skepticism, Greven and Heinelt do not succumb to the temp- tation of pure criticism. In France—and to a lesser extent in Britain and Italy—many scholars have recently described the EU as the gravedigger, not just of democracy but of politics itself. Philosophers like Marcel Gauchet, Pierre Manent, or Paul Thibaud—whose opinions are published by the lead- ing French journals of political theory—see the EU (and transnational gov- ernance more generally) as a framework which substitutes expertise, the market, and judicial adjudication for politics. In Britain, Larry Siedentop's bestseller on *Democracy in the European Union* was in the same tune. In the eyes of these authors, conflict resolution within the EU is unpolitical (and *a fortiori* undemocratic) because it conceals the issues, breaks civic equality, and ultimately undermines the major function of politics: helping people make sense of the collective fate. Some conclude that the EU should be politicized along the lines of a parliamentary state; others support the view that the historical nation-states remain the only forums for democracy. Beyond their divergences, these authors at least agree that new modes of governance have nothing to do with democracy. At their best, they are technocratic routines completing the democratic process; at their worst they threaten the very foundation of modern politics.

Greven and Heinelt are far from these radical positions. Their attitude could be labeled reformist. Indeed, rather than rejecting the institutions and procedures whose compatibility with democratic criteria is disputable, they argue in favor of a stronger reassertion of the democratic principles in the EU, so as to make sure that where new modes of governance subsist, they are submitted to superior democratic standards. How this should be done is not entirely clear, as the two authors do not contemplate the institutional details of a democratically reformed EU. But they seem to agree on at least two points. First, it is necessary to distinguish more clearly different levels of decision-making processes—what Hubert Heinelt calls meta, first, and second order governing. This would make it easier to identify different negotiation styles, associated with different issues, and to refine the diagnosis. Second, once one has reestablished a hierarchy of levels of governance, topped by meta governance (which seems synonymous with what lawyers would call constitutional principles), one could reassert the primacy of the democratic standards, and make sure that they are respected at the lower levels of governance. How exactly these democratic principles should be defined, whether they should be codified in a constitutional charter or not, how they would apply to different modes of governance in the EU, and who should be in charge of guarding them (the governments or parliaments of the Member States, the European Parliament, or the European Court of Justice?) remains unclear, but the basic principle is simple: New modes of governance may be tolerated to the extent that they are submitted to something like a democratic review. Then, the danger to shift from democracy per se towards democracy as an instrument of efficient policy-making would be warded off.

Leaving its empirical vagueness aside, the argument would need two additional clarifications at the normative level to be fully convincing. One would like to know why democratic principles should be put first. After all, what the citizens actually call for, if we can trust Eurobarometer surveys, are efficient policies ensuring their security and defending their socioeconomic interests.

From a social-democratic point of view, this is as important as the inclusiveness and transparency of the decision-making process.[9] Besides, from a liberal point of view, the protection of citizens' rights is the first priority, and liberals, from Benjamin Constant and Alexis de Tocqueville to Judith Shklar, have seen no problem in taking democracy as a means serving this aim. Nowadays, the idea that the EU's legitimacy depends on the capacity the citizens and the states have to limit its encroaching upon their rights remains quite popular in academia[10] and in large sectors of public opinion. Before thinking of how to restate the primacy of democracy as a purpose in itself in the EU, one should explain why democracy should prevail over these equally respectable values.

On the other hand, the authors might also face the question of the transferability of democratic principles formed within states to a nonstate polity. To put it in other words, they might take Dahl's skeptical view seriously. If all that is possible in a multilevel governance is a highly attenuated kind of responsiveness, we might come to the conclusion that describing undemocratic systems as democratic is vain, and begin to think of the standards we should use "to appraise an international organization after we have concluded that it is desirable despite the costs imposed to democracy by its bureaucratic bargaining system of government."[11] After all, conflict prevention and peaceful negotiation have their own value, whose normative foundations are as respectable as those of democracy.

Notes

1. Majone 1998; Craig 1999.
2. Moravcsik 2002.
3. Dahl 1999, 21.
4. Kohler-Koch 1997.
5. Majone 1998.
6. Joerges and Neyer 1997a; Eriksen and Fossum 2000a; Gerstenberg and Sabel 2002.
7. Magnette 2003.
8. Greven, this text, chapter 10.
9. Scharpf 1999c.
10. Moravcsik 2002.
11. Dahl 1999, 34.

11

The Organization of Interests and Democracy in the European Union

Beate Kohler-Koch

IN RECENT YEARS, a new discourse has been introduced to the academic and political debate on European interest intermediation attracting much attention in the media and scholarly debate. The focus is not any longer on the influence of interest groups on public policy-making but on the democratic potential of closer public-private cooperation. Though the trendy catchwords are civil society and participatory democracy, the debate did not originate in a bottom-up process but was initiated by those in power and has the clear characteristics of an engineered discourse: As a response to the slim victories in some referenda which were held in the aftermath of the Maastricht Treaty negotiations and the decreasing popular support of the European integration project indicated by the Eurobarometer surveys since the early 1990s, the heads of states and governments called for "a Union closer to the citizens."[1] The Commission on its part provided an important impetus by framing the debate with the publication of the White Paper on European Governance.[2] It is propagating a wider involvement of civil society for the sake of efficient and democratic governance. The Commission already adhered to that principle when preparing and launching the White Paper: In the preparatory phase it engaged in extensive consultations with representatives of organized interests and the academic community, it organized and stimulated a broad public debate after publication, and since then provides incentives for more thorough investigations on the conditions for and linkages between European citizenship, civil society and EU democracy[3].

More importantly, however, the publication of the White Paper was followed by concrete measures with which the Commission aimed to provide a new foundation for the cooperation with organized interests, referred to by the White Paper as "civil society."[4] The term carries different connotations in EU documents. Sometimes it is used to express the idea of active citizenship and the notion of organized civil society refers to associations working to the benefit of the general interests.[5] When the term is defined explicitly, a broader concept applies and civil society is considered to embrace voluntary associations of all kinds and not just public interest groups.[6] In the follow-up process to the White Paper, the Commission issued guidelines and standards for the consultation of and the cooperation with organized interests[7] and extended related instruments such as online consultations, open online discussions, and an online forum for interactive policy formation.[8]

With the Economic and Social Committee (ESC) the Commission has found an enthusiastic partner in this regard. In the middle of the 1990s[9] the ESC was still clearly seen as a representative of economic and social interests advising the lawmaking institutions on common market policies. In the course of the new debate on civil society it changed its role ascription to become the "indispensable intermediary between the EU institutions and organised civil society."[10] This aspiration is backed up by the treaty revision of Nice[11] and the Constitutional Treaty rephrasing its composition to include "parties representative of civil society."[12] The aspired role change from a consultative body of functional interest representation to "a bridge between Europe and organised civil society"[13] will not be achieved without any frictions given the accentuated role of employers' organizations and trade unions within the tripartite structure of the ESC. Both groups are reluctant to give up their privileged position and have raised concerns that the political weight of the social might suffer from an enhancement of the civil.[14]

Nevertheless, the ESC has successfully launched different kinds of initiatives to close the gap between demands and constitutional reality. It has pressed ahead with the opening up to a broader and mainly EU-level audience by organizing public fora which serve both as platforms and contact points for advocacy networks. Those are predominantly used by representatives of common interest groups committed to the principles of participatory democracy and for whom the ESC—resourceful and well established— is an instrument to enhance their role and status.[15] Since the ESC has no command over its own composition and members only represent national associations, it further aimed to institutionalize closer cooperation with EU-level organizations and networks by creating a "liaison group with organised civil society."[16]

Finally, the idea of direct and close cooperation between EU institutions and European civil society has been reinforced by the adoption of the principle of participatory democracy in the Treaty establishing a Constitution for

Europe.[17] The provisions of Article I-47 carry explicit marks of the new understanding of democratic governance propagating the increasing prominence of unmediated channels for citizen participation. The article stipulates EU support for citizens and representative associations to make known and publicly exchange their views and calls upon the EU institutions to maintain an open, transparent, and regular dialogue and carry out broad consultations with parties concerned.

The notion of participatory democracy is by now widely accepted in the debates about the role of organized interests in European affairs. By taking a closer look at such debates it is evident, however, that the term is used as a label for competing concepts and objectives.[18] From an analytical point of view the involvement of societal groups in the decision-making process at the European level aims likewise at

- expanding the knowledge base to increase the quality of EU policies,
- making public administration accountable to society as a whole,
- achieving an all-embracing mobilization of political interests and enhancement of direct participation of citizens,
- creating a trans-national democratic public sphere.[19]

The conceptual ambivalence of participatory democracy and civil society does not come by chance. Ambivalence is useful since it is open to divergent interpretations and it is inevitable since it reflects an ongoing and dynamic process of conceptual framing. The idea to take rescue to organized interests in order to fight the EU's democratic deficit gained momentum in a few years time. Along with a shift in substantive orientation went a shift in terminology. The debate started with reflections on improving governance performance by enlarging the expert basis of EU institutions with the help of interest groups, then turned from output to input legitimacy by emphasizing open access, transparency, and responsiveness, and finally concluded with the codification of participatory democracy as constitutional principle. The thematic reorientation was accompanied by a change in terminology: The dialogue with "special interest groups"[20] was rephrased to "partnership" with "NGOs"[21] and followed by the slogan of "involving civil society."[22]

In the ensuing sections, it will be asked whether the new strategies of involving civil society have a democratic potential. Democratic potential stands for an improvement in the conditions of governing in a way that the basic criteria of democratic governance are met as they have been formulated by normative theories of democracy. Seeing that there is no theoretical consensus on conditions and criteria, I will take the different perspectives offered by liberal, deliberative, and participatory theories of democracy.

First, in line with liberal theory, I will explore whether the politics of open dialogue and the new consultation strategies are likely to help redress the unequal representation of interests. When democracy is equated with a marketplace that is governed by a regime of fair competition, any provision that improves the representation of the plurality of interests, provides equal access, and furthers representativity will bring a value added.

Secondly, I will turn to deliberative democracy. Proponents of deliberative democracy are more demanding than proponents of liberal theory: Since deliberative democrats want to go beyond the aggregation and trading of given preferences, they ask for institutions that support a discursive structure of opinion formation. The benchmark to be met is not the plurality of actors but the range of competing views that get a fair treatment. A promising consultation regime has to operate in the shadow of the law and in the shadow of the future. Private, informal meetings with EU institutions, one shot interventions, and one way communications will not induce actors to take account of the legitimate interests of others and to communicate about the validity of good reasons.

Thirdly, an equally demanding concept of democracy values participation as an essential part of democratic life. Associations are valued not just because they are instrumental to the well functioning of democratic rule but because political participation marks an essential condition in the making of an emancipated citizen. Procedures and regulations that work against political consumerism, that activate citizens, and that provide incentives to reach out from the grassroot to the EU level would be rated positively.

Lastly, I will discuss the emergence of a European, transnational, public sphere which is considered to be a necessary condition in different strands of democratic theory. European-wide awareness of what is at stake in EU affairs is a minimum condition even in the parsimonious concept of liberal democracy. It is a prerequisite for turning voting power into an instrument of political control. Information is, however, not sufficient to make democracy work. All theoretical concepts ask for a well-functioning system of transnational communication. Any improvement in the patterns of communication that reach beyond elite circles and contribute to the emergence of a European public sphere will be considered a democratic asset.

Assessing Liberal Democracy: The Politics of the Open Dialogue

The cooperation with interest groups is seen as an important ingredient in redressing the democratic deficit. In contrast to former proposals which highlighted the contribution of information exchanges with organized interest groups for the quality of European policies,[23] the White Paper on European Governance provides a new impetus by stressing the Commission's commitment to the "involvement of civil society."[24] This new conception aims at giving greater consideration to representatives of general interests and at the inclusion of the individual citizen into the process of consultation. This envisaged expansion of societal participation promises to yield a double legitimacy gain: The consideration of a broad range of preferences and information confers legitimacy both from a procedural and an output-oriented perspective.

Hitherto, there has been a wide variety of practices of consultation among the various Commission Directorates, ranging from *ad hoc* consultations to institutionalized consultations in committees. Since the 1990s, however, the Commission has increased its efforts to expand and institutionalize the inclusion of organized interests of civil society. Democratic participation shall be attained by following the guiding principles of openness, transparency, and inclusiveness. The debates preceding the adoption of the White Paper and the implementation of the principle of participatory democracy have demonstrated, however, that the new strategy has an Achilles heel and it did not meet the unanimous support of interest organizations on several grounds.[25] Objections were raised against the redefinition of civil society and the commitment to a more formal institutionalization of relations. Whereas the professional lobbyists welcomed the broad definition that put them on an equal footing as legitimate representatives of civil society with general interest groups, the latter qualified it as an usurpation that must be prevented.[26] At the heart of this controversy are different concepts of legitimacy but also competing interests because a change in terminology affects the political standing of an organization and as a consequence its relative weight in the decision-making process. The same holds true for the institutionalization of EU-society relations. Organizations with well-established working relations to EU institutions are not enthusiastic to see their competitors advanced and, therefore, bring up shortcomings such as the lack of flexibility which might exclude newcomers and stakeholder interests on special issues. From the viewpoint of liberal democratic theory, institutionalization may cut both ways: It enhances transparency and has the potential to provide for more equality, yet it undermines the competition between organizations in the political market and conserves the gatekeeping power of a not democratically legitimized authority like the Commission. To limit the discretion of EU institutions a definition of specific criteria have been proposed to guarantee equal opportunities for access and to ensure the representativeness of the included organizations. The question of how to assess the representativeness of those organizations included in the process of consultation and opinion formation has proven to be a particularly contentious issue. Irrespective of the consensus that both quantitative indicators (membership, activities, age) and qualitative indicators (autonomy, internal democratic procedures, expertise) shall be borne in mind, it is considered a difficult task to do justice to them all, given the plurality of organizations.[27] A more comprehensive formalization of criteria, however, is against the interests of organizations that reject interference in their internal affairs.

By introducing the instrument of online consultations, the Commission aims to take equally into account the principles of openness, transparency, and inclusion: Every proposal that is to be decided upon is made public, every citizen and every organization is invited to comment, every petition can be read online, and the Commission reports about the results at the end of the process. However, practice has shown a number of fundamental tradeoffs and procedural shortcomings[28]: Openness does not correct for the inequality in interest representation. The responses to the consultation guidelines provide a case in point. Here, state actors and economic actors tend to be overrepresented while the advocates of more diffuse interests are underrepresented. This imbalance is, on the one hand, a reflection of the different resource endowments of different groups, and, on the other hand, it also reflects differences in political cultures which is indicated by the geographical bias towards the Nordic countries.[29] Inclusion, that is, the invitation to all affected actors to express their concerns, will necessarily lead to an information overload that forces the Commission to select among the inputs.[30] Moreover, online consultations on controversial regulative measures are likely to produce vast input of varying quality.[31] One strategy to avoid this problem in the future would be the use of those devices, such as a questionnaire, that prestructure responses by providing substantive guidelines and formal procedures. However, as the example of the regulation of chemicals has demonstrated, despite great efforts to preserve political neutrality, preformulated response items are likely to restrict choices one-sidedly.[32] No matter how successful the Commission is in ensuring transparency in the preparation and handling of consultations, there is no guarantee that transparency can be preserved in the course of their evaluation. This could only be achieved if legally binding guidelines for the justification of regulatory proposals were developed that are as strict as those formulated by American administrative courts. However, this would come at the price of a further judicialization of European politics.

Assessing Deliberative Democracy: Opening Supranational Deliberation for General Interests?

Fair representation of interests and of opinions is not sufficient alone to allow us to draw conclusions about the possible gain for democracy. John Stuart

Mill has already stressed that among the crucial facets of a representative system is not only the election and control of representatives, but also the institutionalization of deliberation: Policy positions should be heard, weighted, and rejected only in the face of superior, reasonable arguments.[33] Research on deliberative democracy[34] has advanced the debate about EU democracy, since the transfer of a state-centered model of majoritarian decision making does not look promising, given the structural specificities of the EU.[35] However, it is not implied here that a deliberative democratic upgrading of the EU polity will have to move governance to "decentralised processes of decision-making in deliberative arenas."[36] The purpose of this analysis is rather to examine whether new procedures of consultation will provide an impulse for deliberative processes and forms of decision making at the EU level that counterbalance the interstate bargaining processes and self-interested representation of particular interests.

Such a counterbalance is not seen as including ever more interests or giving preeminence to representatives of general interests, but as a choice for procedures that require reason giving for positions and their justification in respect to the solution of the problems at stake.[37] For authors who perceive of deliberation as a convincing response to the objections against the legitimacy of the European project, it is the institutional and normative framework that makes the difference and not the constellation of actors. The theorem of *Deliberative Supranationalism* highlights the contribution of European law for "transforming strategic action into deliberative problem-solving."[38] Within European law rules and principles structure the decision-making processes to the effect that they "narrow down the range of arguments that are admissible within debate so that only generally reproducible and justifiable grounds or concerns . . . can be used."[39] Furthermore, these rules and principles "promote pluralist discourse and the presentation of all relevant viewpoints" and force participants "to generalize their arguments . . . with an eye to the legitimate . . . concerns and interests of those who do not directly participate within the committee system."[40] The authors mention and have tested a range of indicators to make their assumption plausible with respect to the comitology system. But will it also function in institutionalized relations between EU institutions and organized civil society? The general principles of European law and the rules and practice defining appropriate behaviour in EU negotiations quite obviously spill over into arenas of consultation.[41] But other institutional conditions limit deliberative interaction. Consultations, by nature, are open-ended and because the final decision will be taken in another arena, participants are not under pressure to arrive at a common understanding. The Commission cannot afford to leave the consultation process with tight hands and associations will not compromise on an issue when other channels of interest representation are still open and look more promising. Furthermore, participants do not communicate on equal footing because of the asymmetric power relation between the Commission and the representatives of nongovernmental associations in terms of controlling the agenda and making use of consultation input. To make deliberation work, consultations have to deal with substance and have to be organized in an iterative process.

Therefore, it is not so much due to inappropriate institutional design of the respective body that most of the newly created forums for consultation do not live up to the expectations of the participants. For example, members of the European Consumer Consultative Group (ECCG) deplore that it is just a medium for information of a very general nature.[42] The European Consultative Forum on the Environment and Sustainable Development (ECFESD) is another case in point. Even though its structures meet the demands for equal geographical and political representation, openness and transparency, it neither lived up to the standard of deliberation nor did it bring about increased participation of interested actors. The ECFESD was barely consulted by the Commission and, during its first four-year existence, only on two occasions was it able to reach out to the larger public.[43] The shadowy existence of the ECFESD and its insufficient linkages to societal actors at the grassroots raise doubts whether such a forum can meet the expectations of deliberative politics. According to Habermas, "Deliberative politics acquires its legitimating force from the discursive structure of an opinion- and will-formation that can fulfil its socially integrative function only because citizens expect its results to have a reasonable *quality*."[44]

The introduction of procedures for assessing the consequences of proposed legislation is another starting point for procedural rationality.[45] It is intended that these procedures lead to a process of decision making that is as transparent and rational as possible and, at the same time, identifies affected actors that could be approached for specific consultation.[46] Moreover, the creation of specific online services maintained by the respective Commission Directorates providing interested actors with regularly updated data and developments within a policy area is thought to ensure the provision of high-quality information. There is thus an aspiration that in the future, the justification of European policies will not exclusively rest on the knowledge of professional experts but also on reasonable arguments that can be introduced by representatives of general interests. The objective is that participation and efficiency should reinforce each other. Providing easy access to knowledge is, however, just a necessary and not sufficient precondition for a discursive debate that is open to all relevant positions.

Assessing Participatory Democracy: The Contribution
of Organized Interests to Participation and Citizenship

The institutionalization of EU citizenship in the Maastricht Treaty and the adoption of the Charter of Fundamental Rights as well as its inclusion in the Constitutional Treaty is an expression of the qualitative change of the European system of governance and concomitant political demands: Whereas the notion of the "market citizen" was sufficient for the European Economic Community, the creation of a European Union added political rights to existing economic rights. However, the rights to political participation have remained rather rudimentary until today, a fact to which many observers attribute a major share of the EU's democratic deficit.[47] In the light of the historical and theoretical link between citizen rights and the demand for political participation, the political debate about citizenship—which was triggered to a large extent by European institutions—nurtures the hope that their adoption will actually lead to more political participation in the EU. This assumption implies that particularly those nongovernmental organizations that act as advocates for general interests in the EU will become the catalysts for enhanced participatory politics. In the tradition of Tocqueville participation is valued not just as an instrument to give people voice but as the ingredient of true democratic life: When citizens associate freely and are "pursuing in common the object of their common desires."[48] they gain the spirit, the experience, and the skills that elevate them to critical and active political citizens.

In this vein, some observers see the increase of transnational activities of such groups in recent years as evidence for a gradual democratization from below. However, empirical studies analyzing the role of EU associations in the tradition of Alexis de Tocqueville[49] conclude that these organizations are only insufficient schools of democracy in the European multilevel system.

Even though it is true that the public relation efforts of these groups and their advocacy for specific political goals create public attention, yet a considerable number of organizations are not enthusiastic about rendering their own political activities more transparent. Many associations rather aim at improving general support from a large constituency because it promises to yield greater political weight and higher revenues. Another obstacle to include members and supporters in a substantive inner-organizational debate is the lack of knowledge of EU affairs even among politically interested supporters. Thus, within several organizations a lack of incentives, scarce resources, and deficient grassroot response are accumulated: The agenda is set by activists of the association and systematic mechanisms for exchange with supporters are almost non-existent.[50]

Warleigh[51] hence concludes that even organizations that are committed to represent general interests neither contribute to the development of a transnational civil society nor do they act as socializing entities or ensure the participation of their supporters in any other significant way. This assessment is supported by investigations of groups active in European migration and asylum policies respectively.[52] Weak political mobilization is a general phenomenon also in well-established liberal democracies. But the complexity of the European multilevel polity and the well-known obstacles to transnational communication and coalition building aggravate oligarchic predispositions. The empirical studies also point out that the criteria for participation in EU programs discriminate against grassroot organizations: Such groups are usually not able to fulfil the requirement of designing and implementing projects involving transnational cooperation.[53] EU level associations explicitly reject funding criteria demanding the involvement of a high number of national associations because this would prohibit smaller organizations to get access to funds.[54] Though the explicit objective is to further transnational cooperation, EU policies may in practice create additional obstacles and, furthermore, lead to different resource endowments in civil society.

However, other studies are less sceptical. The European Women's Lobby (EWL), for example, has intensified the relations to its national member organizations and improved both mutual communication and transnational cooperation. In particular, the campaign for the inclusion of rules of equality in the Amsterdam Treaty triggered a learning process about the European institutions among their national members. The national associations not only participated in the EWL decision process and helped mobilize female supporters in public rallies for a change of the European Treaties,[55] but they also increased their autonomy from state institutions.

Three conditions for successful member participation can be derived from existing case studies: Vertical communication and cooperation within the multilevel structure of interest group associations will be stronger (1) when the Euro group is dependent on its members' expertise, (2) when successful interest representation demands coordinated action at both the Member State and at the European level, and (3) when the choice of instruments includes the simultaneous use of an insider and an outsider strategy. As long as Euro associations can take recourse predominantly to independent sources of expertise and pursue their interest dominantly with insider strategies on the European level, their linkages to their national members remain weak.

However, the restrictive supply of transmission belts for multilevel interaction is also a response to a lack of demand. Citizens who want to promote general interests such as the protection of the environment or consumer rights, human rights, rights of immigrants, or gender equality look for someone to represent them rather than becoming personally engaged. They do not opt for converting into an activist and equally do not feel obliged to participate directly in decision making and agenda setting. As a survey of European NGOs has revealed, the supply of associations has already saturated the demand for political participation: "NGO supporters do not wish to use these organisations as a means of active citizenship. Instead, supporters wish to delegate responsibility to organisations whose broad aim they support even if they are ignorant of and might conceivable oppose, these organisations' policy stances on a range of issues."[56] Based on a comparative study of national environmental groups, Jochen Rose arrives at the same conclusion.[57] He explains this phenomenon by pointing at diffuse objectives and the general trust evoked by members and supporters respectively.[58] There is also much plausibility in the interpretation that links the behavior of European citizens with that of economic agents: Environmental groups offer themselves as experts for environmental policies with different profiles and of different quality and are purchased for the services they provide. Consequently, the demand for political influence is satisfied and there is no need for further interaction.

Overall, the empirical evidence is sobering, yet it does not come as a surprise. Just like in the national realm, general interest groups are a minority at the European level and they are dependent upon the support of EU institutions. EU-associations have structural difficulties to act as schools of democracy. Their performance is low even when compared to Latin Europe where associational life is much weaker than in the Germanic Northwestern part of the continent[59] and even when sharing the sceptical view that also at the national level associations have a limited capacity to effectively fulfil this function.[60] The reason is obvious: The majority of these EU associations are composed of national groups and not of EU citizens. When they are built on private membership or support they mostly act as political entrepreneurs in the market of public opinion. Their democratic effects are thus highly contingent. They depend on the particular relations to national associations and the structural conditions under which these operate.

Though they may not bring about the democracy enhancing effects that have been attributed to associations by De Tocqueville, they nevertheless can function as agenda setters and provide a counterbalance to state and economic actors. By providing an intermediary infrastructure they support the articulation and bundling of societal interests and are also able to give their own impetus to the definition of these interests.

The Mobilization of a European Public Sphere

Finally, it has to be asked whether the activities of societal groups at the European level contribute gradually to the emergence of a European public sphere. All theories of democracy regard the existence of a public sphere as an integral part of democracy. However, the liberal tradition sees a more modest form of public as sufficient for democracy[61] compared to protagonists of deliberative democracy who ask for an active civil society engaged in public discourse. In the liberal conception of civil society, the public is there to guarantee the weighing of self-interests and the effective control of politics; its main function is to legitimize the exercise of political power. In the democratic conception based on discourse theory, citizen communication strives for a common understanding concerning efficient and appropriate problem-solving strategies and has a substantial impact on the decision-making process of representative institutions.[62]

An impact of interest politics on the EU level—the interaction of European institutions and societal groups—on the evolution of a European public sphere is most likely to happen when controversial issues are at stake and political responsibility is attributed to the European level.

In recent years, the EU institutions initiated several campaigns with the declared goal of creating awareness for specific issues throughout Europe. The European Year against Racism in 1997 serves as a case in point. Usually, such campaigns reach out for an affirmative public and offer an opportunity for the institutions to play to the gallery. However, given a shared view in substance and by providing financial incentives, the EU has been able repeatedly to co-opt a number of societal groups at the European, the national, and subnational level. Their participation not only broadened the range of opinions but also increased the public's awareness of these campaigns. However, if one examines the impact of these campaigns by the amount of media attention they generate, one can quickly realize that the capacity of these campaigns to contribute to a European public sphere are limited. Coverage of national news is still dominating: Most attention is paid to national but not to European actors, activities at the local but not at the European level find their ways into the news, responsibility is attributed to local and national actors but not to the EU.[63] It can thus be concluded that these campaigns contribute only at the margin to the creation of a transnational public.

The response of the public to such campaigns is more lasting when groups in opposition to EU intentions take up the issue and propagate alternative views. The interplay of contrary arguments increases the demand for public justification.[64] The more plausible a debate can be framed as a competition between the *raison d'état* expressing a narrow self-interest of those in power on the one hand and the autochthonic interests of civil society on the other, the easier it is to create a critical public. These findings confirm the general observation that public awareness is often the product of deliberate action. However, only a few interest organizations, such as Transparency International or the European Citizen Action Service (ECAS), see the creation of a public sphere which promotes discursive debates and good governance as a goal in itself. Public relations activities normally aim at the mobilization of societal support to achieve specific policy goals. This is true for farmers' associations, trade unions, and business groups as it is true for the feminist movement campaigning for equal treatment in EU law. The question thus is whether the politicization of single policy issues that do not affect civil rights directly can set in motion a European public sphere. The hypothesis of democratic functionalism assumes that a pluralization of the public will emerge as a consequence of such sector-specific sub-publics.[65] The authors believe that political projects will continue to be accompanied by a critical debate sometimes on core issues, sometimes in response to unintended consequences or side effects; they also believe that the EU institutions themselves will become increasingly aware of the necessity of public justification. According to their view, this will initiate a process of gradual democratization. The argument that public relations activities are used as both a marketing strategy and as a tool of power politics does not invalidate this conclusion.[66] Thus it is an empirical question whether issue-specific controversies promote the emergence of a critical public. When citizens become progressively more receptive for political debate and open to take sides on general issues beyond narrow stakeholder interests our normative aspirations would be satisfied. Over the last decade, the discourse has become increasingly political and the focus is not just on specific EU policies, but also on the shape and structure of the EU polity and its policy-making procedures. Even though many debates are still restricted to a small circle of transnationally connected elite circles, the awareness of EU affairs and the readiness to publicly challenge EU policies has increased significantly. The referenda on the Constitutional Treaty and, in particular, the rejection of the ratification in France and the Netherlands has prompted a controversial and vivid debate across Europe. Yet, the political reality does not fully match the notions about a European public sphere derived from Republican thought or from discourse theory.

To sum up, the role perception of organized interests at EU level has changed dramatically in recent years. The desire to redress the democratic deficit has nourished a debate that attributes organized interests the potential of a transmission belt conveying the plurality of interests to the EU institutions and bringing Europe closer to the people. Since the conceptual framing is ambiguous and vague, it is not surprising that the change in rules and procedures governing EU society relations do not live up to the proclaimed high principles. Furthermore, it is doubtful whether procedural reforms can overcome the institutional impediments of the EU polity and the national self-reference of European societies. Nevertheless, the normative claims and the more inclusive consultation strategies have given general interests a stronger voice and have strengthened the legitimacy of arguing over bargaining. Policy formulation and decision making at EU level has become more transparent and has attracted more public attention. Especially associations interested in the advance of European civil society are eager to exploit the concurrence of growing awareness and normative claims in order to trigger a "virtuous circle." Notwithstanding the good intentions of EU institutions and sympathetic associations, it is quite obvious that they pursue their own agenda. The Commission, in particular, takes a patronizing attitude, is often overselling the democratic quality of its exchange with interest organizations and citizens, and is inclined to give preference to its teaching function. The response to the failed referenda in France and the Netherlands is telling: The Commission issued an action plan to communicate Europe.[67] The wavering dedication to democratic legitimacy and the inclination to oversell achievements in participatory democracy may very well result in undermining the credibility of the whole project.

All things considered, I come to a cautious conclusion: Taking account of the institutional interests of the main EU actors, the unfavorable features of the EU polity, and the low level of societal integration, it is plausible to assume that institutional engineering will not have a strong effect. It might even not work to the benefit of democratic participation and a European public sphere because partly it is based on some glaring misperception of aims and instruments of democratic governance. On the other hand, the normative discourse and changed patterns of behavior have had some positive results and this may build up over time not so much as the result of the intentional strategies but because of unintended consequences due to the dynamics of raising expectations as to what the EU should be about and opposition to what it delivers.

Notes

An earlier German version of this text is incorporated in a joint article with Rainer Eising (Eising and Kohler-Koch 2005). Stefan Goetze's help in translating this contribution and comments by Berthold Rittberger are gratefully acknowledged.

1. The Turin Council 1996.
2. Commission 2001a.

3. Kohler-Koch 2003, 433–437. See, for example, relevant publications (e.g. de Schutter et al. 2001), conference proceedings (e.g. Europe 2004—Le Grand Débat, Commission 2001b), and the topics suggested for research in successive Research Framework Programmes.

4. Commission 2001a, 14.

5. See Commission 2002c, 24.

6. In the White Paper on European Governance the Commission borrowed the description of different categories of civil society organizations arrived at by the Economic and Social Committee (1999, 30). The definition reflects a liberal concept of civil society that rates any voluntary association as good as any other. In this definition the Commission departs from a tradition that conceives of the importance of civil society in terms of promoting the common good and political participation of citizens. See Cohen/Arato (1992) for a comprehensive theoretical treatment of this issue. A more recent overview can be found in Klein (2001).

7. Commission 2002a and more recently: Commission, Green Paper European Transparency Initiative COM (2006).

8. These forums can be accessed under www.eceuropa.eu/yourvoice (last accessed Janury 2007).

9. Art. 193 ECT–Amsterdam.

10. Commission/Economic and Social Committee 2001, paragraph 4.

11. Art. 257 ECT–Nice.

12. CT Art. I-32.

13. ESC homepage www.eesc.europa.eu/index_en.asp (last accessed January 2007).

14. See Economic and Social Committee 2001.

15. See, for example, the conference on "Participatory Democracy: Current Situation and Opportunities Provided by the European Constitution," Brussels, March 8–9, 2004. By organizing the hearings of societal groups as part of the consultation process of the Constitutional Convention, the ESC substantiated its claim to be the mouthpiece of organized civil society. See the ESC's description on its homepage: www.esc.eu.int (June 2005).

16. ESC 2004a.

17. The Constitutional Treaty refers explicitly to both "representative associations" and "civil society" (Art. 47, 2). The reason given is that employer and employee associations as well as the regional and territorial interest groups are different "in kind" from civil society; see CONV 650/03, Art. 34 (12).

18. Kohler-Koch 2004.

19. Art. 47 of the Constitutional Treaty also includes a paragraph on direct democracy which is not mentioned here because it does not relate to the other provisions.

20. See Commission 1992.

21. See Commission 2000.

22. See the respective chapter in the White Paper on Governance (Commission 2001a, 14–15) and the Communication from the Commission (Commission 2002b, 4–6).

23. Commission 1992.

24. Commission 2001, 14.

25. Commission 2002c, ESC 2004b.

26. Michel 2005, 8.

27. In reaction to the Commission's White Paper the ESC produced such a catalogue of criteria (ESC 2001).

28. Kohler-Koch 2003.

29. Commission 2002b, Annex.

30. The implementation of the Sixth Framework Programme provides an illustration of this point: The submission of more than 11,500 proposals outweighed the capacity of the Commission to assess all of them in a systematic and balanced way.

31. The online consultation with regard to the regulation of chemicals provides a case in point: There was a great variety of participants and the quality of the 6,400 responses ranged from substantively and legally sound comments and specific suggestions for improvement to short avowals of ethical concerns.

32. In the case of REACH, for example, the Commission prioritized the question of efficiency. It set the guideline that "in order to ensure the most effective processing of responses stakeholders are invited to concentrate on the efficiency of the mechanism and procedures."

33. Mill 1972, 239–240.

34. Cohen 1989; Habermas 2004; Schmalz-Bruns 1995.

35. Cohen and Sabel 1997; Eriksen and Fossum 2000; Eriksen et al. 2003.

36. Schmalz-Bruns 1999, 189.

37. Joerges 1999, 334.

38. Joerges and Neyer 1997.

39. Joerges and Everson 2000, 182.

40. Joerges and Everson 2000, 182.

41. Interviews with Euro-level NGO representative in late 2004 and early 2005.

42. Interviews in early 2005.

43. Finke, Jung, and Kohler-Koch 2003.

44. Habermas 2004, 304, emphasis in the original.

45. Vibert 2004.

46. Commission 2002a.

47. Shaw 2000, 382.

48. Tocqueville 1963, 199.

49. See, for example, Warleigh 2003.

50. Warleigh 2003, 29.

51. Warleigh 2003, 31.

52. Guiraudon 2001, 165; Trenz 2002, 141.

53. Guiraudon 2001, 173.

54. Commission 2005, 4.

55. Helfferich and Kolb 2001, 154–157.

56. Warleigh 2003, 30.

57. Rose 2003.

58. Rose 155–156.

59. Therborn 1996, 307.

60. Offe 1995.

61. This is particularly true for the elitist branch of liberal democratic theory. See Greven (1998) for an enunciation of more extensive demands in this tradition.

62. Habermas 2004, 296–302.

63. Trenz 2002, 136.

64. Eder and Trenz 2003, 119.

65. Eder et al. 1998, 325. For a clinical evaluation, see Eriksen 2005.

66. Eder and Trenz 2003, 131.

67. See "Action Plan to Improve Communicating Europe by the Commission" www.europa.eu.int/comm/dgs/press_communication/pdf/communication_com_en.pdf. The "teaching approach" is also the most characteristic feature in the Commission's "White Paper on a European Communication Policy" (COM [206]; 35 final, Brussels [1.2.2006]); http://ec.europa.eu/communication_white_paper/doc/white_paper_en.pdf.

A COMMENT ON KOHLER-KOCH

Jeremy Richardson

Beate Kohler-Koch has posed the classic question about interest groups and public policy, namely what is the democratic potential of interest group systems? I remember setting this question to my undergraduates when I first started teaching in 1966. I did not know the answer then and I do not really know it now! I suspect, after reading Beate Kohler-Koch's stimulating chapter, that she too is not sure if the EU interest group system can ever meet specific criteria of democracy which she derives from various theoretical approaches to democracy. There are two main reasons for this uncertainty. First, the term interest group generally covers such a wide range of organizations, from big multinational companies to the so-called public interest organizations such as environmental groups. (However, she uses the European Commission's definition of interest group, which, rather oddly, excludes multinational companies, arguably the best resourced and most active lobbyists in Brussels.) Secondly, we have no reliable quantitative measure of democracy. If democracy is the dependent variable it is not a very robust one in that we can never be sure whether we have more or less of it as a result of institutional change, such as that described in Kohler-Koch's chapter. Moreover, there might be a third, rather subtle, reason for our uncertainty. There does seem to be an unintended bias in much of the discourse in that groups such as producer interests are often regarded as the "baddies" and groups such as public interest groups as the "goodies" (although Kohler-Koch is careful to avoid focussing on the actual quality of actors as her main focus is the relative weight of represented interests and arguments). Indeed the very term "public interest group" appears to reflect this bias by implying that other types of groups do not operate in the public interest. Patently this is nonsense as there is no logical reason to assume that when a group is operating in its own self-interest this must be against the public interest. Whether it is or not is an empirical, case-by-case question. Similarly, we cannot assume that public interest (or to use the currently fashionable term, civil society) groups always act in the public interest. Their leaders are often movement entrepreneurs, as concerned with organizational growth and market penetration (essentially self-interest) as are their producer counterparts, and just as adept at spin and selective use of evidence. (Indeed, their customer base is much more fluid than that of many companies, sometimes forcing them to resort to quite cynical and occasionally dishonest marketing campaigns in order to constantly replace lost members. When your organization loses around 50 percent of its members each year, as do some environmental groups, you might be forgiven for placing self-interest above the public interest in order to survive). Thus, we need to exercise some caution in seeing one of the main problems of the interest group system on the EU as a bias in favor of the "bad guys" or (to pick up Kohler-Koch's concern) a bias in terms of the weight of representation and arguments.

Much of the current discourse in the EU is about the need to introduce institutional innovations which will facilitate greater participation by public interest or civil society groups in order to rebalance the weight of representation and arguments within the EU interest group system. As Kohler-Koch points out, the political debate about the contribution of organized interests to EU democracy is an engineered discourse. Old-fashioned self-interest on the part of bureaucrats is the obvious explanation for this. For its part, the Commission has been a bureaucracy under pressure for some years now and, as Anthony Downs would have predicted, it has been trying to expand its client base by incorporating yet more groups into its policy-making and implementing procedures.[1] Similarly, the Economic and Social Committee (ESC) has historically been a very weak institution, generally ignored by key policy actors, and has spotted a market opportunity (or policy space) created by the current discourse. Thus, as Kohler-Koch's chapter demonstrates, it has become something of an institutional champion of civil society groups and presents itself as some kind of market correcting institution by favoring those groups alleged to have been excluded from EU policy-making in the past.

Clearly we are not going to get a definitive answer to the question about the true potential for interest groups to meet the democratic criteria that Kohler-Koch specifies, if only due to problems of specifying and measuring the relevant variables. However, in 1966 I always sent my students away with another question (the escape clause which all teachers use when in difficulties!) which ran something like "Whatever the faults of the interest group system, can you imagine any democracy without one?" My view now is the same as it was then. Rather like Winston Churchill, who observed that democracy looked an awful form of government until one looked at the alternatives, I think that the EU would be much the worse in the absence of the EU interest group system. Why?

First, it is difficult to overestimate the importance of groups in the supply of a scarce and incredibly valuable good, namely information. I do not know of any study of EU interest groups which does not make this point. All advanced democracies are complex social and economic systems typified by policy-making under uncertainty. It is no surprise at all that EU decision-making elites try to reduce uncertainty by maximizing information prior to taking a decision. The costs of acquiring and processing large amounts of information are small by comparison to the potential costs of unintended consequences of bad (or politically unpopular) policy decisions. This is true for national systems (I return to the comparison between the EU and national systems below) and is especially true for the EU with, now, twenty-five national social and economic systems to govern. Much focus (not least by me!) has been placed on the Commission's incentives to gather information via groups but the incentives are probably just as great for other institutional actors, such as the European Parliament, and the Council and its member governments. Interest groups are a good and cheap source of information, even when it is known that the information is asymmetric. To use an English expression, groups know where the shoe pinches.

Secondly, groups are a potential source of trouble to policy-making elites, particularly in the multivenue EU. Where interinstitutional bargaining is the norm, groups can easily venue shop if they are blocked in a particular venue. In that sense, group bias is as useful information to policy-making elites in the EU as unbiased technical information. It helps elites to construct a political map around a given policy issue, which can be put alongside the technical map. In that way, some technically feasible solutions can be filtered out as political nonstarters. Thus, groups provide elites with a technical and political matrix against which policy proposals can be tested.

The incentives for the groups are obvious. They too gain crucial information (if only to minimize their surprises), itself worth the costs of participating if one has a keen enough interest in policy outcomes. They also gain the opportunity to shape decisions, particularly if they have the resources to get in the policy game early and stay there until the final whistle blows. Thus, there are two payoffs from participating, one certain and one much less so.

It is no wonder then that we have seen a long-run increase in group mobilization (though not at a constant speed) within the EU. All the incentives point that way.[2]

This brings me back to Beate Kohler-Koch's chapter. I think she is absolutely correct to argue that much of the discourse and institutional innovation (such as the Commission's use of web-based consultations and forums, and ESC's somewhat frenetic attempts to become the key institutional venue for EU civil society) is focused on a) a diagnosis which assumes that the EU is not sufficiently democratic and b) that bringing Europe closer to its citizens is the answer. Hence the now rather long period of talk about transparency and participation. As she points out there seems to have been a shift in the Commission, for example, from emphasizing the role of groups in improving the quality of European legislation (1992) to now emphasising the commitment to the inclusion of civil society. In a sense, the Commission appears to be trying to address concerns similar to those expressed in Kohler-Koch's chapter, namely about an imbalance in the relative weights of representation and arguments in the interest group system as a whole. There is clearly a new discourse, but as she also points out, it is a bit more than this as the Commission has been innovative in terms of consultation procedures. The problem, as she argues, is that practicalities turn out to be the Achilles heel because an overformalization of procedures and rules runs counter to the autonomy of groups to run their own affairs. I would add that it runs counter to the Commission's deeply embedded commitment to an open door policy to pretty well any group that comes knocking. An overspecification of rules of access and consultation would leave the Commission much more vulnerable to asymmetric information supplied by those who managed to meet the more restrictive rules. Thus, my prediction is that the old system, largely based on functional need, will continue as before but that we will continue to see institutional innovation in terms of trying to lower the costs of participation (and increase the incentives) for the so-called civil society category in order to create a more level playing field. None of this is likely to change the basic balance of power between different categories of groups within the EU. We have a well-established interest group system in place and only, at best, incremental change is likely and at worst we will see the continued growth of what can be termed "sham" consultation. As Kohler-Koch argues, some of the innovations have proved quite ineffective in terms of the claimed objectives. They enable the Commission (particularly) to sing to the fashionable hymn sheet of wider participation and the inclusion of civil society groups, but probably do not deliver any policy payoffs to the new participants. I see her overall assessment as accurate in that we have seen some changes, a new discourse, and a few successes such as the European Women's lobby, but the basic problems of unbalanced access and participation appear to remain.

Does this matter? First, in trying to answer this question, we need to be very careful not to judge the EU by some especially tough criteria. None of what Beate Kohler-Koch has written surprises me, as someone who has studied lobbying systems for longer than I care to remember! The EU seems to replicate the kind of problems that we see in most national systems in Europe and beyond. For example, producer groups are generally more mobilized with better resources, prefer insider strategies, and have better links with the bureaucracy. Access to state institutions is skewed, producing asymmetric lobbying of state officeholders. There is a concern that so-called public interest or civil society groups are weaker, less well resourced, have less access, and so forth. The EU's problems seem very familiar indeed and are probably less serious than in many of the member states. Indeed, its current procedures for access and consultation are probably not so different to those of, say, Sweden, whose remiss system is at the upper end of good practice in terms of open access and transparency. (Even in Sweden no one would claim that bias in favor of certain types of groups has been eliminated.) So, as Zweifel has argued, the EU might actually score quite highly on some democracy indicators.[3]

Secondly, we need to be a little cautious in assuming that any access bias really does disadvantage public interest or civil society groups. To me, one of the most telling passages in Kohler-Koch's chapter is where she points out that the supply of NGOs has probably already saturated the demand for political participation. She quotes Warleigh as arguing that "NGO supporters do not wish to use these organisations as a means of active citizenship. Instead, supporters wish to delegate responsibility to organisations whose broad aims they support."[4] As I have argued elsewhere,[5] the market for political activism presents a vast array of opportunity structures for modern day citizens, alongside a vast array of nonpolitical activities on offer and competing for their time. Hence the emergence of credit card activism whereby citizens donate money to their currently favorite groups and, as Warleigh argues, delegate representation to group leaders. I would argue that many of these have become part of the EU's policy-making elites, at least in their own policy areas. Thus, it is simply wrong for anyone to believe that groups such as World Wildlife Fund, or the European Consumers' Organisation (BEUC), do not have access and lack clout. If this were true then how can one explain the raft of environmental, consumer, and women's legislation in the EU? It seems unlikely that this all came about with the blessing of producer groups, who continue to squeal protests about excessive EU regulation to this day. The truth is that the allegedly strong producer groups have often failed at that most crucial stage in the policy process—agenda setting—and are forced into essentially reactive modes of lobbying. Thus, I am much more relaxed about the potential effects of the reforms which the Commission has been introducing regarding consultation procedures. It might be argued, as Beate Kohler-Koch implies, that the greater emphasis on openness and transparency actually undermines the influence of public interest groups but we do need more systematic evidence about the outcomes of lobbying before we can conclude that greater resource inputs actually deliver bigger policy gains for lobbyists. Somewhere in John Stuart Mill there is a passage about the importance of the man with the idea. I think the same could be said about EU lobbying. Thus, there can be differential lobbying in the sense that different types of groups are more active at certain stages of the policy process than others. I have lost count of the occasions when I have arrived to interview producer groups (who clearly have greater weight in terms of representation) in Brussels only to find them engaged in what Sammy Finer, nearly half a century ago termed a "fire brigade campaign,"[6] namely rushing around trying to counterattack on an agenda set by others. As Schattschneider[7] said so many years ago, the real power in politics is deciding what politics is about. On that indicator of power, I am not convinced that the EU interest system is such a bad pillar of democracy after all. Like the European Parliament, it aint so bad!

Notes

1. Downs 1967.
2. Richardson 2000; Mazey and Richardson 2005; Richardson 2006.
3. Zweifel 2002.
4. Warleigh 2003, 30.
5. Richardson 1995.
6. Finer 1958.
7. Schattschneider 1960

V

DELIBERATIVE DEMOCRACY

12

The Euro-Polity in Perspective: Some Normative Lessons from Deliberative Democracy

Rainer Schmalz-Bruns

EVEN AFTER MORE THAN A DECADE of very intense debate concerning the basic institutional structure of the emerging Euro-polity and the kind of normativity that can or should be built into it, its unforeseen and *sui-generis* character as well as the conditions of its cultural and historical background, it seems to me that most of these issues are yet unresolved. Beyond the complexity of the phenomenon itself and the perspectival variations arising from a highly differentiated academic discourse, this may in general terms relate to the challenge of novity—a challenge that seems to be of a pragmatic and political imperative, inviting us to fundamentally reinvestigate and rearticulate even the most fundamental concepts and the overall conceptual framework, which for more than three hundred years has been used to articulate, shape, and develop the political project of modernity. Democracy, constitutionalism, and the state in (although ambiguous and tense) combination have informed the institutional framework which was thought necessary for the realization of the promises of the Enlightenment Project and as Habermas put it, the joint realization of the values of self-consciousness, self-perfection, and self-determination.[1] Among the challenges arising from this tradition is the question of precisely why (and of course how) we should advance postnational politics as a solution to the problems we face,[2] a move that urges us to go beyond the state as the organizing center of this conceptual arrangement.

Against this background, it is astonishing that it seems to be part of the *acquis communautaire* to try to avoid, or at least to evade, the issue of the state as unequivocally rejected for either prudential, pragmatic, or normative reasons of feasibility and desirability. To be sure, this picture must be specified and differentiated in several respects. First of all, in a moral or legal perspective of the EU as a rights-based, constitutional system, a metaphysical (be it Hobbesian, Kantian, or Hegelian in inspiration) temptation has always existed to internally link the normativity of moral or legal commitments, obligations, and responsibilities to a notion of statehood. This was introduced as an account of the imperative of pure, social, or prudential forms of practical reason—a conceptual agenda that may well raise skepticism about the possibility of a normative European Constitution. In addition, with reference to the frequently raised concerns regarding the ethical quality of the emerging polity, these ethical properties were very often (although mostly tacitly) confused with issues of state intervention—especially in cases when a preoccupation with the state (and not with community or democracy) determined the recommendation of devolution.

This picture is further complicated by the fact that, once we turn to deliberative democracy and ask if it has to make any contribution to these debates, we are assured that its contribution consists precisely in the conviction that we should rethink and remodel just those rather conventional understandings that are at the heart of a statist account of the meaning of democracy and constitutionalism.[3] However, on closer inspection, it soon turns out that this is at least an overstatement of a conceptual consensus uniting the deliberative view. For example, Habermas has constantly moved back and forth between the basic mechanisms of integration, that is, state and society, a move that is regularly accompanied by a change of perspectives from moral to ethical and pragmatic questions.[4] Of course, there are internal tensions in the idea of deliberative democracy that make it hard to measure its contribution to shaping the Euro-polity unambiguously. There are criticisms concerning its most fundamental assumptions and prescriptions that challenge desirability, necessity, and feasibility. Surely, there is no need to take the polemical fervor too hard. As an example of this, Ladeur[5] recently denounced deliberative democracy as a purely ideological enterprise, restricted to the needs of an intellectual strata that earns its living in the institutions of education and mass media or through the professionalization of social movements, driving societies into the vicious and disenabling circles of juridification and thus undermining the integrative mechanisms of market and community.[6] Still, there remain serious concerns of desirability and feasibility addressing the probable implications of its normative promises—that is, those of equality, freedom, and solidarity—on the one hand and the dangers of a "nirvana fallacy"[7] on the other, where its practical and analytical content is denied.[8]

Now, on the one hand, this does not mean that these criticisms cannot or have not been more or less successfully addressed. Considering the achievement of higher levels of seriousness that have been placed on the demand for an analytical as well as practical "coming of age of deliberative democracy,"[9] there have been useful and convincing clarifications and demonstrations of analytical potential in several dimensions—by more carefully distinguishing and working out heuristic, analytical, reconstructive, constructive, and critical potentials. On the other hand, and despite the internal family quarrels within the deliberative approach, there are some common features to all accounts of deliberative democracy that may serve as a background against which a provisional answer to the question I was asked to address may be projected, and they will be successively refined. Initially, we can take the following suggestions to be relatively uncontroversial. Firstly, any deliberative account is non-republican in the sense that it primarily tries to unfold communicative or administrative rationality at the collective, not at the individual, level.[10] Secondly, while this preserves some room for voluntarism, it definitely adheres to an idea of deliberation that has an important epistemic component. Thirdly, it is certain that the aforementioned character traits of the idea of deliberative democracy directly follow from the moral concept of legitimacy underlying it—a fundamental principle that allows us to set aside an instrumental account of the idea of democracy. Fourthly, this fundamental principle urges us to take political constructivism as one of its main implications. This again, fifthly, also implies that our understanding of democracy cannot be built on a sharp distinction between state and society, although it does not (as I will argue later) force us to completely socialize or horizontalize our understanding of the adequate forms and institutions of democracy.

Against this background I hope to be able to show that there is indeed a distinctive contribution to the major issues of the current debate on democracy and constitutionalism in the European Union. In order to show this I shall proceed in four steps by addressing the issue of democracy, constitutionalism, and the state respectively, but starting from a more general account of the fundamental principles of deliberative democracy. In delineating the argument, I only assume and do not prove that for moral, ethical, and pragmatic reasons the idea of deliberative democracy is, in comparison to its actual competitors,[11] the most plausible candidate for a nascent political philosophy of the Euro-polity.

Deliberative Democracy: Five Components[12]

A generally shared and relatively uncontroversial account of a deliberative understanding of democracy may suggest that it consists

> of a political practice of argumentation and reason giving among free and equal citizens, a practice in which individual and collective perspectives and positions

are subject to change through deliberation and in which only those norms, rules or decisions which result from some form of reason-based agreement among the citizens are accepted as legitimate.[13]

I agree with Forst that the choice between different model-accounts following from the general idea must be based on which of them adequately conceptualizes democracy as the rule of reasons. There exist five components that are not only able to shape the specific idea of democracy against rival communitarian or instrumentalist accounts, but also help to decide between the diverse versions of a deliberative approach that have played an important role in the debates concerning the Euro-polity in recent years.[14]

Normativity, Rationality, and Reasons

From a deliberative perspective, the basic justification of democracy is derived from the assumption that it politically mirrors the fact that under modern conditions normativity cannot but be derived from intersubjectivity, that is, from the rationality assumptions built into language-mediated social interactions in which individuals acquire a sense of themselves as well as of the ideas of rightness and truth expected to govern their social relationships. If that is the sort of normativity distinctive of modernity, it has immediate implications for our understanding of reason in the light of which we judge a political order as justified or accept political decisions as legitimate. The reason precisely lies in the reasons we mutually offer one another in order to collectively convince ourselves of the acceptability of generally binding norms and political decisions; that in turn implies that those reasons must at least meet the formal qualification of being generally and reciprocally justifiable.[15]

The Normative Ground for Democracy

It directly follows that the ultimate foundation for a deliberative account of the idea of democracy resides in a basic moral right to justification. This foundation precludes any instrumental understanding (be it in a liberal, communitarian or technocratic sense) of democracy in which it is thought to serve only as a means to the realization of liberal, or libertarian principles, communitarian, values, or to the implementation of best solutions to common problems of action arrived at independently of a democratic procedure.[16]

Conception of Political Discourse

I depart from Forst where he seems to suggest that we should only use procedural, and not substantive, criteria of legitimacy. Although he is prepared to accept that there might also be substantive criteria that can be derived from the self-application of the principles of reciprocity and generality, his approach does not go far enough. In order for us to accept the outcomes of a procedure as legitimate, we must also be able to convince ourselves of the relative weight and merits (and that implies their quality as measured by independent standards) of (competing) reasons used to justify a concrete decision.[17] So, I think it is a misunderstanding to assume that we are prepared to evaluate democratic procedures and outcomes only in the social dimension of inclusiveness. Although any actual procedure can be evaluated in the light of a more inclusive one, inclusiveness does not, by itself, fully exploit the critical idea of doing better.[18] Rather, procedure-dependent and procedure-independent criteria have to mutually reinforce one another in order to fully unfold the normative force of democratic proceduralism. And this again, as I have argued elsewhere,[19] has two important implications: Epistemic proceduralism as defended here suggests that, while it can be translated into different forms of democracy, it certainly does not supply for an unequivocal support of direct or participatory democracy as such (see below).

Cultural Conditions of Deliberative Democracy

Having made these points, it is nonetheless obvious that we cannot build democracy on transcendental insights alone.[20] Although it is true that the willingness to act on the basis of such insights is itself an important part of our cultural self-understanding, it is not to be regarded simply as a given, completely independent of the form of the political order under which we live. When we refer to democracy as a culturally embedded form of life, what is distinctive of a deliberative approach is not that it disregards ethical concerns altogether, but that it starts from a normative conception of the ethos of democracy that provides a combination of moral and particular ethical-political components.[21] Part of the answer to this problem is that it seeks to display its rationality assumptions primarily on the collective and not on the individual level.[22] The other part of the answer is that it emphasizes the ethical role of normatively credible institutions.[23] This intuitive idea might best be caught in the notion of a community of responsibility that normatively integrates a political community through institutionally mediated willingness to take over discursive responsibilities for justification, the willingness to take responsibility for the institutional realization of such first order responsibilities, and the willingness to take responsibility for the consequences of decisions and action. Of course, the meaning of willingness in this context is normative and explicatory, not explanatory—but this again highlights another crucial component of discourse ethics in general and deliberative democracy in particular: it provides a primarily structural, not a motivational account of the force of the better reason.[24]

Institutional Presuppositions

Finally, these remarks lead us to recommend at least some rules for institutional design (but no blueprint for institution building because that is, in the deliberative understanding, not a theoretical task but it is open to political constructivism, that is, the deliberation among citizens themselves). The most general conclusion is that deliberative politics is best served if there are a variety of institutional spheres, reflexively acting upon one another. Certainly, there should be institutional space for forms of self-government. However, following a principle of "reciprocal objection,"[25] there should also be institutional access points for effectively displaying the individual right to justification and contestation, as well as institutional devices capable of balancing institutional patterns. These access points and devices are required because of the need to improve the epistemic quality of political decisions and because of equality concerns. There is also a need to establish an institutional tier of the polity that makes reflexivity visible,[26] allowing the citizenry to responsibly act collectively and where accountability for decisions concerning the overall institutional arrangement and management of the interdependence of diverse institutional spheres and forum of decision making in a differentiated polity can be guaranteed and secured.

Democratic Problem Solving in the EU

Where does it all leave us when it comes to answering the question of how to solve the democratic deficit or democratic dilemma of the European Union? Part of the answer to this question lies in the distinction itself. Problems arise in the widely held diagnosis[27] that the EU in its current structure is open to charges of regulatory, expertocratic, and legal domination. Once we refer to the democratic tools and institutional devices developed at the level of the nation-state, in order to strengthen and make effective the democratic chain of legitimation, which has to run through the various levels of governance, we may then realize, as many suggest, that even in the best case, problems will arise. The adoption of standard representational solutions to these problems will not only lead to a growing alienation of citizens from politics in a social (regarding the incentives for a more elite-driven political process), in a factual (regarding the growing dependence on forms of expert knowledge), and in a time dimension (regarding the growing spatial and temporal distantiation of citizens from decisive policy choices taken by political elites).[28] This democratic solution will also undermine or overstretch (or both at the same time) democratic resources (in being excessively demanding as to the convictions on which the self-identification of a *demos* as a moral community must rest) and democratic possibilities (where the drawing of the boundaries of a larger union by the constituent and already democratized member parts can be mutually perceived only as an instance of external determination).[29] As we have seen, there are different articulations of this same dilemma. With regard to the EU they all suggest that it is critical for the EU to look more like the modern state or federation if it wishes to make any attempt at overcoming the democratic deficit. In this manner, it will face the danger of the growing alienation of its citizens or the problem of democratic impossibilities, and will have to give up its polycentricity and postsovereignty. Otherwise, if it is to be a novel form of democracy without sovereignty and hierarchy, then it must give up the standard requirement that its polity constitutes a determinate and sovereign *demos*.[30] It is this standard assumption of a unified and sovereign *demos*, in the projection of the idea of the sovereign people, which lies at the heart of the diagnosis of the EU facing a democratic dilemma. It is this fusion of a normative principle with a substantialized notion of a *demos* that the deliberative view tries to confront. This is important because once we give up this view and allow for a more desubstantialized vision of the idea of a sovereign *demos*, centered in the normative principle of general and reciprocal justification as stated above, a deliberative approach helps to establish a conceptual alternative that is based on internally linking the idea of people's sovereignty, the principle of public and inclusive justification, and the idea of a *demos*. A *demos*, then, denotes a reflexively integrated moral (and legal) community, where the sovereignty of dispersed *demoi* is invested into an order of internally deliberative institutions. It is sufficiently reflexive so as to make it democratic in the sense that issues of the nature of the polity, rights, and duties must (and effectively can) be passed through the public deliberation of citizens.[31]

This provisional answer, which establishes the punch line of deliberative republicanism and highlights its special attractiveness in the attempt of coming to terms with the Euro-polity, only triggers a whole series of corollary conceptual questions that have to be answered in order to arrive at a deliberative account of what it would mean to adequately democratize the EU. First of all, any such account must address the rationality assumptions underlying integrative mechanisms on different levels of integration, ranging from policies (or problem solving) to polity building and respecting the demands that arise from moral, ethical-political, or pragmatic concerns. By themselves, these represent different but related aspects of the overall integration process. Secondly, against this background, we can successfully address another important issue that can be derived from the liberal concern of adequately balancing the private and public autonomy of citizens, that is, of balancing epistemic proceduralism and democratic voluntarism. Thirdly, this distinction, and its institutional corollaries, enables us to think of a reflexive institutional order that at various levels allows for different democratic logics or at least a different mix of the two logics alluded to—provided only that they effectively can reflexively act upon one another. Fourthly, this raises the thorny issue of whether reflexive integration can be realized within the confines of a kind of transnational (or horizontal or societal) constitutionalism alone, or whether some form of hierarchical self-intervention by means of state-like structures is also required, in order to make the moral or pragmatic judgments of citizens decisive in the respective dimensions of the integration process.

These are of course huge questions, and I cannot hope to fully and adequately address them here. In one way or another, they build the background against which the conceptual problems to be discussed in the following chapters gain their significance. So, in a first move that is more narrowly confined to the question of how to model democratic processes of problem solving in a multi-level polity characterized by dispersed and fragmented forms of authorities and a plurality of sites of problem solving, I only address one decisive background assumption—namely that an important cognitive or epistemic component to a deliberative account exists. It is obvious that the basic principle of justification has an epistemic meaning that is derived from the account of the integrative force of public reasoning. This meaning is absolutely crucial when we are asked to provide an explication of the assumption that deliberative democracy is well equipped to come to terms with a denationalized vision of a democratic order.[32] Thus, it seems necessary to highlight the epistemic properties of deliberative proceduralism which at the same time allows us to meet the concerns that arise from insights into the reality of pluralism and questions of the feasibility of discursive integration.

Once we admit that the central task of any normative democratic theory is to show how democracy contributes to the moral legitimacy (which can be spelled out by referring to the principle of generally and reciprocally non-rejectability of reasons as stated above) of political decisions,[33] we are left with the choice of arguing that democratic procedures support the conditions for strong political legitimacy expressed in the epistemic account, or denying that these conditions can be democratically achieved. In that case, we would have "to supply an alternative account of democratic legitimacy or . . . settle for the fact that democratic decisions have little or no legitimacy at all."[34] I believe that both alternatives to the epistemic account of the moral value of democratic procedures would severely undermine the idea of deliberative democracy. There is a moral dimension to the idea of legitimacy. It is distinctive in assuming that the fusion of democracy and morality is vested in the idea of reason giving—a practice that is in turn dependent on raising rationally rejectable validity claims, that is, on the cognitive content of these claims. This is necessary in order to answer the deliberative question, namely the question of why political decision making should depend on public discussion at all and not merely in casting votes or flipping a coin as purely proceduralist accounts of justice.[35]

But then we should also understand the reason why democracy cannot simply admit for an idea of truth that is independent of the normative principle of equal and inclusive participation. The argument is simple and straightforward: We should be aware of the dangers of epistocracy (which, besides, can be justified only if it can be proved beyond any reasonable doubt that the epistemic qualifications of an individual or a small elite outreach the epistemic value of broad public and inclusive discussions[36]) and we should be sensitive to the dangers of inequality resulting from correctness theories of political decision making. On balance then, I suggest that we should qualify deliberative proceduralism, which holds that we can generate legitimacy for democratic decisions apart from any independent standard of their qualities. In other words, an epistemic proceduralism holds that outcomes are legitimate on the basis of their derivation from a certain procedure, not on the basis of being correct: "Among the features of the procedure that are held to contribute to the legitimacy of the outcome is the procedure's being, at least as far as can be determined within grounds acceptable to all reasonable citizens, the epistemically best procedure among the procedures that are better than random."[37]

What I have tried to show so far is that any account of the idea of deliberative democracy must be epistemic in some sense. This might be taken as rather uncontroversial. The real question would then be, in what sense and how strong the epistemic conception should be. I suspect that we can come closer to answering that question if we consider two major criticisms of that ideal. First of all, given its epistemic meaning and content, the principle of justification as well as the concomitant idea of a rationally motivated consensus are so demanding that they reach deeply into citizenship competencies and thus into the micro-foundation of the democratic process. In this manner, they may even alter or invert the idea of democratic self-determination; and given the fact of pluralism (in the Rawlsian sense of a plurality of equally plausible and rationally defensible comprehensive doctrines), it is even no longer plausible for normative reasons as well as for reasons of feasibility to submit a rational consensus as the means by which a political community can be integrated. While I think both objections in a strong version are misplaced insofar as they fall victim to the fallacy of misplaced concreteness, one can make good sense of them within the idea of a rationally motivated consensus once one recasts them according to a pivotal distinction between its constitutional and operational role. To indicate how this may work, I will shortly address them in a reverse order.

Concerned about the question of how to present an account of deliberative democracy that is plausible and viable even under conditions of the complexity of modern societies and its inherent and notorious forms of pluralism, Rehg and Bohman[38] set the stage for a debate concerning the normative and practical merits of deliberative politics in a way that resonates with more recent contributions to the European debate on the democratic deficit and the constitutionalization of the EU. These debates are inspired by a normative sensitivity to plurality and difference and try to articulate a dialogical vision of a European democracy rooted in a civic republican or broadly constructivist view. They also attempt to restructure the basic institutional set-up of the Union along the lines of a deliberative polyarchy. The crucial suggestion emerging from their line of reasoning is that, in order to render the deliberative approach plausible in normative and practical terms, that is, under conditions of the fact of pluralism (making it safe for the EU), we must take plurality seriously. In any case, we must avoid that (as in the epistemic account) "real plurality is 'transsubstantiated' into idealized unanimity, and thereby rationalized."[39] The authors contend that this sort of transformation of agreements would require three rather strong assumptions about the force of argumentation that are, however, open to serious doubts when applied to the conditions of real political deliberation. In particular, they contend that an overly epistemic account of the moral and political force of deliberation cannot take the fact of moral pluralism and disagreement seriously. In other words, it is insufficiently sensitive to the differences between moral, ethical-political, and pragmatic aspects of political problems that cannot be rationalized and overcome in a perspective of argumentative rationality alone. Furthermore, they contend that an epistemic account cannot make sense of the notorious observation of the incompleteness of deliberation; an even (or just) open and inclusive public debate will not necessarily increase the chances of a rational consensus.[40] For these reasons they suggest a more dialogical account of rationality in substitution of the epistemic one, an idea which is subsequently substantiated by Bohman with reference to the institutional device of a multiperspectival inquiry. This is where multiperspectivism seems to consist of a fusion of the idea of polyarchical forms of problem solving with dialogical forms of rationality, orientations, and virtues that are anchored in a normative idea of pluralism.[41]

What concerns me is the conceptual contamination of normative and descriptive aspects of the fact of pluralism (which has, as I see it, moral value without being freestanding in a normative sense, cf. Rawls) and the contamination of an ethical perspective with the forms of rationality on which it is based, that is, multiperspectivism as a form of making sense of difference is at first precisely that, a perspective, an orientation, or a disposition, but one that by itself does not tell us very much about the rationalities on which it rests. On closer inspection, one has good reasons to suppose that multiperspectivism based on dialogue cannot, by itself, account for agreement because its qualifying characteristics such as mutual respect, considerate regard, or the solidarity of a nonegoistic commitment can help in the achievement of agreement. However, they cannot solely account for that kind of rationality, which forces us to converge on a distinct view. Of greater importance is that this kind of criticism seems to misinterpret the procedural punch line of the argument from rational consensus. It is, for internal reasons, not meant to directly bring itself to bear on the operational level of trying to achieve agreements, but it only informs those procedural preconditions that must be met in order to qualify factual agreements brought about by different means of argumentation, dialogue or negotiation as legitimate and rationally motivated. This becomes perfectly clear once we turn to those strategies which Habermas has used to come to terms with the same problems that also motivate the dialogical turn of deliberative democracy. These strategies can be called contextual, procedural, and epistemological. The contextual strategy is based on a distinction between types of problems of political action (moral, ethical, or pragmatic in kind) and allows for a contextual specification of the principle of justification by establishing different formal and substantive criteria of what should count as a good argument in the respective cases. The procedural strategy is concerned with the already mentioned procedural transfer of legitimacy from rationally motivated agreement at the constitutional level to modes of interaction and/or forms of political decision making which, by themselves, cannot match the principle of democratic legitimacy and usually take the form of an "as-long-as." Finally, the epistemological strategy is built on a fallible account of the cooperative search for truth or rightness.

In short, this amounts to three suggestions. It is difficult to see that dialogical multiperspectivism or dialogical constitutionalism[42] actually establish a conceptual alternative to the epistemic account of deliberative democracy. While this would, even if successful, not be normatively desirable because it would loosen the grip of the principle of legitimation on the formal and legally circumscribed aspects of political institutions and the institutional system as a whole, it may nonetheless (and rightly) alter our understanding of what we may (and must) expect to occur at the operational level of problem solving. This at least is what is behind a complementary attempt by Eriksen[43] to investigate what he terms the microfoundations of supranationalism. His

line of reasoning is instructive because in his attempt to provide a sociologi-
cally plausible account of the microfoundations of the European integration
process based on communicative action, he convincingly begins from the assumption that the rationality expectations and standards that must be met in
political interaction vary (to a certain degree) with the kind of problems to be
solved.[44] He makes this perfectly clear when discussing the merits of experi-
mental deliberation in deliberative polyarchies where, against the background
of the distinction between problem solving on the level of normal politics and
of integration and agreement at the constitutional level of institutional design
(or, alternatively, deliberation with regard to substantial or factual questions in
contradistinction to deliberation with respect to procedural questions concerning issues of fairness and justice), he raises two important points. Firstly,
as long as problem solving takes place in the shadow of the normative hierarchy of institutionally established rules, and insofar as political conflicts may be
thought to be rationally mediated by the mutual regard of (competing) interests or by reference to well-established criteria of validity where opinions
about facts are controversial, actors can moderate their mutual expectations of
rationality to a degree falling well below the standards of a rational consensus.
Secondly, once political interaction is confronted with moral questions of justice and fairness (and thus directly addresses the issue of democratic legitimacy), then, he suggests, a rational consensus, in the strong sense of an agreement forged in a process of reason giving and built upon reasons that all can
equally share and uphold, is normatively imperative.[45]

Only against this background, Eriksen contends (and I follow him here)
that we can identify different modalities of reaching an agreement, which
mainly differ with respect to the respective standards of rationality. These
modalities include a *modus vivendi* kind of agreement where actors only agree
to mutually respect conflicting interests; a compromise where agreement is
based on different, but convergent reasons; a working agreement which tries
to make sense of the fact of pluralism in that an agreement is expected to rest
on the reasonableness of different understandings of the problem at hand and
which may work as a provisional and temporal agreement; and finally a rationally motivated consensus which refers to the epistemic properties of the
issues to be dealt with and insists that agreement in this sense is only reached
when actors support a common solution to a problem for the same, mutually
acceptable reasons.[46] This strategy of problem sorting seems to me the most
promising attempt to come to terms with the aforementioned objections of
pluralism and difference and the feasibility of deliberative democracy because
it allows us to underline its analytic and reconstructive force while at the same
time keeping the line with the overall epistemic account (or at least the epistemic content and meaning) of the deliberative approach. In so doing, it

nonetheless provides a first step in the attempt to outline at least the rough contours of a deliberative model of democracy for the EU.

Thus, the question of which model of democracy to larger polities on the regional scale the subunits of which are already internally democratized, irrespective of whether these are deliberative polyarchies or nation-states, in any case raises many important second-order questions. And this is why a deliberative perspective puts emphasis not only on internally deliberative procedures, but on an institutional system such that the different parts (on different levels) of the system may reflexively act upon each other and where a variety of democratic forms comes into play—a deliberative system which then also should allow different modes of political interaction and of reaching agreements to play their role.[47]

Reflexive Integration: Constitutional Implications

When it comes to the question of the constitutionalization of the EU, we are again confronted with a bewildering complexity of questions. First, there is the question of whether the EU needs to be constitutionalized at all or, if already constitutionalized, to what degree it is constitutionalized. Even if we answer the second question in the affirmative, there is still room to wonder whether it is constitutionalized in the right way. In order to understand and answer that question, one must determine whether a model account of the idea of constitutionalism exists. Finally, even if we were persuaded that there is something like an ideal of constitutionalism, we are torn into debates concerning its applicability under given circumstances. Taken together, opinions not only diverge on the issue of what is to be regarded as the ultimate authority from which a constitution may derive its normative force—that is, whether we should locate this authority in a moral community, unified and personified in a European *demos* (Dworkin, Habermas, Michelman), or whether we can count on dispersed sources of separately legitimated authorities which are multiple *demoi* (Weiler). There is also disagreement about the scope of constitutionalization as well as the question by which means the aims of constitutionalization are best achieved.

I cannot engage with all of these questions here, and for the sake of brevity I simply assume (but do not argue) that the EU needs to be reconstitutionalized in order to render its evolving structures of governance democratically legitimate. The aim of such a project is to build legally circumscribed forms of reflexivity into its structures and make such forms of reflexive self-regulation democratic, that is, visible and accessible to all. I take these suggestions to be characteristic for any distinctively deliberative approach to constitutionalization, as they allow us to come to terms with internal family quarrels within the deliberative camp. In order to show how this functions, I proceed in two steps. First, I indicate four major problems that are to be solved by (re)constitutionalizing the Euro-polity; and secondly I briefly introduce the idea of reflexive constitutionalization.

Even if one accepts the suggestion that the most important feature of the EU as a postnational political order lies in its horizontally dispersed structures of governance with participatory, civic, associational, and deliberative underpinnings, this might eventually develop into real normative achievements if these elements can be fused into a normatively convincing form of transnational governance.[48] Our expectations concerning the constitutional domestication of these arrangements cannot and should not be too modest, and they should not be too immodest in the wrong way—a wrong way that would consist in simply remodeling the national mode of a strictly hierarchical form of self-intervention on the one hand and evolutionary processes of self-constitutionalization of dispersed polyarchies on the other. To put it in Joerges' words, constitutionalizing the EU implies finding a "third way between constitutionalism 'from above' and blind pragmatism."[49]

Seen in this light, the first aim of such transnational constitutionalization must consist in eliminating legal domination.[50] Legal domination does not result from the imposition of the arbitrary will of an individual or group, but rather from the use of law "to impose a cooperative scheme upon others without their being able to influence its terms."[51] This is obviously also the case in the EU where a supranational form of juridification is based on doctrines like those of direct effect and legal supremacy of EU law, while the legal interpretation of these laws from the contractual sources are not under democratic control. In other words, the problem of administrative juridification and domination arises wherever the constitutive circle between law and legitimate political power is broken. Where the jurisgenerative discourses themselves are inadequately (that is, legally) institutionalized so that it can be taken for granted that public discourses are "temporally, socially and materially specified in relation to political opinion and will-formation . . . in legislative bodies"[52]—that is, the problem of administrative domination. Otherwise, where agents (as in transnational governance arrangements) tend to regulate the very political authorities for which they are agents, this is the problem of the reversal of agency or "incompletely defined democratic authority."[53] While this demand is a direct corollary to the deliberative principle that in order for a law to be legitimate, it must be the case that the addressees of the law can plausibly understand themselves as its authors, it secondly follows from the right to justification that anyone concerned must be effectively able to challenge authoritative political decisions on the ground that they do not meet the criterion of general and reciprocal justification. This right to contestation seems best realized when courts take on the deliberative role to judge whether normatively required and, in that sense, permissible reasons have been used to justify a political decision when they protect the democratic process by reviewing procedures, processes, and institutional devices of accountability.[54] From this it directly follows, thirdly, that, if it occurs, the process of a delegation of authority itself must be organized in a way that allows people to plausibly interpret it as resulting from their own rational will. That is, it must be conceived as an autonomous administrative act not externally administratively imposed on them. If there is an auto-paternalistic dimension to the idea of democratic self-determination, it implies that it can be reasonably expected that fragmentation between horizontally and vertically dispersed sites of authority can be overcome. A layer has to be institutionalized at which the interdependencies become visible and from where interactions could be observed, monitored, and regulated in order to overcome blind pragmatism and to provide an alternative to blind coevolution.[55] While the three aforementioned aims result from the challenge to constitutionally rationalize the interplay between institutionalized discourses in the narrower sense and discourses in the broader public as well as instances of self-legislation from within different and dispersed sites of problem solving and decision making, a final aim should be to internally democratize them. This aim of regulated self-regulation may be best realized through establishing procedural rules that affirm the idea of epistemic proceduralism, as stated above, which put rights to transparency, to access, and to accountability on a regular (i.e. legal) basis as subjective rights to communication, information, and participation.

Together, these four fundamental propositions explain what it means for a process of European constitutionalization to be immodest in the right way, and the idea providing the rationale for it can be best captured by the notion of "reflexive constitutionalization."[56] This notion refers to the intuition that, in order for a democratic system of governance to be fully democratic, it must have the ability to think of it as resulting from the deliberate and deliberatively structured attempts of people continuously and collectively modeling and remodeling the terms of their political interactions. It is important to note that this basic idea has three critical components necessary if the system is to be reflexive in a formal sense, as well as adequately reflexive in a democratic sense. For one, it must be able to meet the liberal challenge that the union of constitutionalism and democracy is at best a paradoxical union (if it is a union at all and not simply a contradiction in terms). In this understanding, through its own process of constitutionalization, democracy reacts to the impossibility of founding itself by democratic means,[57] thus borrowing from a logic of rights that can serve its limiting and self-limiting functions only when they are not contingent upon democratic will formation. I agree with Habermas that, in order to overcome this paradox and not appeal to a kind of moral realism (which would be the only alternative to bring the regress built into the relation between democracy and constitutionalism to a halt), "we have to understand the regress itself as the understandable expression of the future-oriented character, or openness of the democratic constitution. In my view, a constitution that is democratic—not just in its content but also according to its source of legitimation—is a tradition-building project" that can escape the circle of groundless self-constitution only if it "can be understood in the long run as a self-correcting learning-process."[58] Secondly, once we have accepted this theoretical reason for constitutional reflexivity, I think we must also admit the implication that reflexivity can only be unfolded at a collective level in two senses. First, it is collective in the Deweyan sense, that is, a public is constituted by the very fact that it addresses the combined, but unintended effects and consequences of actions taken separately. Secondly, it is also collective in the sense of the use of public reason, which means that it does so in the light of reasons not only acceptable to all, but requiring acceptability not for distributively, but collectively shared (for the same) reasons. Thirdly, it seems to me that once we have accepted these two implications of the idea of reflexivity, we should also be prepared to admit that there is a hierarchical dimension to the idea of reflexive self-intervention. Not only must we be able to sort out moral reasons in the light of which we may be able to devise solutions to the problems at hand, but we should allow them to be decisive—and that is, hierarchically superior.

Reflexive Integration and Hierarchical Self-Intervention

Thus far, I have tried to depict the EU polity as a polycentric democratic order, integrated by a constitution that gives meaning and structure to the idea of reflexive cooperation which is at the heart of any understanding of the EU as a new form of a transnational political entity. This picture also seems to suggest that such a constitutional order can be established without further reference to the idea of stateness. In constitutional terms, this is only a conceptual precursor to constitutional theory. In normative, theoretical, functional, or practical terms it is already absorbed into it. Traditionally, this is a contentious issue (and in some respects still is) because it highlights some important questions concerning constitutional (self-) justification, (self-) enactment, and (self-) application and enforcement. These have led people to have recourse to the state in order to determine the constitutional self who shall be constituted, give authority to the constitution, be the addressee of constitutional rights, and guarantee its structural provisions. Now, some of these problems can be (and of course have been) solved if we move from the idea of the reason of the state to transcendental insights implied in the very idea of cooperation (contractualism), if we dismiss the idea of a homogenous self and put the idea of a multiple self in its place who can reflexively address and constitute itself, and if we substitute a structural and procedural notion of self-application for the legal concept of the personality of the state. The changes these conceptual shifts bring about are significant, because it is no longer the state as a public body that constitutes and constitutionalizes civil society, but it is the civil society that institutes the state as a form by which it can reflexively act upon itself. This is clearly a desubstantialized notion, serving as a civilizing device,[59] but it is nonetheless important not to forget that a substantial residue of administrative hierarchy and uniform application of law remains crucial for a well-ordered constitutional democracy,[60] but that, more generally, without an effective form of organizational law, constitutions are in danger of remaining what they initially are—only words.[61]

Against this background, I want to explore the conceptual relationship of deliberative democracy and the state in normative terms. Even if the notion of stateness acquires some normative content in this respect, it would be an overstatement if we take the state to rest on autonomous sources of normativity as Hegel would like to have it. Instead, what we have to ask in taking the relationship between morality and law as an exemplar and where the law has to compensate for the deficiencies of moral coordination alone (i.e. for weaknesses of the will, for the indeterminacy of moral judgment or at least the cognitive burdens that arise from it, or for its lack of the institutional conditions of a uniform application), is whether the idea of stateness as a means of hierarchical self-intervention into the patterns of societal cooperation is normatively implied in the idea of reflexive integration as outlined so far. However, even if there should be something to this idea, we have come to terms with the normatively important issue of whether compensation here means (as in the case of the law) that the compensating mechanism (i.e. the state) is in itself sufficiently justified for normative reasons (the strong version), or whether we better understand this as a functional requirement only which is at least consonant with the aims of moral coordination and integration without acquiring a moral value of its own. I cannot address this question here and confine myself to reconsider the reasons that speak in favor of taking the issue of the state seriously in this context.

Whenever the issue of a state (or at least of necessary state-like structures) is raised in the context of transnational democratic governance, this contention soon is confronted with major challenges of at least three kinds. The first is an objection from feasibility, pretending that whatever the theoretical merits of the argument, this is not a practically conceivable or viable option for the mediate and intermediate future. This objection may be at least partially countered by the suggestion that in spite of the internal and external weaknesses of the nation-state, actors are nonetheless primarily guided by a sense of the reason of the (national) state. This sense is inimical to transnationally pooling their respective sovereignties or to completely invest it in a supranational structure. What we are really confronted with is a process of the differentiation of the constitutive components of statehood which are selectively institutionalized on a level beyond the nation-state, and thus not with the withering away of the state or its self-assertion in its traditional form, but with its transformation. But even if we were able to settle the issue at that point, we will soon be confronted with normative concerns as well. These again usually take two forms One refers to second-order problems that arise from superimposing a state form on its constituent units, where these units are already internally democratized, and where the normative promise of the idea of the state, residing in fusing statehood, law, constitutionalism, democracy, and solidarity into a whole, cannot be reproduced.[62] The normative force of this kind of criticism is obviously contingent on the contention that such a system is necessarily undemocratic—a contention that I have tried to reject throughout this article. The other is an even more fundamental concern and is liberal and democratic in origin as well as derived from normative individualism and democratic voluntarism. This contention asserts that democracy is a fundamental way of being suspicious and inimical to any form of hierarchically fixed authority and power.[63] To this objection one could reply (as I presuppose throughout this article) that an organized capacity to act is part of the idea of public autonomy as it is understood in the republican tradition and in deliberative democracy respectively.

In light of these provisional responses to the main charges against the idea of statehood we may rephrase the whole issue and instead ask two different questions. We must ask ourselves whether we think of public autonomy as the capacity to effectively act in terms of a hierarchically organized capacity or whether we have reasons to believe that these demands are sufficiently met in horizontal forms of self-coordination as well.[64] If the conditions of a hierarchically organized society are met, we ask whether we would have to pay a price for that acknowledgement; something too high in normative terms and would therefore far exceed its potential gains. Instead of a full-blown answer to these questions I conclude with six propositions showing that, in order for a system of governance to be adequately democratic, there should be hierarchical forms of self-intervention:

- Provide for the possibility to relieve forms of horizontal self-government and coordination and for the possibility to substitute for these if they fail to adequately address political problems at hand.
- Provide for an allocative mechanism under which the allocation of rights, duties, and responsibilities to problem-solving polyarchies, agencies, or expert committees may be thought of as an ideal delegation procedure that establishes an institutional link between delegative decisions and the collective will of the people (expressed, for example, in representative institutions).[65] These decisions should also provide constitutional criteria such as procedural norms regulating the internal and external interactions of units of problem solving, or norms regulating the access to and the composition of the relevant groups.
- Provide for the management of interdependencies and independencies, that is, for a monitoring function which in addition helps to preserve the holistic character of the system.
- Guarantee that rights and responsibilities within self-governing units are observed and ensuring that structural and organizational demands of democracy are met.
- Provide for the visibility of the system as a whole and marking the points of effective access, intervention, and contestation.
- Provide for the moral credibility of the system as a whole and thus inducing necessary relation of horizontal trust between citizens.[66]

And only in this sense may we also contend that there is no democratization without a state.

Conclusion

Common to any understanding of democratic legitimacy is the suggestion that a polity is fully legitimate only under the condition that its members (collectively or individually) may not be subject to any political force or authority that is beyond their reach. That is obvious in cases of external domination in the strict sense, but it also holds against any form of internal domination—be it technocratic, administrative, or even legal. While all these circumstances constitute severe forms of alienation of the citizens' basic right to self-determination, the problem goes even deeper and may be manifested even in a horizontal dimension (and thus between citizens themselves) when in their isolated judgment citizens fail to justify their opinions in the moral perspective of public reason.

Against this background we can see that the idea of democratic legitimacy is challenging because it forces us to think about two issues. First, we have to come about with a suggestion of how citizens can best understand their mutual duties and obligations as members of an integrated political community. And, secondly, we must be able to devise a solution to the paradox of self-foundation, which requires that the will-formation and decision-making process in the constitution of a democratic polity is already guided by those norms and rules that still have to be legally established. Accordingly, this chapter contends that in order to arrive at a normatively convincing answer to the question of democratic legitimacy in the EU, we are well advised to take this foundational paradox as a starting line from which the argument develops in three steps. In a first step, I argue that the best account of democratic legitimacy is to be found in the principle of justification which emphasizes the integrative force of (public) reasons and claims that people best understand their duties as citizens as a duty to respect their fellow citizens as autonomous and reasonable persons who may base their individual judgments on reasons that they can collectively share—that is, reasons that are mutually not rejectable in the sense that they can be generally and reciprocally raised.

Following this, a more contentious issue considers if the principle of justification (in order to acquire and display its full moral worth), does not also imply a further and, in this case, an epistemological qualification of the processes of public reasoning. The answer is that it does, but that, in normative terms, it is required to establish procedural safeguards in order to prevent the polity from declining into an epistocracy. The basic suggestion put forward at this point is that we are best served when we take recourse to the idea of reflexivity, which is already built into the answer to the second fundamental question raised above, namely that the institutionalization of any concrete form of will formation and decision making must be the result of an inclusive democratic process. With this suggestion we then have reached a point from which it is possible to test some of the democratic model accounts of the EU and to draw more constructive conclusions. But, even then, the question of the competing interpretations of the idea of a reflexively integrated polity that best matches the moral point of view from which we derived the basic principle of justification still remains. Again we are confronted with several options, and three are taken into closer consideration. In the first option reflexivity is horizontally projected onto the hierarchical structures of a deliberative polyarchy (call it the model of democratic reflexivity); the second option puts a premium on constitutional reflexivity; and the third option takes recourse to a centralized and hierarchical form of self-intervention—the state model.

The result put forward is that a reflexively integrated democratic polity is best spelled out as a combination of forms of democratic, constitutional, and hierarchical reflexivity, operationalized at different levels of the polity. Following this line of reasoning, this chapter touches upon one of the most controversial issues of the debate concerning the Euro-polity, the question of whether and in which way, in normative terms, we also have to think about it in terms of statehood.

Notes

1. Habermas 1998b, 81.
2. Fine and Smith 2003, 478.
3. See Bohman 2004, 2.
4. See Fine and Smith 2003, 478–483.
5. Ladeur 2002, 3–27.
6. Ladeur 2002, 17–22.
7. Cram 2002, 309–324.
8. Especially with respect to the last objection, cf. Hitzel-Cassagnes forthcoming.
9. Bohman 1998, 400–425.
10. See Pettit 2001, 268–299.
11. See Friese and Wagner 2002, 342–364; Chalmers 2003, 127–189.
12. Here I mainly follow Forst 2001, 345–378, although I shall partly depart from his view in some important respects primarily relating to an adequate (inadequate?) understanding of democratic proceduralism on the one hand and its institutional repercussions on the other (see below).
13. Forst 2001, 346.
14. See sections below. Needless to say that, for example, civic republican accounts centered in the (dialogical) idea of mutual understanding (which, despite its similarities with the Habermasian concept of "Verständigungsorientierung," remains different and derivative from it) differ markedly from pragmatist accounts, centered in the idea of problem solving and from epistemic accounts, centered in the idea of rational persuasion or agreement—a fact that proves far less than trivial if one compares the different recommendations that follow from these perspectives with respect to questions of the *finalité européenne*, to its constitutionalization and basic institutional structure.
15. Forst 2001, 362.
16. See Forst 2001, 374.
17. Estlund 2000a.
18. Forst 2001, 373.
19. See Schmalz-Bruns 2002, 59–74.
20. See Michelman 2001, 253–271.
21. Forst 2001, 367–368.
22. See Pettit 2001.
23. See Offe 1999, 42–87 (73).
24. See Hitzel-Cassagnes, forthcoming.

25. See Forst 2001, 369–370.

26. See Nassehi 2003, 133–169.

27. For a view which denies the reasons normally given in support of the thesis that the supranational features of the EU system undermine the normative principles of self-determination, self-legislation, and self-government (i.e. the idea of popular sovereignty) insofar as these are (at least up to now) institutionally and ethically realized at a level of already adequately democratized member states, compare Moravcsik 2003, 76–97. The problem with this view is that it is insufficiently fact-regarding and insensitive to normative concerns that cannot be met by efficient problem solving alone. Additionally, it does not take the restrictions on democratic self-government that arise from its transnational features seriously enough. An example of this includes an incompletely defined structure of dispersed and fragmented forms of authority. For an instructive criticism of this revisionist view see Ruchet 2004.

28. See Dahl 1999, 22. See also Offe and Preuß 2003, 201–202.

29. See Offe 2003, 153–157.

30. For this formulation of the dilemma see Bohman 2004.

31. This formulation I owe to Bohman 2004.

32. See Habermas 1998c, 91–169; Dryzek 2000.

33. Estlund 2000a, 2; see also Estlund 2000b, 252–275.

34. Estlund 2000a, 16.

35. See also Peters 2004, 20–23.

36. See Estlund 2000a, 14.

37. Estlund 2000a, 13, italics original.

38. Rehg and Bohman 1996, 79–99.

39. Rehg and Bohman 1996, 91.

40. Rehg and Bohman 1996, 91–93.

41. See Bohmann 2004.

42. This result would hardly be altered if we investigated the conceptual foundation of Tully 1995, which he more explicitly confronts in Tully 2002, 204–228.

43. Eriksen 2003, 159–225.

44. Eriksen 2003, 200, 193 and 214–215—although there remain some unresolved tensions in two alternative accounts of the same idea he provides in the paper on page 193 and on page 214.

45. Eriksen 2003, 208–211.

46. Eriksen 2003, 214–216.

47. Bohmann 2004 seems to have something very similar in mind, although his way of rendering the issue as "adequately democratizing" seems to me to be a little bit too defensive in that his version of "adequacy" would be informed by the normative as well as by the emergent structures of the EU. It is not quite clear whether this also means that it is the "ought" that follows the given.

48. Joerges 2003a.

49. Joerges 2003a, 37.

50. Bohman 2004.

51. Bohman 2004.

52. Habermas 2001a, 772–773.

53. Bohman 2004.

54. Bohman 2004.

55. See also Bohman 2004; Cohen and Sabel 2003, 367–368.

56. Bohman 2004.

57. Cf. Offe 2003, 151–181 (154–157).

58. Habermas 2001a, 774.

59. Folke Schuppert 2003.

60. Lord 2003.

61. Brunkhorst 2004, 221.

62. This is of course a concern originally formulated by Kant in his writing on "the eternal peace" and only recently rearticulated and reinvigorated by Habermas 2004b, 135.

63. For a recent articulation of this defensive perspective compare Abromeit 2002.

64. This again more defensive question is Habermas's starting point for developing a vision of a multilevel system of transnational governance which, as a whole, does not and "for very good reasons" must not adopt the character of a state: Habermas 2004b, 134.

65. Pollack 2003, 125–155; Lord 2003, 301ff.

66. See Offe 1999.

A COMMENT ON SCHMALZ-BRUNS

Erik O. Eriksen

I would like to make two interrelated remarks to the chapter of Rainer Schmalz-Bruns. One pertains to whether the EU can be depicted merely as a polycentric, transnational political entity. The other relates to the epistemic account of deliberative democracy as a basis for legitimacy.

Direct Legitimacy

The EU is a new type of organization. It is unprecedented and is demanding in empirical as well as in normative terms. What is really the nature of the beast and what kind of justifications can it possibly draw on? It is not a state, nor is it a nation. But it is more than a common market and it is not merely an intergovernmental organization that solves the perceived problems of the Member States. Increasingly it has developed into an organization in its own right.

The supremacy of EU law is well known. The autonomy of the European legal order constitutes the framework for the integration of national legal orders. EU law prevails in case of conflict. Further, codecision and qualified majority vote are now the standard decision-making procedures. Codecision, which requires the consent of the majorities in the Council and EP, rules out national vetoes. Unanimity among Member States has been turned into a special rule only applicable to certain policy fields such as social, tax, foreign, and security policy. Both developments weaken the position of Member States as masters of European integration. Indeed, the EU has become a polity which performs functions that affect the interests and identities of the citizens as well as the Member States. No one is any longer left untouched by the integration process. Hence, the Union can no longer draw on indirect legitimacy, and it has—post-Maastricht—tried to establish direct links with the citizens. Legitimacy established through domestic channels, through national democracy, has been supplemented with direct chains of influence.

In the standard literature the EU is held to be a polycentric organization with many decision-making centers and several lines of accountability. The proponents of deliberative democracy have made their case both descriptively and normatively in order to make sense of such an entity. Arguing rather than voting and bargaining is the currency of democracy. This is underscored by the EU which it is often described as a consensus democracy. As the bargaining resources are rather slim, the implementation of EU policies and further integration works efficiently only if the enforcement mechanisms resonate with a readiness on the part of the Member States to accept its disciplining role. The many veto points, the lack of forceful compliance mechanisms, representation and problem-solving through committees and networks underscore the deliberative mode of decision making. Reason giving in general is promoted through such mechanisms as public debate, institutionalized meeting places, peer and judicial review, complaint procedures, as well as having been enshrined as a principle of Community law since the very inception of the Communities.

The Deliberative Approach

Also in a normative sense deliberationists have a case as democratic legitimacy cannot stem from direct participation in collective decision making—the people are never present to make choices in modern complex states. It is also hard to see how democratic legitimacy can be based merely on votes, as voting procedures are loaded with aggregation problems. The principle of majority vote does not guarantee full political equality. The theory of deliberative democracy presents itself as an appealing alternative to adversary, economic, or aggregative models of democracy as it is an answer to the quality requirement of democracy, for example, that democratic decisions should be fair and rational. In particular it is a solution to the problem of finding correct answers to normatively charged risk decisions. Such cannot be found in rounds of voting or bargaining over contested issues. It is as nonsensical to hold a vote on the presence of mad-cow disease, as it is to bargain over the levels of dioxin in foodstuffs. Extended participation and more publicity also do not help much in reaching correct decisions in cognitively demanding cases. Nor can such questions be solved in a valid manner by subsuming them under legal statutes. Only deliberation under the strict criteria of truth and justice among competent actors is able to facilitate cogent answers. Hence the virtues of institutionalized deliberation and the merits of transnational deliberative governance as have been praised by many.

The trust of deliberative democracy is to be found in the fact that a free and open discourse brings forth qualitatively better decisions, and that the decisions are justified towards the affected parties. But there are (at least) two different readings of deliberative democracy's basic tenet—or of the discourse principle—that the laws should be justified to the ones bound by them. One—version A—is the participatory reading, which conceives of the democratic procedure as a set of citizenship rights that sets the conditions for justifying the laws. It is based on the moral value of deliberation revolving on the equality of the participants and where will formation is qualified with regard to what all can agree to and not with regard to what is universally valid. Democratic rights not only enable but also constrain the will formation process and hence establish criteria for legitimacy. Version B, the rationalistic reading, builds on the epistemic value of deliberation. Deliberation is held to lead to improvements in information and judgment conducive to a rational consensus and where the quality of the reasons makes for acceptability. On this reading institutionalized deliberation (among experts and representatives, in for example, committees) may be seen as contributing to a vital aspect of modern government, a part that is also intrinsic to the principle of representation.

Schmalz-Bruns subscribes to version B based on the epistemic account of the moral value of democratic procedures. However, the problem is how to link this in with democracy in the material sense, that is democracy as an organizational principle allowing for a state-like organization—or for the organized capacity to act, as it is framed. In particular how do we justify the principle of majority vote which goes to the core of the polity's capacity to act? The strong dependence on rational consensus, which is the criterion of legitimacy, does not seem to be very realistic under modern conditions.

Participation Versus Deliberation

Schmalz-Bruns' alternative is based on a changed conception of representation which he sees to be captured by the idea of public accountability. This as an alternative to standard representational solutions that will exceed the limit of the democratic resources available in Europe. Political decisions can be vindicated and justified in a public debate due to their epistemic quality. Deliberation contributes to the rationality of decision making which is intrinsic to democracy. The *raison d'être* of democratic procedures is to produce good or fair results. According to Jürgen Habermas the legitimating force of the democratic procedure is not merely to be found in participation and preference aggregation but in the access to processes that are of such quality that publicly acceptable decisions presumably can be reached.

But can practical discourses yield correct answers in the sense that argumentation makes clear what is just or equally good for all by securing the impartiality of judgment (version B), or must argumentation rather be seen as a requirement that makes participation possible (version A)? In the latter case, deliberation is needed for respecting and integrating the wants and beliefs of the citizens in collective decision making. On this reading, deliberation is a way to ensure that the reasons of each of the participants count in forging a qualified common will.

The epistemic reading of the discourse principle holds that a practical discourse is a way to improve judgment and reach correct—or fair—decisions. Deliberation makes impartiality of judgment possible when the actors adhere to the principles of rational argumentation. In order to find out what is equally good for all it is requested that everyone have a say. Deliberation has, then, cognitive or epistemic value as it examines whether claims and norms can pass the impartiality test; hence it makes for a rational appraisal of reasons. This proposal is an invaluable contribution to moral and political philosophy. The problem is how far one can stretch this perspective in order to justify practical political arrangements. Alternatively one could ask whether the discourse principle only indirectly can be applied to political affairs as the reality of others' will must be handled in a normative theory of democracy.

Schmalz-Bruns finds the critique of the epistemic approach to correctness misplaced as it neglects the level at which such perspective is applied: It is mainly thought of with regard to the constitutional essentials—citizens can reach a qualified consensus on the basic structure of society because it raises questions that can be settled with reference to deontological principles like individual freedom, human rights, solidarity, and equality. But still there is a big jump from the basic principles of deliberative democracy to the practical principles of modern democracy. There is a conceptual link between deliberation and state as there is no need for actors to comply with obligations unless others comply and there is no way to know what is right unless there is a legal specification of obligations. This can only be accomplished by a system of authoritative norm interpretation and one which also has the capability to sanction norm violations. Without sanctioning of strategic action, no communicative action. But these are merely functional arguments as are the ones given for justifying majority vote. Decisions are needed and technical devices for reaching them are required when consensus does not occur. What is lacking is a normative link— or autonomous reasons—for the state as well as for the majority principle.

Another problem is how one can know the quality of reasons in non-ideal situations. If we cannot know whether norms really are in the equal interest of all because the demanding requirements of a rational discourse cannot be approximated—even under ideal conditions it is impossible to include all affected (or their advocates)—maybe there is a case for the participatory reading of the deliberative ideal—version A. This version allow for equal procedures of decision making that revolve on the actual preferences (volitions) and interests of the citizens regardless of their normative quality. In this perspective, majority vote, constitutional rights, legal protections, and others can be seen as control forms that hinder technocracy and paternalism as they block that rationality shall put aside all other concerns. Constitutional barriers prevent relapse into ethnocentrism and political power can be camouflaged as rationality. This is important as also an intellectual instrumentalization is an instrumentalization after all and cannot be sustained insofar as democracy entails that the reasons for binding norms should be generally and reciprocally justifiable. Only the possibility to block and to revise on the basis of a popularly enacted government can redeem the claim of moral value of democratic procedures. The majority vote on its part is a way to avoid the unanimity requirement of a rational consensus, which also gives the right of veto to quarrelers, from preventing rational decisions from being made.

Without egalitarian procedures of lawmaking there is no democracy, because only then can the citizens effectively influence the laws that affect them, and determine whether the reasons provided are good enough. Thus, deliberation cannot replace institutionalized forms of control (including veto positions) and participation that are equally open to all. One might think of version B of the discourse principle as reserved for the procedure of testing the basic norms of the political order. That is, in a discourse on the constitutional essentials under idealized presuppositions, actors can reach a rational consensus on what is in the equal interest of all the affected parties. By abstracting from present constraints, by discussing typical situations and anticipating future states of norm application, actors may come to a rational agreement. (However, here we encounter another problem pertaining to whether the ideal discourse can ever actually be carried out or should merely be thought of as a device for the representation of free and equal citizens—a fictional situation for the anticipation of all situations where the norms are to be discovered according to a criterion of validity external to discourse á la Rawls' or Scanlon's contractualism.)

On the basis of these reflections the crucial question with regard to legitimacy can be posed: Is it the quality of the debate and that the outcomes are rational or fair that bears the burden of justification—without efficiency and rationality in decision making there is no legitimacy; or is it still the law-based, publicly accountable, and popularly enacted form of government that we know from the state level that is the main container of democratic legitimacy? Not surprisingly, the EU itself has been moving towards meeting the latter claim.

A Union in Motion

For Schmalz-Bruns the EU is a polycentric democratic order or a transnational political union. This is not a flat empirical depiction of the system in place, but a normative contention based on the insight that the social and cultural preconditions for standard representational solutions are not in place in Europe. The EU cannot or should not be more than a polycentric union. But is this an apt notion of the system in place and its normative topoi?

The institutional structure of the EU embodies a complex mixture of supranational, transnational, and intergovernmental elements. It is a supranational entity that does not fit the customary concept of state. The Union does not possess the required means, such as monopoly of violence and taxation, and a well-developed collective identity necessary for majority vote—to enforce its will. It is not sovereign within a fixed, contiguous, and clearly delimited territory. However, the EU has moved beyond an intergovernmental organization and is no longer merely a polycentric union. This started with the constitutionalization of the treaty system, which transformed the EC from an international regime into a quasi-federal legal system based on the precepts of higher law–constitutionalism.

Even though the EU is not a federation as it is based on a dual principle of legitimation and as the states control the Council—the most powerful body of the Union—it is a supranational polity. It has got a charter of fundamental rights, a (not yet fully developed) competence catalogue delimiting the powers of the various branches and levels of government, a two-chamber system of legislation, and it has authoritative dispute resolution mechanisms through the Court of Justice. Furthermore, Article 177 of the Treaty of Rome (EEC) states that whenever Community law is needed for the resolution of a dispute before a national court, the presiding judge may (sometimes must) request the ECJ for an adequate and authoritative interpretation. All legal persons and not just states, have judicially enforceable rights. The unity of law is (still) missing but the protracted constitutionalization processes, that can be seen to have been going on since the very inception of European integration—from the Paris Treaty of 1952 and onwards culminating with the Constitutional Convention 2002–2003—directs us to the fact that the reform process of the Union becomes comprehensible only when seen in light of a variant of standard representational, parliamentarian democracy.

Now this may be puzzling and indeed imply a technocratic overstretch of democratic resources, but since the early 1990s, the EU has changed from an organization whose legitimacy was derived from the Member States to an entity whose legitimacy is increasingly reflected in its own institutional and constitutional make-up. Initially the EP was a consultative body with very limited powers made up of representatives of national parliaments. Over time, and in particular after the introduction of the direct election of MEPs in 1979, its decision-making powers have grown. Recently, it has achieved codecision-making power with the Council in many areas and is increasingly curtailing the power of the Commission. To put it bluntly, democratizing the Union means its parliamentarization. This fact testifies to the strong model power of the democratic *Rechtsstaat* and the parliamentary principle. They establish the codes for proponents as well as opponents, for critique as well as justification of the European integration process and the structure in place. They, so to say, establish the conditions for comprehensiveness and acceptability, and I think a theory of a democratic European polity must resonate with such deeply embedded convictions because they are also part of what makes up the resources for democracy. Normatively speaking, the parliamentary principle does of course not exhaust the concept of democracy but may be seen to play a vital part of it as it makes it possible to expel the scoundrels when needed.

The challenge is to integrate such insights and intuitions with the theory of deliberative democracy premised on a reason-giving practice that warrants rational results. I think there is more work to do in order to redeem the claim of an epistemic account of the moral value of democratic procedures. To this endeavor Rainer Schmalz-Bruns, unequivocally, has provided significant food for thought.

13

Reconceptualizing the Supremacy of European Law: A Plea for a Supranational Conflict of Laws

Christian Joerges

IN THIS CHAPTER, I defend the assertion that deliberative supranationalism offers a viable alternative in the search for the constitutionalization of the European Union (EU) because it can be understood as a response to the problems of legitimacy concerning transnational governance in post-national constellations. What I undertake here is to present the gist of my thesis by stating my plea for a new (European) species of conflict of law without contrasting it with competing or neighboring projects.[1] I have de-liberately chosen to prioritize my argument and its underlying logic, which is a chronological reconstruction of its genesis.[2] Indeed, my starting point is to consider the judicial origin of the very notion of deliberative supranationalism in a discipline much older than that of European law, that of conflict of laws, in a specific approach to the choice-of-law problem. I will then turn to legal theory and recall the debates concerning the crisis of legal interventionism in the 1980s and the search for a postinterventionist legal theory and methodology, and it is only on that basis that I will enter the European arena. European law should be understood as a new species of conflict of laws—this is the thesis building on step one. In addition, this new type of law should learn the lessons of step two and proceduralize Europe's legal responses to the integrationist agenda. European law should adopt a conflict-of-laws methodology, and this methodology should incorporate the critique of legal interventionism; this synthesis of conflict of laws and legal theory should lead to a law of law production in the integration process, thus en-suring its law-mediated legitimacy.

Conflict of Laws versus Private International Law
and International Public Law

For students of international relations and European integration, international law and European law represent the legal dimension of their inquiries. However, the legal system is much richer: Each and every field of law (private law, economic law, labor law, administrative law) has an international branch, and private international law (PIL) figures as the mother of all of them. The (recent) legal history of international law and PIL is part of the political history of the sovereign nation-state, and the conceptualization of international relations in the various legal disciplines is based on the same paradigm as traditional theories of international relations. International law (*ius gentium*) was traditionally confined to an ordering of interstate relations and its contents and validity was based on the will of the states. National public law (and in particular the administrative law of nation-states) was perceived from outside and in transnational contexts as an emanation of sovereignty. A truly international public law was unthinkable because the very notion of an authority higher than that of the sovereign nation-state was inconceivable. Instead, the realm of all international public and administrative law and mandatory law was engaged in the one-sided delineation of the sphere of application of national provisions. This is because a state may recognize another sovereign but cannot exercise that state's sovereign power.[3]

In contrast, private international law (PIL) in the Von Savigny tradition was more universalistic in its orientation. This universalism was based upon an understanding of private law as the organizer of strictly private relations in what was, by definition, an apolitical (civil) society—*Gesellschaft*—and an application of foreign private law was not perceived as a threat to the sovereignty of the forum state. This ensuing type of PIL universalism is fully compatible with the refusal to support foreign regulatory objectives, considering such political dimensions beyond the scope of private law.

Private international law has, of course, developed enormously since its so-called classical era, but in Germany in particular the prevailing view has retained its Savignian legacy. It will suffice here to restate the main points as given in the leading textbook[4]: PIL determines the applicable law in cases with foreign elements, that is, links to or relationships with different legal systems. Its rules of rule selection are, in principle, indifferent as to the contents of the potentially applicable laws. In that respect PIL justice is categorically different from substantive justice: what it seeks to determine is not which law is better or more just but, rather, which legal system should govern. It is exactly this indifference towards content that enables national courts to accept and apply foreign law; indeed, it is thanks to this indifference that PIL's selection rules can be accepted by all jurisdictions, thus furthering the equality of decisions over legal controversies all over the world (*Entscheidungseinklang*). This type of universalism, however, is conceivable only in private law because only in private law, where the rules are dedicated to justice between private parties and thus apolitical, was it assumed that sovereignty is not affected by the application of a foreign law. In contrast, in all fields of public law and wherever political objectives are pursued through law, all the courts can do is unilaterally determine their own law's scope of application; they are not supposed to implement the commands of a foreign sovereign. As Germany's *maître penseur* puts it so succinctly, "Every State is an association of the citizens within it. . . . Every State promotes its own commonwealth in its own country; is free (master in its own house), accepts no orders from outside, and tolerates no judge over itself."[5]

This is, however, not the notion of conflict of laws I want to suggest should be brought to bear in the law of the EU. On the contrary, Europe and its law have, in effect, established quite contrary principles to those cited above. The most visible break with the tradition is Article 28 (ex Art. 30) and the duty to recognize (i.e., to apply) the law of other Member States; however, that rule responds to a conflict of laws. The discrepancy that exists between PIL traditionalism and European law has not done away with the necessity of developing rules to deal with differences between legal systems. Norm collisions are omnipresent within the EU, where diversity has become a value with constitutional status,[6] and it is not the elimination of diversity and norm collisions but the responses to diversity and the treatment of collisions that characterize the postnational quality of EU law.

In explaining my thesis I need to take a detour and present an American alternative to the Savignian tradition in PIL. In 1959, Brainerd Currie published an article in which he summarized his "misgivings concerning our method of handling problems in the conflict of laws."[7] In what was an important move, Currie started to make such misgivings public in 1958, continuing to do so until 1973, and he was successful in that he provoked intense debates, primarily in the United States, but also occasionally abroad.[8] Indeed, this move can be considered all the more successful by the fact that Currie's insights and queries have even had an impact on competing approaches and still presently continue to preoccupy the agenda of the discipline.

The strength of Currie's influence need not concern us here in any detail.[9] However, two elements of his approach are of crucial importance to my argument. The first is quite simple: All law, even private law, has become politicized in the sense that we understand it as a response not only to private quarrels but also to issues of social significance. This is why one can attribute policies to private law rules and even talk of an interest of a polity in the application of its policies. Currie utilized the (rather unfortunate) term "governmental interest" for this commitment, stating that

> 1. Normally, even in cases involving foreign elements, the court should be expected, as a matter of course, to apply the rule of decision found in the law of the forum . . . 4. ["False problems"] If the court finds that the forum state has no interest in the application of its policy, but that the foreign state has, it should apply the foreign law. 5. ["True conflicts"] If the court finds that the forum state has an interest in the application of its policy, it should apply the law of the forum, even though the foreign state also has an interest in the application of its contrary policy.[10]

All of these directives, amounting as they did to an assault on the most precious values and achievements of PIL, namely its tolerance towards foreign law, provoked heated debates. They brought a political dimension into the citadel of private law without indicating how the law could cope with this unruliness. These objections caused Currie to modify his position in his later writings, where he conceded that in cases of true conflicts, courts should resort to a "moderate and restrained interpretation" especially where their own jurisdiction was disinterested, thus avoiding conflicts.[11]

Nevertheless, despite this moderated stance, Currie's second query, namely his concern about the epistemic and constitutional limits of the judiciary, remains in place:

> [C]hoice between the competing interests of co-ordinate states is a political function of a high order, which ought not, in a democracy, to be committed to the judiciary . . . the court is not equipped to perform such a function; and the Constitution specifically confers that function upon Congress.[12]

Currie is not as hostile towards foreign public law as traditional PIL. But his call to accept the reign of foreign policies in the forum is based upon a kind of supremacy of governmental interests and policies concerning law. In cases of false and avoidable conflicts, the forum state does not need to decide upon a conflict of laws proper but simply respects the concerns of states. In a more legalized terminology: the forum does not apply legal principle but exercises *comitas*.[13]

European law, however, cannot tolerate this type of indifference towards the mandatory law of European Union Member States. In cases of true conflicts it amounts to blunt rejection, while also being unable to overcome the epistemic impasses of adjudication and enhance the policy-solving capacities of courts by means of treaty amendments or legislative fiat. Instead, European law must resort to alternative legal strategies and institutional devices, which has already been accomplished to a substantial degree. An explanation of this optimistic statement requires a second brief detour into legal theory.

Concepts of a Postinterventionist Law:
Reflexive Law, Proceduralization, and the Discovery Procedure
of Practice and the Turn from Government to Governance

The legal debates of the late 1960s and most of the 1970s, in Germany and elsewhere, were focused on the critique of legal formalism and the search for a new substantive or material legal rationality, which would further a socially progressive agenda. The optimism of that period, however, was not to last long. There was widespread disappointment over the implementation of purposive legal programs aimed at social change problem solving (*Zweckprogramme*),[14] and a growing concern regarding law's "intrusions into the life-world"[15] through social policy prescriptions. It became common ground in sociological jurisprudence and among the proponents of "law and . . ." studies that economic processes were embedded within societies in far more complex ways than a simple market-state dichotomy might have suggested.

The normative and pragmatic critiques of both purposive programs and command-and-control regulation motivated a search for alternatives, such as self-regulation, soft law, and what is now called governance arrangements. In terms of legal theory, this movement stimulated the development of the theory of reflexive law[16] and of proceduralization as a new legal paradigm.[17] Both of these concepts based themselves upon more indirect and organizational forms of legal programming through which the law could avoid overburdening itself.

A related (albeit not as famous) idea should also be mentioned, one that much later inspired my discovery and interpretation of comitology. In contrast to the mechanisms Friedrich A. von Hayek praised as the "discovery procedure of competition,"[18] complex democratic societies resort to coordinated forms of problem solving, to a discovery procedure of practice in which political and societal actors accommodate their interests and balance conflicting policy goals, while the law has to content itself with supervising the fairness of such activities.[19]

All of the concepts mentioned delegate problem-solving endeavors to nonlegal operations and re-integrate their outcome into the legal system by assigning legal validity to the solution found. They use law as an organizer and supervisor of processes but do not expect that exercises in classical legal methodologies suffice to generate the answers the law has to produce.[20] The term "governance" was not yet *en vogue* at the time, and what we are by now used to calling governance arrangements were already widely established. Since then the debate on the legitimacy (the constitutionalization, as I prefer to characterize this task) of these practices has become deeper and more differentiated.[21] The theoretical considerations of the 1980s have not become outdated, however, but continue to inspire the search for yardsticks and criteria with which governance arrangements must comply if they are to deserve recognition.

The links between our notes on the debates of the 1980s and the previous and following sections should be stressed here. Firstly, conflicts between the policy objectives pursued by legislatures are by no means restricted to international constellations; rather, these conflicts are a constitutive feature of the law of democratic societies—law has to endure pluralism and ongoing contestation. The legal systems of such polities cannot and should not prioritize one objective over others but, rather, should take account of the fact that the wisdom and power of the law are limited. In terms of conflict resolution, therefore, the law should encourage the concerned actors to take up the search for problem solving and interest mediation themselves. It should ensure that their activities respect principles of fairness, enhance their deliberative quality, and eventually acknowledge such societal norm generation. It is in this way that law can respond to collisions and contestations, and it can thus be characterized as conflicts law.

Europeanization as Process: Deliberative versus Orthodox Supranationalism

You can't have it all. Europe cannot aspire to become a unitary state underpinned by a unitary cultural identity and at the same time defend its diversity, its poststate quality, and cultural diversity. Nicolaus von Cues's *unitas in diversitas* or "united in diversity"[22] seems to be the more appealing formula. However, how could that appealing formula be substantiated?

Conceptualizing the EU

As lawyers we have heard the messages so often and, indeed, (some of us) have even taken them seriously: Europe is no federation, but it is more than a regime.[23] It is a heterarchical multilevel system *sui generis*[24] that must organize its political action in networks.[25] And since the powers and resources for political action are located at various and relatively autonomous levels in the EU, coping with functionally interwoven problem constellations will depend on communication between the various actors. This observation concerns something like normative fact, suggesting as it does that the interdependence of the concerned actors will produce a normative fabric that can exert factual power. In his account, Jürgen Neyer posits that the EU-specific conditions for political action favor a deliberative mode of communication that is bound by rules and principles, where arguments are only accepted if they are capable of universal application,[26] and where such considerations can be easily reconstructed in the language of the law. The European legal framework is neither designed merely to secure fundamental freedoms, nor to create a new European state. Instead, the purpose of European law is to discipline the actors within the Community in their political interactions and to guide strategic action towards a deliberative style of politics. European law should leave vertical (orthodox) supranationalism behind and, instead, found its validity as law on the normative (deliberative) quality of the political processes that create it.[27]

This being said, it is also clear that no state in Europe can make or refrain from making decisions without causing extra-territorial effects on its neighbors.[28] Provocatively put, perhaps, but brought to its logical conclusion this means, in effect, that nationally organized constitutional states are becoming increasingly incapable of acting democratically. They cannot include all those who will be affected by their decisions in the electoral processes, and vice versa—citizens cannot influence the behavior of those political actors who are making decisions on their behalf. It would, therefore, appear to be a legitimate step for Europe to require its Member States to design their national laws with the view of accommodating Community law. In the same vein, it would also seem sensible to afford to citizens of Member States legal rights that are truly European, given that they allow national citizens to compare their own laws with laws and experiences in other Member States.

These normative claims of deliberative supranationalism should not be portrayed as wishful thinking. They are both well documented and somewhat canonized in real existing European law, albeit in other terms. Examples may be found in doctrines where Member States of the Union cannot enforce their interests and laws unboundedly: They are bound to respect European freedoms; they may not discriminate; they may only pursue legitimate regulatory policies approved by the Community; they must coordinate in relation to what regulatory concerns they can follow; and they must design their national regulatory provisions in the most Community-friendly way.

So, what is the meaning of all this for the relationship between European and national law in general, and the Europeanization of private law in particular? How do these very abstract suggestions relate to the conflict of laws problematic and to the theoretical debates referred to in the previous sections? To answer these questions, I will, first of all, begin with a presentation of a rough typology of conflict constellations, and then restate an analytical distinction between deliberative supranationalism I (DSN I) and deliberative supranationalism II (DSN II).[29]

Three Types of Conflicts

Bundesrecht bricht Landesrecht or European law trumps national law. The supremacy principle suggests a vertical conflict between European law and national law, as supremacy is a conflicts rule. The advocates have justified it continuously and so successfully that we tend to take it for granted. But are there not some limits? Does this conflicts rule actually mean that European secondary law trumps national constitutional law? Was it really surprising that the German Constitutional Court in its Maastricht judgment claimed a competence in the interpretation of the fundamental rights of Germany's basic law?[30]

Horizontal conflicts between national legal systems are no longer governed exclusively by traditional PIL rules and principles. European law, especially through its nondiscrimination provisions, can exert corrective effects. Most importantly, European law cannot tolerate the principled refusal not to apply another Member State's public law in the present context. It even empowers European citizens with the right to expose the laws enacted by their own sovereign to judicial scrutiny.[31] To this conflict-of-laws revolution we will return under the heading of deliberative supranationalism I.

In terms of its problem-solving ambitions and capacities, European law is typically incomplete as it cannot cover all aspects of interdependent problem constellations. This can be illustrated by means of two very simple examples. European competition law may legalize the contractual conditions of distribution agreements that national contract law holds to be unfair and thus invalid, and European law may approve a new drug when it is national law that decides on the remuneration of patients by national insurance schemes. Such conflict constellations I have called diagonal.[32] They result from the assignment of competences to different levels of governments and, in these cases, it follows from the principle of enumerated European competences that the supremacy rule must not be applied.

Deliberative Supranationalism I: European Law as Conflicts Law and Conflicts Law as a Law of Lawmaking

I will first restate the normative foundations of deliberative supranationalism before explaining how this perspective changes our perception of European primary law and Europeanization.

The Case against Orthodox Supranationalism Restated

The basic claim of this chapter is that deliberative supranationalism offers a revised understanding of the supremacy of European over national law. It conceptualizes a form of European law that responds to differences in the laws of the EU Member States by resorting to principles and rules that are acceptable to all the national polities concerned. The normative basis for this correction of democratic polities is a nation-state failure; this failure comes to bear in the extra-territorial effects that any closed polity is bound to produce.[33]

Deliberative supranationalism can hence be conceptualized as a supplement to the model of the constitutional nation-state. It respects the nation-state's constitutional legitimacy while simultaneously clarifying and sanctioning the commitments arising from its interdependence with other democratically legitimate states, and with the supranational prerogatives that the institutionalization of this interdependence requires. The legitimacy of supranational constraints imposed upon the sovereignty of constitutional states seems obvious: Extra-territorial effects of national policies might be unintended but they are real and unavoidable in an economically and socially interdependent community. This raises the question of how a constitutional state could legitimize the burden it unilaterally imposes upon its neighbors. This is an old question, but one that presents a new urgency to the discussion. The globalization of markets has led to an even greater intensity in the interchange of extra-territorial effects between states, such as environmental costs and the energy used in the production of goods for export. From this perspective, territorial boundaries have become an ambiguous category of polity boundaries. The principle of no taxation without representation can claim universal validity because the very idea of democratic constitutionalism requires that constitutional states apply this principle in their own actions and hence take the interests and concerns of extra-territorial stakeholders into account. A supranational constitutional charter, therefore, does not need to represent a new state nor does supranationalism require democracies to concede a right to vote to nonnationals. However, it does require that the interests and concerns of nonnationals be considered even within the national polity and in this sense supranationalism does convey political (procedural) rights—and not just economic freedoms—to Community citizens. In this conception, supranationalism is a fundamentally democratic concept and so being, the supremacy of European law should be re-interpreted as giving a voice to foreign concerns and imposing corresponding constraints upon Member States.

Supremacy is not properly understood if it is ascribed to some transnational body of law. European law requires the identification of rules and principles that ensure both the coexistence of different constituencies and the compatibility of these constituencies' objectives with the common concerns they share. In that sense it is supreme.

Juridifying Deliberative Supranationalism

Community law should provide a legal framework so as to structure political deliberation around these issues. The ECJ has a constitutional mandate to protect such legal structures and principles, and to resolve controversies surrounding their contents. Here we will have to refrain from presenting our evidence in much detail and simply claim that European law has repeatedly managed to civilize national idiosyncrasies, with good reasons and considerable de facto success.[34]

One legendary example may serve to illustrate these contentions. In 1979 the Cassis de Dijon case[35] saw the European Court of Justice declare a German ban on the marketing of a French liqueur—the alcohol content of which was lower than its German counterpart—to be incompatible with the principle of free movement of goods.[36] The ECJ's response to the conflicts between French and German policies was as convincing as it was trifling: Any confusion on the part of German consumers could be avoided, and a reasonable degree of protection against erroneous decisions by German consumers could be achieved simply by disclosing the low alcohol content of the French liqueur. With this observation, the Court redefined the constitutional competence to review the legitimacy of national legislation, which presented a non-tariff barrier to free intra-Community trade. This represents a development of principled theoretical importance that had far-reaching practical impact. In order to translate the argument into the language of conflict of laws, the ECJ essentially identified a meta-norm that both France and Germany, as parties to the conflict, could accept. Since both countries were committed to the free trade objective, they were also prepared to accept that restrictions of free trade must be based on credible regulatory concerns.

The implicit rejection of the legacy of traditional doctrines on the treatment of foreign public law has become a necessity since product regulation, market-creating, and market-correcting regulatory policies are nothing exceptional. There is no such thing as an unregulated product. With ever more sophisticated products, trade requires the development of regulatory machinery ensuring the trustworthiness of such products—and the Member States of the EU must all recognize these concerns. The ECJ has, in fact, dealt with these implications quite sensitively, acknowledging that the autonomy of Member States deserves recognition but also, as Fritz Scharpf[37] has put it, that its exercise must be community compatible.

Two further discrepancies between European and traditional conflicts law should be underlined. European law does not typically choose between the given rules of two jurisdictions but requires amendments of national law. These changes may look marginal but can have far-reaching effects. European conflict solutions have an instigating function: They require changes, initiate learning, further transformations, organize diversity. To conclude with a defensive remark, DSN I is not about constituting some transnational democracy, as conflict of laws has never aspired to such a thing. Instead, DSN I is about the respect of constitutional democracies and the limitation of one of their failures. It is neither antidemocratic nor technocratic. Indeed, this second point can be more properly explained in the context of the discussion of comitology.

Deliberative Supranationalism II

Member States are being asked to make changes to their legal systems—changes that should in principle take place in order to guarantee that Europe's innovative impact will help national legal systems to evolve sensibly. European secondary law is widely understood as an alternative to the organization of *unitas in diversitas* just described. It is perceived and studied in terms of compliance and implementation, and the differences are by no means as fundamental as this terminology may suggest. Texts adopted in the European legislative process cannot reflect a uniform understanding. These legislative acts always and necessarily look different from the perspective of national legal systems simply because the adaptation of each of the national systems to the European prerogatives must reflect national traditions and be incorporated into non-unitary contexts. This is why comparative studies of compliance with European directives have revealed significantly different compliance patterns and Europeanization processes which mirror Europe's diversity quite faithfully.[38] For exactly that reason, European legislation has been content with adopting directives and legislative frameworks (especially in the realm of regulatory politics) which did not foresee just one central authority but gave rise to the infamous committee system that organizes the implementation of Community law as an ongoing process. Diversity, however, is just one reason for this phenomenon. The second is the nature of the problems to which this type of legislation must respond. The failures of legal interventionism which have preoccupied legal theory and sociological jurisprudence since the early 1980s and prompted the turn from government to governance are all present at the European level, and they are particularly burdensome because the Community lacks the competences and the resources to build up some genuine administrative machinery of its own—it simply has to resort to institutionally unforeseen governance arrangements. However, it should also reflect upon its constant institutional innovations and seek to ensure legitimacy so that they deserve recognition.[39]

New Modes of Transnational Governance in the EU

To repeat, it seems unsurprising that transnational governance structures have developed in Europe, and that these structures have their own logic and significance. The dynamics of this development cannot be described comprehensively here, let alone analyzed in their full complexity.[40] In order to characterize the differences between the adaptation processes that European law initiates at the national level of governance and the level of transnational dynamics, and the process of coordination between both levels, it is necessary to reiterate the distinction between DSN I and DSN II that I have been making since 2001[41]; namely that DSN I is a law of conflicts mediation, while DSN II is a law that responds to the apparently irresistible transformation of institutionalized government into transnational governance arrangements. This differentiation is not meant to overrule the grounding of deliberative supranationalism in a conflict-of-laws methodology, but rather pays tribute to what has been characterized above[42] as Brainerd Currie's second concern, namely his reluctance to accept any judicial evaluation of conflicting foreign policies and governmental interests. His terminology can be restated to show that the courts have neither the legitimacy to subject their home jurisdictions to some transnational governance arrangement, nor are they equipped with the management capacities and epistemic resources needed to find out what good transnational governance might require.

However, while these are all still valid in principle, what Currie did not observe and could hardly have predicted was the transformation and evolution of regulatory practices during the last decades—and, in particular, the turn from government to governance which both enabled and forced the legal system to content itself with proceduralized controls. That turn has affected national legal systems substantially, but the case for governance proved to be even more compelling at the European and international levels. This is because institutional frameworks that establish the common European market ensure the functioning of international trade and a globalizing economy. These frameworks cannot be built upon the administrative infrastructures nation-states have at their disposal. The forms vary enormously. Within Europe we witness the establishment of ever more agencies and the design of ever-new regulatory strategies and forms of cooperation between and across all levels. What they have in common, however, is that they delegate problem solving to non-legislative levels, and engage experts and societal experts in the consideration of these responses.

The paradigmatic institutional setting in Europe is currently a broad legislative framework with generalizing answer of such vagueness that the implementation process will require additional decision making, which cannot be adequately understood as a mere application of the legislatively approved principles. Can such a process be understood in the terms of conflict of laws? Yes, if one subscribes to the characterizations substantiated above. To reiterate, conflict of laws is not about the selection of rules, the proper choice among a given set of ready-made responses to regulatory issues. It is about the search for a response to legal diversity that ensures compatibility with Community concerns while respecting the autonomy of democratically legitimated actors. So, what else is at stake when implementation is delegated to a composite of European and national governmental and nongovernmental actors? The answer will depend on the governance arrangements under scrutiny, and cannot be comprehensive and general. The only case that will be addressed here is comitology, a case that, it is submitted, fits into the conflict-of-laws paradigm.[43]

The Example of the Committee System—Comitology

Comitology is just one of the new modes of governance, albeit a particularly prominent one. Its institutional history is old and well documented[44] and our knowledge as to its functioning is comparatively solid.[45] The academic debate is intense, however, because comitology is a moving target, within which all institutional actors continue to pursue their particular strategies.[46] The European Parliament pleads for more supervisory powers, whereas the European Commission would like to become the head of Europe's regulatory machinery and work with executive agencies rather than committees in which the Member States remain influential. The Draft Constitutional Treaty, in Articles 32–36, has adopted the recommendations of the Working Group XI of the Convention on simplification,[47] in which three types of nonlegislative acts are listed: delegated regulations, European implementing regulations, and European implementing decisions to be adopted by the Commission.[48] It is difficult to see what is to be simplified by these proposals. And it would be misleading to present the suggested substitution of comitology by Commission-led European administrative machinery as a purely technical innovation. It seems safe, however, to predict that the proposed amendments will have very limited effects. Their framing and wording can only camouflage but not remove the political and normative dimensions of implementing acts. The assignment of these acts to the Commission cannot overcome the objections and anxieties, which so far have been articulated through representatives of the Member States. It thus appears certain that the issues discussed in the debates on comitology will remain on the European agenda.

These issues all concern Europe's aspiration to realize its *unitas in diversitas,* and four points in particular deserve to be mentioned:

Is it reasonable or even conceivable to conceptualize unitary European market governance? The comitology system had fostered a bundling of resources and the involvement of the national level of governance while retaining the supervisory and ultimately autonomous decision-making powers of the Member States.

The type of activity performed via comitology does not fit into our inherited understandings of legislation, adjudication, and rule-bound administration. This phenomenon both mirrors and embodies the functional, structural, and normative tensions that characterize modern markets. These markets are politicized and thus, politically accountable while economic actors cannot simply disregard the concerns and anxieties of market citizens (consumers). However, neither the political nor the legal systems can provide the epistemic and managerial capacities that would ensure their effective functioning and social responsibility. Hence it is unsurprising that comitology is being composed of technical experts and (political) governmental bodies, and also that societal actors take an interest in its functioning. Comitology hovers between technical and political considerations and between functional needs and ethical/social criteria. The system represents an underworld,[49] albeit one that ensures the social embeddedness of markets, and without which Europe's common market would cease to function. In order to link these observations and theses to the introductory sections on conflict of laws and on legal theory, it can be stated that comitology responds to the nonunitary social embeddedness of the European common market. In the European constellation, market governance continues to require that the concerns of various jurisdictions be accommodated, but these responses can neither be produced nor attributed to some superior and unitary authority. Instead they result from the search responses that the polities concerned can endorse. In view of its affinities to the horizontal conflict of law in the EU, comitology can be understood as a conflict-of-laws mechanism.

The committees have to respect the pertinent legal framework within which they operate as well as general principles of European law. However, they need to be productive and cannot deduce the contents of their responses from these texts. This is why their search activities can be understood as a "discovery procedure of practice,"[50]—although this is, of course, not to say that these searches will always be successful!

The third issue is the thorniest: does comitology deserve recognition and how can its legitimacy be enhanced? Some objections are easy to refute, others less so. First, comitology is often portrayed as technocratic governance. National and European administrators and all kinds of experts are involved in comitology. This composition looks Kafkaesque; indeed, its critique as a technocratic machinery suggests this itself. The point that comitology appears to be technocratic, and operates within a hegemonic organizational structure has often been repeated, most recently by Hauke Brunkhorst.[51] However, this is not what Jürgen Neyer and I observed and described almost a decade ago.[52] To restate a later defense, "[C]ommittees do not just have the so-called 'implementation' function of Community framework provisions to deal with (comitology proper), they also operate much more comprehensively as fora for political processes and as coordinating bodies between supranational and national and governmental and social actors."[53] Competing scientific schools of thought, risk management strategies, and public concerns raised by public bodies and societal actors need to be and are, in fact, addressed.

Second, Joseph Weiler argues that comitology "is not a discreet phenomenon which occurs at the end of the decision-making process. . . . It is more like the discovery of a new sub-atomic particle, a neutrino or a quark, affecting the entirety of molecular physics which requires an account of both the phenomenon itself and the way it impacts the rest of nuclear understanding. *Comitology* argues for a rewriting of the entire decision-making field because of the importance of the committee particle in all its stages."[54] Weiler's observations are valid, and often approvingly registered,[55] but what follows from them? Do they simply rephrase what I have characterized as the social embeddedness of markets? If it is true that economy and society are being infused with more norms, the constant noise concerning deregulation and liberalization notwithstanding, then we are not free to reject such phenomena but should instead try to understand their causes and aim to cure their deficiencies. As we have argued repeatedly, the turn to governance even within constitutional states is a response to the politicization of markets and to the saliency of concerns that the state regulatory machinery is unable to cope with. Comitology is an accompanying phenomenon in the European market-building process, a mode of generating resources and organizing interactions that support and domesticate market building. If these assumptions have some *fundamentum in re*, it seems all the more important to explore the potential of law to ensure the legitimacy of the committee system.

Third, it is often argued that comitology is undemocratic. Rainer Schmalz-Bruns was the first to underline the fact that deliberative supranationalism cannot be equated with democratic governance.[56] Since then many others have followed suit.[57] His observation is valid in that it would be absurd to interpret deliberative modes of interaction within comitology as the advent of deliberative democracy in the EU. The conflict-of-laws approach to European law and comitology governance, which I have restated here, cannot and does not claim to establish what the protagonists of the theories of deliberative democracy have in mind. Does it follow, then, that conflict of laws is undemocratic? A better question is, is it conceivable to practice conflict of laws in general and comitology in particular in a democracy compatible way?

A final question restates the challenge Jürgen Neyer and I have addressed in our quest for a constitutionalization of comitology.[58] What is at issue for a conflict-of-laws perspective is not the establishment of a European constitutional state within which governance arrangements could be supervised the same way as within national democracies. Instead, our queries concern the normative legitimacy of a conflict-of-laws approach to transnational governance. Only from such a perspective does it make sense to explore the legal structuring of the discovery procedures through which we expect comitology to arrive at detailed responses to complex conflict constellations. The following should all be considered: the composition of communications and their interactions, the openness of their agenda, the access of concerned societal actors, the pluralism of expertise, judicial protection, safeguard procedures, a supervision of the whole process by national and European parliamentary bodies and exit options in cases where conflicts cannot be resolved.[59]

The validity of this approach does not depend on the gradual rise or sudden fall of comitology. Instead, deliberative supranationalism strives for a conceptualization of the *unitas in diversitas* formula; it seeks to conceptualize Europeanization as process, methodologically speaking, and a discovery procedure of practice in which law generates and supervises public power. The conflict-of-laws approach to the problematic of good transnational governance certainly has its *lacunae* and deficiencies but, to cite Brainerd Currie again, "Let me stick with it until someone else comes along with a better idea."[60]

Notes

I would like to thank Florian Rödl, PhD Researcher at the European University Institute, for his many helpful comments and his colleague Jennifer Hendry for her manifold assistance in the production of this essay.

1. See first and foremost Gunther Teubner's perspectives for a legal reconstruction of (his version of) systems theory in a conflict of laws terminology, Teubner 1996b, 199–220; Teubner 1996a, 901–918; Teubner 2003, 1–28; and the English version, Teubner 2004a, 3–28; Teubner and Fischer-Lescano 2004, 999–1046. See also Amstutz 2003, 213–237.

2. I have attempted this previously: Joerges 1999a, 185–242 [English version: Joerges 2001]; Joerges 2002a, 133–151; Joerges 2003a, 501–540.

3. See Vogel 1965, 176–239; for alternative traditions, cf. Tietje 2001. See also Joerges 1979, 6–79; for a surprisingly similar recent reconstruction, see Humrich 2004, 17ff. Humrich restricts his—otherwise enormously rich—analysis to "international law in the narrow sense of interstate law" (3). In that respect international law and international relations scholars tend to share the same benign neglect of international economic law (*Wirtschaftskollisionsrecht*) that accompanied the transformation from the liberal to the interventionist state.

4. Kegel and Schurig 2004, in particular page 4 on the definition of PIL, page 131 ff on PIL justice, and page 139 on uniformity of decision making.

5. Kegel and Schurig 2004, 1094.

6. Cf. Article I-8 of the "Treaty Establishing a Constitution for Europe" (OJ C 310/1 of 16–12, 2004).

7. Currie 1963b, 177–187.

8. For example, Joerges 1971; Schnyder 1990.

9. The most constructive contributions to this tradition that I am aware of are by Kramer 1991, 245–278; Kramer1990, 277–345.

10. Currie 1963b, 183–184; see also Currie 1963a, 1233, at 1242 ff.

11. Currie 1963c, 754, 763. The term "avoidable conflicts" is, however, from Cavers 1965, 73.

12. Currie 1963b, 272.

13. This is an ancient doctrine with a complex history and an ambivalent heritage (critically reviewed by Paul 1991, 1–79). Its dark side is a subordination of law under political prerogatives and the denial of legal duties to respect foreign law and interests. Its brighter side, which we recall, are commitments that do not arise out of juridified obligations but, rather, out of friendship and trust among nations.

14. This is famously summarized and analyzed by Teubner 1987, 3–48.

15. Habermas 1985, 203–220; Habermas 1981, 332–368; Habermas 1981, 257–296 and esp. 504–521.

16. Teubner 1983, 239–285.

17. Wiethölter 1989, 501–510; Habermas 1992, 516–537; Habermas 1998a, 13–25.

18. von Hayek 1969, 249–265.

19. Joerges 1981, 111–115; Joerges 1986, 142–163.

20. Rudolf Wiethölter captures this point elegantly in his term *Recht-Fertigungs-Recht* (law of law production); see Wiethölter 2003, 13–21. The term *Gesellschafts-Recht* (societal law) points to the generation of law and the involvement of societal actors.

21. For a recent instructive and thoughtful account of primarily German contributions cf. Folke Schuppert 2004 (on file with author).

22. Preamble of the Treaty Establishing a Constitution for Europe, paragraph 4.

23. Wallace 1983, 403–436.

24. Instructive are contributions to Jachtenfuchs and Kohler-Koch 2003; for earlier summaries see Jachtenfuchs 2001, 221–240 and Scharpf 2001b, 1–26.

25. Cf. for an adaptation in legal science, see Ladeur 1997, 33–54; Teubner 2004b, 17–22 and *passim*.

26. Neyer 2003, 687–706; more detailed in his habilitation thesis, see Neyer 2004.

27. See Joerges and Neyer1997a, 273–299; Joerges 2002b, 219–242.
28. See Joerges 1997b, 378–406.
29. Joerges and Sand 2001.
30. Judgment on the Maastricht Treaty of 12 October 1993, *Entscheidungen des Bundesverfassungsgerichts* 89, 155, (1994).
31. Cf. Joerges, 2004b, Sections II 2 and III.
32. Cf., Joerges, 1997b, 378–406 (Section IV A 2); Schmid 1998, 185–191.
33. Similarly, Zürn 1999.
34. Cf., Poiares Maduro 1998, 150–220.
35. European Court of Justice, Cassis de Dijon (Case 120/78, ECR [1979] 649), 1979.
36. Article 30 EC Treaty, now 28 EC.
37. Scharpf 1994, 219–242.
38. Cf., very instructively, Falkner 2005.
39. The formula is taken from Habermas 2001b, 113–129.
40. For a generalizing overview, cf. Joerges and Everson forthcoming; for a critical discussion of the OMC cf. Joerges 2004c.
41. Joerges and Sand 2001.
42. Currie 1963b, 272.
43. The same holds true for diagonal conflicts. Such conflict constellations require a coordination of national with Europeanized competencies. Uniform substantive rules cannot provide adequate answers. For an exemplary discussion cf. Joerges 2004b, Sections II.3 and III.3.
44. For example, see Falke 1996, 117–165.
45. Cf., for example, Joerges and Falke 2000; Trondal 2001; Töller 2000, 313–342.
46. Cf., for a topical overview, see Vos 2005.
47. The "Amato-Report"—CONV 424/02, available at european-convention.eu.int/.
48. Cf. Vos 2004, 111–121.
49. J.H.H. Weiler 1998, 9.
50. Cf., the very early and productive sociological study by Roethe 1994.
51. Brunkhorst 2004.
52. Joerges and Neyer 1997a.
53. Joerges 2002a, 141.
54. Weiler 1999a, 340.
55. Most prominently, perhaps, Mestmäcker 2003, 69–71.
56. Schmalz-Bruns 1999, 185–242.
57. For example, Gerstenberg and Sabel 2002, 295.
58. Joerges and Neyer 1997a.
59. Joerges 1999b, 326–338.
60. Currie 1963a, 1243.

A COMMENT ON JOERGES

Damian Chalmers

Joerges has remarked that his is not an essay about deliberative democracy, but one about the relationship between law and the authority of public power. To be sure, the subject matter is the reconceptualization of the European Union, yet the central concern is the control of public power. He is particularly concerned with the legal limitation of territorial power: both how law may control its abuse within the European law and also how law is contributing to its unbundling within the European Union. Joerges's work, however, and this is part of its genius, is also about the limits of law. Law cannot effectively control territorial power through setting out substantive policies. Instead, law's legitimacy derives from its being able to set out the places where choices about these policies are made and the procedural terms under which these choices are made. The innovativeness and multidimensionality of his approach, combined with the rich detail of his case studies, has led to Joerges's work being the most significant and interesting in helping us understand how institutional power is restructured and played out within the European integration process. This essay will argue that his natural modesty has perhaps led him to understate the radical potential of his work.

The unconfined and polyfaceted nature of supranational governance has led not so much to its limiting the territorial power of the nation-state as to its undercutting territoriality's claim to be the central source of political and legal authority within the European Union. The traditional territorial sovereign has increasingly little say in the constellations of norms that will apply to an expanding array of disputes within its territory. This affects how one views the constellations of power emerging within the European Union more radically than Joerges implies, as the unbundling of territoriality makes territorial/extra-territorial dichotomies increasingly difficult to apply.

It also affects how one views the authority of law. Territoriality has been the central pillar upon which law's claim to have the capacity to exercise authority has traditionally rested. If it can no longer do this, law must look to other structures to enable it to exercise authority over its subjects. This essay will argue that two have emerged in the world of supranational governance: actors accept the authority of law as it both allows them to confine contestation to manageable proportions and also allows them to come together to solve problems. Yet, just as the territorial authority of law excluded extra-territorial stakeholders, this essay will argue that these two new sources of authority generate their own patterns of exclusion and division, which are no less problematic than those raised by territoriality, and it is increasingly to these that the mission of democratic legitimacy must turn its eye.

Deliberative Supranationalism: An Essay about Territorial Power?

Although Joerges does not make it explicit, there is a strong link here between his work on deliberative supranationalism and his work on the influence of National Socialism in European law.[1] National Socialism sacralized the political as a form of public power in quite terrible ways, but was also alert to the repressive and invidious consequences of other forms of public power, most notably techno-administrative power.[2] By contrast, his interest in supranationalism rests in the ways it has problematized the territorial power of the state. Territoriality, the assertion of control over a geographical area, allows two forms of intense public power to be harnessed.[3] It is the basis for state sovereignty: that coercive power which impacts so directly upon the senses of its subjects that territorial sovereignty has become the power to let live. It is also the basis for governmental power. Territory provides the jurisdiction over which a government acts over its subjects for the benefit of its subjects, and, which through its panoply of welfare and regulatory institutions, government has traditionally induced broader patterns of routinization, hierarchy, and proto-organization on the parts of its subjects.[4]

Joerges, on my reading, is concerned with the authority of these forms of power: authority both as something which constitutes an institutionally recognized right to influence the actions of others and something which provides subjects with good reasons, other than fear, to obey these forms of power. Traditional accounts have done this through locating the authority of both state sovereignty and government in the constituent power of the people. Sovereignty's existence depends upon its acceptance by its collective subjects,[5] so the sovereignty of EC law is contingent for its existence upon its acceptance as such by its subjects. Doubts lie, therefore, in part in the contestation of its power by national courts and others, and, in part, by the lack of any clear constituent power which can be ascribed to confer sovereignty upon EC law. The authority of governmental power rests in its public nature. It is done in the public interest and the government is accountable to the people and can be changed by the people. It is done for a public subject and is accountable to a public subject. Administrative power exercised for private ends is seen as corruption, whilst governments no longer hold power once they have been voted out of power.

The position of the foreigner poses real challenges for the authority of these two types of power. Not considered to form part of the public subject, there are no clear reasons that can be given for the foreigner accepting the authority of either, other than brute force. The solution of the Westphalian system to this bind was to deny the foreigner's existence. Individuals were not treated as legal subjects in international law. They were not part of an international society with reciprocal rights and duties. They existed only as the chattel of states who could choose whether to intervene upon their behalf. Even then, the forms diplomatic protection could take were extremely limited as the central organizing principle of international law was nonintervention and nonaggression. The foreigners could not, thus, ask their home states to intervene too directly on their behalf.

EU law changes this through the grant of legal subjectivity to the foreigner. *Van Gend en Loos* created the idea of a European legal subject, who could invoke certain indefeasible rights wherever she is in the territory of the Union.[6] They can be invoked against her home state or against other states. To be sure, these rights are highly partial ones. The European legal subject is not a freestanding subject, but is constituted by the patchwork of rights given by substantive provisions of EU law. Nevertheless, the change is revolutionary. The foreigner's subjectivity is recognized and the national administration must now provide reasons to her why she should accept its authority and these reasons must be regarded as good reasons by an independent arbiter, namely EU law. This characterization of EU law has been the central determinant on most writing on supranationality. Supranationality is seen as corrective against boundary abuse by the nation-state. Weiler has argued that it acts to prevent three types of abuse: violence against other states; actions where the state invokes the images of nationhood for ends that are clearly not for the public good, and abuses against strangers who do not form part of the collective "Us."[7] Similar reasoning has been used by other writers, most notably Maduro and Somek. Maduro conceives supranationalism, therefore, as curbing representation deficits that emerge from the insular perspectives of the nation-state. It acts to protect the interests of foreigners where these have not been represented or have been unrepresented.[8] Somek, by contrast, has argued that supranationality curbs those disadvantages which are a systemic consequence of the co-existence of nation-states. He argues, most notably, that states cannot prohibit discrimination on grounds of nationality without denying their existence. Supranationality is concerned to do something that the nation-state cannot do: prohibit discrimination on grounds of nationality. Somek is concerned, in particular, with securing equality around two sorts of entitlement that he sees as the prerogative of the modern liberal state. The one derives from what he terms the constitution of liberty, and includes classic civil liberties and property rights. The other derives from the constitution of inclusion, and includes all those social rights that correct disadvantages and externalities that emerge from the functioning of the market.[9]

Joerges can be characterized as a skillful exponent of this tradition. If the others focus on the policing of imagined communities, institutional malfunction, and membership rights, his concern is the limits of territorial authority in an interdependent world. His two models of deliberative supranationalism parallel, in this regard, two dimensions of territoriality problematized by the European Union.

Deliberative supranationalism I (DSN I) reflects the manner in which territorial integrity has been compromised in the modern world. Territorial integrity is historically central to state self-government. It implies that the state has complete freedom over the actions that take place on its territory, whilst respecting the equivalent freedom of other states over their territories. Joerges observes that the extra-territorial effects of state actions, whether they like it or not, compromise that integrity. They compromise other states' capacities to govern themselves and affect the interests of extra-territorial stakeholders who lose the capacity to govern themselves. DSN I responds to this bind by requiring a state to respect the rights that extra-territorial stakeholders have acquired in their home territory provided these do not impair the state's capacity for self-government legitimately carried out for the general good.

DSN II concerns itself with the problem of territorial unity. Territorial unity would require that the law be applied equally across the territory of the Union. Joerges observes that this is impossible for Union law for a number of reasons. When seen from the national context, Union law must accommodate a number of non-unitary contexts. These pull it in diverse ways in different territories. In addition, there is the problem of diagonal law. Union law rarely comprehensively regulates a legal problem.[10] Instead, it intersects with different legal provisions, which will result in unique constellations of legal norms governing any individual problem. DSN II responds to there being more than one legal authority governing any part of the territory of the Union. It seeks to secure compatibility with Union concerns while respecting the autonomy of democratically legitimated actors. Joerges observes that governance has been the turn that has allowed this. Governance is concerned with mediating these concerns. It is characterized by, on the one hand, a multiplicity of forms, and, on the other, by a shared use of experts and societal experts (eg NGOs, industry) to coordinate decision making between these centers of power.

Even at this level, Joerges' work operates at a level of sophistication that is unmatched. The location of supranationalism around territoriality allows it to be seen as something that polices not only nation-states (DSN I) but also center-periphery relations in the exercise of Union competencies (DSN II). It is a norm governing all political decision making within the Union rather than simply targeted at the nation- state. It also operates at a level of reconstructive sophistication that none of the other work musters in that it is based on detailed case studies of institutional practice. As a consequence, it can suggest the ends and means for the realization of supranationalism in far more convincing and practical ways than almost all other writing.

Interpreted in this way, Joerges's model of deliberative supranationalism is still one that rests within rather than challenges classic liberal political theory. Deliberative supranationalism is seen as something external to the state, which does not challenge the state's traditional constitutional authority. It merely engages in an exercise of enfranchisement by granting the classical liberal rights and duties to extraterritorial stakeholders that states have traditionally granted to their own citizens. However, this takes it as something that is external to the nation-state. It does not reconstitute nation-state authority in any deep way, but is at times a check on it and at other times an important alternate center of political gravity. Joerges suggests, therefore, that deliberative supranationalism does not challenge the constitutional legitimacy of the nation-state. Some critics have taken this interpretation as the basis for their criticism. They claim that deliberative supranationalism is too timorous from a liberal perspective. It exalts technocratic arguments and interests too much, and is insufficiently attentive to either the range of interests or plurality of arguments required by deliberative democracy. Only Weiler has taken an alternative interpretation. He has argued that the central dynamics of deliberative supranationalism are infranational ones. The dynamos of decision making are not Community versus nation-state, but those of sectoralism, functionalism, and managerialism.[11] Yet even Weiler then considers that it is a quark that must be tamed according to the traditional values of the nation-state. The task is to infuse it with the political values of equality of access, transparency, and political accountability.[12]

I wonder if such views are not too concerned with the formal architecture of decision making, and take, consequently, too static an interpretation. They fail to take account sufficiently of the material dimension of these phenomena. That is to say, they are government practices concerned with doing things, structured, above all, by the contingency and parameters of the events with which they deal. They are not merely novel spatially, insofar as they reterritorialize law and politics. They are also novel materially in that they are reacting to new challenges. Some of these are inspired by technology (e.g., biotechnology, internet regulation, futures markets in financial services) while others are inspired by the need to create new public goods (e.g., the single market, the precautionary principle). The consequence is that these phenomena are too diverse and fluid to be fitted into neat territorial versus extra-territorial stakeholder packages. Three scenarios can illustrate this point, none of which fit comfortably into the models suggested by Joerges.

1. *Domestic Redistribution Through Foreign Law:* The first scenario is one set out in *Cassis de Dijon.*[13] To be sure, one has a situation where a foreign good is marketed in Germany according to conditions largely set by French law. But is this really a case of deliberative supranationalism? A case where Germany is being required to take account of non-German stakeholders? The case was, after all, not between the French producers of Cassis de Dijon and the German authorities. The parties to the dispute were exclusively German. It was between Rewe, a German distributor, and the German regulatory authorities. It was not only the parties to the dispute that were domestic, the center of gravity of the dispute was also domestic. Cassis de Dijon is not a widely sold drink. Instead, it was used as the touch paper to resolve a wider redistributive question between German distributors and German producers, namely whether the former could increase their profits through selling a wider array of alcoholic drinks at the expense of the latter's profits. It is difficult to see the center of the dispute as one protecting marginalized stakeholders. Instead, the more interesting question is why a dispute between two constellations of powerful domestic interests should be decided to be determined by the law of another Member State.

2. *Domestic Redistribution Through Deregulation:* Cassis de Dijon concerned a distributor. It was therefore relatively easy to point to a foreign good that they were distributing, which imported its legal regime with it. Increasing numbers of cases involving the economic freedoms do not involve distributors, but retailers. This is not simply an arcane point about the remit of the economic freedoms. It also goes to the nature of the conflicts of law developed by Joerges. He rightly points out that Cassis de Dijon was not about deregulation about choosing whether to apply German or French law in the German court. In these other cases, the choice is not that. It is about whether to legally regulate or not to legally regulate. *Anomar* is a case in point. The Portuguese Gambling Machines Assocation (Anomar) challenged a Portuguese law which provided that gambling machines could only be operated in casinos in designated areas.[14] They argued that it breached Article 49 EC, the pro-

vision requiring free movement of services. The matter appeared wholly Portuguese in nature, as it was a case brought by Portuguese companies against a Portuguese law. It was also essentially a redistributive domestic dispute. Casinos had historically monopolized the market for gaming machines, and Anomar wished to break this stranglehold. The Court held that for Article 49 EC to apply, it was unnecessary to point to particular foreign service providers who might be unable to operate gambling services, if there were identifiable foreign operators who might do so. If the measure fell within Article 49 EC, the Court observed, it would still be lawful, as it could be justified as necessary to meet a variety of public interests, notably the protection of consumers, the prevention of fraud and crime, and the protection of public morality. The extraterritorial interest protected in this case is so small as to be almost invisible. More interestingly, the choice of laws regulating the conditions of competition between machine operators is not between Portuguese law and another state's law, but between Portuguese law and no law. The case is one about the limits of legal authority.

3. *Denationalization and Reterritorialization*: The final scenario concerns the possibility of EU law creating its own territorial unities. Joerges gives comitology as an example of a mechanism to deal with the lack of territorial unity within the Union, whereby the committees overseeing the Commission are a mixture of national representative, social expert, and technical expert. What happens, however, when one of these dimensions becomes so powerful that it dominates the other two? There is, indeed, a strong suspicion that increasingly the process is becoming colonized by scientific expertise at the expense of values of national representation and societal pluralism. The Commission is increasingly bound by the views of the scientific committees or regulatory agencies it is required to consult in adopting draft measures.[15] These bodies are increasingly unrepresentative bodies.[16] To be sure, the measures must pass the Standing Committees before they can be adopted as law. These are composed of national representatives, but studies have shown that processes of socialization have led to these becoming increasingly deliberative rather than terrains for negotiating representative interests.[17] In such circumstances, a territorial unity is created. It is created not by representative institutions but by scientific expertise, and is a *Grossraum* centered around the political virtue of expertise, which, insofar as it is based upon more general beliefs, transcends and incorporates the Union.[18] The central questions within this *Grossraum* are not the accommodation of different centers of power and plural societal interests, but rather the boundaries of its operation: to what extent is rule by law being replaced by rule by

expertise and with what are technical experts replacing representatives in the making of collectively binding decisions.

The consequence is that the scenarios discovered by Joerges are much more multiple, contingent, and fluid than he suggests. They involve a wider array of interests, a wider variety of legal norms, wider forms of social conflict, and also conflicts between legal and other forms of institutional norm. It becomes impossible, thus, to see these conflicts as something that occurs beyond the nation-state. They happen within the nation-state and are transforming institutional authority within the nation-state. Representative surpluses, where actors who can arbitrage between different fora are enfranchised at the expense of those who cannot, are as much a problem as representative deficits.[19] Consequently, territoriality ceases to be constitutive of legal and political authority.[20] It is not merely that a variety of norms apply over the territory of any Member State and that these govern a wide array of matters, but the choice of applicable norm to apply is highly uncertain and contingent. The slightest difference in factual circumstances can alter which is applicable. Consequently, if a state or the Union no longer has the power to determine which norms apply within its territory, it becomes difficult for it to harness the resources which allow and justify both sovereign and governmental authority. It can neither determine authoritatively the circumstances when the coercive power of the state will be brought to bear upon the individual nor does it have the capacity to allocate power for the realization of public goods, as this is now dispersed to a wide variety of actors, each with their own powers of norm setting and organization.

Deliberative Supranationalism and the Rediscovery of the Authority of Law

Law's authority cannot rely upon the background territorial power of the state, but must depend upon some other power. Joerges's concern with Brainerd Currie's work on the conflicts of law suggests this is also beginning to trouble him. Conflicts of law are unlike other forms of legal specialization as they are concerned with the limits of legal authority. In what circumstances should a legal norm have authority? By drawing upon Currie's work, Joerges is concerned to show that this question is extra-legal, not simply because, logically, the authority of law cannot be a legal question, but also because the matter is one of the highest political importance. Yet if this matter should not be left to courts, then how does the law control the public power making this choice? For, in a world of multiple sources of normative authority, this power is as dangerous as the power to set and apply the norms themselves.

In controlling this power, Joerges argues that the law must recognize its limits. The failure of goal-oriented law as a project entails that the setting of broad policy objectives would be counterproductive. Law should, instead

> encourage the concerned actors to take up the search for problem-solving and interest-mediation. . . It should ensure that their activities respect principles of fairness, enhance their deliberative quality, and then eventually acknowledge such societal norm generation. It is in this way that law can respond to collisions and contestations, and it can thus be characterised as conflicts law.[21]

Law is thus not to make active choices itself, but bound the arenas in which these choices are made and set the rules for how these choices are made. This begs the question of what gives law the authority to do even this: the taken-for-granted qualities that lead actors to accept it. If it is such a big task, why should law do this and why should actors accept its place here? Joerges's work leaves this question largely unexplained: Possibly it is the next project in his amazing intellectual odyssey. But what are the political and sociological bases for the place of law in his model of the Union? I think that the authority of law in his model can be explained by the emergence of two phenomena which are beginning to replace territoriality in the EU as the basis for law's right to determine the terms of conflict resolution.

The first is the bounding of conflict. Joerges rightly notes that the presence of conflict and contestation is a necessary and desirable part of a plural society. They cannot, however, be too much in conflict. Nobody wants the Hobbesian jungle where anarchy leads merely to survival of the fittest. Law's authority derives, in part, from its ability to contain and channel conflict. It sets out the places and forms in which this can legitimately take place. Recognition of this by all central parties of the undesirability of alternatives provides strong reasons for law's authority. This authority increases as societies become more complex and interdependent. In the era of primitive, atomized societies, law is merely the avoidance of physical harm to human beings. The growth of the liberal, territorial state led to concerns about avoidance of territorial conflict; intra-administrative conflict between different parts of government, and conflicts between the state, society and economy. Class differentiation deriving from both the dispersion of the means of consumption and production has led to further complexity. Finally, the increased differentiation and recoupling of social systems has led to new sources of contestation.

In such circumstances, law is the only institution that can hold everything together in balance and prevent the tensions from becoming unmanageable. All parties have a strong interest in this because of their interdependence. The paradox of modern societies is that most interests, values, and systems are irreducibly opposed to each other: economy versus society, capital versus labor,

France versus Germany. They cannot be integrated into some synthetic unity. Their proximity combined with the potential for destruction of each by the other leads to the terms of cooperation.[22]

The bounding of conflict leads to law acquiring two other qualities that bolster its authority. One is coherence. Law only retains its authority if it is seen to be formally fair (e.g., treat like cases alike). Parties defect if they feel they are not treated equally before the law. It must produce results, therefore, which seem mutually supportive. Through this, law creates a narrative that makes sense of the whole enterprise. The other is value and interest pluralism. Parties defect from law if they feel it has not taken their interests into account. This leads to law having to be concerned with balance. No interest, value, or system can predominate over the others.[23]

The second phenomenon supporting law's authority is the growth of problem solving. Problem solving is a form of politics that accords a high degree of normative force to empirically derived knowledge.[24] It either involves setting out an identifiable bad that must be resolved or an identifiable good that is seen as attainable through collective action. Knowledge is at the heart of both forms of problem solving. As we know more, we become more aware of what needs to be averted and what can be averted with the consequence that the expansion and specialization of knowledge has led to an increase in this forms of politics. In a world of contestation, law becomes integral to the realization of this project in two ways. It sets out the patterns of cooperation and the role of the parties that enable collective action. Crucially, as many problems take time to solve, law's stickiness and its difficulty to change also limit intertemporal problems by making it difficult for parties to act on a unilateral change of preferences. Equally importantly, law sets out the ideals and teleologies that justify party participation in problem solving and provides a set of commitments against which defection and good faith can be measured.[25] Parties have to argue for the poverty of those goods, namely that they are not worth pursuing, if their defection is to be taken seriously by other parties. This both restricts the types of arguments that may be used, but also provides new spaces for debate. A governance regime on safe food, for example, limits arguments about food to questions of safety, but it also leads to the notion of safety being explored more richly, with debates extended to questions of nutrition or whether ethically unsafe food should be produced.

Challenging Deliberative Supranationalism

If the need to contain conflict and to solve problems are the central pillars enabling law to find its place and its authority in the world of transnational governance, these bases raise further challenges for law and suggest its position is not unproblematic.

One challenge emerges from the sheer plurality of the sites of governance. To be sure, law might be the vehicle for the broad visioning of a governance regime, setting its overall direction and goals.[26] It is also dragged into the micro-capillaries of every dispute in every single arena. Within such disputes, parties rarely lift their eyes before the horizons of that dispute to consider the wider benefits, costs, or values at stake. In *Cassis de Dijon*, it is doubtful to think that either Rewe or the German Government considered the dispute as anything other than one about the marketing of alcoholic drinks. The wider implications for the structure of the overall single market project or the regulation of market externalities were background considerations at best. This leads, on the one hand, to government by stealth. Judgments with broad implications are given without much prior consideration to these implications. It also leads, in turn, to displacement of conflict. This lack of consideration generates new conflicts or leads to pre-existing tensions re-emerging, with unpredictable consequences, in other fora. Finally, it can lead to parties miscalculating the costs of a conflict. The compulsion for battle in a particular dispute can lead to parties, particularly governments, challenging the authority of EU law, precisely because the wider consequences are seen as beyond the horizon of the dispute.

The second challenge is the plurality of knowledge. For transnational governance imposes an epistemic overload on law. Problems are difficult to resolve. This is not simply because of the technical complexity and specialization of the information that may have to be used, but because of the multifaceted nature of knowledge. Any corpus of knowledge will have a technical dimension concerned with extending control over the natural processes in question; a practical dimension concerned with fostering mutual understanding by locating these against wider social processes; and an emancipatory one concerned with identifying the undesirable consequences of any process. These elements interact in such a way that it is impossible to disentangle one from the other so that the identification and resolution of any problem involves in each case a unique blend of these three elements with the knowledge being assessed in terms of its plausibility and relevance to the problem rather than its universal veracity.[27] The situatedness and action-orientated nature of this process limits those who can participate in the formulation of problem solving; for it to emerge as knowledge, as justified true belief, all participants must be sufficiently convinced by the end result that they believe it to be true. It also inevitably entails that they will miss many forms of knowledge that other stakeholders consider to be important. These tensions come to the fore in a transnational governance regime that is dispersed across time and space, as these other stakeholders will often be dominant in other sites, where they can challenge the veracity and authority of the knowledge used to solve the problem and bolster the authority of law.

The final challenge is the redistributive one. The turn to governance has, in essence, been a flight from questions of contestation and redistribution: an attempt to purge politics of these unsavory questions. If Joerges is astute enough to re-introduce the former, it is not clear where the latter fits in. For the narrowness of the parameters of each site of governance both obscure its capacity to dwell upon the broader redistributive implications of any of its decisions and its capacity to realize any redistributive strategy that will involve and incorporate other sites. Yet if individual sites cannot effectively engage in redistribution, it is not clear that law can. For, as Joerges notes, the history of the welfare state indicates that law is functionally poorly equipped to realize substantive goods. Yet redistributive questions do not and should not go away: The question of how to accommodate them cannot therefore be left unaddressed.

The challenges of coherence of vision, pluralism of knowledge, and redistribution may ultimately be undefeatable, but this does not mean that there should not be an attempt to address them through institutional design. It is at this point that deliberative supranationalism seems to send out contradictory messages.

DSN I suggests that the most effective way to deal with these issues is through a system of checks and balances. As no single site can simultaneously address these overall needs and satisfactorily resolve local challenges, a system of counteraction is put in place where subsequent sites can revisit other decisions in the light of their own needs. In *Cassis de Dijon*, the authorization to market Cassis de Dijon would have been considered in the light of the French markets, first, with the needs of the single market a secondary consideration. The authorities could be mindful of the claims of other regulatory authorities but could not possibly be knowledgeable about them or anticipate how they might change. The German authorities have the possibility to put their needs first, when the application to market Cassis de Dijon is made. They have both a greater local knowledge and, intertemporally, their decision is closer to the event of marketing. It makes sense, therefore, that they should have the right to trump the French decision. They cannot do it in an autarkic manner. Instead, they must first recognize that the French decision is something which should have legal authority in Germany unless it fails to take account of German needs as the Germans see them. They, then, have the right to say that it has failed to do this, but the duty of coordination, which occurs as result of Article 28 EC, requires they provide good reasons why this is the case. They are given, moreover, wide parameters within which to do this. It must not merely be that it failed to respect a public interest recognized in Germany and that the German authorities were mindful of their responsibilities to other economic operators in regulating this public interest.

To be sure, questions can be raised with this model. Is sufficient account taken of redistributive questions in the case law? Is the Court sometimes too restrictive in its interpretation of the proportionality principle? Is there enough room for macro-systemic visioning? It has, however, great merits. It is, above all, a dynamic model. Every decision is authoritative, but no decision is determinative. It can be revisited in the light of changes as they occur. It is also a local model. The priority of the local over the transnational has been spelled out by Balibar:

> [Local determinations] refer to the specific historical and geographical roots of the conflict, which are also, dialectically, the premises of its solution, and because they allow us to assign responsibilities and make concrete forces accountable for their actions, whereas the primacy of the "global" nourishes passivity by suggesting that everything is determined at the global level, that is nowhere.[28]

DSN I reaffirms this, but suggests also that supranationalism is above all a form of accountability. Local actors may have priority for their actions, but their actions do not merely affect themselves. They must be open to the interests of others and account to others for their actions.

DSN II adopts an entirely different approach to the tensions of transnational governance. It is the approach of synthetic unity. An assembly place is created at the apex of any regime for the different interests to frame the problems and values of the regime. This does not have to take place in a central setting, but it must create a European frame (e.g., open method of coordination (OMC))—a standard that claims to have taken all the different interests into account and is therefore best practice. The lack of territorial unity is then provided for by allowing different actors leeway as to how they apply and comply with these frames—be this through the room provided by the framework directives or the mandate in OMC to tailor European standards according to local standards. In all instances, the golden thread running through these different sites of governance is a European line of reason which is assumed to be sufficiently flexible and open to incorporate all concerns. The premises of such an approach are the opposite to those in DSN I. A golden line of reason can only be found if it is assumed there is neither incommensurability nor incompatibility between the interests, beliefs, and values of different stakeholders. If it is neither possible to iron out differences nor evaluate the weight of the respective values and interests at stake, then it is simply not possible to have a single view on what is best practice. In addition, there is limited trust in the capacities, responsibilities, or will of local actors to resolve many disputes. Comparative advantage is attributed to the transnational level with its broader horizons.

While it is true that one level of decision making should not be fetishized at the expense of the other, the global can be as rich, wise, and plural as the local, and vice versa, the basis for these assumptions is left surprisingly unclear. More disturbingly, the deep level of incompatibility between DSN I and DSN II and their opposing approaches to the problematics of problem solving are left unexplored. It may be that the diversity of transnational governance is such that a dual system is needed, where a checks and balances approach applies in some areas and a synthetic unity approach applies in others. It is too simplistic to assume, however, that what has taken place in EU governance is some clever allocation along these lines.

Conclusion

The deliberative supranationalism project remains an unfinished but exciting and evolving project. At its basis lies a tension, for it is simply not possible to argue that important new institutional arrangements are emerging which curb territorial authority, without considering whether the very idea of territorial authority is not being challenged by these as well. As these arrangements create their own territorialities of power and their own dynamics of governance, if they have become one of the central motors of Europe, then territoriality as the basis for legal and political authority has lost its hegemony. In keeping with the scepticism of Joerges about public power, the discovery of these new arrangements requires that we also consider both the origins and the working of their power, and what is problematic about it. If supranationalism emerged from the love-hate embrace between territoriality and its discontents, the implicit message of Joerges is that the central relationship should be between governance and its discontents. This essay suggests there are three vectors along which discontent at governance may be challenged: its banalization of political virtue, its dishonesty about the consequences of rule by expertise, and its elitist absence of concern with any form of redistribution.

Notes

1. Joerges and Ghaleigh 2003.
2. On the latter and the Nazi notion of honour see Whitman 2003, 243–266.
3. Sack 1986, 19.
4. On territoriality and the modern State see Mann 1984, 185; Taylor 1994, 151.

5. Pottage 1998, 16.

6. European Court of Justice. *Case 26/62 Van Gend en Loos v. Nederlands Administratie der Belastingen*, ECR 1, 1963.

7. Weiler 1999b, 99.

8. Maduro 1998, 166–174.

9. Somek 2001.

10. Schmid 2000, 155; Joerges 2003c.

11. Weiler 1999a, 399, 341–42.

12. Weiler 1999a, 346.

13. European Court of Justice, *Case 120/78 REWE-Zentral AG v. Bundesmonopolverwaltung für Branntwein*, ECR 649, 1979.

14. European Court of Justice. *Case C-6/01 Anomar v. Estado Português*, ECR I-8621, 2003.

15. European Court of Justice. Case *T-13/99 Pfizer Animal Health v. Council*, ECR II-3305, 2002.

16. For example, the GMO Panel of the European Food Safety Authority contains four Brits, three Germans, three Dutch, two Danes, and then one from Belgium, Greece, Spain, France, Italy, Austria, Finland, Sweden, and Ireland. www.efsa.eu.int/science/gmo/gmo_members/catindex_en.html (10 March 2005).

17. Trondal and Veggeland 2000.

18. On the Schmittian idea of *Grossraum* as a territory governed by a hegemony of belief see Joerges 2003b.

19. de Areilza 1995.

20. Unsurprisingly, this was realized first by international relations scholars for whom territoriality has been the building block of their trade. Ruggie 1993, 139.

21. Joerges, this volume, p. chapter 13

22. Balibar 2004, 222–224.

23. Broome 1991.

24. Ewald 1987, 91, 104–105.

25. In Cassis de Dijon, the law does not only contain conflict. It also sets out a series of positive goods, the realization of a single market which protects the consumer and public health, to which parties commit themselves.

26. Walker 2002, 317.

27. For the vast literature on this see Yanow 2000, 247.

28. Balibar 2004, 229.

References

Abromeit, H. "Ein Vorschlag zur Demokratisierung des Europäischen Entscheidungssystems." *Politische Vierteljahresschrift* 39, no. 1 (March 1998a): 80–90.

———. *Democracy in Europe: Legitimising Politics in a Non-State Polity.* Oxford: Berghahn Books, 1998b.

———. *Wozu braucht man Demokratie?* Opladen: Leske+Budrich, 2002.

Agh, A. "National Parliaments and the EU: The Role of the ECE Parliaments in the EU Integration." Paper presented at the annual conference of the Central European Political Science Association on EU Accession and National Parliaments, Budapest, 22–24 April 2004.

Agrikoliansky, E. et. al. ed. *Radiographie du movement altermondialiste: Le second Forum social européen.* La Disput, 2005.

Allott, P. "The European Community Is Not the True European Community," *Yale Law Journal* 100 (1991): 2485–2500.

Amstutz, M. "Zwischenwelten. Zur Emergenz einer interlegalen Rechtsmethodik im europäischen Privatrecht." Pp. 213–237 in *Rechtsverfassungsrecht-Recht-Fertigung zwischen Privatrechtdogmatik und Gesellschaftstheorie,* edited by C. Joerges and G. Teubner. Baden-Baden: Nomos, 2003.

Andersen, S. S. and T. Burns. "The European Union and the Erosion of Parliamentary Democracy: A Study of Post-Parliamentary Democracy." Pp. 227–51 in *The European Union: How Democratic Is It?* edited by S. S. Andersen and K. A. Eliassen. London: Sage, 1996.

Andeweg, R. B. and L. Nijzink. "Beyond the Two-Body Image: Relations between Ministers and MPs." Pp. 152–178 in *Parliaments and Majority Rule in Western Europe,* edited by H. Döring. Frankfurt: Campus/New York: St Martin's Press, 1995.

Andretta, M. et. al. *Global, Noglobal, New Global, La protesta contro il G8 a Genova.* Roma-Bari: Laterza, 2002.

———. *Global, Noglobal*. Frankfurt a.M.: Campus, 2003.

Arendt, H. *Vita Activa oder vom tätigen Leben*. München: Beck, 1967.

Arneson, R. J. "Equality." Pp. 489–507 in *A Companion to Contemporary Political Philosophy*, edited by R. E. Goodin and P. Pettit, Oxford: Blackwell, 1993.

Arter, D. "The Folketing and Denmark's 'European Policy': The Case of an 'Authorising Assembly'?" Pp. 111–123 in *National Parliaments and the European Union*, edited by P. Norton. London: Frank Cass, 1996.

Auel, K. and A. Benz. "National Parliaments in EU Multi-Level Governance: Dilemmas and Strategies," FernUniversität Institut for Political Science polis-Arbeitspapiere No. 59, 2004.

Auel, K. "Strategische Anpassung Nationaler Parlamente and das Europäische Mehrebenensystem-ein Deutsch-Britischer Vergleich." Pp. 259–280 in *Politische Steuerung und neue Staatlichkeit*, edited by E. Grande and R. Prätorius. Baden-Baden: Nomos, 2003.

Augustin, A. *Das Volk der Europäischen Union*. Berlin: Duncker und Humblot, 2000.

Bache, I., and M. Flinders, ed. *Multi-Level Governance*. Oxford: Oxford University Press, 2004.

Bachrach, P. *Die Theorie demokratischer Elitenherrschaft*. Frankfurt a.M.: Europäische Verlagsanstalt, 1970.

Balibar, E. *We, the People of Europe? Reflections on Transnational Citizenship*. Princeton, NJ: Princeton University Press, 2004.

Balkin, J.M. "Agreements with Hell and Other Objects of Our Faith," *Fordham Law Review* 65 (1997): 1703–1738.

Balme, R., and D. Chabanet. Introduction. Action collective et gouvernance de l'Union Européenne. Pp. 21–120 in *L'action collective en Europe*, edited by R. Balme and D. Chabanet. Paris: Presses de Sciences Po, 2002.

Bardi, L., and P. Ignazi *Cosa è il parlamento europeo*. Bologna: Il Mulino, 1999.

Bartolini, S. "Lo stato nazionale e l'integrazione europea: un'agenda di ricerca." *Quaderni di Scienza Politica* 9 (2002): 397–414.

Bauer, H. "Art. 50." Pp. 1020–1036 in *Grundgesetz-Kommentar*, edited by H. Dreier. Tübingen: Mohr Siebeck, 1998.

Beetham, D. *The Legitimation of Power*. Basingstoke: Macmillan, 1991.

———. *Defining and Measuring Democracy*. London: Sage/ECPR, 1994.

Bendix, R. *Nation Building and Citizenship*. New York: Wiley and Son, 1964.

Benz, A. "Compounded Representation in EU Multi-Level Governance." Pp. 81–110 in *Linking EU and National Governance*, edited by B. Kohler-Koch. Oxford: Oxford University Press, 2003.

———. "Path-Dependent Institutions and Strategic Veto-Players—National Parliaments in the European Union," *West European Politics* 27, no. 5 (2004): 875–900.

Bergman, T. and T. Raunio. "Parliaments and Policy-Making in the European Union," in J. Richardson ed. *European Union: Power and Policy-Making*. London: Routledge, 2001.

Bergman, T. and E. Damgaard, ed. *Delegation and Accountability in European Integration: The Nordic Parliamentary Democracies and the European Union*. London: Frank Cass, 2000.

Bila, J. et. al. *Der Ausschuss für die Angelegenheiten der Europäischen Union des Deutschen Bundestages*, 2nd ed. Bonn: Sekretariat des Ausschusses für die Angelegenheiten der Europäischen Union, 1998.

Birner, R. and H. Wittmer. "Converting Social Capital into Political Capital: How Do Local Communities Gain Political Influence? A Theoretical Approach and Empirical Evidence from Thailand and Columbia." Paper submitted to the 8th Biennial Conference of the International Association for the Study of Common Property, Indiana, 2000.

Blondel, J., R. Sinnot, and P. Svensson. *People and Parliament in the European Union: Participation, Democracy and Legitimacy*. Oxford: Clarendon Press, 1998.

Blyth, M. *Great Transformations: Economic Ideas and Political Change in the Twentieth Century*, Cambridge: Cambridge University Press, 2002.

Böckenförde, E. W. "Sozialer Bundesstaat und parlamentarische Demokratie." Pp. 182–199 in *Politik als gelebte Verfassung*, Festschrift für Friedrich Schäfer, edited by J. Jekewitz, M. Melzer and W. Zeh. Opladen: Westdeutscher Verlag, 1980.

———. *Recht, Staat, Freiheit. Studien zur Rechtsphilosophie, Staatstheorie und Verfassungsgeschichte*. 3rd ed. Frankfurt a.M.: Suhrkamp, 1992.

Bohman, J. "Survey Article: The Coming of Age of Deliberative Democracy." *Journal of Political Philosophy* 6, no. 4 (1998): 400–425.

———. "Constitution Making and Democratic Innovation." *European Journal of Political Theory* 3, no. 3 (2004): 315–337.

———. "Constitution Making and Democratic Innovation: The European Union and Transnational Governance." in *Making the European Polity: Reflexive Integration in Europe*, edited by E. O. Eriksen. London: Routledge, 2005.

Booth, J. A., and P. Bayer Richard. "Civil Society, Political Capital, and Democratization in Central America." *Journal of Politics* 60, no. 3 (1998): 780–800.

Bothe, M. "Art. 20, para. 1–3 II (Bundesstaat)." Pp. 1–19 in *Kommentar zum Grundgesetz für die Bundesrepublik Deutschland, Reihe Alternativkommentare*. 3rd ed. edited by E. Denninger et. al. Neuwied, Kriftel: Hermann Luchterhand Verlag, loose-leaf collection, updated: August 2002.

Bourgignon-Wittke, R. et al. "Five Years of the Directly Elected European Parliament: Performance and Prospects." *Journal of Common Market Studies* 24, No. 1 (1985): 39–60.

Bové, J. and F. Dufour. *Le monde n'est pas une marchandise. Des paysans contre la malbouffe*. Paris: La découverte, 2000.

Bowler, S. and H. Farrell. "The Organizing of the European Parliament: Committees, Specialisation and Coordination." *British Journal of Political Science* 25, No. 2 (1995): 219–243.

Branch, A. P. "The Impact of the European Union on the Trade Union Movement," Pp. 279–312 in *L'action collective en Europe*, edited by R. Balme and D. Chabanet. Paris: Presses de Sciences Po, 2002.

Britz, G. and M. Schmidt. "Die institutionalisierte Mitwirkung der Sozialpartner an der Rechtsetzung der Europäischen Gemeinschaft." *Europarecht* 34, no. 4 (July–August 1999): 467–498.

Bröhmer, J. "Das Europäische Parlament: Echtes Legislativorgan oder bloßes Hilfsorgan im legislativen Prozeß? Zur Matthews-Entscheidung des Europäischen

Gerichtshof für Menschenrechte." *Zeitschrift für Europarechtliche Studien* 2, no. 2 (1999): 197–217.

Broome, J. *Weighing Goods: Equality, Uncertainty and Time.* Oxford: Blackwell, 1991.

Brunkhorst, H. "Verfasst ohne Verfassung. Europäische Union zwischen Evolution und revolutionärer Umgründung." *Blätter für deutsche und internationale Politik,* no. 2 (2004): 211–222.

Búrca, G. de. "The Constitutional Challenge of New Governance in the European Union." *European Law Review* 28, No. 6 (2003): 814–839.

Burns, C. "More Power, Not Less? The European Parliament and Co-Decision." Ph.D. thesis. University of Sheffield, 2002.

Burns, T. R. "The Future of Parliamentary Democracy: Transition and Challenge in European Governance." Green Paper prepared for the Conference of the Speakers of EU Parliaments, 22–24 September 2000, Rome, 2000.

Burt, R. *The Constitution in Conflict,* Cambridge/Mass: Harvard University Press, 1992.

Bush, E. and P. Imi. "European Farmers and Their Protests," Pp. 97–121 in *Contentious Europeans. Protest and Politics in an Emerging Polity,* edited by D. Imig and S. Tarrow. Lanham: Rowman & Littlefield, 2001.

Cain, B. E., R. Dalton and S. E. Scarrow, ed. *Democracy Transformed? Expanding Political Opportunities in Advanced Industrial Democracies.* Oxford: Oxford University Press, 2003.

Carter, A. and S. Stokes, ed. *Democratic Theory Today: Challenges for the 21st Century.* Cambridge: Polity Press, 2002.

Cavers, D. F. *The Choice-of-Law Process.* Ann Arbour: University of Michigan Press, 1965.

Cederman, L. E. "Nationalism and Bounded Integration: What It Would Take to Build a European Demos," *European Journal of International Relations* 7, no. 2 (2001a): 139–74.

———. *Constructing Europe's Identity: The External Dimension.* Boulder: Lynne Riener, 2001b.

Chabanet, D. "Les marches européennes contre le chômage, la précarité et les exclusions," Pp. 461–494 in *L'action collective en Europe,* edited by R. Balme and D. Chabanet. Paris: Presses de Sciences Po, 2002.

Chalmers, D. "The Reconstruction of European Public Spheres." *European Law Journal* 9, no. 2 (2003): 127–189.

Church, C. and D. Phinnemore. *European Union and European Community: A Handbook and Commentary on the Post-Maastricht Treaties,* New York: Prentice Hall, Harvester Wheatsheaf, 1994.

Cocca, L. "La protesta per le quote latte in Italia: Il movimento degli allevatori tra difesa della cultura localistica tradizionale e ricerca di una nuova identità a vocazione sovranazionale." Tesi di laurea, Facoltà di scienze politiche, Università di Firenze, 2001.

Cohen, J. and Arato, A. *Civil Society and Political Theory.* Cambridge: MIT Press, 1992.

Cohen, J. "Deliberation and Democratic Legitimacy," Pp. 17–34 in *The Good Polity: Normative Analysis of the State,* edited by A. Hamlin and P. Pettit. Oxford: Basil Blackwell, 1989.

Cohen, J. and C. Sabel. Directly Deliberative Polyarchy. *European Law Journal* 3, No. 4 (1997): 313–343.

Cohen, J. and C. F. Sabel. "Sovereignity and Solidarity: EU and US," Pp. 376–406 in *Governing Work and Welfare in a New Economy: European and American Experiments*, edited by J. Zeitlin and D. M. Trubek. Oxford: Oxford University Press, 2003.

Commission. "An Open and Structured Dialogue Between the Commission and Special Interest Groups", SEC (92) 2272 final, Brussels, (2 December 1992), 1992.

———. "Evolution in Governance. What Lessons for the Commision? A First Assessment." Working Paper compiled by Notis Lebessis and John Paterson. Brussels: European Commission, 1997.

———. "The Commission and NGOs: Building a Stronger Partnership," COM (2000) 11 final, (18 January 2000), 2000.

———. "European Governance: A White Paper." COM(2001) 428 final. Brussels (25 July 2001), 2001a.

———. "Europe 2004—Le Grand Débat. Setting the Agenda and Outlining the Options." Brüssels (15–16 October 2001), 2001b; http://europa.eu.int/comm/governance/whats_new/europe2004_en.pdf .

———. Communication from the Commission on impact assessment (COM [2002]) 276 final). Brussels (5 June 2002), 2002a.

———. Consultation Document: Towards a reinforced culture of consultation and dialogue—Proposal for general principles and minimum standards for consultation of interested parties by the Commission (COM [2002]277 final). Brussels (5 June 2002), 2002b.

———. Report from the Commission on European Governance , (COM [2002] 705 final). Brussels (11 December 2002), 2002c.

———. European Consumer Consultative Group (ECCG) Minutes of the Meeting of 16 March 2005, (ECCG 2005 031), 2005.

Commission/Economic and Social Committee. Joint Declaration of the presidents of the Commission and the ESC, CES 1235/2001, Brussels (24 September 2001), 2001.

Committee of Independent Experts. "Second Report on Reform of the Commission." (10 September 1999), 1999; www.europarl.eu.int/experts/default_en.htm (16 December 2004).

Corbett, R., F. Jacobs, and M. Shackleton. "The European Parliament at Fifty: A View from the Inside." *Journal of Common Market Studies* 41, no. 3 (2003): 353–373.

Corbett, R. *The Treaty of Maastricht: From Conception to Ratification: A Comprehensive Reference Guide.* Essex: Longman, 1992.

———. *The European Parliament's Role in Closer Integration.* Basingstoke: Palgrave, 1998.

Coultrap, J. "From Parliamentarism to Pluralism: Models of Democracy and the European Union's Democratic Deficit." *Journal of Theoretical Politics* 11, no. 1 (January 1999): 107–135.

Cox, G. *Making Votes Count: Strategic Co-ordination in the World's Electoral Systems.* Cambridge: Cambridge University Press, 1997.

Craig, P. "The Nature of the Community: Integration, Democracy and Legitimacy," in *The Evolution of EU Law*, edited by P. Craig and G. de Burca. Oxford: Oxford University Press, 1999.

Cram, L. "Introduction to Special Issue on the Institutional Balance of the Future of EU Governance: The Future of the Union and the Trap of the 'Nirvana Fallacy.'" *Governance* 15, no. 3 (2002): 309–324.

Crombez, C. "The Codecision Procedure in the European Union." *Legislative Studies Quarterly* 1 (1997): 97–121.

———. "Understanding the EU Legislative Process: Political Scientists' and Practioners' Perspectives." *European Union Politics* 3 (2000): 363–381.

Crum, B. "Legislative-Executive Relations in the EU." *Journal of Common Market Studies* 41, no. 3 (2003): 375–95.

Currie, B. "Comment on Babcock v. Jackson." *Columbia Law Review* 63 (1963a).

———. "Notes on Methods and Objectives in Conflicts of Law," Pp. 177–187 in *Selected Essays on the Conflict of Laws*, edited by B. Currie. Durham, N.C.: Duke University Press, 1963b.

———. "The Disinterested Third State." *Law and Contemporary Problems* 28 (1963c).

Curtin, D. M. *Postnational Democracy: The European Union in Search of a Political Philosophy*. The Hague: Kluwer Law International, 1997.

Dahl, A., T. Næss, and K. Tangen. "Europeanisation in Denmark: Participation in EU Energy and Environmental Policy Processes." Fridtjof Nansen Institute Report No. 03, 2001.

Dahl, R. A. *Democracy and Its Critics*. New Haven: Yale University Press, 1989.

———. *On Democracy*. New Haven: Yale University Press, 1989.

———. "A Democratic Dilemma: System Effectiveness versus Citizen Participation." *Political Science Quarterly* 10, no. 1 (1994): 23–34.

———. *On Democracy*. New Haven: Yale University Press, 1998.

———. "Can International Organizations Be Democratic? A Skeptic's View," Pp. 19–36 in *Democracy's Edges*, edited by I. Shapiro and C. Hacker-Cordon. Cambridge: Cambridge University Press, 1999.

Dalton, R., S. E. Scarrow, and B. E. Cain. "New Forms of Democracy? Reform and Transformations of Democratic Institutions," Pp. 1–20 in *Democracy Transformed? Expanding Political Opportunities in Advanced Industrial Democracies*, edited by B. E. Cain, R. Dalton, and S. E. Scarrow. Oxford: Oxford University Press, 2003.

Dalton, R. *Democratic Challenges, Democratic Choices: The Erosion of Political Support in Advanced Industrial Democracies*. Oxford: Oxford University Press, 2004.

Damgaard, E. and A. S. Nørgaards. "The European Union and Danish Parliamentary Democracy." *Journal of Legislative Studies* 6, no. 1 (2000): 33–58.

Dann, P. "The Political Institutions." in *Principles of European Constitutional Law*, edited by A. von Bogdandy and J. Bast. Oxford: Hart, 2006.

De Areilza, J. "Sovereignty or Management? The Dual Character of the EC's Supranationalism—Revisited." Jean Monnet Working Paper no. 2 (1995).

Dehousse, R. "Constitutional Reform in the European Community: Are There Alternatives to the Majoritarian Avenue?" in *The Crisis of Representation in Europe*, edited by J. Hayward. London: Frank Cass, 1995.

————. *The European Court of Justice.* New York: Macmillan, 1998.

Della Porta, D. and M. Caiani. "L'europeizzazione della sfera pubblica in Italia: un processo "top-down"?" *Rivista italiana di Scienza Politica* 34, no. 4. (2004): 459–490.

Della Porta, D. and M. Diani. *Social Movements.* Oxford: Blackwell, 1999.

Della Porta, D., and H. Kriesi. "Social Movements in a Globalizing World: An Introduction." Pp. 3–22 in *Social Movements in a Globalizing World,* edited by D. Della Porta, H. Kriesi, and D. Rucht. New York: Macmillan, 1999.

Della Porta, D. and S. Tarrow. "Transnational Movements and Global Activism: An Introduction," in *Transnational Movements and Global Activism: An Introduction,* edited by D. della Porta and S. Tarrow. New York: Rowman and Littlefield, 2004.

Della Porta, D. "Europeanization and Social Movements," in *Comparing European Societies: Actors, Institutions and Change,* edited by G. Bettin Lattes and E. Recchi. Bologna: Monduzzi, 2003.

————. "From Corporatist Unions to Protest Unions? On the (Difficult) Relations between Labour and New Social Movements," in *The Diversity of Democracy: A Tribute to P. C. Schmitter,* edited by C. Crouch and W. Streek. 2006 (forthcoming).

Dellavalle, S. "Für einen normativen Begriff von Europa: Nationalstaat und europäische Einigung im Lichte der politischen Theorie," Pp. 237–266 in *Die Europäische Option,* edited by A. von Bogdandy. Baden-Baden: Nomos, 1993.

Delorme, H. "Les agriculteurs et les institutions communautaires: du corporatisme agricole au lobbyisme agro-alimentaire," Pp. 313–375 in *L'action collective en Europe,* edited by R. Balme and D. Chabanet. Paris: Presses de Sciences Po., 2002.

De Schutter, O., Lebessis, N., and Paterson, J., ed. *Governance in the European Union.* "Cahiers" of the Forward Studies Unit. Luxembourg: Office for Official Publications of the European Commission, 2001.

Deutsch, K. *Nationalism and Social Communication: An Inquiry into the Foundations of Nationality.* Cambridge: MIT Press, 1953.

Deutscher Bundestag, ed. *Der Weg zum EU-Verfassungskonvent, Berichte und Dokumentationen.* Berlin: Referat Öffentlichkeitsarbeit, 2002.

Dewey, J. *The Public and Its Problems.* London: George Allen and Unwin, 1927.

Dimitrakopoulos, D. "Incrementalism and Path Dependence: European Integration and Institutional Change in National Parliaments." *Journal of Common Market Studies* 39, no. 3 (2001): 405–422.

Downs, A. *An Economic Theory of Democracy.* New York: Harper, 1957.

————. *Inside Bureaucracy.* Boston: Little Brown, 1967.

Dryzek, J. S. *Deliberative Democracy and Beyond: Liberals, Critics and Contestations.* Oxford: Oxford University Press, 2000.

Duff, A. "Building a Parliamentary Europe," Pp. 251–266 in *Démocratie et Construction Européenne,* edited by M. Télo. Bruxelles: Edition de l'Université de Bruxelles, 1995.

Earnshaw, D. and D. Judge. "From Co-operation to Co-decision: The European Parliament's Path to Legislative Power," Pp. 96–126 in *Policy Making in the European Union,* edited by J. Richardson. London: Routledge, 1996.

Economic and Social Committee. Opinion on "The Role and Contribution of Civil Society Organisations in the Building of Europe," OJ C329, Brussels (17 November 1999), 1999.

———. ESC report. "Economic and Social Committee and Organised Civil Society," CES 1009/2001 rev., Brussels (10 July 2001), 2001.

———. "Final Report of the ad hoc group on Structured cooperation with European civil society organisations and networks," CESE 1498/2003 fin, Brussels (17 February 2004), 2004a.

———. Conference on Participatory Democracy: Current situation and opportunities provided by the European Constitution, Summary Memo, Brussels (8–9 March 2004), 2004b.

Eder, K. and C. Kantner. "Transnationale Resonanzstrukturen in Europa. Eine Kritik der Rede vom Öffentlichkeitsdefizit in Europa," Pp. 306–331 in *Die Europäisierung nationaler Gesellschaften.* Kölner Zeitschrift für Soziologie und Sozialpsychologie, Sonderheft 40, edited by M. Bach. Opladen: Westdeutscher Verlag, 2000.

Eder, K. "Chancenstrukturen für Bürgerbeteiligung und Protestmobilisierung in der EU. Überlegungen zu einigen Besonderheiten transnationaler Streitpolitik," Pp. 45–75 in *Politische Partizipation und Protestmobilisierung im Zeitalter der Globalisierung,* edited by A. Klein, R. Koopmans, and H. Geiling. Opladen: Leske+Budrich, 2001.

Eder, K., K. U. Hellmann, and H. J. Trenz. "Regieren in Europa jenseits öffentlicher Legitimation? Eine Untersuchung zur Rolle von politischer Öffentlichkeit in Europa," Pp 321–244 in *Regieren in entgrenzten Räumen,* Special Issue of the Politische Vierteljahresschrift, No. 29, edited by B. Kohler-Koch. Opladen: Westdeutscher Verlag, 1998.

Eder, K., H. J. Trenz. "The Making of a European Public Space: The Case of Justice and Home Affairs," Pp. 111–134 in *Linking EU and National Governance,* edited by B. Kohler-Koch. Oxford: Oxford University Press, 2003.

Eising, R. and B. Kohler-Koch. *Interessenpolitik in Europa.* Baden-Baden: Nomos, 2005a.

———. "Interessenpolitik im Europäischen Mehrebenensystem," Pp. 11–75 in *Interessenpolitik in Europe,* edited by R. Eising and B. Kohler-Koch. Baden-Baden: Nomos, 2005b.

Eriksen, E. O. "Integration and the Quest for Consensus—On the Micro-Foundations of Supranationalism," Pp. 159–225 in *European Governance, Deliberation and the Quest for Democratization,* edited by E. O. Eriksen, C. Joerges and J. Neyer. ARENA Report no. 02, Oslo, 2003.

Eriksen, E. O. and J. E. Fossum, ed. *Democracy in the European Union: Integration Through Deliberation?* London: Routledge, 2000a.

———. "Post-National Integration," Pp. 1–28 in *Democracy in the European Union: Integration Through Deliberation,* edited by E. O. Eriksen and J. E. Fossum. London: Routledge, 2000b.

———. "Democracy Through Strong Publics in the EU? " *Journal of Common Market Studies* 40, no. 3 (2002): 401–423.

———. "Europe in Search of Legitimacy: Strategies of Legitimation Assessed." *International Political Science Review* 25, no. 4 (2004): 435–459.

Eriksen, E. O., "An Emerging European Public Sphere." *European Journal of Social Theory* 8, no. 3 (2005): 341–363.

Eriksen, E. O., J. E. Fossum and A. J. Menéndez, ed. *Developing a Constitution for Europe*. London: Routledge, 2004.

Eriksen, E. O., C. Joerges, and J. Neyer, ed. *European Governance, Deliberation and the Quest for Democratisation*. ARENA Report No 02/2003. Oslo, 2003.

Estlund, D. "Democratic Authority: Toward a Philosophical Framework." Paper presented at the research conference "Deliberating About Deliberative Democracy," University of Texas, Austin, 4–6. February 2000a.

———. "The Insularity of the Reasonable: Why Political Liberalism Must Admit the Truth." *Ethics* 108 (2000b): 252–275.

European Commission. "European Governance, A White Paper." COM(2001) 428 final. 2001. http://europe.eu.int/eur-lex/en/com/2001/com2001_428en01.pdf

European Parliament. White Paper on the 1996 Intergovernmental Conference, http://europa.eu.int/en/agenda/igc-home/eu-doc/parlmentpeen2.htm, Vol. II, 1996.

———. Report on the moderation of procedures for the exercise of implementing powers—comitology (Aglietta report). Brussels, European Parliament, 1998.

———. Report on the European Parliament's proposals for the Intergovernmental Conference (Dimitrakopoulos-Leinen report). Brussels, European Parliament, 2000.

———. Delegation to the Conciliation Committee Activity Report, 1999–2004. Brussels: European Parliament, 2004.

European Union. Commission of the European Communities. "European Governance, A White Paper." (KOM(2001) 428). Brussels, 2001.

Ewald, F. "Justice, Equality, Judgment: On Social Justice" in *Juridification of Social Spheres: A Comparative Analysis in the Areas of Labour, Corporate, Antitrust and Social Welfare Law*, edited by G. Teubner. Berlin-New York: de Gruyter, 1987.

Falke, J. "Comitology and Other Committees: A Preliminary Empirical Assessment," Pp. 117–165 in *Shaping European Law and Policy: The Role of Committees and Comitology in the Political Process*, edited by R. H. Pendler and G. F. Schaefer. Maastricht: EIPA, 1996.

Falkner, G., et al. *Complying with Europe? The Impact of EU Minimum Harmonisation and Soft Law in the Member States*. Cambridge: Cambridge University Press, 2005.

Farrell, H., and A. Héritier. *Inter-Organizational Negotiation and Intra-Organizational Power in Shared Decision-Making: Early Agreements under Codecision and Their Impact on the European Parliament and the Council of Ministers*. Vienna: Institut für Höhere Studien, March 2004.

Fearon, J., and A. Wendt. "Rationalism and Constructivism in International Relations Theory," Pp. 52–72 in *Handbook of International Relations Theory*, edited by W. Carlsnaes, T. Risse, and B. Simmons. London: Sage, 2002.

Ferry, J.-M. *La question de l'État Européen*. Paris: Gallimard, 2000.

Finder, S. E. *Anonymous Empire: A Study of the Lobby in Great Britain*. London: Pall Mall, 1958.

Fine, R. and W. Smith. "Jürgen Habermas´ Theory of Cosmopolitanism." *Constellations* 10, no. 4 (2003): 469–487.

Finke, B., N. Jung, and B. Kohler-Koch. (2003): Europäisierung des intermediären Raums: Steuerungsinstrumente der Europäischen Kommission. Paper presented at the Drei-Länder-Tagung der deutschen, österreichischen und schweizerischen Vereinigungen für politische Wissenschaft, Berne (14–15 November 2003).

Finnemore, M. and Sikkink, K. "International Norm Dynamics and Political Change," *International Organization* 52, no. 4 (1998): 887–917.

Fischer, J. "From Confederacy to Federation: Thoughts on the Finality of European Integration, 2000, www.jeanmonnetprogram.org/papers/00/joschka_fischer-_en.rtf;

Flora, P., ed. *State-Formation, Nation-Building and Mass Politics in Europe: The Theory of Stein Rokkan*. Oxford: Oxford University Press, 1999.

———, ed. "Externe Grenzbildung und interne Strukturierung—Europa und seine Nationen: Eine Rokkanische Forschungsperspektive," *Berliner Journal für Soziologie* 2 (2000): 151–66.

Florini, A. "The Evolution of International Norms," *International Studies Quarterly* 40, no. 3 (1996): 363–389.

Foley, P. and S. Martin. "A New Deal for the Community? Public Participation in Regeneration and Local Service Delivery," *Policy and Politics* 28, no. 4 (2000): 479–491.

Folke Schuppert, G. *Staatswissenschaft*. Baden-Baden: Nomos, 2003.

———. *Governance im Spiegel der Wissenschaftsdisziplinen*. Berlin: Wissenschaftszentrum, 2004.

Follesdal, A. and S. Hix. "Why There Is a Democratic Deficit in the EU: A Response to Majone and Moravcsik." Eurogov, *European Governance Papers*. No. C-05-02. 2005. www.connex-network.org/eurogov/pdf/egp-connex-C-05-02.pdf

Forst, R. "The Rule of Reasons. Three Models of Deliberative Democracy." *Ratio Juris* 14, no. 4 (2001): 345–378.

Forster, A. *Britain and the Maastricht Negotiations*. Basingstoke: Macmillan, 1999.

Franck, T. *The Power of Legitimacy Among Nations*, New York: Oxford University Press, 1990.

Frankenberg, G. *Die Verfassung der Republik*. Frankfurt: Suhrkamp, 1997.

———. "Art. 20, para. 1-3 I (Republik)," Pp. 1–19 in *Kommentar zum Grundgesetz für die Bundesrepublik Deutschland, Reihe Alternativkommentare*, 3rd edition, edited by E. Denninger et. al. Neuwied, Kriftel: Hermann Luchterhand Verlag, loose-leaf collection, updated: August 2002.

Frankenfeld, P. J. "Technological Citizenship: A Normative Framework for Risk Studies." *Science, Technology & Human Values* 17, no. 4 (1992): 459–484.

Friese, H., and P. Wagner. "The Nascent Political Philosophy of the European Union." *Journal of Political Philosophy* 10, no. 3 (2002): 342–364.

Fuchs, D. "Demos und Nation in der Europäischen Union," Pp. 215–236 in *Zur Zukunft der Demokratie, Herausforderungen im Zeitalter der Globalisierung*, edited by H. D. Klingemann and F. Neidhardt. Berlin: Ed. Sigma, 2000.

Fuchs, E. R., L. C. Minnite, and R. Y. Shapiro. "Political Capital and Political Participation." Paper presented at APSA annual meeting, Washington, DC., 2000.

Fung, A. and E. O. Wright. "Deepening Democracy: Innovations in Empowered Participatory Governance," *Politics and Society* 29, no. 1 (March 2001): 5–41.

Garrett, G., and G. Tsebelis. "An institutional Critique of Intergovernmentalism." *International Organization* 50, no. 2 (1996): 269–299.

Garrett, G. "From the Luxembourg Compromise to Co-decision: Decision Making in the European Union." *Electoral Studies* 14, No. 3 (1995): 289–308.

Gbikpi, B. and J. R. Grote. "From Democratic Government to Participatory Governance," Pp. 17–34 in *Participatory Governance: Political and Societal Implications*, edited by J. R. Grote and B. Gbikpi. Opladen: Leske+Budrich, 2002.

Geertz, C. *The Interpretation of Cultures*, New York: Basic Books, 1973.

———. *Local Knowledge: Further Essays in Interpretative Anthropology*, New York: Basic Books, 1983.

Gellner, E. *Nations and Nationalism*. Ithaca: Cornell University Press, 1983.

Gerhards, J. "Westeuropäische Integration und die Schwierigkeiten der Entstehung einer Europäischen Öffentlichkeit." *Zeitschrift für Soziologie* 22 (1993): 96–110.

———. "Missing a European Public Sphere," Pp. 145–158 in *Will Europe Work? Integration, Employment and the Social Order*, edited by M. Kohli and M. Novak. London: Routledge, 2001.

Gerstenberg, O. "Law's Polyarchy: A Comment on Cohen and Sabel." *European Law Journal* 3, no. 4 (1997): 343–358.

Gerstenberg, O. and C. Sabel. "Directly Deliberative Polyarchy: An Institutional Ideal for Europe," in *Good Governance in Europe's Integrated Market*, edited by C. Joerges and R. Dehousse. Oxford: Oxford University Press, 2002.

Giugni, M. and F. Passy. "Le champ politique de l'immigration en Europe: opportunités, mobilisations et héritage de l'Etat national," Pp. 433–460 in *L'action collective en Europe*, edited by R. Balme and D. Chabanet. Paris: Presses de Sciences Po, 2002.

Gosepath, S. "Equality," in *Stanford Encyclopedia of Philosophy* (Winter 2001 Edition), edited by E. N. Zalta. http://plato.stanford.edu/archives/win2001/entries/equality/.

Grabenwarter, C. "National Constitutional Law Relating to the European Union," in *Principles of European Constitutional Law*, edited by A. von Bogdandy and J. Bast. Oxford: Hart, 2006.

Grabitz, E. et. al. *Direktwahl und Demokratisierung. Eine Funktionsbilanz des Europäischen Parlaments nach der ersten Wahlperiode.* Bonn: Europa Union Verlag, 1988.

Greven, M. Th. "Mitgliedschaft, Grenzen und politischer Raum: Problemdimensionen der Demokratisierung der Europäischen Union," Pp. 249–270 in *Regieren in entgrenzten Räumen*. Politische Vierteljahresschrift Sonderheft 29, edited by B. Kohler-Koch. Opladen: Westdeutscher Verlag, 1998.

———. *Die politische Gesellschaft. Kontingenz und Dezision als Probleme des Regierens und der Demokratie.* Opladen: Leske+Budrich, 1999.

———. "Informalization of Transnational Governance—A Threat to Democratic Government," Pp. 261–284 in *Complex Sovereignty: Reconstituting Political Authority in the 21st century*, edited by Edgar Grande and Louis W. Pauly. Toronto: Toronto University Press, 2004.

Grieco, J. M. "Anarchy and the Limits of Cooperation. A Realist Critique of the Newest Liberal Institutionalism." *International Organization* 42, no. 3 (1988): 485–507.

Grimm, D. "Does Europe need a constitution?" *European Law Journal* 1, no.3 (September 1995): 282–302.

Große Hüttmann, M. "Das Subsidiaritätsprinzip in der Europäischen Union—eine Dokumentation," Occasional Papers Nr. 5. Tübingen: Europäisches Zentrum für Föderalismus-Forschung, 1996.

Grote, J. R., and B. Gbikpi, ed. *Participatory Governance: Political and Societal Implications*. Opladen: Leske+Budrich, 2002.

Guiraudon, V. "Weak Weapons of the Weak? Transnational Mobilization around Migration in the European Union," Pp. 163–186 in *Contentious Europeans. Protest and Politics in an Emerging Polity*, edited by D. Imig, S. Tarrrow. Lanham: Rowman & Littlefield. 2001.

Gutmann, A. "Democracy," Pp. 411–421 in *A Companion to Contemporary Political Philosophy*, edited by R. E. Goodin and P. Pettit. Oxford: Blackwell, 1993.

Haas, E. *The Uniting of Europe: Political, Economic and Social Forces*. Stanford: Stanford University Press, 1958.

Habermas, J. "Über den Begriff der Politischen Beteiligung," Pp. 11–55 in *Student und Politik*, edited by J. Habermas et al. Neuwied am Rhein und Berlin: Luchterhand, 1961.

———. *Theorie des Kommunikativen Handelns*, Vol. 1. Frankfurt: Suhrkamp, 1981.

———. "Law as Medium and Law as Institution," Pp. 203–220 in *Dilemmas of Law in the Welfare State*, edited by G. Teubner. Berlin: de Gruyter, 1985.

———. *Faktizität und Geltung: Beiträge zur Diskurstheorie des Rechts und des demokratischen Rechtsstaats*. Frankfurt a.M: Suhrkamp, 1992.

———. *Faktizität und Geltung*. Frankfurt a.M.: Suhrkamp, 1994.

———. *Between Facts and Norms: Contributions to a Discourse Theory of Law and Democracy* (transl. W. Rehg), Cambridge/Mass: MIT Press, 1996a.

———. *Die Einbeziehung des Anderen: Studien zur politischen Theorie*, Frankfurt: Suhrkamp, 1996b.

———. "Drei normative Modelle der Demokratie," Pp. 277–292 in *Die Einbeziehung des Anderen: Studien zur politischen Theorie*, edited by Jürgen Habermas. Frankfurt: Suhrkamp, 1997.

———. "Paradigms of Law," Pp. 13–25 in *Habermas on Law and Democracy: Critical Exchanges*, edited by M. Rosenfeld and A. Arato. Berkeley, CA: University of California Press, 1998a.

———. "Jenseits des Nationalstaats? Bemerkungen zu Folgeproblemen der wirtschaftlichen Globalisierung," Pp. 67–84 in *Politik der Globalisierung*, edited by U. Beck. Frankfurt a.M.: Suhrkamp, 1998b.

———. "Die postnationale Konstellation und die Zukunft der Demokratie." Pp. 91–169 in *Die postnationale Konstellation. Politische Essays*, edited by J. Habermas. Frankfurt: Suhrkamp, 1998c.

———. *Die postnationale Konstellation: Politische Essays*. Frankfurt: Suhrkamp, 1998d.

———. "Constitutional Democracy: A Paradoxical Union of Contradictory Principles?" *Political Theory* 29, no. 6 (2001a): 766–781.

———. "Remarks on Legitimation through Human Rights," Pp. 113–129 in *Postnational Constellation: Political Essays*, edited by J. Habermas. Cambridge: MIT Press, 2001.

————. "Warum braucht Europa eine Verfassung?" *Die Zeit* 27. 2001b. www. zeit.de/archiv/2001/27/200127_verfassung_lang.xml (16 Dec 2004).

————. *Between Facts and Norms: Contributions to a Discourse Theory of Law and Democracy.* Cambridge: Polity Press, 2004a.

————. "Hat die Konstitutionalisierung des Völkerrechts noch eine Chance?" Pp. 113–193 in *Der gespaltene Westen,* edited by J. Habermas. Frankfurt: Suhrkamp, 2004b.

Habermas, J. and J. Derrida. "Eine attraktive Vision für ein künftiges Europa kann nur aus dem beunruhigenden Empfinden der Ratlosigkeit geboren werden," *Frankfurter Allgemeine Zeitung,* June 30, 2003.

Hall, P. A. *The Political Power of Economic Ideas.* Princeton: Princeton University Press, 1989.

————. "Policy Paradigms, Social Learning, and the State," *Comparative Politics* 25, no. 3 (1993): 275–296.

Hallstein, W. *L'Europe Inachevée.* Paris: Robert Laffont, 1970.

Haltern, U. "Pathos and Patina: The Failure and Promise of Constitutionalism in the European Imagination," *European Law Journal* 9, no.1 (2003): 14–44.

————. "The Dawn of the Political: Rethinking the Meaning of Law in European Integration," *Schweizerische Zeitschrift für internationales und europäisches Recht* 14 (2004): 585–614.

————. *Europarecht und das Politische.* Tübingen: Verlag Mohr Siebeck, 2005a.

————. "Rechtswissenschaft als Europawissenschaft, in Europawissenschaft" in *Europa-wissenschaft,* edited by G. Folke Schuppert, I. Pernice, and U. Haltern. Baden-Baden: Nomos, 2005b.

————. "On Finality," in *Principles of European Constitutional Law,* edited by A. von Bogdandy and J. Bast. Oxford: Hart, 2006.

Hanebeck, *Der demokratische Bundesstaat des Grundgesetzes.* Berlin: Ducker & Humblot, 2004.

Haus, M., and H. Heinelt. "How to Achieve Governability at the Local Level: Theoretical and Conceptual Considerations on a Complementarity of Urban Leadership and Community Involvement," Pp. 12–39 in *Urban Governance and Democracy: Leadership and Community Involvement,* edited by M. Haus, H. Heinelt, and M. Steward. London: Routledge, 2005.

Healey, P. *Collaborative Planning: Shaping Places in Fragmented Societies.* London: Macmillan, 1997.

Hedström, P. and R. Swedberg, ed. S*ocial Mechanisms: An Analytical Approach to Social Theory.* Cambridge: Cambridge University Press, 1998.

Heinelt, H. and R. Smith, ed. *Policy Networks and European Structural Funds: A Comparison between Member States.* London: Avebury, 1996.

Heinelt, H. and A. E. Töller. "Sustainability, Innovation, Participation and EMAS," Pp. 11–21 in *Sustainability, Innovation and Participatory Governance,* edited by H. Heinelt and R. Smith. Aldershot: Ashgate, 2003.

Heinelt, H., et.al. ed. *European Union Environment Policy and New Forms of Governance.* Aldershot: Ashgate, 2001.

Heinelt, H. et.al. ed. *Participatory Governance in Multi-Level Context: Concepts and Experience.* Opladen: Leske+Budrich, 2002.

Heinelt, H. et.al. *Die Entwicklung der EU-Strukturfonds als kumulativer Politikprozess.* Baden-Baden: Nomos, 2005.

Heinelt, H. Results of the Conference "Democratic and Participatory Governance: From Citizens to 'Holders'?" held at the European University Institute in Florence, 14–15 September 2000 (unpublished paper, Institute for Political Science, Darmstadt University of Technology, October 2000).

———. "Achieving Sustainable and Innovative Policies through Participatory Governance in a Multilevel Context," Pp. 17–32 in *Participatory Governance in Multi-Level Context: Concepts and Experience,* edited by H. Heinelt, P. Getimis, and G. Kafkalas. Opladen: Leske+Budrich, 2002a.

———. "Civic Perspectives on a Democratic Transformation of the EU," Pp. 97–120 in *Participatory Governance: Political and Societal Implications,* edited by J. Grote and B. Gbikpi. Opladen: Leske+Budrich, 2002b.

———. "Preface," Pp. 13–16 in *Participatory Governance. Political and Societal Implications,* edited by J. Grote and B. Gbikpi. Opladen: Leske+Budrich, 2002c.

———. ed. *Sustainability, Innovation and Participatory Governance: A Cross-National Study of the EU Eco-Management and Audit Scheme.* Aldershot: Ashgate, 2003.

Held, D. *Democracy and the Global Order: From the Modern State to Cosmopolitan Governance.* Cambridge: Polity Press, 1995.

———. *Models of Democracy,* 2nd ed. Cambridge: Polity Press, 2002.

Helfferich, B. and F. Kolb. "Multilevel Action Coordination in European Contentious Politics: The Case of the European Women's Lobby," Pp. 143–161 in *Contentious Europeans: Protest and Politics in an Emerging Polity,* edited by D. Imig and S. Tarrow. Lanham: Rowman & Littlefield, 2001.

Hennis, W. *Demokratisierung.* Köln, Opladen: Westdeutscher Verlag, 1970.

Héritier, A. "Policy-Making by Subterfuge: Interest Accommodation, Innovation and Substitute Democratic Legitimation in Europe—Perspectives from Distinctive Policy Areas," *Journal of European Public Policy* 4, no. 2 (1997): 171–189.

———. "Elements of democratic legitimation in Europe: An alternative perspective." *Journal of European Public Policy* 6, no. 2 (1999): 269–282.

Hesse, K. *Grundzüge des Verfassungsrechts der Bundesrepublik Deutschland.* 20th ed. Heidelberg: C.F. Müller, 1999.

Hirst, P. *Associative Democracy.* Cambridge: Polity Press, 1994.

Hitzel-Cassagnes, T. "The Reconstruction of Discursive Processes in the European Institutional System: The 'Right of Access to Information' and Its Transformations," in *Making the Euro-Polity: Reflexive Integration in Europe,* edited by E. O. Eriksen. London: Routledge (forthcoming).

Hix, S., T. Raunio, and R. Scully. "Fifty Years On: Research on the European Parliament," *Journal of Common Market Studies* 41, no. 2 (2003): 191–202.

Hix, S. "Parties at the European Level as an Alternative Source of Legitimacy." *Journal of Common Market Studies* 4 (1995): 525–554.

———. "Elections, Parties and Institutional Design: A Comparative Perspective on European Union Democracy." *West European Politics* 21, no. 3 (1998a): 19–52.

———. 'The Study of the European Union II: The New Governance Agenda and Its Rival, *Journal of European Public Policy*, vol. 5, no. 1 (1998b): 38–65.

———. *The Political System of the European Union.* London: Macmillan, 1999.

———. "Legislative Behavior and Party Competition in the European Parliament: An Application of Nominate to the EU." *Journal of Common Market Studies* 39, No. 4 (2001): 663–688.

———. "Why the EU Should Have a Single President, and How She Should Be Elected." Paper for the Working Group on Democracy in the EU for the UK Cabinet Office. 2002. http://personal.lse.ac.uk/hix/Working%20Papers/Why%20the%20EU%20Should%20Have%20a%20Single%20President.pdf

Hodson, D. and I. Maher. "The Open Method as a New Mode of Governance," *Journal of Common Market Studies* 39, no. 4 (2001): 719–746.

Hofmann, H. "A Critical Analysis of the New Typology of Acts in the Draft Treaty Establishing a Constitution for Europe." *European Integration Online Papers* 7, no. 9 (2003).

Holland-Cunz, B. "Feministische Demokratietheorie—Thesen zu einem Projekt." Opladen: Leske+Budrich, 1998.

Hooghe, L., and G. Marks. "Birth of a Polity: The Struggle over European Integration," in *The Politics and Political Economy of Advanced Industrial Societies,* edited by H. Kitschelt et. al. Cambridge: Cambridge University Press, 1995.

———. *Multi-Level Governance and European Integration.* Boulder: Rowman & Littlefield, 2001.

———. "Unraveling the Central State, But How? Types of Multi-Level Governance," *American Political Science Review* 97, no. 2 (2003): 233–243.

Hooghe, L. "The Mobilization of Territorial Interests and Multilevel Governance." Pp. 347–374 in *L'action collective en Europe,* edited by R. Balme and D. Chabanet. Paris: Presses de Sciences Po, 2002.

House of Commons. Second Report from the Foreign Affairs Committee, European Council, Rome 14–15 December 1990, Minutes of Evidence, Session 1990–91, 5 December 1990, 1990a.

———. Second Report from the Foreign Affairs Committee, Session 1989–90, "The Operation of the Single Market," Observations by the Government, 1990b.

House of Lords. Select Committee on the European Communities, 14th Report, 1985.

———. Select Committee on the European Communities, "Economic and Monetary Union and Political Union," 27th Report, 1990.

———. Select Committee on European Union, 7th Report, 2001.

Hovey, J. A. *The Superparliaments. Interparliamentary Consultation and Atlantic Cooperation.* New York: Frederick A. Praeger, 1966.

Huber, P. M. "Demokratie ohne Volk oder Demokratie der Völker?" Pp. 27–57 in *Europäische Demokratie,* edited by J. Drexl et. al. Baden-Baden: Nomos, 1999.

———. "Das institutionelle Gleichgewicht zwischen Rat und Europäischem Parlament in der künftigen Verfassung für Europa." *Europarecht* 38, no. 4, (2003): 574–599.

Hubschmid, C. and P. Moser. "The Co-operation Procedure in the EU: Why Was the European Parliament Influential in the Decision on Car Emission Standards?" *Journal of Common Market Studies* 35, no. 2 (1997): 225–242.

Humrich, C. "Legalization and the Evolution of Law in International Society: A Habermasian approach." Paper presented at the 5th Pan-European International Relations Conference, The Hague, 2004. www.sgir.org/conference2004.

Imig, D. and S. Tarrow. "The Europeanization of Movements? Contentious Politics and the European Union. October 1983–March 1995." in *Social Movements in a Globalizing World*, edited by D. Della Porta, H. Kriesi, and D. Rucht. New York: Macmillan, 1999.

———. *Contentious Europeans: Protest and Politics in an Emerging Polity*. Lanham: Rowman and Littlefield, 2001.

———. "La contestation politique dans l'Europe en formation," Pp. 195–223 in *L'action collective en Europe*, edited by R. Balme and D. Chabanet. Paris: Presses de Sciences Po, 2002.

Imig, D. "Contestation in the Streets: European Protest and the Emerging Euro-Polity," Pp. 216–234 in *European Integration and Political Conflict* edited by G. Marks and M. Steenbergen. Cambridge: Cambridge University Press, 2004.

Ipsen, H. P. *Europäisches Gemeinschaftsrecht*. Tübingen: Mohr/Siebeck, 1972.

———. "Zur Exekutiv-Rechtsetzung in der Europäischen Gemeinschaft." Pp. 425–441 in *Wege und Verfahren des Verfassungslebens*, Festschrift für Peter Lerche, edited by P. Badura and R. Scholz. München: C.H. Beck, 1993.

Israel, J. *Der Begriff Entfremdung*. Reinbek bei Hamburg: Rowolth, 1972.

Jachtenfuchs, M. and B. Kohler-Koch. "Regieren im Dynamischen Mehrebenensystem," Pp. 15–44 in *Europäische Integration*, edited by M. Jachtenfuchs and B. Kohler-Koch. Opladen: Leske+Budrich, 1996.

———, ed. *Europäische Integration*, 2nd ed. Opladen: Leske+Budrich, 2003.

Jachtenfuchs, M., T. Diez, and S. Jung. "Which Europe? Conflicting Models of a Legitimate European Political Order," *European Journal of International Relations* 4, no. 4 (1998): 409–445.

Jachtenfuchs, M. *Ideen und Integration. Verfassungsideen in Deutschland, Frankreich und Großbritannien und die Entwicklung der EU*. Habilitationsschrift: Universität Mannheim, 1999.

———. "The Governance Approach to European Integration." *Journal of Common Market Studies* 39 (2001): 221–240.

———. *Die Konstruktion Europas. Verfassungsideen und Institutionelle Entwicklung*. Baden-Baden: Nomos, 2002.

Jacobs, F. B. "Development of the European Parliament's Powers: An Incomplete Agenda?" European Union Studies Association (EUSA) Biennial Conference, Nashville, Tennessee, March 27–29, 2003. http://aei.pitt.edu/archive/00000441/.

Jacobson, J. K. "Much Ado About Ideas: The Cognitive Factor in Economic Policy." *World Politics* 47, no. 2 (1995): 283–310.

Jacqué, J. P. "Strategien für das Europäische Parlament: Abschied von nationalen Konfliktlinien," in *Das Europäische Parlament im dynamischen Integrationsprozeß: Auf der Suche nach einem zeitgemäßen Leitbild*, edited by O. Schmuck and W. Wessels. Bonn: Europa Union Verlag, 1989.

Jekewitz, J. "Art. 50." Pp. 1–7 in *Kommentar zum Grundgesetz für die Bundesrepublik Deutschland, Reihe Alternativkommentare*, 3rd edition, edited by E. Denninger et al.

Neuwied, Kriftel: Hermann Luchterhand Verlag, loose-leaf collection, updated: August 2002.

Jessop, B. "Governance and Metagovernance: On Reflexivity, Requisite Variety, and Requisite Irony." Pp. 33–58 in *Participatory Governance in Multi-Level Context. Concepts and Experience*, edited by H. Heinelt et al. Opladen: Leske+Budrich, 2002.

Joerges, C. and M. Everson. "Challenging the Bureaucratic Challenge." Pp. 164–188 in *Democracy in the European Union: Integration through Deliberation?* edited by E. O. Eriksen and J.E. Fossum. Routledge: London, 2000.

———. "The European Turn to Governance and Unanswered Questions of Legitimacy: Two Examples and Counter-Intuitive Suggestions," in *The Economy As A Polity: The Political Construction of Modern Capitalism*, edited by C. Joerges, B. Stråth and P. Wagner. London: UCL Press, forthcoming.

Joerges, C. and J. Falke. *Das Ausschußwesen der Europäischen Union. Praxis der Risikoregulierung im Binnenmarkt und ihre rechtliche Verfassung*. Baden-Baden: Nomos, 2000.

Joerges, C. and N. S. Ghaleigh ed. *Darker Legacies of Law in Europe*. Oxford: Hart Publishing, 2003.

Joerges, C., Y. Mény, and J.H.H. Weiler. "Mountain or Molehill? A Critical Appraisal of the Commission White Paper on Governance." New York School of Law, Jean Monnet Working Paper Series, no. 6/1, 2001, www.jeanmonnetprogram.org/papers/01/010601.html

Joerges, C. and J. Neyer "From Intergovernmental Bargaining to Deliberative Political Processes: The Constitutionalisation of Comitology," *European Law Journal* 3, no. 2 (1997a): 273–99.

———. "Transforming Strategic Interaction into Deliberative Problem-Solving: European Comitology in the Foodstuffs Sector," *Journal of European Public Policy* 4, no. 4 (1997b): 609–625.

———. "Politics, Risk Management, World Trade Organisation: Governance and the Limits of Legalisation." *Science and Public Policy* 30 (2003): 219–225.

———. "Free Trade: The Erosion of National and Birth of Transnational Governance," in *Transformation of the State*, edited by Stephan Leibfried and Michael Zürn. Cambridge: Cambridge University Press, 2005.

Joerges, C. and I. J. Sand. "Constitutionalism and Transnational Governance." Paper presented at the Conference on Constitutionalism and Transnational Governance, European University Institute, Florence, December 2001.

Joerges, C. *Zum Funktionswandel des Kollisionsrechts. Die 'Governmental Interest Analysis' und die 'Krise des Internationalen Privatrechts'*. Berlin/Tübingen: de Gruyter-Mohr-Siebeck, 1971.

———. "Vorüberlegungen zu einer Theorie des Internationalen Wirtschaftsrechts." Rabels *Zeitschrift für Ausländisches und Internationales Privatrecht* 43 (1979): 6–79.

———. *Verbraucherschutz als Rechtsproblem*. Heidelberg: Verlagsgesellschaft Recht und Wirtschaft, 1981.

———. "Quality Regulation in Consumer Goods Markets: Theoretical Concepts and Practical Examples." Pp. 142–163 in *Contract and Organization*, edited by T. C. Daintith and G. Teubner. Berlin: de Gruyter, 1986.

———. "From Intergovernmental Bargaining to Deliberative Political Processes: The Constitutionalisation of Comitology." *European Law Journal* 3 (1997a): 273–299.

———. "The Impact of European Integration on Private Law: Reductionist Perceptions, True Conflicts and a New Constitutional Perspective." *European Law Journal* 3 (1997b): 378–406.

———. "Deliberative Supranationalism." *Zeitschrift für Internationale Beziehungen* 6 (1999a): 185–242.

———. "'Good Governance' Through Comitology?" Pp. 311–338 in *EU Committees: Social Regulation, Law and Politics*, edited by C. Joerges and E. Vos. Hart Publishing: Oxford, 1999b.

———. "'Deliberative Supranationalism'—A Defence." *European Integration online Papers* (EIoP) 5, no. 8 (2001).

———. "'Deliberative Supranationalism'—Two Defences." *European Law Journal* 8 (2002a): 133–151.

———. "'Good Governance' in the European Internal Market: Two Competing Legal Conceptualisations of European Integration and their Synthesis." Pp. 219–242 in *European Integration and International Co-ordination*. Studies in Transnational Economic Law in Honor of Claus-Dieter Ehlermann. ZaöRV 62. The Hague: Kluwer Law International, 2002b.

———. "Comitology and the European Model? Towards a Recht-Fertigungs-Recht in the Europeanisation Process." Pp. 501–540 in *European Governance, Deliberation and the Quest for Democratization*, edited by E. O. Eriksen, C. Joerges, and J. Neyer. ARENA Report no. 2, Oslo, 2003a, 133–151.

———. "Europe a Grossraum? Shifting Legal Conceptualisations of the European project," in *Darker Legacies of Law in Europe: The Shadow of National Socialism and Fascism over Europe and Its Legal Traditions*, edited by C. Joerges and N. S. Ghaleigh. Portland-Oxford: Hart, 2003b.

———. "On the Legitimacy of Europeanising Private Law: Considerations on a Justice-Making Law for the EU Multi-Level System." *Electronic Journal of Comparative Law* 7, no. 3 (2003c), www.ejcl.org/ejcl/73/art73-3.html.

———. "Juridification Patterns for Social Regulation and the WTO: A Theoretical Framework." Paper presented at the Conference on "Legal Patterns of Transnational Social Regulation and International Trade," EUI/RSCAS, Florence, September 2004a.

———. "The Challenges of Europeanization in the Realm of Private Law: A Plea for a New Legal Discipline." EUI Working Paper LAW 2004/12, 2004b. available at www.iue.it/PUB/law04-12.pdf.

———. "What is Left of the European Economic Constitution?" EUI Working Paper LAW 2004/13, 2004c. available at www.iue.it/PUB/law04-13.pdf.

Judge, D. and D. Earnshaw. *The European Parliament*. Houndsmills, Basingstoke: Palgrave, 2003.

Kadelbach, S. "Annotation." *Common Market Law Review* 38, no. 1 (2001): 179–194.

———. "Union Citizenship," in *Principles of European Constitutional Law*, edited by A. von Bogdandy and J. Bast. Oxford: Hart, 2006.

Kaelberer, M. "The Euro and European Identity: Symbols, Power, and the Politics of European Monetary Union," *Review of International Studies* 30, no. 2 (2004): 161–178.

Kahn, P. W. "American Hegemony and International Law. Speaking Law to Power: Popular Sovereignty, Human Rights, and the New International Order." *Chicago Journal of International Law* 1, no. 1 (Spring 2000): 1–18.

———. "Comparative Constitutionalism in a New Key," *Michigan Law Review* 101 (2003): 2677–2705.

———. *Putting Liberalism in Its Place*, Princeton: Princeton University Press, 2005.

Kaiser, J. H. "Bewahrung und Veränderung Demokratischer und Rechtsstaatlicher Ver-Fassungsstruktur in den internationalen Gemeinschaften." *Veröffentlichungen der Vereinigung der Deutschen Staatslehrer* 23 (1966): 1–33.

Kamann, H. G. *Die Mitwirkung der Parlamente der Mitgliedstaaten an der europäischen Gesetzgebung*. Frankfurt: Peter Lang, 1997.

Katz, R. "Models of Democracy: Elite Attitudes and the Democratic Deficit," *European Union Politics* 2, no. 1 (2001): 53–80.

Keck, M. and Sikkink, K. *Activists Beyond Borders: Advocacy Networks in International Politics*, Ithaca: Cornell University Press, 1998.

Kegel, G., and K. Schurig. *Internationales Privatrecht*. 9th ed. München: C. H. Beck, 2004.

Keohane, R. O. and J. S. Nye. *Power and Interdependence. World Politics in Transition.* Boston: Little Brown, 1977.

———. *After Hegemony: Power and Discord in the World Political Economy*. Princeton: Princeton University Press, 1984.

Kielmansegg, P. Graf. "Integration und Demokratie." Pp. 47–71 in *Europäische Integration*, edited by M. Jachtenfuchs and B. Kohler-Koch. Opladen: Leske+Budrich, 1996.

Kielmansegg, P. Graf. "Integration und Demokratie." Pp. 49–83 in *Europäische Integration*, edited by M. Jachtenfuchs and B. Kohler-Koch. Opladen: Leske+Budrich, 2003.

King, A. "Modes of Executive-Legislative Relations: Great Britain, France, and West Germany," *Legislative Studies Quarterly* 1 (1976): 11–36.

Kiser, L. and E. Ostrom. "The Three Worlds of Action." Pp. 179–222 in *Strategies of Political Inquiry*, edited by E. Ostrom. Beverly Hills: Sage Publications, 1982.

Klein, A. *Der Diskurs der Zivilgesellschaft: Politische Hintergründe und Demokratietheoretische Folgerungen*. Opladen: Leske+Budrich, 2001.

Klein, E. "Die Kompetenz—und Rechtskompensation." *Deutsches Verwaltungsblatt* 96, no. 14 (Juli 1981): 661–667.

Kohler-Koch, B. "Catching Up with Change: the Transformation of Governance in the European Union", *Journal of European Public Policy* 3, no. 3 (1996): 359–380.

———. "Organized Interests in European Integration: The Evolution of a New Type of Governance?" in *Participation and Policy-Making in the European Union*, edited by H. Wallace and A. R. Young. Oxford: Clarendon Press, 1997.

———. "Europäisierung der Regionen: Institutioneller Wandel als Sozialer Prozess." Pp. 13–30 in *Interaktive Politik in Europa: Regionen im Netzwerk der Integration*, edited by B. Kohler-Koch. Opladen: Leske+Budrich, 1998.

———. "The Evolution and Transformation of European Governance." Pp. 14–35 in *The Transformation of Governance in the European Union*, edited by B. Kohler-Koch and R. Eising. London: Routledge, 1999.

———. "Framing: The Bottleneck of Constructing Legitimate Institutions," *Journal of European Public Policy* 7, no. 4 (2000): 513–531.

———. "Legitimes Regieren in der EU: Eine Kritische Auseinandersetzung mit dem Weißbuch zum Europäischen Regieren." Pp. 432–445 in *Demokratietheorie und Demokratieentwicklung: Festschrift für Peter Graf Kielmansegg*, edited by A. Kaiser and T. Zittel. Wiesbaden: VS Verlag für Sozialwissenschaften, 2003.

———. Synthesis of the debates, Conference on "Participatory Democracy: Current Situation and Opportunities Provided by the European Constitution." Brussels (8–9 March 2004), www.esc.eu.int/pages/en/acs/events/08_03_04_democracy/Intervention_Kohler-koch_en.pdf.

Kohler-Koch, B. and R. Eising, ed. *The Transformation of Governance in the European Union*. London/New York: Routledge, 1999.

Kolm, S. C. "Distributive Justice." Pp. 438–461 in *A Companion to Contemporary Political Philosophy*, edited by R. E. Goodin and P. Pettit. Oxford: Blackwell, 1993.

Kooiman, J. "Governance. A Social-Political Perspective." Pp. 71–96 in *Participatory Governance in Multi-Level Context: Concepts and Experience*, edited by H. Heinelt et. al. Opladen: Leske+Budrich, 2002.

———. *Governing as Governance*. London: Sage, 2003.

Koselleck, R. "Geschichte." Chapters I. und V–VII in *Geschichtliche Grundbegriffe*, Vol. 2, edited by O. Brunner, W. Conze, and R. Koselleck. Stuttgart: Klett-Cotta, 1975.

Kramer, L. "Rethinking Choice of Law." *Columbia Law Journal* 90 (1990): 277–345.

———. "More Notes on Methods and Objectives in Conflict of Laws." *Cornell International Law Journal* 24 (1991): 245–278.

Kraus, P. A. "Political Unity and Linguistic Diversity in Europe." *Archives européennes de sociologie* 41 (2000): 138–63.

Kreppel, A. "Rules, Ideology and Coalition Formation in the European Parliament: Past, Present and Future," *European Union Politics* 1, no. 3 (2000): 340–362.

———. *The European Parliament and Supranational Party System: A Study in Institutional Development*. Cambridge: Cambridge University Press, 2002a.

———. "Moving Beyond Procedure: An Empirical Analysis of European Parliament Legislative Influence." *Comparative Political Studies* 35, No. 7 (2002b): 784–813.

Ladeur, K. H. "Towards a Legal Theory of Supranationality—The Viability of the Network Concept." *European Law Journal* 3 (1997): 33–54.

———. "'Deliberative Demokratie' und 'Dritter Weg'—eine neue Sackgasse?" *Der Staat* 41, no. 1 (2002): 3–27.

Landshut, S. "Kritik der Soziologie—Freiheit und Gleichheit als Ursprungsproblem der Soziologie." Pp. 43–188 in *Politik: Grundbegriffe und Analysen*, edited by S. Landshut. Berlin: Verlag für Berlin Brandenburg, 2004.

Langenbucher, K. "Zur Zulässigkeit Parlamentsersetzender Normgebungsverfahren im Europarecht." *Zeitschrift für europäisches Privatrecht* 10, no. 2 (2002): 265–286.

Laughland, J. *The Tainted Source: The Undemocratic Origins of the European Idea*. London 1998.

Laursen, F. and S. A. Pappas, ed. *The Changing Role of Parliaments in the European Union.* Maastricht: European Institute of Public Administration, 1995.

Laursen, F. "Parliamentary Bodies Specializing in European Union Affairs: Denmark and the European Committee of the Folketing." Pp. 43–60 in *The Changing Role of Parliaments in the European Union,* edited by F. Laursen and S. A. Pappas. Maastricht: European Institute of Public Administration, 1995.

———. "The Danish Folketing and Its European Affairs Committee: Strong Players in the National Policy Cycle." Pp. 99–115 in *National Parliaments on Their Ways to Europe: Losers or Latecomers?* edited by A. Maurer and W. Wessels. Baden-Baden: Nomos, 2001.

Le Torrec, V. et. al. "Framing Europe: News Coverage and Legitimacy of the European Union in Five Countries." Paper presented at the European Community Studies Association, Madison, Wisconsin, May 31–June 2, 2001.

Lefébure, P. and E. Lagneau. "Le Moment Volvorde: Action Protestataire et Espace Publique Européen." Pp. 495–529 in *L'Action Collective en Europe,* edited by R. Balme and D. Chabanet. Paris: Presses de Sciences Po, 2002.

Leggewie, C. "Transnational Movements and the Question of Democracy." *Transit* 24, Winter 2002/2003. www. eurozine.com/article/2003-02-06-leggewie-de.html.

Legro, J. W. "Which Norms Matter? Revisiting the 'Failure' of Internationalism," *International Organization* 51, no. 1 (1997): 311–363.

Lepsius, R. M. "Bildet Sich eine Kulturelle Identität in der Europäischen Gemeinschaft?" in *Identität und Interesse: Der Diskurs der Identitätsforschung,* edited by W. Reese-Schäfer. Opladen: Leske+Budrich, 1999.

———. "Die Europäische Union als Herrschaftsverband Eigener Prägung." Pp. 203–212 in *What Kind of Constitution for What Kind of Polity?* Harvard Jean Monnet Working Paper 7/00, edited by C. Joerges, Y. Mény, and J. H. H. Weiler, 2000. www.law.harvard.edu/Programs/JeanMonnet/ or www.jeanmonnetprogram.org/papers/01/010701.html (15 Dec. 2004).

Lijphart, A. *Democracies: Patterns of Majoritarian and Consensus Government in Twenty-One Countries.* New Haven: Yale University Press, 1984.

———. *Patterns of Democracy: Government Forms and Performance in Thirty-Six Countries.* New Haven: Yale University Press, 1999.

Lindblom, C. E. *The Intelligence of Democracy: Decision Making Through Mutual Adjustment.* New York: Free Press, 1965.

Lipset, S. M. "The Social Requisites of Democracy Revisited." *American Sociological Review* 59 (1994): 1–22.

Lord, C. *Democracy in the European Union.* Sheffield: Sheffield Academic Press, 1998.

———. "Assessing Democracy in a Contested Polity." *Journal of Common Market Studies* 39, no. 4 (November 2001): 641–61.

———. "New Governance and Post-Parliamentarism." Paper presented at the International Conference on "Debating the Democratic Legitimacy of the European Union," Mannheim, Germany, 27–29 November 2003.

———. *A Democratic Audit of the European Union.* Basingstoke: Palgrave, 2004.

Lovan, W. R., M. Murray, and R. Shaffer, ed. *Participatory Governance: Planning, Conflict Mediation and Public Decision-Making in Civil Society.* Aldershot and Burlington: Ashgate, 2004.

Lowdes, V., L. Pratchett and G. Stoker. "Trends in Public Participation: part 1—Local Government Perspectives." *Public Administration* 79, no. 1. (2001): 205–222.

Lübbe-Wolff, G. "Europäisches und Nationales Verfassungsrecht." *Veröffentlichungen der Vereinigung der Deutschen Staatsrechtslehrer* 60 (2000): 246–287.

Maduro, M. P. *We the Court: The European Court of Justice and the European Economic Constitution.* Oxford: Hart, 1998.

Magnette, P. "L'Union européenne: Un Régime Semi Parlementaire" in *À Quoi Sert le Parlement Européen?* edited by P. Delwit, J. M. DeWaele, and P. Magnette. Bruxelles: Éditions Complexes, 1999.

———. "European Governance and Civic Participation: Beyond Elitist Citizenship?" *Political Studies* 52, no. 1 (2003): 144–161.

Majone, G. "The European Community: An Independent Fourth Branch of Government?" Pp. 23–43 in *Verfassungen für ein Ziviles Europa,* edited by G. Brüggemeier. Baden-Baden: Nomos, 1994a.

———. "The Rise of the Regulatory State in Europe." *West European Politics* 17 (1994b): 77–101.

———. *Regulating Europe.* London: Routledge, 1996a.

———. "Regulatory Legitimacy." Pp. 284–301 in *Regulating Europe,* edited by G. Majone. London and New York: Routledge, 1996b.

———. "Europe's 'Democratic Deficit': The Question of Standards," *European Law Journal* 4, no. 1 (March 1998): 5–28.

———. "The Credibility Crisis of Community Regulation." *Journal of Common Market Studies* 38, no. 2 (2000): 273–302.

———. "Delegation of Regulatory Powers in a Mixed Polity." *European Law Journal* 38, no. 3 (2002): 319–339.

Major, J. *John Major—The Autobiography.* London: Harper Collins, 1999.

Manin, B. *Principes du Gouvernement Représentatif.* Paris: Flammarion, 1995.

Mann, M. "The Autonomous Power of the State: Its Origins, Mechanisms and Results." *European Journal of Sociology* 25 (1984).

March, J. G., and J. P. Olsen. *Rediscovering Institutions: The Organizational Basis of Politics.* New York: Free Press, 1989.

———. *Democratic Governance.* New York: Free Press, 1995.

———. "The Institutional Dynamics of International Political Orders." *International Organization* 52, Special Issue (1998): 943–59.

Marks, G. and D. McAdam. "On the Relationship of the Political Opportunities to the Form of Collective Action," in *Social Movements in a Globalizing World,* edited by D. Della Porta, H. Kriesi, and D. Rucht. New York: Macmillan, 1999.

Marks, G. and M. Steenbergen, ed. *European Integration and Political Conflict.* Cambridge: Cambridge University Press, 2004.

Marshall, T. H. *Class, Citizenship and Social Development.* New York: Doubleday, 1964.

———. "Citizenship and Social Class." Pp. 3–51 in *Citizenship and Social Class,* edited by T.H. Marshall and T. Bottomore. London: Pluto Press, 1992.

Martin, A., and G. Ross. "Trade Union Organizing at the European Level: The Dilemma of Borrowed Resources." Pp. 53–76 in *Contentious Europeans: Protest and*

Politics in an Emerging Polity, edited by D. Imig and S. Tarrow. Lanham: Rowman & Littlefield, 2001.

Mattila, M. and Lane, J. E. "Why Unanimity in the Council? A Roll-Call Analysis of Council Voting." *European Union Politics* 2, no. 1 (2001): 31–53.

Maurer, A. and W. Wessels, ed. *National Parliaments after Amsterdam: From Slow Adapters to National Players?* Baden-Baden: Nomos, 2001.

Maurer, A. "Die Demokratisierung der Europäischen Union: Perspektiven für das Europäische Parlament." Pp. 15–38 in *Legitimationsprobleme und Demokratisierung der Europäischen Union*, edited by A. Maurer and B. Thiele. Marburg: Schüren, 1996.

———. "Die Institutionellen Reformen: Entscheidungseffizienz und Demokratie," in *Die Europäische Union nach Amsterdam*, edited by M. Jopp, A. Maurer, and O. Schmuck. Bonn: Europa Union Verlag, 1998.

———. "National Parliaments in the European Architecture: From Latecomers' Adaptation towards Permanent Institutional Change?" Pp. 27–76 in *National Parliaments on their Ways towards Europe: Loser or Latecomers?* edited by A. Maurer and W. Wessels. Baden-Baden: Nomos, 2001.

———. *Parlamentarische Demokratie in der Europäischen Union: Der Beitrag des Europäischen Parlaments und der Nationalen Parlamente.* Baden-Baden: Nomos, 2002.

———. "Mass Media Publicized Discourse on the Post-Nice Process." Austrian Academy of Sciences Working Paper No. ICE/IWE 40, 2003a.

———. "The Legislative Powers and Impact of the European Parliament." *Journal of Common Market Studies* 41, No. 2 (2003b): 227–247.

Mayntz, R. and F. W. Scharpf. "Steuerung und Selbststeuerung in staatsnahen Sektoren." Pp. 9–38 in *Gesellschaftliche Selbstregulierung und Politische Steuerung*, edited by R. Mayntz and F. W. Scharpf. Frankfurt/New York: Campus, 1995.

Mazey, S., and J. Richardson. "Interest Groups and EU Policy-Making: Organisational Logic and Venue Shopping," in *European Union: Power and Policy-Making*, 3rd ed., edited by J. Richardson. London: Routledge, 2005.

Mazey, S. "L'Union Européenne et les Droits des Femmes: De L'européanisation des Agendas Nationaux à la Nationalisation d'un Agenda Européen?" Pp. 405–432 in *L'action Collective en Europe*, edited by R. Balme and D. Chabanet. Paris: Presses de Sciences Po, 2002.

McAdam, D., S. Tarrow and C. Tilly. *Dynamics of Contention.* Cambridge: Cambridge University Press, 2001.

McNamara, K. *The Currency of Ideas: Monetary Politics in the European Union.* Ithaca: Cornell University Press, 1998.

Mearsheimer, J. J. "The False Promise of International Institutions." *International Security* 19, no. 1 (1995): 5–49.

Mestmäcker, E. J. "On the Legitimacy of European Law." *Rabels Zeitschrift für Ausländisches und Internationales Privatrecht* 58 (1994): 615–635.

———. "Wandlungen in der Verfasstheit der Europäischen Gemeinschaft," in *Wirtschaft und Verfassung in der Europäischen Union. Beiträge zu Recht, Theorie und Politik der Europäischen Integration.* Baden-Baden: Nomos, 2003.

Michel, H.(2005): "The Lobbyists and the Consultation on the White Paper: Objectivization and Institutionalisation of 'Civil Society,'" paper prepared for the workshop, "The Institutional Shaping of EU–Society Relations," CONNEX Research Group 4, Mannheim, 14–15 October 2005.

Michelman, F. "Morality, Identity and 'Constitutional Patriotism.'" *Ratio Juris* 14, no. 3 (2001): 253–271.

Mill, J. S. (1972): *Utilitarianism: On Liberty and Representative Government*. London: Dent.

Milward, A. S. *The European Rescue of the Nation-State*. London: Routledge, 1992.

Mitrany, D. A *Working Peace System*. Chicago, 1943.

Moravcsik, A. "Why the European Community Strengthens the State: Domestic Politics and International Cooperation." Center for European Studies Working Paper Series No. 52, 1994.

———. "In Defence of the Democratic Deficit: Reassessing Legitimacy in the European Union," *Journal of Common Market Studies* 40, no. 4 (2002): 603–624.

———. "In Defence of the Democratic Deficit: Reassessing Legitimacy in the European Union." Pp. 76–97 in *Integration in an Expanding European Union*, edited by J.H.H. Weiler, J. Peterson, and I. Begg. Oxford and Malden: Blackwell Publishers, 2003.

Moser, P. "The European Parliament as a Conditional Agenda Setter: What Are the Conditions?" *American Political Science Review* 90, No. 4 (1996): 834–838.

Muecke, D.C. Irony. London: Methuen, 1970.

Müller-Ibold, T. *Die Begründungspflicht im Europäischen Gemeinschaftsrecht und im Deutschen Recht*. Frankfurt: Lang, 1990.

Muschg, A. "Europa ist das, was Europa wird," *Neue Züricher Zeitung*, May 30, 2003.

Nannestad, P. "Das Politische System Dänemarks." Pp. 55–92 in *Die Politischen Systeme Westeuropas*, edited by W. Ismayr. Opladen: Leske+Budrich, 2003.

Napolitano, G. "European Parliament." Initiative Report on Relations between the European Parliament and the National Parliaments in the European Constitution, No. A5-0023/2002, 2002.

Naschold, F. *Organisation und Demokratie*. Stuttgart et al.: Kohlhammer, 1969.

Nassehi, A. "Der Begriff des Politischen und die Doppelte Normativität der 'Soziologischen' Moderne." Pp. 133–169 in *Der Begriff des Politischen*, edited by A. Nassehi and M. Schroer. Baden-Baden: Nomos, 2003.

Nennen, H. U. and D. Garbe, ed. *Das Expertendilemma*. Berlin, Heidelberg: Springer, 1996.

Nettesheim, M. "Anmerkung." *Juristenzeitung* 58, no. 19 (October 2003): 952–956.

Neyer, J. "Discourse and Order in the EU: A Deliberative Approach to Multi-Level Governance." *Journal of Common Market Studies* 41, no.4 (2003): 687–706.

———. *Postnationale Politische Herrschaft: Vergesellschaftung und Verrechtlichung Jenseits des Staates*. Baden-Baden: Nomos, 2004.

Nickel, D. "The Amsterdam Treaty—A Shift in the Balance between the Institutions!?" Jean Monnet Center for International and Regional Economy Law & Justice. Working Paper 98–14, 1998. www.jeanmonnetprogram.org/papers/98/98-14-The.html.

———. "Das Europäische Parlament als Legislativorgan: Zum neuen institutionellen Design nach der Europäischen Verfassung." *Integration* 26, no.4. (2003): 501–509.

Nicotra, I. "Il Diritto di Recesso e il Trattato che Institutisce la Constituzione Europea." Pp. 447–458 in *Studi sulla Constituzione Europea*, edited by A. Lucarelli and A. Patroni Griffi. Napoli, Italy: Edizioni Scientifiche Italiane s.p.a, 2003.

Norman, P. *The Accidental Constitution: The Story of the European Convention*. Brussels: Eurocomment, 2003.

Norris, P., S. Walgrave, and P. van Aelst. "Who Demonstrates? Anti–State Rebels or Conventional Participants? Or Everyone?" presented at the Midwest Political Science Association meeting, Chicago, 2003.

Norton, P., ed. *National Parliaments and the European Union*. London: Frank Cass, 1996.

Nugent, N. *The Government and Politics of the European Union*. Durham, NC: Duke University Press, 1994.

Oeter, S. "Federalism and Democracy," in *Principles of European Constitutional Law*, edited by A. von Bogdandy and J. Bast. Oxford: Hart, 2006.

Offe, C. "Some Skeptical Considerations on the Malleability of Representative Institutions." Pp. 114–132 in *Associations and Democracy*, edited by J. Cohen and J. Rogers. London: Verso, 1995.

———. "Demokratie und Wohlfahrtsstaat: Eine Europäische Regimeform unter dem Stress der Europäischen Integration." Pp. 99–136 in *Internationale Wirtschaft, Nationale Demokratie*, edited by W. Streeck. Frankfurt, New York: Campus, 1998.

———. "How Can We Trust Our Fellow Citizens?" Pp. 42–87 in *Democracy and Trust*, edited by M. E. Warren. Cambridge: Cambridge University Press, 1999.

———. "'Homogeneity' and Constitutional Democracy: Coping with Identity Conflicts through Group Rights." Pp. 151–181 in *Herausforderungen der Demokratie*, edited by C. Offe. Frankfurt and New York: Campus, 2003.

Offe, C. and U. K. Preuß. "Democratic Institutions and Moral Ressources." Pp. 182–209 in *Herausforderungen der Demokratie: Zur Integrations—und Leistungsfähigkeit Politischer Insitutionen*, edited by C. Offe. Frankfurt, New York: Campus, 2003.

Olson, M. *The Logic of Collective Action*. Cambridge: Harvard University Press, 1965.

Ostrom, E. *Governing the Commons: The Evolution of Institutions for Collective Action*. Cambridge: Cambridge University Press, 1990.

———. "Vulnerability and Polycentric Governance Systems." IHDP Update. Newsletter of the International Human Dimensions Programme on Global Environmental Change, No. 3 (2001): 1–4.

Padoa-Schioppa, T. "The Institutional Reforms of the Amsterdam Treaty." *The Federalist* 1, no. 1 (1998).

Palonen, K. S. *History, Politics, Rhetoric*. Cambridge: Polity, 2003.

Papadopoulos, Y. "Problems of Democratic Accountability in Network and Multi-Level Governance," paper presented at the CONNEX session "EU Multi-Level Governance and Democracy"; 20th IPSA World Congress, Fukuoka (Japan), July 9–13, 2006.

Paul, J. "Comity in International Law." *Harvard Journal for International Law* 32 (1991): 1–79.

Peers, S. "W.T.O Dispute Settlement and Community Law." *European Law Review* 26, no. 6 (December 2001): 605–615.

Pernice, I. "Art. 23." Pp. 325–474 in *Grundgesetz-Kommentar*, edited by H. Dreier. Tübingen: Mohr Siebeck, 1998.

———. "Europäisches und Nationales Verfassungsrecht." *Veröffentlichungen der Vereinigung der Deutschen Staatsrechtslehrer* 60 (2000): 148–193.

Peters, A. *Elemente einer Theorie der Verfassung Europas*. Berlin: Duncker und Humblot, 2001.

———. "European Democracy after the 2003 Convention." *Common Market Law Review* 41, no. 1 (February 2004): 37–85.

Peters, B. "Public Discourse, Democracy, Identity, and Legitimacy in National and Supranational Political Systems: What are the Questions?" in *Making the Euro-Polity: Reflexive Integration in Europe*, edited by E. O. Eriksen. London: Routledge, 2004.

Peters, G., and J. Pierre. "Multi-Level Governance and Democracy: A Faustian Bargain?" Pp. 79–92 in *Multi-Level Governance*, edited by I. Bache and M. Flinders. Oxford: Oxford University Press, 2004.

Peterson, J. and E. Bomberg. *Decision-Making in the European Union*. London and New York: Palgrave, 1999.

Peterson, J. "Decision-Making in the European Union: Towards a Framework for Analysis", *Journal of European Public Policy* 2, no. 1 (1995): 69–93.

Petersson, B. and A. Hellström. "The Return of the Kings: Temporality in the Construction of EU Identity." *European Societies* 5, no. 3 (2003): 235–252.

Pettit, P. *Republicanism. A Theory of Freedom and Government*. Oxford: Oxford University Press, 1997.

———. "Deliberative Democracy and the Discursive Dilemma." *Philosophical Issues* (supp. Nous) no. 11 (2001): 268–299.

Pharr, S. J. and R. D. Putnam, ed. *Disaffected Democracies: What's Troubling the Trilateral Countries?* Princeton: Princeton University Press, 2000.

Pierre, J. and B. G. Peters. *Governance, Politics and the State*. London: Macmillan, 2000.

Pierre, J., ed. *Debating Governance. Authority, Steering, and Democracy*. Oxford: Oxford University Press, 1999.

Pizzorno, A. "Mutamenti nelle Istituzioni Rappresentative e Sviluppo dei Partiti Politici." Pp. 961–1056 in *La Storia dell'Europa: L'età Contemporanea*. Secoli XIX-XX, edited by P. Bairoch and E. J. Hobsbawn. Torino: Einaudi, 1996.

Poiares Maduro, M. *We, the Court: The European Court of Justice & the European Economic Constitution*. Oxford: Hart, 1998.

Pollack, M. "Representing Diffuse Interests in EC Policy-Making," *Journal of European Public Policy*, vol. 4, no. 4 (1997): 572–90.

———. "Deliberative Democracy and the Discursive Dilemma." *Philosophical Issues* (supp. Nous) no. 11 (2001): 268–299.

———. "Control Mechanism or Deliberative Democracy? Two Images of Comitology." *Comparative Political Studies* 36, no. 1/2 (2003): 125–155.

Polsby, N. "Legislatures." Pp. 277–296 in *Handbook of Political Science*, edited F. Greenstein and N. Polsby. Reading, Mass: Addison Wesley, 1975.

Post, R. "Democracy and Equality." *Annals of the American Academy of Political and Social Sciences* 603 (2006): 24–36.

Pottage, A. "Power as an Art of Contingency: Luhmann, Deleuze, Foucault." *Economy & Society* 27, no. 1 (1998).

Putnam, R. D. (with R. Leonardi and R. Y. Nanetti). *Making Democracy Work: Civic Traditions in Modern Italy*. Princeton, NJ: Princeton University Press, 1993.

Putnam, R. D. "Diplomacy and Domestic Politics: the Logic of Two-Level Games." International Organization 42 (1988): 427–460.

———. *Bowling Alone: The Collapse and Revival of American Community*. New York: Simon & Schuster, 2000.

Quermonne, J. L. *La Système Politique de l'Union Européenne*. Paris: Montchrétien, 1994.

Randelzhofer, A. "Zum behaupteten Demokratiedefizit der Europäischen Gemeinschaft." Pp. 39–55 in *Der Staatenverbund der Europäischen Union*, Beiträge und Diskussionen des Symposiums am 21./22. Januar 1994 in Heidelberg, edited by P. Hommelhoff and P. Kirchhof. Heidelberg: Müller, Jur. Verl., 1994.

Ranney, A. *The Doctrine of Responsible Party Government*. Urbana: University of Illinois Press, 1962.

Raunio, T. and Hix, S. "Backbenchers Learn to Fight Back: European Integration and Parliamentary Government." *West European Politics* 23 (2000): 142–68.

Raunio, T. "Parliamentary Questions in the European Parliament: Representation, Information and Control." *Journal of Legislative Studies* 2, No. 4 (1996): 356–382.

———. "Two Steps Forward, One Step Back? National Legislatures in the EU Constitution," *The Federal Trust*, www.fedtrust.co.uk/uploads/constitution/Raunio.pdf, 2004.

Rehg, W. and J. Bohman. "Survey Article: Discourse and Democracy: The Formal and Informal Bases of Legitimacy in Habermas's 'Faktizität und Geltung.'" *The Journal of Political Philosophy* 4, no. 1 (1996): 79–99.

Ress, G. "Das Europäische Parlament als Gesetzgeber." *Zeitschrift für Europarechtliche Studien* 2, no. 2 (1999): 219–230.

Rhodes, R. "The New Governance: Governing without Government," *Political Studies* 44, no. 4 (1996): 652–68.

———. "Governance and Public Administration." Pp. 54–90 in *Debating Governance*, edited by J. Pierre. Oxford: Oxford University Press, 2000.

Richardson, J. "The Market for Political Activism: Interest Groups as a Challenge to Political Parties." *West European Politics* 18, no. 1 (1995): 116–139.

———. "Eroding EU Policies: Implementation Gaps, Cheating and Re-Steering." Pp. 278–295 in *European Union, Power and Policy Making*, edited by J. Richardson. London: Routledge, 1996.

———. "Government, Interest Groups and Policy Change." *Political Studies*, 48, no. 5 (2000): 1006–1025.

———. "Organised Interests in the EU." in *Handbook of European Politics*, edited by K. E. Jorgensen, M. Pollack, and B. Rosamund. Sage: London, 2006.

Ridder, H. "Was die Euro-Rhetorik Nicht an die Große Glocke Hängt—Faktoren der Europäischen Einigung von den Pariser Verträgen bis zu Maastricht." *Blätter für deutsche und internationale Politik*, 5 (1995): 554–565.

Rifkin, J. *The European Dream: How Europe's Vision of the Future Is Quietly Eclipsing the American Dream*, London: Jeremy P. Tarcher/Penguin, 2004.

Riker, W. H. *Liberalism against Populism: A Confrontation Between the Theory of Democracy and the Theory of Social Choice*. Prospect Heights: Waveland Press, 1982.

Risse, T. et al., ed. *The Power of Human Rights: International Norms and Domestic Change*, Cambridge: Cambridge University Press, 1999.

Risse, T. "'Let's Argue!': Communicative Action in World Politics." *International Organization* 54, no. 1 (2000): 1–39.

Rittberger, B. and F. Schimmelfennig. The Constitutionalization of the European Union: Explaining the Parliamentarization and Institutionalization of Human Rights. IHS Working Paper, no. 104, Vienna, 2005.

Rittberger, B. "The Creation and Empowerment of the European Parliament," *Journal of Common Market Studies* 41, no. 2 (2003): 203–225.

———. *Building Europe's Parliament: Democratic Representation beyond the Nation-State*, Oxford: Oxford University Press, 2005.

Roethe, T. "EG-Ausschußwesen und Risikoregulierung: Ein Problem von Handlungsstruktur und Rationalität." EUI Working Paper LAW 94/7, 1994.

Roose, J. (2003): "Umweltorganisationen zwischen Mitgliedschaftslogik und Einflusslogik in der Europäischen Politik." Pp. 141–158 in *Bürgerschaft, Öffentlichkeit und Demokratie in Europa*, edited by A. Klein et. al. Opladen: Leske+Budrich.

Rootes, C. A. "The Europeanization of Environmentalism." Pp. 377–404 in *L'Action Collective en Europe*, edited by R. Balme and D. Chabanet. Paris: Presses de Sciences Po, 2002.

Rorty, R. *Contingency, Irony, and Solidarity*. Cambridge: Cambridge University Press, 1989.

Roth, R. "Participatory Governance and Urban Citizenship." Pp. 75–82 in *Participatory Governance in Multi-Level Context: Concepts and Experience*, edited by H. Heinelt, et. al. Opladen: Leske+Budrich, 2002.

Ruchet, O. "Europeanization and Democracy: Andrew Moravcsik and the Legitimacy of the European Union." Paper presented at the ECPR-SGEU Second Pan-European Conference on EU Politics, Bologna, Italy, 24–26 June 2004.

Rucht, D. "Lobbying or Protest? Strategies to Influence EU Environmental Policies." Pp. 125–142 in *Contentious Europeans*, edited by D. Imig and S. Tarrow, Lanham: Rowman & Littlefield, 2001.

Ruggie, J. G. "Territoriality and Beyond: Problematising Modernity in International Relations." *International Organisation* 47 (1993).

Saalfeld, T. "The Bundestag: Institutional Incrementalism and Behavioural Reticence." Pp. 73–96 in *Germany, Europe and the Politics of Constraint*, edited by K. Dyson and K. Goetz. Oxford: Oxford University Press, 2003.

Sack, R. D. *Human Territoriality: Its Theory and History*. Cambridge: Cambridge University Press, 1986.

Saretzki, T. "Technological Governance—Technological Citizenship?" Pp. 83–106 in *Participatory Governance in Multi-Level Context: Concepts and Experience*, edited by H. Heinelt, et. al. Opladen: Leske+Budrich, 2002.

Scelo, M. "Le Parlement Européen Face à L'avenir de l'Europe: De la Convention Européenne à L'adoption d'une Constitution pour l'Europe." *Revue du Marché Commun et de l'Union Européenne* 462 (2002): 578 582.

Scharpf, F. *Demokratietheorie zwischen Utopie und Anpassung.* Konstanz: Konstanzer Universitätsverlag, 1970.

———. "Community and Autonomy: Multi-Level Policy-Making in the European Union." *Journal of European Public Policy* 1 (1994): 219–242.

———. *Governing in Europe: Effective and Democratic?* Oxford: Oxford University Press, 1999a.

———. "Demokratieprobleme in der Europäischen Mehrebenenpolitik." Pp. 672–694 in *Demokratie in Ost und West,* edited by W. Merkel and A. Busch. Frankfurt: Suhrkamp, 1999b.

———. *Governing in Europe: Effective and Democratic?* Oxford: Oxford University Press, 1999c.

———. "European Governance: Common Concerns vs. The Challenge of Diversity," Jean Monnet Working Paper 6 (2001a).

———. "Notes Toward a Theory of Multilevel Governing in Europe." *Scandinavian Political Studies* 24 (2001b): 1–26.

———. "Verso una Teoria Della Multi-Level Governance." *Rivista Italiana di Politiche Pubbliche* 1, no. 13 (2002): 11–42.

———. "Legitimationskonzepte jenseits des Nationalstaates." MPIfG Working Paper 04/6. 2004. www.mpi-fg-koeln.mpg.de/pu/workpap/wp04-6/wp04-6.html

Schattschneider, E. E. *The Semi-Sovereign People: A Realist's View of Democracy in America.* New York, Holt, 1960.

Scheffler, H.-H. *Die Pflicht zur Begründung von Maßnahmen nach den Europäischen Gemeinschaftsverträgen.* Berlin: Duncker und Humblot, 1974.

Schelsky, H. "Mehr Demokratie oder mehr Freiheit?" *Frankfurt Allgemeine Zeitung,* December 20, 1973, 7–8.

Schimmelfennig, F. "Legitimate Rule in the European Union: The Academic Debate." Tübinger Arbeitspapiere zur Internationalen Politik und Friedensforschung 27 (1996) www.uni-tuebingen.de/uni/spi/taps/tap27.htm (visited 16 Dec 2004).

———. *The EU, NATO, and the Integration of Europe: Rules and Rhetoric.* Cambridge: Cambridge University Press, 2003.

Schmalz-Bruns, R. *Reflexive Demokratie: Die demokratische Transformation Moderner Politik.* Baden-Baden: Nomos, 1995.

———. "Deliberativer Supranationalismus: Demokratisches Regieren Jenseits des Nationalstaats," *Zeitschrift für Internationale Beziehungen* 6, No. 2, (1999): 185-244.

———. "The Normative Desirability of Participatory Democracy," Pp. 59–74 in *Participatory Governance in Multi-Level Context: Concepts and Experience,* edited by H. Heinelt et al. Opladen: Leske+Budrich, 2002.

Schmid, C. "Vertical and Diagonal Conflicts in the Europeanization Process." Pp. 185–191 in *Private Governance, Democratic Constitutionalism and Supranationalism,* edited by Christian Joerges and Oliver Gerstenberg. Luxembourg: European Commission, 1998.

———. "Diagonal Competence Conflicts between European Competition Law and National Regulation: A Conflict of Laws Reconstruction of the Dispute on Book Price-Fixing." *European Review of Private Law* 8, no. 1 (2000): 155–172.

Schmidt, M. G. *Demokratietheorien*, Opladen: Leske+Budrich, 1995.

———. *Demokratietheorien*, 3. Aufl. Opladen: Leske+Budrich, 2000.

Schmitt, C. *Verfassungslehre*. 8th ed. Berlin: Duncker & Humblot, 1993.

———. "Vertical and Diagonal Conflicts in the Europeanization Process." Pp. 185–191 in *Private Governance, Democratic Constitutionalism and Supranationalism*, edited by C. Joerges and O. Gerstenberg. Luxembourg: European Commission, 1998.

Schmitt, H. and Thomassen, J. "Dynamic Representation: The Case of European Integration," *European Union Politics* 1, no. 3 (2000): 340–363.

Schmitter, P. C. *Some Propositions about Civil Society and the Consolidation of Democracy*. Wien: Institut für Höhere Studien. Reihe Politikwissenschaft. Forschungsberichte Nr. 10, 1993.

———. "Examining the Present Euro-Polity with the Help of Past Theories," in *Governance in the European Union*, edited by G. Marks, F. W. Scharpf, P. C. Schmitter, and W. Streeck. London: Sage, 1996.

———. *How to Democratize the European Union . . . and Why Bother?* Lanham: Rowman & Littlefield, 2000.

———. "What Is There to Legitimise in the European Union and How Might This Be Accomplished?" Jean Monnet Working Paper No.6/01, Symposium: Responses to the European Commission's White Paper on Governance. Harvard, 2001.

———. "Participation in Governance Arrangements: Is There Any Reason to Expect It Will Achieve 'Sustainable and Innovative Policies in a Multilevel Context'?" Pp. 51–70 in *Participatory Governance: Political and Societal Implications*, edited by J. Grote and B. Gbikpi, Opladen: Leske+Budrich, 2002.

———. "Democracy in Europe and Europe's Democratization." *Journal of Democracy* 14, no. 4 (2003): 70–85.

Schmuck, O. and W. Wessels. *Das Europäische Parlament im Dynamischen Integrationsprozeß. Auf der Suche nach einem Zeitgemäßen Leitbild*. Bonn: Europa Union Verlag, 1989.

Schnyder, A. K. *Wirtschaftskollisionsrecht*. Zürich: Schulthess-Schaffer, 1990.

Schoo, J. "Das Institutionelle System aus der Sicht des Europäischen Parlaments." Pp. 63–74 in *Der Verfassungsentwurf des Europäischen Konvents: Verfassungsrechtliche Grundstrukturen und Wirtschaftsverfassungsrechtliches Konzept*, edited by J. Schwarze. Baden-Baden: Nomos, 2004.

Schweller, R. L. "Bandwagoning for Profit: Bringing the Revisionist State Back In." *International Security* 19, no. 1 (1994): 72–107.

Scott, W. R. "Institutions and Organizations: Towards a Theoretical Synthesis." Pp. 55–80 in *Institutional Environment and Organizations. Structural Complexity and Individualism*, edited by W. Richard Scott and John W. Meyer. Thousand Oaks, London, New Delhi: Sage, 1994.

Scully, R. "Policy Influence and Participation in the European Parliament." *Legislative Studies Quarterly* 22, No. 2 (1997a): 233–252.

———. "The EP and Codecision: A Rejoinder to Tsebelis and Garrett." *Journal of Legislative Studies* 3, No. 3 (1997b): 93–103.

———. "The European Parliament and the Co-Decision Procedure: A Re-Assessment." *Journal of Legislative Studies* 3, No. 3 (1997c): 58–73.

———. "Democracy, Legitimacy and the European Parliament." Pp. 228–245 in *The State of the European Union*, edited by M. Green Cowles and M. Smith, Vol. 5. Oxford: Oxford University Press, 2000.

Seidendorf, S. "Europeanisation of National Identity Discourses? Comparing French and German Print Media." Paper presented at the ECPR Joint Sessions, Edinburgh March 28–April 2 2003.

———. "Defining Europe against Its Past?—Memory Politics and the Sanctions against Austria in France and Germany." *German Law Journal* 6, no. 2 (2005): 207–230.

Shackleton, M. "The European Parliament's New Committees of Inquiry: Tiger or Paper Tiger?" Paper presented at the ECSA Fifth Biennial Conference, Seattle, May 29–June 1 1997.

———. "The Politics of Codecision." *Journal of Common Market Studies* 38, No. 2 (2000): 325–342.

Shapiro, I. *The State of Democratic Theory*. Princeton: Princeton University Press, 2003.

Shapiro, M. "Comparative Law and Comparative Politics." *Southern California Law Review* 53 (1980), 537–542.

Shaw, J. "Postnational Constitutionalism in the European Union." *Journal of European Public Policy* 6, no. 4 (1999): 579–97.

———. *Law of the European Union*, Basingstoke: Palgrave, 2000.

———. "Process, Responsibility and Inclusion in EU Constitutionalism." *European Law Journal* 9, no. 1 (February 2003): 45–68.

Shore, C. *Building Europe: The Cultural Politics of European Integration*. London/New York: Routledge, 2000.

Siaroff, A. "Varieties of Parliamentarianism in the Advanced Industrial Democracies." *International Political Science Review* 24, no. 4 (2003): 445–464.

Siedentop, L. *Democracy in Europe*. London: Penguin Books, 2000.

Skinner, Q. *Visions of Politics*. Vol. 1–3. Cambridge: University Press, 2002.

Slater, D. *Consumer Culture and Modernity*. Cambridge: Polity Press, 1997.

Smith, E., ed. *National Parliaments as Cornerstones of European Integration*. London: Kluwer Law International, 1996.

Sobotta, C. *Transparenz in den Rechtsetzungsverfahren der Europäischen Union*. Baden-Baden: Nomos Verl.-Ges., 2001.

Somek, A. "On Supranationality." *European Integration Online Papers* 5, no. 3 (2001).

Sommier, I. *Le Renouveau des Mouvements Contestataires a l'heure de la Mondialisation*. Flammarion, 2003.

Soysal, Y. N. "Locating Europe." *European Societies* 4, no. 3 (2002): 265–284.

Steppat, S. "Execution of Functions by the European Parliament in Its First Electoral Period." *Revue d'Intégration Européenne* 1 (1988): 5–35.

References

Stoker, G. "Distributing Democracy: Seeking a Better Fit for All Tiers of Government." Unpublished paper. 2003. www.ipeg.org.uk/Paper%20Series/Distributing%20democracy.pdf

Strøm, K. "Parliamentary Democracy and Delegation." Pp. 55–106 in *Delegation and Accountability in Parliamentary Democracies*, edited by K. Strøm, W. C. Müller, and T. Bergman. Oxford: Oxford University Press, 2003.

Swyngedouw, E., B. Page, and M. Kaika. "Sustainability and Policy Innovation in a Multi-Level Context: Crosscutting Issues in the Water Sector." Pp. 107–132 in *Participatory Governance in Multi-Level Context: Context and Experience*, edited by H. Heinelt et al. Opladen: Leske+Budrich, 2002.

Sypris, P. "Legitimising European Governance: Taking Subsidiarity Seriously within the Open Method of Coordination." Unpublished manuscript, 2002.

Tarrow, S. "Confessions of a Recovering Structuralist." Prepared for *European Political Science*, 2005

Taylor, P. J. "The State as Container: Territoriality in the Modern World-System." *Progress in Human Geography* 18 (1994): 151–162.

Teubner, G. "Substantive and Reflexive Elements in Modern Law." *Law and Society Review* 17 (1983): 239–285.

———. "Juridification—Concepts, Aspects, Limits, Solutions." Pp. 3–48 in *Juridification of Social Spheres*, edited by G. Teubner. Berlin, New York: de Gruyter, 1987.

———. "De Collisione Discursum: Communicative Rationalities in Law, Morality and Politics." *Cardozo Law Review* 17 (1996a): 901–918.

———. "Altera Pars Audiatur: Das Recht in der Kollision anderer Universalitätsansssprüche." *Archiv für Rechts– und Sozialphilosophie*, 65 (1996b): 199–220.

———. "Globale Zivilverfassungen: Alternativen zur staatszentrierten Verfassungstheorie." *Zeitschrift für ausländisches öffentliches Recht und Völkerrecht* 63 (2003): 1–28.

———. "Societal Constitutionalism: Alternatives to State-Centered Constitutional Theory?" Pp. 3–28 in *Constitutionalism and Transnational Governance*, edited by C. Joerges, I.-J. Sand, and G. Teubner. London: Hart, 2004a.

———. *Netzwerk als Vertragsverbund: Virtuelle Unternehmen, Franchising, Just-in-time in Sozialwissenschaftlicher und Juristischer Sicht*. Baden-Baden: Nomos, 2004b.

Teubner, G. and A. Fischer-Lescano. "Regime Collisions: The Vain Search for Legal Unity in the Fragmentation of Global Law." *Michigan Journal of International Law* 25 (2004): 999–1046.

Theiler, T. "Why the European Union Failed to Europeanize its Audiovisual Policy." Pp. 115–140 in *Constructing Europe's Identity: The External Dimension*, edited by L.-E. Cederman. Boulder: Lynne Rienner, 2001.

———. *Political Symbolism and European Integration*. Manchester: Manchester University Press, 2004.

Therborn, G. *European Modernity and Beyond: The Trajectory of European Societies, 1945–2000*. London: Sage, 1996.

Thucydides. *The History of the Peloponnesian War: Revised Edition*. London: Penguin Classics, 1954.

Tietje, C. *Internationales Verwaltungshandeln*. Berlin: Duncker & Humblot, 2001.

Tilly, C. "Social Movements and National Politics." Pp. 297–317 in *Statemaking and Social Movements: Essays in History and Theory*, edited by C. Bright and S. Harding. Ann Arbor: University of Michigan Press, 1984.

———. *Social Movements, 1768–2004*. Boulder, CO: Paradigm, 2004.

Tocqueville, A. de. *Democracy in America*. New York: The New American Library, 1963.

Töller, A. "Der Beitrag der Komitologie zur Politischen Steuerung in der Europäischen Umweltpolitik." Pp. 313–342 in *Wie Problemlösungsfähig Ist die EU? Regieren im Europäischen Mehrebenensystem*, edited by E. Grande and M. Jachtenfuchs. Baden-Baden: Nomos, 2000.

Treaty Establishing a Constitution for Europe. 2400/C310/01.

Treaty of Amsterdam amending the Treaty on European Union, the Treaties establishing the European Communities, and Certain Related Acts. 1997/C340.

Treaty of Nice amending the Treaty on European Union, the Treaties establishing the European Communities, and Certain Related Acts. 2001/C80/01.

Trenz, H. J. "Protestmobilisierung in Netzwerken: Revitalisierung oder Selbstblockade Zivilgesellschaftlicher Protestformen in der EU?" *Forschungsjournal Neue Soziale Bewegungen* 15, no.1 (2001): 87–98.

———. *Zur Konstitution Politischer Öffentlichkeit in der Europäischen Union. Zivilgesellschaftliche Subpolitik oder Schaupolitische Inszenierung?* Baden-Baden: Nomos, 2002.

———. Europäische Integration und Öffentlichkeit. Institutionelle Selbstdarstellung und Mediale Repräsentation der Politischen Gesellschaft Europas. Habilitationsschrift, Humboldt Universität zu Berlin, 2004a.

———. "'Qua vadis Europe?' Quality Newspapers Struggling for European unity," in *One EU—Many Publics* (Cidel Conference Proceedings. Arena Reports), edited by J. E. Fossum and P. Schlesinger. Oslo: University of Oslo, 2004b.

Trenz, H. J. and K. Eder. "The Democratising Dynamics of a European Public Sphere: Towards a Theory of Democratic Functionalism." *European Journal of Social Theory* 6 (2004): 5–25.

Trif, M. and D. Imig. "Demanding to Be Heard: Social Movements and the European Public Sphere." Prepared for *Developing the European Public Sphere*, edited by R. Koopmans and P. Statham, 2003.

Trondal, J. "Administrative Integration Across Levels of Governance: Integration through Participation in EU Committees." ARENA Report no. 7/2001, 2001.

Trondal, J. and F. Veggeland. "Access, Voice and Loyalty: The Representation of Domestic Civil Servants in the EU Committees." ARENA Working Paper no. 8, 2000.

Tsebelis, G. and G. Garrett. "Agenda Setting, Vetoes and the European Union's Co-Decision Procedure." *Journal of Legislative Studies* 3, No. 3 (1997): 74–92.

Tsebelis, G. "The Power of the European Parliament as a Conditional Agenda-Setter." *American Political Science Review*, no. 1 (1994): 128–142.

Tully, J. *Strange Multiplicity: Constitutionalism in an Age of Diversity*. Cambridge: Cambridge University Press, 1995.

———. "The Unfreedom of the Moderns in Comparison to Their Ideals of Constitutional Democracy." *The Modern Law Review* 65, no. 2 (2002): 204–228.

Turin Council: White Paper on the 1996 Intergovernmental Conference, 29. March 1996, Vol. II, www.europarl.eu.int/igc1996/pos-intr_en.htm.

UK Government. Cabinet Office. *The Guide to Better European Regulation.* London: Stationary Office, 1999.

UK Parliament. 6th Report: European Documents on Economic and Monetary Union: The Scrutiny Process. (HC 36-vi/96). December 9, 1996a.

———. First Special Report: The Government's Reply to the Twenty-Seventh Report from the Committee. (HC 140/96). December 9, 1996b.

———. House of Commons. Select Committee on European Legislation. 27th Report: The Scrutiny of European Business. (HC 51–xxvii, 95/96). July 18, 1996c.

———. House of Commons. European Scrutiny Committee. The European Scrutiny System in the House of Commons—A Short Guide for Members of Parliament by the Staff of the European Scrutiny Committee. London: House of Commons, 2001; www.parliament.uk/documents/upload/ESC%20GreenGuide.pdf.

———. 30th Report: European Scrutiny in the House of Commons. (HC 152-xxx/02). May 22 2002a.

———. House of Commons. Standing Orders of the House of Commons—Public Business. London, 2002b.

Urry, J. *Consuming Places.* London/New York, 1995.

Van Der Eijk, C. and M. N. Franklin. "Potential for Contestation on European Matters at National Elections in Europe." Pp. 32–50 in *European Integration and Political Conflict,* edited by G. Marks and M. Steenbergen. Cambridge: Cambridge University Press, 2004.

Verhoeven, A. *The European Union in Search of a democratic and Constitutional Theory.* The Hague: Kluwer Law International, 2002.

Vibert, F. *The EU's System of Regulatory Impact Assessment—A Scorecard.* London: European Policy Forum, 2004.

Vilmar, F. *Strategien der Demokratisierung.* 2 Vol. Darmstadt: Luchterhand, 1973.

Vogel, K. *Der Räumliche Anwendungsbereich der Verwaltungsrechtsnorm.* Frankfurt, Berlin: Metzner, 1965.

von Bogdandy, A. "The European Union as a Human Rights Organization?" *Common Market Law Review* 37 (2000a), 1307–1338.

———. *Gubernative Rechtsetzung.* Tübingen: Mohr Siebeck, 2000b.

———. "Globalization and Europe: How to Square Democracy, Globalization, and International Law." *European Journal of International Law* 15, no. 5 (November 2004): forthcoming.

———. "Constitutional Principles." in *Principles of European Constitutional Law,* edited by A. von Bogdandy and J. Bast. Oxford: Hart, 2006.

Von Hayek, F. A. "Wettbewerb als Entdeckungsverfahren." Pp. 249–265 in *Freiburger Studien. Gesammelte Aufsätze,* edited by F. A. von Hayek. Tübingen: Mohr Siebeck, 1969.

Vos, E. "The Fall of Committees?" Pp. 111–121 in *The European Union—An Ongoing Process of Integration.* Liber Amicorum F. Kellermann, edited by J. de Swaan, J. Jansen, and F. Nelissen. Den Haag: Asser Press, 2004.

———. "The Role of Committees in European Governance," in *Good Governance in the European Union: Concept, Implications and Applications*, edited by D. Curtin and W. Wessels. Antwerpen: Intersentia, 2005.

Walker, N. "The Idea of Constitutional Pluralism," *Modern Law Review* 65 (2002).

Wallace, H. "Politics and Policy in the EU: The Challenge of Governance." Pp. 3–36 in *Policy-Making in the European Union*, edited by H. Wallace and W. Wallace. Oxford: Oxford University Press, 1996.

Wallace, W. "Less Than a Federation. More than a Regime: The Community as a Political System." Pp. 403–436 in *Policy-Making in the European Community*, edited by H. Wallace and W. Wallace. Oxford: Oxford University Press, 1983.

Wallrabenstein, A. *Das Verfassungsrecht der Staatsangehörigkeit*. Baden-Baden: Nomos Verl.-Ges., 1999.

Waltz, K. N. *Theory of International Politics*. New York: Random House, 1979.

Ward, I. "Beyond Constitutionalism: The Search for a European Political Imagination," *European Law Journal* 7 (2001), 24–40.

Warleigh, A. Informal Governance: What Contribution to the Legitimacy of the EU? Pp. 22–35 in *Informal Governance in the European Union*, edited by T. Christiansen and S. Piattoni. Aldershot: Edward Elgar Publications, 2003.

Warren, M. "Democratic Theory and Self-Transformation." *American Political Science Review* 86, no. 1 (1992): 8–23.

———. *Democracy and Association*. Princeton: Princeton University Press, 2001.

Weale, A. *Democracy*. London: Macmillan, 1999.

Weber-Panariello, P. A. *Nationale Parlamente in der Europäischen Union*. Baden-Baden: Nomos, 1995

Wehner, B. *Nationalstaat, Solidarstaat, Effizienzstaat*. Darmstadt: Wissenschaftliche Buchgesellschaft, 1992.

Weiler, J.H.H. (1997), "The Reformation of European Constitutionalism," *Journal of Common Market Studies* 35 (1997), 97–131.

———. "In der Umwelt der Ausschüsse." *Die Zeit* 44, October 22 1998.

———. "Epilogue: 'Comitology' as Revolution—Infranationalism, Constitutionalism and Democracy," in *EU Committees*, edited by C. Joerges and E. Vos. Oxford: Hart, 1999a.

———. *The Constitution of Europe: Do the New Clothes Have an Emperor? and Other Essays on European Integration*. Cambridge: Cambridge University Press, 1999b.

———. "Federalism and Constitutionalism: Europe's Sonderweg," Harvard Jean Monnet Working Paper 10/00, 2000.

Weiler, J. H. H., U. Haltern, and F. Mayer. "European Democracy and Its Critique." *West European Politics* 18, no. 3 (1995): 4–39.

Wessels, W. "The Modern West European State and the European Union: Democratic Erosion or a New Kind of Polity?" Pp. 57–72 in *The European Union: How democratic Is It?*, edited by S. S. Andersen and K. A. Eliassen. London: Sage, 1996.

———. "Comitology: Fusion in Action. Politico-Administrative Trends in the EU System," *Journal of European Public Policy*, vol. 5, no. 2 (1998): 209–34.

Westlake, M. "Mad Cows and Englishmen—The Institutional Consequences of the BSE Crisis." *Journal of Common Market Studies* 35, no. 1 (1997): 11–36.

Whitman, J. "On Nazi 'Honour' and New 'European' Dignity." Pp. 243–266 in *Darker Legacies of Law in Europe: The Shadow of National Socialism and Fascism over Europe and Its Legal Traditions*, edited by C. Joerges and N. S. Ghaleigh. Portland-Oxford: Hart, 2003.

Wiethölter, R. "Proceduralisation of the Category of Law." Pp. 501–510 in *Critical Legal Thought: An American-German Debate*, edited by C. Joerges and D. M. Trubek. Baden-Baden: Nomos, 1989.

———. "Recht´–Fertigungs–Recht eines Gesellschafts–Rechts." Pp. 13–21 in *Rechtsverfassungsrecht Recht–Fertigung zwischen Privatrechtsdogmatik und Gesellschaftstheorie*, edited by C. Joerges and G. Teubner. Baden-Baden: Nomos, 2003.

Wolf, K. D. "The New Raison d'Etat as a Problem for Democracy in World Society," *European Journal of International Relations* 5, no. 3 (1999): 333–363.

———. "Contextualizing Normative Standards for Legitimate Governance beyond the State." Pp. 30–50 in *Participatory Government*, edited by J. R. Grote and B. Gbikpi. Opladen: Leske+Budrich, 2002.

Wouters, J. "Constitutional Limits of Differentiation: The Principle of Equality." Pp. 301–345 in *The Many Faces of Differentiation in EU Law*, edited by B. de Witte, D. Hanf, and E. Vos. Antwerpen. Oxford, New York: Intersentia, 2001.

Yanow, D. "Seeing Organizational Learning: A 'Cultural View'." *Organization* 7 (2000).

Zimpel, G. *Selbstbestimmung oder Akklamation*. Stuttgart: Enke, 1972.

Zuleeg, M. "Demokratie ohne Volk oder Demokratie der Völker?" Pp. 11–25 in *Europäische Demokratie*, edited by J. Drexl et. al. Baden-Baden: Nomos Verl.-Ges., 1999.

Zürn, M. "Über den Staat und die Demokratie im Europäischen Mehrebenensystem." *Politische Vierteljahresschrift* 37, no. 1 (March 1996): 27–55.

———. *Regieren Jenseits des Nationalstaates*. Frankfurt: Suhrkamp, 1998.

———. "The State in the Post-National Constellation—Societal Denationalization and Multi-Level Governance." ARENA Working Paper no. 35/1999 (1999).

Zweifel, T. *Democratic Deficit? Institutions and Regulation in the European Union and the United States*. Oxford: Lexington Books, 2002.

Index

accountability: democratic, 6–9, 11, 102, 116, 118, 124, 196, 205; political, 5, 8–9, 333; public, 9, 189, 306
accountability deficit, 9, 205, 224
agenda-setting, 90, 159, 170, 242, 276, 159, 180
Amsterdam, Treaty of, 1, 34, 39–40, 57, 78, 80, 83–84, 86, 96, 114–15, 121–22, 124–26, 128–29, 131–32, 135, 210, 264, 269, 367–69, 377
Austria, 68, 97, 126
autonomy: of citizens, 288; personal and social, 144; principle of, 12–14; public, 288, 298

Bundesrat, 67, 69, 73–74, 107
Bundestag, 66–69, 107–8, 120

Cassis de Dijon. *See* community law
Charter of Fundamental Rights, 40, 50, 263, 309
citizen(s): as holders, 225–30; initiatives, 11, 19, 40; national, 58, 107, 317; participation, 10–11, 23, 218, 235, 237, 257; rights, 35, 199, 253; transnational, 10

citizenship, 52, 198, 224–30, 244, 255–56; active, 265, 276; civil, 226; concept of, 218; jurisprudence, 52; political, 226; social, 226; supranational/EU, 33, 36, 49, 50, 206, 263
civil rights, 33, 36, 267
civil society, 2, 11, 14–15, 19, 22, 24, 71, 100, 104–5, 150, 172, 192, 197, 241, 244, 251, 255–59, 261, 264, 266–68, 272–76, 297, 312
collective learning, 22, 71, 149, 166, 173, 184
comitology, 141, 160, 168, 172, 261, 315, 321, 323–26, 335
Commission: appointment and investiture of the, 77–78, 103, 114, 152; as a collegiate body, 83; Commissioners, 68, 78, 114, 170; consultations, 24, 260–61, 274–75; president of the, 7, 83, 152, 170; White Paper on European Governance, 10–11, 23, 48, 161, 168, 233, 236, 249, 255
Common Foreign and Security Policy (CFSP), 141, 170

About the Contributors

Rudy B. Andeweg is professor of political science at the University of Leiden. His research interests include executive-legislative relations, parliamentary behavior, and political representation. His recent publications include "Modes of Political Representation: Toward a New Typology," *Legislative Studies Quarterly* 30 (2005) (with J. Thomassen) and *Governance and Politics of the Netherlands* (2005) (with G. Irwin).

Katrin Auel is lecturer in politics at the University of Oxford and Fellow at Mansfield College, Oxford. Her research interests include legislative studies and democratic theory, in particular the democratic legitimacy of systems of multilevel governance such as the European Union. Her publications include *Regionalisiertes Europa—Demokratisches Europa?* (2003) and *The Europeanisation of Parliamentary Democracy*, special issue of the *Journal of Legislative Studies* 11 (2005) (co-edited with A. Benz).

Arthur Benz is professor of political science at the University of Hagen. During the last years he has concentrated his research on problems of democracy in systems of multilevel governance. His publications on government, federalism, and multilevel governance include *Der moderne Staat* (2001) and *Governance and Democracy—Comparing National, European and Transnational Experiences* (co-edited with Y. Papadopoulos) (2006).

Lars-Erik Cederman is professor of international conflict research at ETH Zurich. His research focusses on political macro-processes such as state formation, nationalism, democratization, and integration. He is the editor of *Constructing Europe's Identity: The External Dimension* (2001) and the author of *Emergent Actors in World Politics: How States and Nations Develop and Dissolve* (1997).

Damian Chalmers is a professor in EU law at the London School of Economics and Political Science. He is the author of *European Union Law* (with C. Hadjiemmanuil, G. Monti, and A. Tomkins) (2006). His other recent publications include "The Reconstitution of Europe's Public Spheres," *European Law Journal* 9 (2003), "Food for Thought: European Risks and National Ways of Life," *Modern Law Review* 66 (2003), "Risk, Anxiety and the European Mediation of the Politics of Life," *European Law Review* 30 (2005), "The Court of Justice and the Constitutional Treaty," *I-CON* 4 (2005), "Private Power and Public Authority in European Union Law," *Cambridge Yearbook of European Legal Studies*, 8 (2005-6).

Deirdre Curtin is professor of international and European governance at the Utrecht School of Governance, University of Utrecht, and is Vice Chairperson of the Standing Committee of Experts on Matters Relating to International Immigration, Refugee and Criminal Law in the Netherlands. She has written extensively on issues relating to the constitutional and institutional development of the European Union including *Postnational Democracy: The European Union in Search of a Political Philosophy* (1997). She is currently working on a book on accountability of EU executive(s).

Donatella della Porta is professor of sociology at the European University Institute. Her main areas of interest include social movements, political violence, policing, political corruption. Among her recent publications are *Globalization from Below* (2006), *Police et manifestants* (2006), *Quale Europa? Europeizzazione, identità e conflitti* (2006), *Social Movements: An Introduction*, second ed. (2006), *Transnational Protest and Global Activism* (2005).

Klaus Eder is professor of comparative macrosociology at Humboldt University, Berlin. He has written extensively on sociological theory, public sphere, symbolic power, citizenship, and social movements. Recent publications include "From the Common Market to the Political Union: The shifting opportunity structure of contentious politics in Europe." In C. Tilly and M. Kousis (Eds.), *Threats and Opportunities in Contentious Politics* (2004), *Die Einhegung des Anderen: Türkische, Polnische und Russlanddeutsche Einwanderer in Deutschland* (with V. Rauer, O. Schmidtke, et al. (2004), *Collective*

Memory and European Identity: The Effects of Integration and Enlargement (co-edited with W. Spohn) (2005).

Erik O. Eriksen is professor of political science at ARENA, University of Oslo. His main fields of interest are political theory, democratic governance, public policy, and European integration. Recent publications include *Democracy in the European Union* (co-edited with J. E. Fossum) (2000), *Understanding Habermas* (co-edited with J. Weigard) (2003), *The Chartering of Europe* (co-edited with J. E. Fossum and A. J. Menéndez) (2003), *Developing a Constitution for Europe* (co-edited with J. E. Fossum and A. J. Menéndez) (2004), and *Making the European Polity: Reflexive Integration in the EU* (2005).

Michael Th. Greven is professor of political science and political theory at the Institut für Politikwissenschaft at the University of Hamburg. His is the author of *Die Politische Gesellschaft. Kontingenz und Dezision als Probleme des Regierens und der Demokratie* (1999), *Kontingenz und Dezision: Beiträge zur Analyse der politischen Gesellschaft* (2000), and *Democracy Beyond the State? The European Dilemma and the Emerging Global Order* (edited together with L. W. Pauly 2000).

Ulrich Haltern is professor of German and European constitutional and administrative law at Hanover University and Director of the Hanover Institute for National and Transnational Integration Studies. His main areas of research include EU law, constitutional law and theory, and a cultural study of law. Recent publications include *Europarecht: Dogmatik im Kontext* (2005), *Europarecht und das Politische* (2005), *Europawissenschaften* (co-edited with G. F. Schuppert and I. Pernice) (2005), "On Finality." In A. von Bogdandy and J. Bast (eds.), *Principles of European Constitutional Law* (2006).

Hubert Heinelt is professor of public administration, public policy, and urban research at the Institute of Political Science, Darmstadt University of Technology. His recent publications include *Urban Governance and Democracy: Leadership and Community Involvement* (together with M. Haus and M. Stewart) (2005), *Metropolitan Governance: Capacity, Democracy and the Dynamics of Place* (together with D. Kübler) (2005), *Legitimacy and Urban Governance: A Cross-National Comparative Study* (together with P. Getimis and D. Sweeting) (2006).

Doug Imig is professor of political science at the University of Memphis, and Fellow at the Urban Child Institute in Memphis, Tennessee. His teaching and research concern social movements and the representation of marginalized voices in the United States and Western Europe. He is the author of *Poverty and Power* (1996) and co-author of *Contentious Europeans* (2001).

Christian Joerges is professor of European economic law at the European University Institute. His present research deals with transnational risk regulation, the Europeanization of private law, and antiliberal traditions of legal thought in Europe. Recent publications include *Constitutionalism, Multilevel Trade Governance and Social Regulation* (co-edited with E. U. Petersmann) (2006), "What Is Left of the European Economic Constitution? A Melancholic Eulogy," *European Law Review* 30 (2005), *Law and Governance in Postnational Europe: Compliance Beyond the Nation-State* (co-edited with Michael Zürn) (2005).

Beate Kohler-Koch is professor of international relations and European affairs at the University of Mannheim. Her recent research activities concentrate on the transformation of governance both at EU and national levels as a consequence of deeper European integration. She has initiated and currently coordinates the EU-funded Network of Excellence "CONNEX" on "Efficient and Democratic Governance in a Multi-Level Europe" (2004–2008). Recent book publications cover constitutional politics (2002), a state-of-the-art reflection on European integration (2003), an exploration of *Linking EU and National Governance* (2003), a textbook on integration and European governance (2004), and an assessment of interest intermediation in Europe (2005).

Christopher Lord is professor of politics at the University of Reading. He has published extensively on Democracy and Legitimacy and the European Union, including *A Democratic Audit of the European* (2004) and *Democracy in the New Europe* (co-authored with E. Harris) (2006).

Paul Magnette is professor of political science and director of the Institute for European Studies at the Université Libre de Bruxelles. He is the author of a number of articles and books on the EU and its democratic deficit. His last book is *What is the European Union?* (2005).

Andreas Maurer is head of unit "EU Integration" at the German Institute for International and Security Affairs (SWP), Berlin. His areas of research are multilevel and multi-actor governance in the European Union; concepts and practice of EU soft law; rules of procedure and interinstitutional agreements, perspectives, roles, and functions of the European Parliament and of the national parliaments in EU integration; EU policy-making with regard to immigration, asylum, and international environmental crime; negotiations and reform of European treaties; German and British policies toward European integration. Recent publications include *Postnational Constitution-Building in the Enlarged Europe: Foundations, Legitimacy, Prospects* (co-edited with U. Liebert and J. Falke) (2005); "Failing Collectively at Nice: The Search for Efficiency Building." In F. Laursen (ed.) *The Treaty of Nice: Actor Preference, Bargaining and Institutional Choice* (2006), "In Detention, Repeating the Year, or Expelled? Perspectives for the Realisation of the Constitutional Treaty" (2006).

Jeremy Richardson is professor emeritus and fellow of Nuffield College, Oxford and Editor of the *Journal of European Public Policy*. His main fields are public policy in the EU, comparative public policy, and the role of interest groups in the policy process. His most recent book is *European Union: Power and Policy-Making*, third ed. (2005). He is currently editing (with D. Coen) a second edition of *Lobbying in the European Union*.

Berthold Rittberger is professor of political science and contemporary history at the University of Manheim. His main fields of research include the constitutional development of the European Union and theories of European integration. His most important publications are *The Constitutionalization of the European Union*, Special Issue of the *Journal of European Pubic Policy* (co-edited with Frank Schimmelfennig) (2006), *Building Europe's Parliament: Democratic Representation Beyond the Nation-State* (2005), "The Creation, Interpretation and Contestation of Institutions: Revisiting Historical Institutionalism," *Journal of Common Market Studies* 41 (2003) (together with Johannes Lindner).

Rainer Schmalz-Bruns is professor at the department of political science, Leibniz University, Hanover. His current research areas cover transnational constitutionalism, cosmopolitanism, and the legal development in the enlarged European Union. His recent publications include *Politik der Integration: Symbole, Repräsentation, Integration* (2006), "An den Grenzen der Entstaatlichung: Bemerkungen zu Jürgen Habermas Modell einer Weltinnenpolitik ohne Weltregierung." In P. Niesen and B. Herborth (eds). *Anarchie der kommunikativen Freiheit: Jürgen Habermas und die Theorie der Internationalen Politik* (forthcoming).

Hans-Jörg Trenz is research professor at ARENA, Center for European Studies, University of Oslo. Major publications include "The EU's Fledgling Society: From Deafening Silence to Critical Voice in European Constitution Making," *Journal of Civil Society* 2 (together with John Erik Fossum) (2006), *Europa in den Medien: Das Europäische Integrationsprojekt im Spiegel nationaler Öffentlichkeit*

(2005), "Media coverage on European Governance: Testing the Performance of National Newspapers," *European Journal of Communication* 19 (2004).

Armin von Bogdandy is director of the Max Planck Institute for Comparative Public Law and International Law, Heidelberg and Professor for International Law at the Karls-Ruprecht-Univerität, Heidelberg. His fields of interest are international economic law, comparative law in Europe, European constitutional law, and theory of international law. Among his recent publications are *European Constitutional Law* (2006), "The European Constitution and European Identity," *International Journal of Constitutional Law* 3 (2005), "The Prospect of a European Republic: What European Citizens Are Voting On," *Common Market Law Review* 42 (2005), "Globalization and Europe: How to Square Democracy, Globalization, and International Law," *European Journal of International Law* 15 (2004).